THE UPPER ROOM

Disciplines

2020

UPPER
ROOM BOOKS®
NASHVILLE

An Outline for Small-Group Use of *Disciplines*

Here is a simple plan for a one-hour, weekly group meeting based on reading *Disciplines*. One person may act as convener every week, or the role can rotate among group members. You may want to light a white Christ candle each week to signal the beginning of your time together.

Opening

Convener: Let us come into the presence of God.

Others: Lord Jesus Christ, thank you for being with us. Let us hear your word to us as we speak to one another.

Scripture

Convener reads the scripture suggested for that day in *Disciplines*. After a one- or two-minute silence, convener asks, "What did you hear God saying to you in this passage? What response does this call for?" (Group members respond in turn or as led.)

Reflection

- What scripture passage(s) and meditation(s) from this week was (were) particularly meaningful for you? Why? (Group members respond in turn or as led.)
- What actions were you nudged to take in response to the week's meditations? (Group members respond in turn or as led.)
- Where were you challenged in your discipleship this week? How did you respond to the challenge? (Group members respond in turn or as led.)

Praying Together

Convener says, "Based on today's discussion, what people and situations do you want us to pray for now and in the coming week?" Convener or other volunteer then prays about the concerns named.

Departing

Convener says, "Let us go in peace to serve God and our neighbors in all that we do."

THE UPPER ROOM DISCIPLINES 2020

© 2019 by Upper Room Books®. All rights reserved.

Upper Room Books website: upperroombooks.com

Cover design: Left Coast Design, Portland, Oregon

Cover photo: © Tomas Picka / Shutterstock.com

At the time of publication all websites referenced in this book were valid. However, due to the fluid nature of the internet some addresses may have changed, or the content may no longer be relevant.

Revised Common Lectionary copyright © 1992 Consultation on Common Texts. Used by permission.

Scripture quotations not otherwise identified are from the New Revised Standard Version Bible © 1989, Division of Christian Education of the National Council of the Churches of Christ in the United States of America. Used by permission. All rights reserved.

Scripture quotations marked NIV are taken from the Holy Bible, New International Version®, NIV®. Copyright © 1973, 1978, 1984, 2011 by Biblica, Inc.™ Used by permission of Zondervan. All rights reserved worldwide. www.zondervan.com.

Scripture quotations marked AP are the author's paraphrase.

Scripture quotations marked KJV are from the King James Version of the Bible.

Scripture quotations marked RSV are from the Revised Standard Version of the Bible, copyright 1952 [2nd edition, 1971] by the Division of Christian Education of the National Council of the Churches of Christ in the United States of America. Used by permission. All rights reserved.

Scripture quotations from THE MESSAGE. Copyright © by Eugene H. Peterson 1993, 1994, 1995, 1996, 2000, 2001, 2002. Used by permission of NavPress Publishing Group.

Scripture quotations marked ESV are from The Holy Bible, English Standard Version® ESV®, copyright © 2001 by Crossway, a publishing ministry of Good News Publishers. Used by permission. All rights reserved.

Scripture quotations marked CEB are from the Common English Bible. Copyright © 2010 Common English Bible. Used by permission.

Scripture quotations marked NLT are taken from the Holy Bible, New Living Translation, copyright © 1996, 2004, 2007. Used by permission of Tyndale House Publishers, Inc., Carol Stream, Illinois 60188. All rights reserved.

Hymns designated UMH are taken from *The United Methodist Hymnal*, Copyright © 1989 by The United Methodist Publishing House, Nashville, Tennessee.

The weeks of November 9–15 and December 28–31 first appeared in *The Upper Room Disciplines 2002* and *1999–2000*, respectively. Reprinted and used by permission.

Writers of various books of the Bible may be disputed in certain circles; this volume uses the names of the biblically attributed authors.

ISBN: 978-0-8358-1873-5 (print)

978-0-8358-1875-9 (mobi) | 978-0-8358-1876-6 (epub)

Printed in the United States of America

Contents

FOREWORD

On the sixteenth anniversary of my ordination, I received the gift of a small, leather-bound Bible from my husband, John. He had intended it as a travel-friendly essential for a spouse engaged in ministry and had inscribed it with these words: "To my dearest Marjorie—Here you will find your daily bread and your eternal joy. With all my love, John." I treasure this little Bible, which has accompanied my travels ever since. Scripture is indeed "daily bread" for my spirit and therefore sustenance for every kind of journey in my life, including my journey through grief.

Five years after John's untimely death, I take comfort in knowing how central the Word was to his life and work, thus how profoundly prepared he was to enter that "eternal joy" proclaimed by the Word incarnate. Like a strong, fragrant tea, John's mind and heart were well steeped in scripture. He brought that knowledge and distinctive flavor with him into the pages of *Weavings: A Journal of the Christian Spiritual Life* that he conceived and launched in 1986.

To celebrate the sixtieth anniversary of *The Upper Room Disciplines*, this 2020 edition honors the contribution *Weavings* made over the course of its thirty-year history to the renewal of spiritual life and practice. You will find in its pages the voices of former *Weavings* writers, editors, staff, and interns. Given that the journal ceased publication at the end of 2016, I am delighted by the prospect of once again engaging the fine minds and grace-filled hearts of many authors who fed my spirit through *Weavings* over the course of three decades. I trust that many of you who loved *Weavings* will feel similar anticipation and that those of you unfamiliar with the journal will find here writers whose work you might like to know better.

In his editorial introduction to the inaugural issue, John laid out his vision for a journal in which a community of contributors and readers could explore together "the many ways in which God's life and our lives are woven together in the world." Unfolding the metaphor further, he wrote, "*Weavings* seeks to thread together some of the unraveled ends of Christian life—personal formation and social transformation, individual renewal and church renewal, prayer and ministry, contemplation and mission, Sunday and Monday." In helping to reweave the frayed fabric of our life with God and with one another, John aspired to offer hope for the reintegration of human life as intended by God. Such integrity and connection remains a sorely needed vision for our time.

For *Weavings* authors, this integration included combining the best of contemporary scriptural exegesis with deep spiritual reflection. While scholarly in many ways, John was never motivated by primarily intellectual pursuits. He was highly intuitive, swimming naturally in the waters of metaphor, story, and poetry—those vessels of communication known to the wise as the language of the soul. John invited his writers to root their articles in scripture; solid classical theology from Eastern and Western Christianity; the rich, broad heritage of spiritual practices from our ecumenical traditions; and the realities of contemporary life, with all their challenges and fresh perspectives. From this invitation came forth deeply personal yet remarkably universal reflections on life and faith.

Deeply personal reflection on life and faith is precisely what this book invites you to explore for yourself. Starting with a scripture text, continuing with the author's meditation, and concluding with a brief prayer or questions for reflection, each page invites you to reflect and integrate your daily reality with your life in Christ. This practice is a variation on the classic, time-honored tradition of *lectio divina* or "spiritual reading."

From the start, John believed that the content of *Weavings* offered the opportunity for spiritual reading. In 2003, he lifted the practice into full view. He designed and field-tested a contemplative small group process using selected *Weavings* articles as texts for spiritual reading. Following an enthusiastic response, *Weavings* Reading Groups were formed and promoted. For six years, the final page of each issue offered aids to a range of individual and corporate spiritual practices: scripture texts for sermon preparation, retreat designs, and individual or group *lectio divina*, along with reflection questions based on selected articles. The inside back cover of the journal provided a summary description of spiritual reading that made clear the larger purpose of this time-honored practice: to encourage contemplative receptivity to the Spirit's work—the graced labor of seeding insight into the reader's personal condition and guiding the reader's life toward greater integrity and maturity in Christ. This is the work earlier generations called "sanctification" and that we have come to call "spiritual formation." John intended *Weavings* to encourage regular spiritual reading, prayerful contemplation, and deep formation in the spirit and character of Jesus Christ.

A dear friend recently told me that for her, *Weavings* was the next best thing to personal spiritual direction. The content of each issue invited her to pay attention to her own spiritual life—the quality of her relationship with God and the contours of her spiritual journey. Deep spiritual writing often serves as a guide to us, as it rises from the Spirit's work in the author and resonates with the Spirit in our own heart.

Marilyn McEntyre, a faithful contributor to *Weavings* over many years and author of the meditations from October 19–25 in this book, articulates for us simply and clearly the nature of spiritual reading as it has historically been practiced with scripture—the original context for *lectio divina*. I have spread her words out here to help you pause with them:

I have come to see the great legacy we have in the Bible as an invitation:
Dwell in these stories.
Explore them.
Wrestle with them.
Imagine your way into them.
Talk about them with one another.
Seek the wisdom of scholars. . . .
Let the Spirit breathe in the sentences and the spaces between them.
Carry the stories in your heart. . . .
Treasure them and let them teach you. . . .
Let them mystify, invite, unnerve, and delight you.
It's all yours to enter . . . but not to own or control.
When I read the Bible in that spirit,
I find what I need: bread and breath and song.

What a magnificent description of the invitation to you in this devotional guide!

I too find bread and breath, music and poetry, light and life, in the pages of scripture—just as John trusted I would, evidenced in his inscription in that little travel Bible. But there is more to the gift of the Word than the receiving of God's grace. In the only week of meditations John himself contributed to *The Upper Room Disciplines*, specifically in his meditation for December 31, 1990, John reflected on the Epiphany text "Arise, shine; for your light has come" (Isa. 60:1). Noting that "the verb *shine* may also be translated 'become light,'" he suggested that "we are called to do more than merely reflect God's truth; we are called to *become* God's truth, so that the light coming *for* us becomes the light coming *from* us." More than ever, the world needs us to shine forth! May our daily practice of *lectio* with the Word of Life so fill us that we come to embody Jesus' recognition of our deepest truth (Matt. 5:14): "You are the light of the world."

—MARJORIE J. THOMPSON
Author, Teacher, Spiritual Mentor

As It Was in the Beginning . . .

JANUARY 1–5, 2020 • ANNE BURKHOLDER

SCRIPTURE OVERVIEW: Jeremiah delivers happy news, a promise from the Lord of a brighter future day. God will bring back the scattered peoples to their homeland, and their mourning will turn into joy. The psalmist encourages those in Jerusalem to praise God for all that God has done. God gives protection, peace, and the law to the children of Israel. The author of Ephesians encourages readers with confidence in God's eternal plan. God's will is to send Christ and adopt us into God's family. We have been sealed with the Holy Spirit. The opening to John helps us understand the eternal scope of God's plan. From the beginning, the Word has been with God but then becomes flesh and lives among us to reveal divine glory.

QUESTIONS AND SUGGESTIONS FOR REFLECTION

- Read Jeremiah 31:7-14. How do you continue to celebrate God's goodness, even if the Christmas season has been difficult for you?
- Read Psalm 147:12-20. What is your doxology—your command and faith claim—today?
- Read Ephesians 1:3-14. Consider the author's question, Who makes up your family? Do you define your family by looking back to your heritage or looking forward to your legacy and future generations' inheritance?
- Read John 1:1-18. What does it mean for you that Jesus is cocreator in the beginning and takes on human life and suffering as Emmanuel?

Associate dean of Methodist Studies at Candler School of Theology, Emory University; ordained elder in the Florida Conference of The United Methodist Church.

NEW YEAR'S DAY

Is your Christmas tree still up? Are you still overindulging in Christmas goodies? Are you celebrating throughout this week too? I hope so. In stark contrast to the secular season of Christmas, which begins in October and ends on December 25, the Christian season of Christmas begins on December 25 and lasts twelve days until Epiphany on January 6. These two weeks are meant to be an extended time of celebration of God's extraordinary gift—God's entrance into the world as Emmanuel, God with us. That should take twelve days to celebrate!

As someone who struggles with depression at Christmas, I know it can be hard to imagine such ongoing celebration. I, like many others, know the "languish" of which Jeremiah speaks.

Like the promise of redemption through God's incarnation as Jesus, Jeremiah's promises are of God's abundance and the resulting celebration of the redeemed people of Israel. After being led home to Israel from exile in Babylon, they will gather at the center of Jerusalem, "the height of Zion," and they will be "radiant over the goodness of the Lord." Rejoicing, merriment, joy, comfort, and gladness are expressions of a grateful people responding to a God who has heard their cries for redemption and responds.

Christmas calls us into celebration. Christmas calls us into the joy of knowing that God loves us so much that God takes the extraordinary initiative to enter the world as a baby; live among us as one of us; and experience our ugliness, pain, and suffering. And so, even if we struggle with the holidays, we can claim the joy and seek the radiance of knowing the goodness of God. We will languish no more.

Emmanuel, thank you for entering our complicated and difficult world, for being with us, and for calling us into the joy of knowing your love. Amen.

I listened with awe as a young man shared his testimony. His wife died from cancer several years ago. He spoke of the holiness of the moment of her death; he praised God and spoke of his growing faith.

Doxology is a form of praise that we often sing on Sunday mornings. One contemporary version is: "Praise God from whom all blessings flow. Praise God, all creatures here below. Praise God above ye heavenly hosts. Praise Creator, Christ, and Holy Ghost." Grammatically speaking, "Praise God!" is both a command and a faith claim. We praise God during times of well-being and claim that blessings are present even when they are hard to recognize.

Today's scripture is a doxology, the third stanza of a praise hymn sung by the restored, postexilic community in Jerusalem. The passage begins and ends with the sentence "Praise the LORD," both a command to praise and an act of praise by the community. The first two stanzas of Psalm 147 express praise for God's creative initiative, redemptive acts, and abundance. However, the third stanza of the doxology demands and offers praise for God's Word that comes to the people of Jerusalem through the laws that frame their intimate relationship with God.

For Christians, Jesus is the incarnate, redemptive, living expression of God's Word. As disciples of Jesus, we experience through him the most grace-filled expression of God's love in all of creation. As our relationship with Jesus grows stronger and deeper, we grow in our ability to recognize and claim the blessings among us. Our lives are increasingly framed by praise that sustains us, emboldens us, and gives voice to our gratitude and joy—whether surrounding a newborn baby or encircling the deathbed of a loved one.

Praise to you, O God, our Creator, Christ, and Holy Ghost! I praise you amid my struggles, even as I praise you in times of laughter and peace. Amen.

Today's reading introduces a discussion about the relationship between God and Jesus and describes how God and Jesus are united as the Word from the beginning. The Word is with God and is God. The Word speaks, and all things—light and life—come into being. (See Genesis 1.) John testifies that Jesus is the Word made flesh once again as the true light. Jesus is cocreator with God in the beginning of the world and is the true light who enters the world as Emmanuel.

The first few verses of this Gospel drive us to a deeper understanding of God's willingness to relinquish sovereignty, to empty God's self to take on the struggles of human existence, and to testify as the true light to God's all-encompassing love for humanity and all of creation. (See Philippians 2:1-11.) God as Jesus enters the world as a human baby and dies as a criminal. In between, he grows up, attends worship and weddings, struggles with his call on earth, teaches lessons, suffers hunger and homelessness, heals people, breaks laws, and invites himself to dinner with despised people.

Jesus' taking human form means that God, as Jesus, knows us in our greatest weakness, pain, and sin. Nothing about us has been or ever will be hidden from God. And Jesus, as the true light that enlightens everyone—even you and me, provides the means for us to discover the grace of God.

O God, I give up trying to hide myself from you. Help me draw closer to you through Jesus, so that I may know your grace and love forevermore. Amen.

Jesus Christ is God's complete expression of grace and truth. Jesus makes God known to us and to the world. The law is given through Moses, but we receive God's grace and truth through Jesus. But many do not recognize Jesus, including "his own" people, his neighbors in Nazareth and the Pharisees, Sadducees, and high priests in Jerusalem.

Laws provide boundaries and rules that seek to control behavior and protect society. We can all acknowledge that societies need laws in order to function. Some law also shapes identity. The "Law of Moses" shapes the identity of the Jews. But the law does not reveal God to the people. John proclaims that the grace and truth that comes through Jesus Christ makes God known to us.

We live in an age that *New York Times* journalist Thomas Friedman calls "the Age of Accelerations." Friedman describes how humans are losing the capacity to adapt to the pace of technological innovation and expanding information. One way to react is to tighten laws that have proven dependable in the past in order to protect identity and prevent change.

The struggle between the followers of the law and Jesus becomes a key theme of John's Gospel, which concludes with Jesus' resurrection. The resurrection proves the Jewish leaders wrong and implores Peter to demonstrate his love for Jesus by feeding and tending others. (See John 21:15-19.)

How do you feed and tend others in ways that demonstrate your love for Jesus and reveal the grace and truth of God to them? If Jesus is how God is made known to us, how do you now feed and tend to others in a world facing such difficult and complex challenges?

O God, may I see you so fully revealed in Jesus that I cannot help but strive to reveal you to others through my love. Lead me to others who need feeding and tending. Amen.

I love working on my genealogy as a way of discovering my heritage. I have learned a lot about my family members. I am quite proud of some; others, not so much. Most of us define who we are based on whom and where we have come from, from the identity and heritage of our "people." And yet, today, families are changing. Within my own so-called "traditional" family, we now have members from five different countries and four racial/ethnic groups. Most of us don't share heritage and identity. Our shared commitment is to the future of our children and grand-children—our legacy and their inheritance.

Who makes up your family? I am increasingly aware that shared gene pools or heritages do not a family make. Today we often form families through formal or informal extended relationships of trust, nurture, and love. We see this most often among those who have been ostracized by or who live far away from their families of origin.

Ephesians speaks of an inheritance granted originally to Jewish Christians (the "we" of the chapter) that is now shared with Gentile Christians (the "you" of v. 13) through their redemption received "in Christ." Jews had always defined themselves by their differences with rigid laws in place to prevent interaction with Gentiles. But Ephesians insists that when we come together in Christ, we are defined not by a shared heritage but by a shared inheritance. Heritage looks backward; inheritance looks to the future. Heritage, though meaningful, fades in importance compared with what we share and will grow into as we live together in Christ.

So, who makes up your family? Who makes up your church family? Do all these family members share the same heritage or the same inheritance?

God of us all, plant in me your vision of the ingathering that leaves out no one. Help me honor the beauty of our differences and the unity that can ground us in Christ. Amen.

Jesus' Baptism and Ours

JANUARY 6–12, 2020 • E. GLENN HINSON

SCRIPTURE OVERVIEW: As we celebrate the Baptism of the Lord, the readings draw our attention to the connection between baptism and the pouring out of the Spirit. The prophet points forward to the day when God's servant will come, empowered by the Spirit, and bring justice to all people, both Jew and Gentile. In the psalm, the same heavenly voice that will speak over Jesus at his baptism resounds on the earth with might and power. Peter realizes in Acts that he is witnessing the fulfillment of the promise in Isaiah, for through Jesus, God's favor is poured out on people from every nation. Matthew tells the story of Jesus' baptism and of the arrival of the Spirit, confirmed by the heavenly voice of affirmation.

QUESTIONS AND SUGGESTIONS FOR REFLECTION

- Read Isaiah 42:1-9. What does it mean for Jesus to be a Servant Messiah? In what ways does God suffer with or for you?
- Read Psalm 72:1-7, 10-14. As children of God, we are called to reflect God's righteousness. How do you defend the poor and deliver the needy?
- Read Acts 10:34-43. Consider the author's proposal that those who fear God and do what is right may include people of other faiths. What would this mean for your faith and your relationships with those of other faiths?
- Read Matthew 3:13-17. Remember your baptism. Did you make the decision to be baptized or did someone else make the decision for you? How does remembering your baptism guide you to do what God wants?

Author of autobiography, *A Miracle of Grace*; frequent contributor to *Weavings*.

EPIPHANY

Early Christians added the visit of the magi to Bethlehem to the baptism of Jesus as a second interpretation of Epiphany. (The first interpretation of Epiphany was the day of Jesus' baptism, which we now celebrate the first Sunday after Epiphany.) The star-guided trek of the magi from the East to Bethlehem to see the child born in a manger adds to our understanding of God: God not only is the God of the Hebrew people and nation but also the God of people everywhere, in every nation. When we consider the star that guides the magi, we recognize that God is also the God of the universe.

The wise men come from ancient Persia (modern Iran) where Zoroastrianism, which accounts for the strong apocalyptic currents in Judaism and early Christianity, prevails. The story of Herod's murderous plot to eliminate a competitor has garnered most of the attention paid to their visit, but something else deserves serious attention. True to their Zoroastrian training, the wise men look to the heavens for guidance. After a conference with Herod, they set out, "and there, ahead of them, went the star that they had seen at its rising, until it stopped over the place where the child was." Joy overwhelms them. They kneel down and honor the child with gold, frankincense, and myrrh.

In an age informed by science, we treat star-guidance with considerable skepticism. In Matthew's age, however, reliance on astrology made perfect sense. God, the God of the whole universe, uses nature to direct humans. In our own time we are learning anew that all the world is alive with God. It behooves us to pay attention to what God says to us through nature as well as through history and our own lives. Our survival will depend on it.

Sensitize us, O God, to your presence in our whole world lest we miss your word in the natural world. Amen.

Readers of the Gospels will recognize readily the impact the Servant Poems of Isaiah (42:1-4; 49:1-6; 50:4-11; 52:13–53:12) exert on Jesus' understanding of himself and God's expectations of him. Scholars hold differing views on the identity of the Servant. Some think the Servant is the nation; others, an individual. Yet it is clear that Jesus applies this identity to himself. God does not intend for him to be a Messiah like David who restores the kingdom of Israel but a Servant Messiah, one suffering with and for the people.

At Jesus' baptism, the voice from heaven certifies him with the opening words of the poem: "My chosen, in whom my soul delights" becomes "my Son, the Beloved, with whom I am well pleased" (Matt. 3:17). God puts the Spirit upon the Servant with the promise that "he will bring forth justice to the nations"; in Jesus' words, he will "fulfill all righteousness" (Matt. 3:15).

As the temptations in the desert will convince Jesus, his way will not be the way of power perfected by might but the way of power perfected through weakness and vulnerability. This idea in this poem and also in Jesus' life is one we humans find difficult to grasp. The Servant will not break a bruised reed or quench a burning wick and yet "he will faithfully bring forth justice." He will not give up, no matter how great the suffering, until he achieves God's purpose—"justice in the earth."

We do well to note that the Servant works for justice everywhere, not only among God's chosen people. Through him we gain this remarkable insight about God: God is our Fellow Sufferer. God may not cure every ill, put an end to death, or turn all our nights into day; but God can and does suffer with us and for us.

Pour your Spirit into our hearts, O loving God, that we may accept your vulnerability along with our own. Amen.

Devout Jewish Christians find it hard to believe that God accepts people into the Christian fold without the Jewish requirements for admission—baptism for all and circumcision for males. One of Jesus' most dedicated followers, Simon Peter, is among the skeptical. It takes a dramatic dream to change his mind.

When an angel tells the Roman centurion Cornelius in a vision to go to Simon Peter (see Acts 10:1-8), Peter undoubtedly still has reservations about the wideness of God's mercy. But his dream of a sheet let down from heaven filled with all sorts of ritually forbidden foods he is told to eat (10:9-16) settles the matter. When Peter finally meets with Cornelius, Peter makes the speech of his life: He boldly asserts that God, the God he has come to know in and through Jesus Christ, "shows no partiality." Quite the contrary, as Isaiah declares long before, God reaches out to embrace all people and all nations. What does God require? Not observance of certain food laws or customs such as circumcision of males but that "in every nation anyone who fears [God] and does what is right is acceptable to [God]."

The kind of fear Peter talks about is not groveling in terror, but showing reverence. We display such reverence not when we recite a creed of some kind but when we do justice, love mercy, and walk humbly with God. (See Micah 6:8.) Like Peter, we need to ask in our day whether those who fear and do what is right include people of other faiths—Muslims, Buddhists, Hindus, Taoists, Confucians—and perhaps even people who may list themselves as "nones." How wide is God's mercy? Is it like the wideness of the sea?

O God, liberate us from conceptions and ideas that make you smaller than you are, and open our minds to praise you for mercy wide enough to include all people as your children. Amen.

The words of this prayer for a newly installed king apply just as readily to leaders of countries with a different form of government. They surely embody hopes and aspirations that I would wish for the United States of America. Yet many Americans, influenced deeply by the "gospel" of Ayn Rand, might find the focus on the poor and needy hard to accept and apply. The Israelite people, to be sure, pray for other concerns connected with their concept of righteousness (*tzedek*), or fair judgment. But the author of this psalm equates righteousness specifically with defending the poor and delivering the needy. Likewise, in the Sermon on the Mount, Jesus defines giving of alms for the needy as "righteousness" (*dikaiosune*). (See Matthew 6:1-2.) Prayer for the poor and needy is not a casual element in Jewish piety; it is central.

The question is this: Where does such concern come from? The psalmist asserts that human concern for the poor and needy stems from God's concern. God instills righteous and compassionate character. So the prayer opens with the plea, "Give to the king your justice, O God, and your righteousness to a king's son." Righteousness belongs to God's very nature, and if we claim to know God, we should reflect it instinctively. Jesus once again echoes such thinking in the parable of the last judgment. (See Matthew 25:31-46.) Those invited into the kingdom of heaven will be those who feed the hungry, give drink to the thirsty, clothe the naked, and welcome strangers into their homes without even thinking about it. Indeed, these actions are so natural for those who will enter the kingdom of heaven that when the Master says they have been invited because they do these things for him, they have to ask, "When?"

O God, grant our leaders your righteousness, so that they will defend the cause of the poor and deliver the needy who have no helper. Amen.

All of us experience darkness at some time in our lives. One of my moments stands stark in my memory. My wife of sixty-one years died May 17, 2018, after a long walk deep into the forest of dementia. Watching the light of life go out in a loved one's life is what the psalmist called "the valley of the shadow of death" (Ps. 23:4, KJV).

Second Isaiah has watched Jerusalem, his beloved city, be destroyed by its enemies. At times he has delivered stern warnings to his people for their failings. But in grand poems he celebrates the glory of Jerusalem and God's people. (See Isaiah 60:1–62:12.) "Arise, shine"; the prophet exclaims, "for your light has come, and the glory of the LORD has risen upon you." Turned in on their own miseries, people who have watched their city torn down and have been carried away into captivity may find such words hard to comprehend. Darkness has swallowed up their hopes and dreams. The prophet recognizes their suffering. Darkness envelops the earth and its peoples.

Such depictions accurately define what we see happening today in our world, where we witness nations torn apart by war, schools decimated by weapons of mass destruction, and more refugees than at any period in history except World War II. In such circumstances, dare we believe that the Lord will arise upon us? Yes, we dare! How could we face such happenings with any other confidence than that God is our light and our hope? When the light of God illumines us, it may shock us to find that other people may make their way to the brightness of our dawn.

O God, may we not fear as we pass through life's dark vales. Rather, may your light so shine in us and through us that others may see the dawn. Amen.

No one knows the boundlessness of God's grace better than the apostle Paul. He knows it experientially through what he has done and what he has become. According to Luke, those who stone Stephen "[lay] their coats at the feet of a young man named Saul" (Acts 7:58). In his letter to the Philippians, Paul confesses that he has been "a persecutor of the church" (3:6) but that he has put aside his former life and counted it as rubbish "because of the surpassing value of knowing Christ Jesus my Lord" (3:8).

The way Paul, self-described "prisoner for Jesus Christ for the sake of you Gentiles," speaks about his commissioning by God's grace prompts us to ask what grace is and how it works in our lives. In Paul's understanding, grace is not merely a "gift," as the Greek word *charis* signifies. Grace is God's gift of Godself, God present and at work in human lives through the Holy Spirit. Such an understanding breaks through to Paul in his urgent prayer for removal of his "thorn in the flesh." We do not know for sure what the "thorn in the flesh" is, but it is clear he wants it removed. He says, "Three times I appealed to the Lord about this, that it would leave me" (2 Cor. 12:8). Paul's asking God three times signifies that he has pulled out all the stops. Yet he does not get the answer he wants. Instead, God answers, "My grace is sufficient for you, for my power is made perfect in weakness" (12:9). Grace is God with us, sharing our human vulnerability.

O God, help me to become attentive to your presence and your grace in moments both high and low in my life. Amen.

BAPTISM OF THE LORD

As early as the third century CE, Christians in the East celebrated January 6 as the date of Jesus' baptism. In time that celebration joined Easter and Pentecost as one of the three most important feasts in the Christian calendar. In the West, we now celebrate Jesus' baptism on the first Sunday after January 6. The main feature of the feast is the blessing of the baptismal waters.

In our text from Matthew 3:13-17, John the Baptist voices this question: Why is Jesus baptized? It seems fairly clear that a sect composed of followers of John the Baptist consider him the Messiah and Jesus one of his followers. John's words and the events surrounding Jesus' baptism negate such thinking. Matthew takes care to distinguish John's baptism from Christian baptism, as Paul does in Ephesus for some who are baptized "into John's baptism" but "have not even heard that there is a Holy Spirit" (Acts 19).

According to Matthew, John the Baptist makes the distinction between his and the Messiah's baptisms: "I baptize you with water for repentance," but he "will baptize you with the Holy Spirit and fire" (Matt. 3:11). When Jesus presents himself for baptism, John dissents: "I need to be baptized by you, and do you come to me?" (v. 12). In response Jesus explains why he has come for baptism—"to fulfill all righteousness." His baptism signifies his desire to do what God wants him to do with his life. Confirmation of God's desire for Jesus to be baptized comes in the baptism itself. A voice from heaven says, "This is my Son, the Beloved, with whom I am well pleased." Is this not also what our baptism should mean—that we want to do what God wants us to?

Dear God, in baptism you put a seal on my life. May I faithfully honor this day the vow I took to do what is right. Amen.

Called in the Sight of God

JANUARY 13–19, 2020 • KATHLEEN R. FLOOD, OP

SCRIPTURE OVERVIEW: These readings contain the common theme of the power of spoken testimony. Isaiah begins by telling his audience, "Listen to me!" He then recounts not only his own story but also the promises of restoration given to him by God. The psalmist gives testimony of his experience. Although he has been in a difficult place, God has called him out and has given him a new song of praise to proclaim. Paul and Sosthenes write to the Corinthians to remind them of the powerful testimony that they had given them in person, which was confirmed by God. John the Baptist cries out that Jesus is the Lamb of God and bears testimony to the miraculous signs at the baptism. Our testimony as believers today can be just as powerful.

QUESTIONS AND SUGGESTIONS FOR REFLECTION

- Read Isaiah 49:1-7. What does it mean to be God's servant? How does this Servant Song speak of your experiences of serving God?
- Read Psalm 40:1-11. When has scripture sustained you? What words have become a real presence to you?
- Read 1 Corinthians 1:1-9. When have you turned your gifts inward as a sign of spiritual or social status? How can gratitude help you use your gifts in service to God and others?
- Read John 1:29-42. How have you experienced Jesus saying to you, "Come and see"?

Member of the Dominican Sisters of Sinsinawa, Wisconsin.

One crisp wintry day when I was a young girl, I decided to go for a walk after school. Shortly after I started my walk, snow began to fall. Within a few minutes, the snowfall became heavy, and I found it difficult to see. I became disoriented, and I was not sure how to find my way home. I was afraid and did not know what to do. My mother became concerned, so she turned on the porch light. I had just started to get my bearings when I saw the glow of the porch light in the distance. I followed that light and found my way home.

In today's reading, the Israelites are caught—not in a snowstorm but in storms of captivity and loss. They experience disorientation and fear too. Like my mother did for me, God provides a light for the Israelites. God's people, Israel, have experienced defeat, the destruction of the Temple, the loss of their land, and exile. The hopes of the people are pinned on their return to Jerusalem. In today's passage, Isaiah prophesies for the third time the coming of a Servant. (The first, second, and fourth Servant Songs are found in Isaiah 42:1-4, Isaiah 50:4-11, and Isaiah 52:13–53:12.) The third Servant Song is prophesied amid the people's despair. It brings a glimmer of hope. The prophet describes an agent, a Servant whom God is raising up. The task of the people of Israel is to listen and believe the message. Isaiah prophesies that God's Servant will shout the message from the mountaintops to the coastlands. The Servant will make it known that Israel is still the people of God.

Have you experienced a time of disorientation? What words or events brought you a glimmer of hope?

Yesterday we reflected on Isaiah's prophecy of a Servant whom God sends to live among a people who have experienced disorientation and exile. We learn in verse 4 that this prophecy includes a sense of personal disillusionment: "I have labored in vain." There are days when we feel the same. Not only do we doubt our work; we feel exiled from the land of our hopes and dreams.

Amid this lament a new sense of hope rises. God sends this Servant with a promise of transformation. Hope rises in us too as we read the address to "you peoples from far away." The Servant's mission is not just for the restoration of Israel; it is for the whole world. The story of exile comes to an end with a new story of restoration on the horizon. The description of the Servant brings us some clues.

The Servant's mouth will be "like a sharp sword." His words will cut through all the chattering voices to speak the truth. The message will be like a "polished arrow" and land where it is aimed. Its target is the restoration of the tribes of Jacob and all creation. God has dreamed of Israel's freedom from even before the Servant was born. "God called me before I was born, while I was in my mother's womb God named me."

The task will not be easy. The Servant will be honored "in the sight of the LORD," and God will provide the strength. The rulers of Israel's time will not be impressed with the message and will despise the Servant. On that day, though, the leaders of all nations will honor the God who is faithful.

God chooses the Servant; God chooses us too.

What message does our world need to hear today? What message is God calling you to proclaim?

Called in the Sight of God   31

One Sunday when I was a child, the pastor of my church announced that a missionary would be visiting us. She was a professor in India. I asked my mother two questions: "Where is India?" and "What is a professor?" She showed me where India is on a globe. Then she told me that a professor was someone who was very smart and taught adults. Years later I learned another definition. In his book *The Promise of Paradox*, Parker J. Palmer writes, "*Professor* originally meant someone who professed a faith."*

Today we meet missionary and professor Paul. Paul preaches and teaches in Corinth for over a year. His work in Corinth is entrusted to him by a mysterious encounter with Jesus. (See Acts 18:9-11.) The Christian community grows, and Paul continues his missionary journey.

Paul begins this letter, like all his letters, with a word of thanksgiving. He gives thanks for the grace the Corinthians have received in Christ Jesus. They are blessed with knowledge and speech and other spiritual gifts. (Later in the letter Paul will name many of these gifts.) Paul wants the believers at Corinth to remember the source of their gifts.

In our short passage we get some clues about Paul's concerns that he will develop in the body of the letter. One concern is that the Corinthians seem to be enamored with the gifts themselves rather than the reason for the gifts. They are content with what they have and turn away from further manifestations of the Spirit. "Already you have all you want! Already you have become rich (4:8). You think you are in charge!"

*p. 117

How can you begin your communications with others by first giving thanks?

When I was a child, I would wait with great expectation at the end of the sidewalk in the front of my house. I was waiting for my dad to come home from work. We had a daily ritual: I would put my feet on top of his, and we would walk together to the front steps. As hard as I tried I could only go a couple of steps, and then I would fall off. One day, after several attempts, my dad made a suggestion. He told me to hold his hands, lean back, and look into his eyes. We walked together, with no falls, to the steps. I know now my dad wanted me to look up instead of down at my feet. When I looked down I lost my balance. The secret was in seeing each other.

Our passage from the Gospel of John shows scenes from a journey. John the Baptist has been testifying and baptizing in the area of Bethany. When he is questioned by the authorities about his message, he tells them he is not the one God is sending. The next day John sees Jesus and says to his followers, "Here is the Lamb of God who takes away the sin of the world." John continues to describe Jesus. He tells of his baptism of Jesus. I can only imagine them leaning in and listening to John describe the event: I saw a dove descend and remain. Jesus is not only baptized with water; he receives the Holy Spirit.

The next day after the baptism the writer tells us that John is walking with his disciples. John sees Jesus and says to his disciples: "Look, here is the Lamb of God." After hearing this, two of John's disciples start following Jesus.

When was the last time you heard a testimony about Jesus? How did it affect you?

Jesus notices the two disciples following him and asks, "What are you looking for?" It is a pivotal question in any encounter. It opens up the possibility for dialogue. We learn an important lesson here: Our task is to focus on what people are looking for instead of assuming we know what they need or want. John's disciples reply, "'Rabbi' (which translated means Teacher), 'where are you staying?'" When we hear these ancient words we realize how contemporary they are. So many people are looking for answers to their spiritual questions. The world can seem chaotic and gloomy like it was at the time of Isaiah. We ask, "Where are you, God?"

Jesus answers their question and ours: "Come and see." He invites them into a relationship where they will find fulfillment of their longings. Andrew is convinced by his experience of Jesus and invites his brother to join them. I often wonder about what they see. I believe they begin to see with the eyes of their heart. They see Jesus' concern for the widow and orphan, his feeding of people hungry for hope, and people crippled by fear and despair lifted up.

The words of an old hymn come to mind. "Turn your eyes upon Jesus, look full in his wonderful face, and the things of earth will grow strangely dim in the light of his glory and grace" (UMH, no. 349).

I close with an invitation offered by John Mogabgab in his editor's introduction to the January/February 2004 edition of *Weavings*: "During this holy season, let us listen and understand, look and perceive the one who even today responds to our heart's desire with the words, 'Come and see.'"

How will you answer Jesus' question, "What are you looking for?" What do you need to see?

Two years ago I was diagnosed with a severe infection. It took me over six moths to recover fully. When I was in the hospital, the nights were long and lonely. I found comfort in praying the Compline, the last prayer of the night in a monastic community. The words of the psalms I carried in my heart became companions. I also remembered what Henri Nouwen wrote about the psalms and the Compline in August of 1974: "I start realizing that the psalms of Compline slowly become flesh in me . . . slowly these words enter the center of my heart. They become a real presence."*

The most difficult part of healing from an illness is the waiting. It can be "the pits." Waiting is not easy for anyone. We wait for the results of tests. We wait to feel better. We all have experiences of waiting. The psalmist waited with patience, yet that can be extremely difficult. "I waited patiently for the Lord; he inclined to me and heard my cry."

The psalmist then tells the story of God's presence and deliverance: "I have told the glad news of deliverance in the great congregation . . . I have not hidden your saving help within my heart." The story of God's saving help echoes the prophecy we read in Isaiah. The words of Psalm 40 may have been the same words the exiles sang on their way home.

What about us? There are days when we feel in the pits, sinking in a muddy bog. On such days, we can reach into our hearts and bring forth words of hope, mercy, and faithfulness. We sing along with the ancient words that God "put a new song in my mouth, a song of praise."

*The Genesee Diary, 99–100.

What psalm(s) of praise do you have in your heart?

The believers at Corinth have every gift they need to be a community of life and light. They turn their gifts inward and use them to claim status instead of turning them outward to be a beacon, a witness to the work of the Spirit among them. Paul seems to question why they would boast about something that was a gift. Do they not know that their knowledge and wisdom, their spiritual gifts, are from God? They are given by grace to manifest Christ.

When I was a new campus chaplain, a student came to talk with me about a big problem. She obviously was upset. I asked her about the problem. "I have failed at prayer," she replied. (I was not sure how one could fail at prayer.) "I do not have the 'gift.' I have not experienced speaking in tongues, so I have failed. Everybody else has received that gift. I cannot go back to that group again." I reminded her that the Spirit gives many gifts and named some that I saw in her. I do not know the end of her story, but I believe what I told her that day.

Paul writes to a community that may have made the same judgment, that some were blessed more than others and that some spiritual gifts were more important than others. Paul cautions them and us not to be too self-impressed. When we read a little forward in the text we find Paul's "bottom line": "I decided to know nothing among you except Jesus Christ, and him crucified" (2:2).

Paul's words bring us back to where we began this week's reflections: We are called to be people of gratitude for the work of the Spirit of God among us.

What gifts has God given you and others in your church to bless your community? What gifts among your members might be overlooked?

The Light of Liberation

JANUARY 20–26, 2020 • KRISTEN E. VINCENT

SCRIPTURE OVERVIEW: Sometimes we struggle with the challenges we face. If God is good and God is for us, then why do we experience pain and loss? Isaiah feels the sting of darkness and despair, and the psalmist has experienced days of distress. Yet both encourage themselves with the promise that God has not forgotten them. The light will come, as will the shouts of joy. The New Testament readings warn against following human leaders to the extent that we take our eyes off Christ. The Corinthian church has divided into factions that identify primarily with Paul or Peter, not Christ! The Gospel reading shows that Peter, like all other human leaders, is merely a disciple himself. Jesus is the one we should seek to follow.

QUESTIONS AND SUGGESTIONS FOR REFLECTION

- Read Isaiah 9:1-4. How has God's love freed you to find your calling?
- Read Psalm 27:1, 4-9. When have you called out to God? How has God helped you turn your cries to praise?
- Read 1 Corinthians 1:10-18. How have you experienced division within the body of Christ? How might a focus on Christ rather than particular faith leaders or denominations help you to repair division and work through differences?
- Read Matthew 4:12-23. How have significant changes in your life (like a loved one's death or a career change) allowed your ministry to grow?

Award-winning author, retreat leader, and artisan in spiritual formation, prayer beads, and helping others heal from trauma; graduate of Duke Divinity School and the Academy for Spiritual Formation (#34); lives in Atlanta with husband, Max, a UMC pastor, and son, Matthew.

Freedom from Darkness

As I write, the sun is shining. Given our recent weather in Atlanta, Georgia, this is no small thing. For five straight days we have endured dark clouds and rain. By day three, the grey days had begun to affect me. I felt sleepy and somber, overcome by the dreariness and wanting nothing more than to stay in bed and hibernate. I know I was not alone because this morning the sidewalks are full of people walking dogs, running, and riding bikes. People are in the park, chatting, laughing, and throwing frisbees. As I walk, people smile at me and wave, many commenting on the arrival of the sun. We are grateful to be in the light again.

Isaiah is speaking to people who have been living in another type of darkness for a very long time. The tribes of Zebulun and Naphtali have been conquered and forced to endure poverty and harsh treatment by those in power. This has gone on for generations, long enough for the people to feel as if they are in a "pitch-dark land" (CEB) with no way out. I imagine that many of them have given up or even have accepted that life is nothing more than their oppression.

Yet Isaiah is proclaiming that the people will see a great light. This light will be like no other. It will break through the darkness and shine across the land. It will bring freedom from their oppressors. And it will come in time; Isaiah declares the light will come before the people become "exhausted," before they give up. The light will be a light of liberation, freeing them for a whole new way of being.

Lord, there are times in my life when I feel like I am in darkness, a darkness that will not lift. Yet you are the light that will never be extinguished. Help me to be still and recognize the signs of your light around me. Amen.

Freedom from Fear

A quote that used to hang in my office read, "What would you do if you weren't afraid?" For many years that quote held meaning for me. I recognized I had a lot of fear in my life, and I knew it was holding me back. Sitting with that quote, I imagined how different my life would be without fear. I dreamed of things I would do, risks I would take. And I realized that without fear I would be free to live boldly into the life God intends for me.

David certainly understands the power of fear as he writes Psalm 27. As a teenager taking on Goliath, as the ruler of a kingdom facing various threats, and as the veteran of many battles, David has experienced fear many times. Still, David has killed the giant. He has become a powerful king and has defeated many adversaries. David explains that this success has been possible because of the light of the Lord, a light that repeatedly has protected and saved him from his enemies. Because of this, David has learned to trust in the Lord, moving forward with confidence into his calling.

Still, there are moments when David is afraid, times when he cries out to the Lord. Rather than indicating a loss of faith, his cries are modeling faith for us: In moments of darkness, we cannot help but call out to God. In doing so, we acknowledge that God exists even though we may not feel God's presence. As we call out, God brings us toward the light. Though it may not happen as quickly as we'd like or in the way we'd like, God will always bring us into the light, free us from fear, and free us to live into God's calling.

Lord of light, help me to cry out to you in the darkness. Deliver me from fear so that I may live boldly into your calling for me. Amen.

Freedom from Bondage

Can You Ever Forgive Me? is a true story about celebrity biographer Lee Israel. After enjoying success writing biographies of people like Katherine Hepburn and Estée Lauder, Israel discovers that her audience's tastes have changed. They no longer want to read about such figures, but Israel seems incapable of shifting to new subject matter. Unable to pay her rent and other bills and becoming more of an alcoholic, Israel begins forging letters from deceased celebrities and selling them to collectors. After selling more than 400 letters, Israel is arrested.

In the movie scene where Israel is being sentenced by the court, she admits she wrote in other people's voices because she feared writing in her own and thus opening herself up to criticism. Israel is sentenced to house arrest and five years probation. During this time, she writes her own autobiography detailing her career as a literary forger. *The New York Times Book Review* called it "exquisitely written" and "fabulous."

This story is tragic for me. Clearly, Israel was a talented writer and found satisfaction in the writing process. But she got so caught up in writing in other people's voices that she lost her own. It isn't until she's left with no other choice that she finally writes her own story in her own voice. And the critics praise her for it. Freed from the bondage of her ego, fear, and addiction, Israel is able to be authentic. I wonder what her life would have been like had she been able to do that sooner.

The people of Zebulun and Naphtali are bound, both literally and figuratively. But Isaiah promises that one day they will be freed from bondage. And then they will live into their calling and find great joy.

Dear Lord, help me to recognize what binds me and keeps me from living into my calling. Free me so that I reflect you more clearly. Amen.

Freedom from Death

John the Baptist has been arrested, which appears to set two things in motion. First, upon learning of John's arrest, Jesus relocates to Galilee. This move signals a fulfillment of Isaiah's prophecy to the people of Zebulun and Naphtali. Jesus is the light Isaiah referenced, the one who would deliver the people from darkness. And that light is now in Galilee, as promised.

Second, Matthew tells us that once Jesus arrives in Galilee, he immediately begins preaching. In other words, we are witnessing the genesis of Jesus' ministry. Indeed, immediately following this passage, Jesus starts to call the first of his disciples.

What interests me most about this passage is the relationship between John and Jesus. John's ministry had always been about pointing toward Jesus, foretelling his coming, calling people to repentance as a way of preparing for the Messiah. Now Jesus is here, ready to live into his calling as the Anointed One. He has been baptized, God has called him God's beloved Son, and he has spent forty days in the desert being tempted and gaining clarity about his purpose. The time has come. There is nothing more for John to do. He is arrested and eventually killed.

It seems that Jesus waits for John to finish his ministry before beginning his own. With John gone, the people are free to shift their focus to Jesus. With John gone, Jesus can fulfill his calling. This means John's arrest and death are not in vain. They open the way for Jesus, who is the Light. He is the Light who will brighten the darkness, the Light who will overcome the shadow of death. John was not the Light; he could only point to this Light that will free us from death. Now the Light is with us. Thanks be to God.

Lord, free me from the darkness of death so that I can point others toward your light. Amen.

Freedom to Receive

Jesus has begun his ministry, but he's not going to do it alone; he clearly plans to involve others in this venture. This makes sense on a number of levels: He is a teacher, a rabbi, and thus must have students so they can learn from him and continue his ministry. Also, he wants to spread the good news of God's kingdom, which, as they say, takes a village. I imagine he recognizes how hard this journey will be and knows he will need the support of a community to fulfill his calling.

Walking along the Sea of Galilee, Jesus sees Simon and Peter casting their nets. Using a fishing metaphor, he invites the two to follow him, and they do. Eventually, the new trio comes across two more fisherman brothers—James and John—and calls them. They too stop what they are doing and immediately join the group.

What's striking is how quickly the four join him; they do so without reservation. They do not question him or ask for clarification. They do not take time to finish their work or say goodbye to their loved ones. They just go.

Clearly, something about Jesus leads them to respond so confidently. It could be his voice, the look in his eyes, the way in which he holds himself. I imagine it is the light shining through him. I imagine that Simon, Peter, James, and John all look up and recognize something brilliant about this man, and so they do not hesitate to step out of their boats, their identities, their ways of life, and follow him.

The Light is like that. It is so brilliant we can't help but want to follow it. This frees us to let go of things that keep us from following the Light.

Lord, help me to let go of anything that keeps me from walking in your light. Free me for joyful obedience. Amen.

Freedom to Praise

About ten years ago I heard "Revelation Song" by Jeannie Lee Riddle for the first time. Although it was beautiful, I thought the lyrics didn't make sense; they seemed to be a jumble of words. Then a friend explained that the lyrics are from Revelation, chapters 4 and 5. Turning to the passage, I read about the point in John's vision when all of creation comes before Jesus, who is sitting on his throne in heaven, and begins to praise him.

Suddenly, I got it; I understood why the song lyrics had sounded so jumbled. In the scripture passage, there is much repetition: "Holy, holy, holy, the Lord God the Almighty, who was and is and is to come" (Rev. 4:8) and "Worthy is the Lamb that was slaughtered!" (Rev. 5:12). And it's no wonder. I have no doubt that when all of creation is gathered up into God's kingdom and we are in Christ's presence, we will not be able to help ourselves: We will want to praise, praise, and praise some more. With so much praising, we will run out of words because there are not enough available to adequately express our praise of God. And so we will repeat ourselves and jumble our words. We will shout and sing and dance and laugh. We will be free to praise in a way we have never experienced before.

This is what I imagine David has in mind as he writes the words of Psalm 27. He wants just one thing: to live in the Lord's house for eternity and be able to offer constant praise. He wants to see the Lord's beauty, offer sacrifices, shout with joy, and sing. David understands that when he is in God's presence, he will be free to praise God however and whenever he can, over and over, forever and ever. Amen.

God of all creation, free me to praise you forevermore. Amen.

Freedom to Be in Community

The sun was shining high over Jerusalem. The poor guy sitting on the roof just wanted some relief from the heat. So he moved his chair a few feet over into the shade. Immediately, he heard shouting. As he turned to look, he saw several angry men rushing toward him. They began hurling stones and iron bars at the young guy, whose friends jumped in to defend him. In the end, eleven people were sent to the hospital for injuries.

This could be a scene from a movie, but it's not. This incident took place in 2002 at Jerusalem's Church of the Holy Sepulchre, one of the holiest sites in Christian tradition. The church is believed to stand on the site where Jesus Christ was crucified, buried, and resurrected. Rather than serve as a place to unify Christians, the church has become the center of deep division. For centuries, members of six denominations have fought over property rights to the church. Because they do not trust one another, a Muslim family keeps control of the key to the church.

The church in Corinth appears to be similarly divided. Paul has learned that people are arguing over whose minister is better. Paul reminds the Corinthians that it doesn't matter who their minister is; it's not their ministers who gave their lives upon the cross and in whose name people are baptized. They should be focused on Jesus. In Jesus there are no divisions, only unity.

I imagine that was good news for the Corinthians. I hope it is for us. Disagreements and divisions require a lot of energy; you have to be concerned about boundaries, careful about what you say and how you say it, worried about where you place your chair. Jesus breaks through such division, freeing us to live in community.

Lord Jesus, help me to focus on you so that I may be free to embrace my community. Amen.

Holy Relationship Rules 101

JANUARY 27—FEBRUARY 2, 2020 • ENUMA OKORO

SCRIPTURE OVERVIEW: We must beware counterfeit gospels. According to one current counterfeit gospel, we deserve God's favor based on our deeds or intellect or status. The readings for this week remind us that this is false. Yes, the Israelites offer sacrifices, but they are first and foremost called to show mercy because they have received divine mercy. The psalmist asks who can stand in God's holy dwelling and so provides a list of ways to live morally. Ultimately no one can stand before God on merit alone. Paul reminds the Corinthians that human wisdom is foolishness compared to the wisdom of God, and thus we should not puff ourselves up based on our intellect. Jesus teaches that those who may seem insignificant in the eyes of the world are great in the kingdom of heaven.

QUESTIONS AND SUGGESTIONS FOR REFLECTION

- Read Micah 6:1-8. How have you let down God? What changes can you make to recommit to your relationship with God?
- Read Psalm 15. Consider the notion that the requirements for dwelling with God are in how we treat our friends and neighbors. How does this change the ways you seek God?
- Read 1 Corinthians 1:18-31. When have you seen God's work in the world in a way that is antithetical to human standards?
- Read Matthew 5:1-12. How do you maintain a poverty of spirit in your relationship with God? How does this help you to serve God and others?

Writer, speaker, and teacher; spiritual director in the Ignatian Tradition; 2003 graduate of Duke Divinity School; member of the Roman Catholic Church.

In the sixth chapter of Micah, God is taking the people to court. Their behavior has been unwarranted and offensive, and God wants to make a plea against them. So God calls the mountains and the hills to be witnesses in the case against the Israelites. This passage reveals to us that God is upset and perhaps even angry, enough to make a formal complaint against God's own children. But before we focus on the valid anger, it is important to remember that God is so upset because God takes the relationship with humanity seriously. During the time of this passage, that relationship is in jeopardy because the Israelites aren't living as though the relationship matters as much to them.

We all know what it's like to have a supposed friend who claims to be committed to the friendship but then never quite makes the effort to work on its weaknesses. Some of us currently are in relationships just like that. The "friend" or partner just does not care enough to react. But God is committed to having a strong and life-giving relationship with us and will let us know when we've hurt or offended God and will hold us accountable in our relationship. We may find it strange to think of hurting God, but love comes with vulnerability. Loving others gives them the power to hurt us. And God loves us deeply. While it may be mind-blowing to think of God's choosing to be vulnerable with us, this passage reminds us that God has been choosing vulnerability since Creation, even before the Incarnation, which was the ultimate act of holy vulnerability.

Lord, convict me where I've grown complacent in my relationship with you. I am committed to you. Amen.

God begins the case against the Israelites by reminding them of God's saving acts of service, mercy, and love toward them. It is as though God is asking the beloved people, "Do you not remember who I am and who I have been to you?"

When we've been in a relationship a long time, we can easily forget the attributes that make us love, appreciate, and rely on our loved ones. Familiarity breeds comfort—but not always in a good way. The Israelites' seeming loss of memory is doubly astounding because God has saved their lives time and again. God delivers them from slavery in Egypt and gives them not one but three leaders to help them. Moses teaches and instructs them. Aaron atones for them, and Miriam demonstrates the call to worship and praise in constant recognition of God's provision and deliverance. Even when others plot against the Israelites or they sin and should be punished, God still chooses to protect them. God's complaints are justified, and God wants answers.

We may be uncomfortable with thinking about where we have let God down. But self-reflection on how we may or may not be nurturing that relationship is an important practice in our relationship with God; it is a healthy practice for any important relationship. Our relationship with God should be our most important one because it helps us remember who we are, whose we are, and who we are called to be in all areas of our life.

God, thank you for your mercy and grace. Forgive me when I take your loving actions toward me for granted. You watch over me even when I'm unaware of it. Remind me of all your good works toward me, and help me to be faithful in my relationship with you. Amen.

Scholars suggest that Psalm 15 is an "entrance liturgy," a psalm offered in preparation for the faithful to enter the house of God. The question posed in the psalm is both an earnest imploring and a teaching moment. Who is worthy enough to abide in God's presence? There is a beautiful aspect to this question: It presumes that we can abide and dwell in God's presence. As if it weren't grace enough that God permits us to know God and speak to God, God also permits us to abide and dwell, to stay in God's presence, and to be in continual worshipful relationship with God. But what does that presence mean? How do we get to abide there?

As with all things, we have been given free choice to live by God's tenets or to do things our way. We can dwell in the holy presence if we're willing to do what God requires of us. The choice to do things God's way always seems costly. We may have to live in ways that do not come easily for us, like putting others' needs before our own or choosing vulnerability and humility over self-protection and pride. But eventually we learn that God holds us to these terms because God knows that we are our best selves when we are in healthy relationship with God and with one another. So it makes sense that the requirement for who gets to dwell with God is wrapped up tightly with how well we live in relationship with one another. How we treat our friends and our neighbors, even those who may not be our friends, has direct repercussions on how we dwell with God.

Lord, you call me to be a better version of myself because you want me to experience fullness of life in relationship with you and others. Open my heart to receive your call to dwell in you through my words and actions with others. Amen.

We often have our own ideas of how God should show up in our lives, but God chooses the boundaries of our relationship. The Corinthian church has both Greek and Jewish members, and each group of believers has its own ideas of how God should show up in the world. The Jews want a God recognizable by power. The Greeks want a God known by wisdom.

God is indeed known by power and wisdom but not in ways the world expects such attributes to play out. Christ crucified on the cross is God's idea of power and wisdom through humility, servanthood, and love. The crucified Christ is God's central way of revealing God's self to humanity and seeking relationship with us. But for the Corinthians' culture and time, the cross is a symbol of failure, weakness, and defeat. Paul's message about God's choosing the cross makes no sense to believers. But that is the point: The God of the Incarnation, Crucifixion, and Resurrection makes little sense to human minds.

The wisdom of the world is often at odds with the wisdom of God. Paul's message to the church in Corinth is as relevant today as it was then. If we believe we are made in the image of God and called to mimic God, then we have to abide by the way God chooses to reveal God's self to us. God has chosen the servant way of the cross. Success in the kingdom of God may look different than success in the world. To follow Christ means to agree to new standards of what it means to be powerful and wise, even in ways that may look weak and foolish by the world's standards. The world's benchmarks no longer apply to how we judge and live our lives. Christ is our benchmark. Christ is the power and the wisdom of God.

Lord, help me to discern between your ways and the ways of the world, and turn my heart toward your ways. Amen.

God's ways are the opposite of the world's. So Paul is trying to teach the Corinthians that they shouldn't try to discern God's working by looking at the usual people and places that the world says produce great outcomes. As the ultimate object lesson, Paul instructs the Corinthians to take a good look at themselves to better understand how God works in the world. Most of the Corinthian Christians are average, ordinary citizens. Theirs isn't a congregation of wealthy businessmen, socialites, celebrated academics, or politicians. Yet God is present among them and uses them to spread the gospel and bear witness to a life lived by God's standards. Paul wants believers to understand that God initiates our work because God defines the boundaries of our relationship with God and the terms by which we dwell and abide in God and God's ways. This reminder contains a lesson in recognizing our inherent value and worth in God despite what the world says makes someone valuable and useful and worthy.

We so often gauge our usefulness by the world's standards. Are we making enough money to be worthy? Are we saying the right things to be considered intelligent? Are we doing enough to be seen as useful and valuable? Are we attractive enough to be noticed and lauded and wanted? But for God, none of these attributes is required for us to be called and used to change the world.

We might be rich and intelligent. We might have jobs with plenty of responsibility. We might be physically beautiful. God can use us with all of that. But, according to scripture, God can also use people who don't seem to have anything extraordinary to offer by the world's standards. God's work in and through us is not about our own abilities. The power always comes from God. We just have to be willing and obedient.

Lord, thank you for calling and equipping me. Help me believe that I am capable of being who you are forming me to be. Amen.

A ll week we have been reading about how God sets boundaries for our relationship with God and guidelines for abiding in God's presence—being in the kingdom of God. With all these boundaries and guidelines, God tells us repeatedly that the righteousness of Christ and the power of the Holy Spirit enable us to be in ongoing relationship with God. It's good to hold in mind these promises as we read today's passage.

The Beatitudes, which are part of the larger Sermon on the Mount that makes up Matthew 5–7, are among the most famous of Jesus' teachings. Jesus lays out for the disciples eight defining characteristics of those who are blessed in the reign of God. It can seem like an impossible list of character traits for us to live up to. But blessedness of which Jesus speaks is both a reality of the present and a fulfillment yet to come in the fullness of God's kingdom.

When Jesus declares these blessings, he speaks to a depth of joy that comes from being in right relationship with God— something we continually are living into as we work out our salvation with fear and trembling. The joy is the result of growing discipleship. It is not the same thing as being happy in the way the world might describe happiness, a giddy and transitory emotion. Jesus offers another reminder that the ways of God can appear foolish to the world. We can consider the Beatitudes as a growing progression of life in Christ as we are transformed into Christ's image by Christ's righteousness. When we read this passage, we do not need to feel downcast because of the ways we do not yet measure up to these defined traits. Jesus offers an image of what it looks like to be at home in the kingdom of God. Our work is in the transformation.

Holy Spirit, show me where I most need to be transformed in my heart to be at home in the kingdom of God. Help me on my journey to become more like Christ. Amen.

The first beatitude sets the foundation for understanding the kind of life to which God calls us and the primary condition for access to that life and relationship with God. Poverty of spirit is the key to getting into the kingdom of God. It speaks to the posture of our heart before God.

To be poor in spirit is to recognize our utter lack of anything sufficient to earn God's love. It is the recognition of complete dependence on God because nothing we can do or say or be can redeem us from ourselves and our brokenness. We turn to God because we know that nothing other than the righteousness of Christ can bridge that gap between ourselves and God. Not our own intelligence, wealth, relationships, or physical attributes.

Poverty of spirit is the prerequisite for confession, repentance, and pursuing life with God. The kingdom of God belongs to those of us who recognize our brokenness and our complete need for redemption and who understand that our access to the kingdom comes from God's initiating love and grace. We do not foster a right relationship with God by relying on our own abilities or setting our own terms for relating with God.

The longer we have been believers, the easier it can be to forget that we need to maintain a poverty of spirit in our ongoing relationship with God. To be a Christian is to weigh continually the ways in which we are at odds with the temptations of who the world tells us we should be. We constantly face the choice of living our lives in the world's way rather than relying on God's way of servant leadership, abundance mentality, forgiveness, generosity, hospitality, and peacemaking. Maintaining a poverty of spirit takes an ongoing active life of discipleship. From that posture, we grow to embody the rest of the Beatitudes.

Lord, it is not easy to put down my pride, my desire to accomplish things my way and by my own means. Help me to be poor in spirit so that I always find myself before you in humility and gratitude. Amen.

Living the Faith

FEBRUARY 3–9, 2020 • LUTHER E. SMITH JR.

SCRIPTURE OVERVIEW: According to another counterfeit gospel, our inward convictions about God are enough, so our actions do not really matter. Isaiah chastises his audience for being half-hearted in their religious observance. They ignore the plight of the oppressed and the poor, and by doing so they betray that they do not grasp the heart of God. The psalmist argues that the true faithful are steadfast and generous, and as a result God establishes them and their cause. The understanding of God's view of the world, Paul writes, must be spiritually discerned, for it opposes the normal thinking of the world. In Matthew, Jesus tells his followers that living faith is shown by bringing flavor and light to the world. Otherwise, our faith is useless to those around us.

QUESTIONS AND SUGGESTIONS FOR REFLECTION

- Read Isaiah 58:1-12. What can you do to be a foundation of many generations, the repairer of the breach for your community?
- Read Psalm 112:1-10. How have you seen God's blessings abound from your faithfulness? How do you remain faithful when God's blessings seem absent?
- Read 1 Corinthians 2:1-16. Consider the many ways wisdom comes. How do you seek to understand God's wisdom?
- Read Matthew 5:13-20. When does your faith community resist the call to be the salt of the earth and light of the world? How can you transform yourself or those around you to fulfill God's commandments?

Professor Emeritus of Church and Community, Candler School of Theology, Emory University, Atlanta; clergy member of the Christian Methodist Episcopal Church.

The crises of God's people result from a crisis of faith. Despite fervent rituals of prayer, fasting, and submission, the faithful living that God desires does not occur. God is angry. Isaiah makes dramatic pronouncements that the religious rituals do not conform to God's passion for justice, humility, liberation from oppression, and care for those who live in poverty.

How does such a crisis of faith occur? How do our rituals become empty of what God most wants? How do we know what God desires? Israel's prophets continually reference the laws and covenants in their faith's history as providing what is necessary for living the faith. In the ancestors' history with God we come to know what is expected of us. Responding faithfully to God's passion requires remembering.

The requirement to remember is not just about the ability to recite tenets of faith. Neither is remembering primarily about ritualizing the tenets. Living the faith involves enacting in our relationships with others what we remember from our faith heritage. Our faith is rooted in and nourished by commitment to justice, humility, freedom, and compassion for the poor.

Most often, we fail to live faithfully not because we have forgotten what must be remembered. Our failure arises from ignoring what we remember. We sanctify behaviors that value privilege over justice, domination over humility, status quo over liberation from oppression, and self-interest over compassion. Continuing on this path is untenable for people of faith and for society. Ignoring is unacceptable to God—so much so that God considers it as "rebellion" against the path of faith that God has traveled with us. To our numerous questions about God and the circumstances of our lives comes a clear response: God remembers us. And God desires for us to remember to live the faith and practice righteousness.

Help us, O God, to remember faithfully on our journey with you. Amen.

God promises that living the faith results in joy. Living the faith changes the world. The oppressed go free, the hungry are fed, the homeless are sheltered, and the naked are clothed because they all have come to experience compassionate hearts amid cruel circumstances. God's passion for justice and kindness is exhibited.

Faithful living changes us. God promises that "your light shall break forth like the dawn, and your healing shall spring up quickly." Our relationships are healed. Our needs do not overwhelm us. We have strength for the journey with God.

The movement from complaint to promise in this passage of Isaiah is cause for hope. Our sins do not determine what the world is and what we can become. God calls us into a future where the rubble of our lives is transformed into means for vital living. We must remember that we have been instructed on what God desires of us, and then do that. The opportunities to please God are near, abundant, and within our capacities. God has promised to be near with help sufficient for all our needs.

Living the faith is not just for our immediate personal and societal well-being. We are the ancestors that either inspire or misguide coming generations. How will our witness serve as an example for those confronting ancient and new challenges? As coming generations struggle with the alienating realities of racism, classism, sexism, and isolationistic nationalism, what creative resources will they discover from us? Living the faith transports us into the future with a life-giving legacy that gains us life-giving titles: "You shall be called the repairer of the breach, the restorer of streets to live in."

As we live the faith, may our hearts rest in the assurance of God's promises.

Praise for God's loving presence pours forth with assurances of joy. We delight in following the commandments of God. Joy comes not only from the consequences of righteous living but also from the commitment to be on the path of righteousness. The blessed life is not only the one that lives in a time of justice but also the life that interacts justly with others. By living faithfully, we are assured a blessed life.

Being devoted to God is a joy that does not avoid the consequences of difficult and even deadly realities. The righteous have foes and face "evil tidings." The psalmist assures, however, that the faithful witness prevails both in an immediate situation and "forever." Our living the faith affects future generations.

Have you ever felt anchored by your faith in a situation full of threat and tumult? If so, to what do you attribute the ability to feel secure and do what is right even amid virulent opposition? How do you continue to nourish your spiritual life so that your heart and mind are resolute in being faithful through all the seasons of life?

If you are unable to recall feeling such steadiness amid conflict, what do you name as the reasons? How might you begin to address the difficulty of being clear and steadfast in your faith witness under challenging circumstances? Do you know individuals whose witness in such circumstance is inspiring? How might you discuss with them the spiritual practices that inform their witness?

Committing ourselves to God is our work and sacred privilege. All matters of security, joy, and hope rely ultimately on the ultimate Source of life. May it be so with us.

Present God, whether I am resting or in fierce turmoil, may your joy be ever with me. Help me to live each day as a blessing for the time at hand and for all time to come. Amen.

The apostle Paul was so focused on succeeding in his mission to persuade listeners about the person and significance of Jesus Christ that he stripped his message and himself to essentials. He abandons "lofty words" and complex spiritual probing and forsakes relying upon his strength and confidence. This stripping not only eliminates impressive yet confusing forms of speech but also makes a way for the power of the Spirit to be evident. Paul's testimony is an example of subtracting in order to add, of decreasing in order to increase.

Over the years I have heard effusive introductions that noted a person's educational attainment, vocational accomplishments, achievement awards, and so on. The contents of someone's résumé were spoken of to authenticate the person's significance. However, I have been most inspired by introductions in which someone was simply introduced as "genuine" or "tender-hearted" or "a loving spirit" or "my dearest friend" or "passionate for justice." The single word or phrase expressed more about one's essential character than a long list of achievements.

Simplicity can be the most effective means of delivering a message—simplicity in delivery and simplicity of the message itself. What do you interpret as the simple message of living the faith? Write it in your journal or on a piece of paper. Speak it. Plan to revisit what you have written to affirm and/or revise this message. If your message is based upon a biblical text, identify it. Reflect on how your message is based on your experience of the Spirit of God being active in your life and in the world.

Dear God, so often our overflowing thoughts and feelings about your presence in our lives impel us to use a mound of words to capture the experience. Relieve us from such futile efforts, and release in us the simple truth that instructs us on the journey. Amen.

Yesterday's emphasis on simplicity does not dismiss the value of wisdom. Wisdom resides in simplicity and in the complex. Our challenge is to understand our readiness for the different manifestations of wisdom. The outpouring of ideas about wisdom to persons whose minds and hearts are unprepared to receive it can be bewildering if not alienating.

Paul's proclamations to mature persons present a message of wisdom that is sensitive to their preparedness to understand. However, hearers will not understand the message if they interpret wisdom by cultural values that are not God's values. The capacity to know God's wisdom, according to Paul, depends upon submitting to and being led by the Spirit of God. Those who are not led by the Spirit interpret God's wisdom as "foolishness." In a culture that values domination, sacrificing for others is foolishness. Where identification with people of prestige and influence is admired, living in solidarity with the poor is foolishness. Where avoiding confrontation and discomfort epitomizes happiness, offering oneself to the painful and lengthy work of racial reconciliation is foolishness.

Living the faith requires a commitment to pursue spiritual wisdom despite disparaging social consequences. Becoming spiritually wise involves being in relationship with God's guiding Spirit. God is ever active in revealing what God wants known. The pursuit of spiritual wisdom is more than the pursuit of ideas about spirituality. Ultimately, the pursuit entails a way of life that responds faithfully to God's presence and guidance.

Dear God, the pressure to conform to society's standards of success has hounded us from our earliest days of memory. In these standards we perceive deadly traps and what seem to be promising possibilities for advancing your shalom. The options can be confusing. Help us to discern rightly so that our choices and our lives are aligned with your instruction and your passion for the world. Amen.

Many words characterize the sacred and purposeful significance of being a follower of Jesus; *calling, vocation, disciple,
pilgrim, saint,* and *convert* are just a few. In today's reading, Jesus
tells us to be "salt" and "light." As in Thursday's focus on Paul's
choosing simplicity to instruct, Jesus refers to what is common
and simple to illustrate what living the faith means.

As salt, we preserve and bring forth flavor to what is essential to sustenance. As light, we illuminate what needs to be
seen by the world. Both metaphors portray followers of Jesus
as essential in enabling others to perceive what God has given.
Fulfilling the purposes of salt and light entails being diligent in
keeping their powers active for the world. Sustain and use salt.
Shine light where it most illumines. Jesus instructs us to be who
God made us to be. And he instructs us to be what is needed in
the world.

Reflecting on this past week, identify times when you were
salt and light. What occurred in these times that led you to interpret them as examples of the scripture message? If you have difficulty identifying such times, why is this the case? How might
you prepare to live each day as salt and light? Who are examples
of salt and light in your life and the world? What do they say and
do that leads you to characterize them in this way? How has your
life been affected by their saltiness and illumination?

*At our earnest best we often struggle, O God, to give ourselves
to life as you have desired. At times we are bewildered by the
complexity of challenges. At other times we are indifferent to
the opportunity to make our full selves available to what is
immediately before us. Help us to see ourselves as you see us
and to offer ourselves each day as salt and light. Amen.*

SUNDAY, FEBRUARY 9 ~ *Read Matthew 5:17-20*

Often we have ignored or distorted God's laws for so long that we only come to know them as false surrogates for what God intended. "Love your neighbor," "Welcome strangers," and "Do justice" are examples of God's commands that too few churches enact. In many churches, if some members insist on outreach to neighbors, extending hospitality to the homeless, or confronting disparities in the justice system, these members are denounced as disruptors and fanatics. Their efforts to fulfill God's commands are judged to be efforts to destroy the calm, like-mindedness, and security that have become sacred idols.

How determined are you to fulfill today's scripture as you read and understand it as instruction related to what follows in the Sermon on the Mount? (See Matthew 5–7.) Today's passage says that how we honor or fail to honor what God has commanded is a matter of spiritual vitality or spiritual death. Fulfilling God's laws is not ultimately for the sake of the laws but for our own sake and for the world. What God wants fulfilled is to be fulfilled in us and is fulfilled for us.

Living the faith is the way to fulfill the law and experience God's joy for us. Knowing this should embolden our discipleship even when our motives are misunderstood and the likelihood of transformation seems dismal. We were created to be salt and light. Settling for anything less is unworthy of us.

Release us, O God, from whatever hinders our enthusiasm to fulfill the guidance you have given us. Help us to rest in the assurance that comes from yielding our anxieties and fears to you. Enliven us by the certainty that your loving presence is constant and your joy is even beyond our imagination. Amen.

Covenant of the Heart

FEBRUARY 10–16, 2020 • CHRISTINE AND JOHN VALTERS PAINTNER

SCRIPTURE OVERVIEW: This week we continue to explore the importance of Christian morality. We do not earn God's grace by our actions; rather, our obedience is a response to God's grace. In Deuteronomy, we read that the choice of life will bring prosperity and is the proper response from a heart of gratitude. The psalmist echoes this sentiment, for blessed are those who follow the Lord not just with words but also with actions. The Corinthians have not understood this so they continue to act like those in the world around them, living by the flesh instead of by the Spirit. Jesus pushes us even further. God sees not only what we do on the outside but who we are on the inside. A true life of obedience begins on the inside and flows outward.

QUESTIONS AND SUGGESTIONS FOR REFLECTION

- Read Deuteronomy 30:15-20. When have you experienced the choice God sets before us of life or death, prosperity or adversity, blessings or curses? How have you discerned how to obey God?
- Read Psalm 119:1-8. How does following God's commandments bring you joy?
- Read 1 Corinthians 3:1-9. Consider the forms of love Paul and Saint Valentine display in their letters. What types of love help you serve God, who gives growth?
- Read Matthew 5:21-37. When have you experienced legalistic interpretations of scripture? How do you get to the heart of scripture?

Directors of AbbeyoftheArts.com, a virtual monastery cultivating contemplative practice and creative expression; Christine is the author of a dozen books on spirituality, and John often contributes biblical knowledge to these; residents of the west coast of Ireland; leaders of pilgrimages and writers' retreats.

This passage from the Hebrew scriptures comes toward the end of the book of Deuteronomy and is part of a section known as the Final Words of Moses. Here, the author is making closing arguments as to why future generations should agree to the covenant offered by Yahweh. The author reminds the people of the great works of God, particularly how God freed them from captivity in Egypt and led them back to the land of their ancestors.

If for no other reason, the rationale goes, your freedom and life warrant that you live according to the covenant—a sign of gratitude for all Yahweh has done for you. But God does more than free individuals; God forms our spiritual ancestors into a community. The fates of these recently freed Israelites and their descendants rely on two things at the heart of the covenant: They must be faithful to Yahweh, and they must act with justice toward one another. By doing the latter they demonstrate the former.

This passage seems to be a dire pronouncement of punishment for those who stray. But there is more to this warning. God frees the Israelites from captivity, a great act of love for the people. In return, the Israelites and their descendants (both biological and spiritual) are asked to return God's love and to pay it forward by loving one another. They act out this love through observance of the commandments. How we treat one another is a sign of our love for God.

Holy One, give me a heart of gratitude for the overflow of blessings in my life. Help me remember especially those whose freedom is threatened and those who have died fighting for that gift. May I be renewed this day to share these blessings with others. Amen.

Psalm 119 is the longest psalm. Each of the twenty-two eight-verse stanzas corresponds to a letter of the Hebrew alphabet. The entirety of Psalm 119 sings God's praises, particularly the joy found in following God's instructions. Happiness is found in faithfulness to the covenant. Faithfulness uplifts the heart.

Faithfulness to the covenant sets up a cycle of love and spiritual prosperity. The psalmist argues that we should obey the commandments because of the good things God has done for us. Through our fidelity to the commandments, future spiritual fruit will be harvested, not just for the individual but for the community. Scripture consistently supports the message that what we are given by God is not for us alone.

While this week's passage from Deuteronomy contains a not-so-subtle threat to those who disobey God's commandments, this passage from Psalms offers a different perspective. Where yesterday's reading was more "stick," today's reading is more "carrot."

According to the psalmist, following the commandments isn't an obligation full of dread; faithfulness to the commandments is a source of joy. Love in practice always generates more love. Gratitude in practice generates more gratitude. The joy comes not only in the rewards it delivers but also in the concrete doing itself. With our hearts full of gratitude, the commandments become a blessing in themselves.

As a creative practice, consider writing your own Alphabetic Acrostic of Blessings, using each letter of the alphabet to start each stanza or verse.

Source of Joy, may my prayer join with the psalmist to seek you with my whole heart. May I find my true joy in faithfulness to you, for you love me without end. And may that joy overflow into my life so that it touches the lives of others. Amen.

After establishing the proto-church in Corinth, Paul moves on to spread the good news to other communities. But he stays in touch. The epistles, like this one, are Paul's correspondence to the early churches he helps start. In these letters he generally encourages the new community and answers specific questions that arise. We don't have the other half of this written conversation, but we can deduce the issues by Paul's responses.

In this portion of his first letter to the church in Corinth, Paul addresses a divided community. There appears to be a growing schism between two factions. Paul asserts his authority while empowering the whole community of believers. He does not get into a petty dispute with Apollos but rather lifts up his work and calls on the whole community to be united in Christ.

Paul's epistles are proof of his continued love for the communities he forms. He loves them so much that he doesn't care who takes credit for them. In this letter, Paul is not upset that some Corinthians favor Apollos over him; he cares that they treat one another with love, as exemplified by Jesus. Paul's focus is not glory for himself but faith in Christ.

The love for God that burns in Paul's heart drives him to travel the world, spreading the good news and establishing communities in the way of Christ Jesus. It is this same burning love that motivates him to stay in contact with these communities when he moves on to spread the gospel elsewhere.

God the Great Artist, lift up all of our divided and broken places. Transform them into a great mosaic crafted from your love, a witness to the beauty of our faithfulness to your work in our hearts. Amen.

The first Gospel begins with a genealogy of Jesus and then quickly moves on to the infancy narratives involving magi from the East coming to visit the new King of kings. This news enrages the jealous King Herod, so the Holy Family flees to Egypt.

Skipping ahead a few decades, Jesus goes to the Jordan River to receive a baptism from his cousin John and the blessing of God. From there, Jesus goes into the desert for forty days to prepare for his public ministry. When he returns from his time of retreat, Jesus begins calling his disciples.

All of this, from Jesus' birth to his baptism, from his time in the desert to the gathering of the first disciples, seems to be leading to this moment where Jesus preaches to the multitudes in what becomes known as the Sermon on the Mount. Here is the core, the heart of the good news. Jesus begins with the Beatitudes and teaches about the Law before discussing anger, adultery, divorce, and oaths.

Religiosity can often be heady or legalistic. This legalism can lead us to (or sometimes can even be motivated by) the search for loopholes. That is to say, we might find ourselves asking: If the commandment only restricts or prohibits a certain activity, then is there a way around it?

But here in Matthew's Gospel, Jesus proposes a deeper, more heartfelt spirituality. It is a faith that isn't looking to get away with something or to avoid the legalism of sinning. Jesus' teaching means we aren't trying to game the system or get one over on God. Instead, we are invited to look beyond particular actions to the heart of each commandment. What is the attitude, the mind-set at the core of our faith? Jesus calls us to integrity between our mind and heart.

Divine Spirit, you are the source of all goodness. Help me to align my attitude to the source of all love. Guide me to discover the shadow places of my heart and offer them up to you for illumination and healing. Amen.

Today, Valentine's Day, is the feast day of Saint Valentine. As with most early Christian saints, there is some controversy around who exactly Saint Valentine was. While we may never know the exact historical facts, several legends emerge that have been passed down through the centuries and have made him a significant figure in both religious and secular calendars.

Like the apostle Paul, but to a lesser extent, Saint Valentine is famous for writing letters. One letter in particular stands out. Valentine had been asked to help heal and later educate the blind daughter of a jailer. The young girl and the saint became friends. So when Saint Valentine was later arrested, he wrote the girl letters from jail. Again, like the apostle Paul, Saint Valentine wrote out words of encouragement to another when he could not physically be there for her.

How Saint Valentine's feast day became intertwined with romantic love, cards, flowers, and candy is more about modern marketing than theology. But perhaps now is the time to break out of this narrow definition of love that amplifies the loneliness many single people feel and the pressure put on couples to meet unrealistic expectations of romantic love.

The ancient Greeks had many different words for the awkward, all-encompassing English word *love*. We can make this feast day about more than just buying gifts for our significant others (or fretting about not having one).

Consider writing a letter of love and support to someone whom you wish to comfort through a difficult period even though you cannot be with her or him in person.

Source of Expansive Love, guide us deep into your heart of compassion and care for those who are lonely, those who feel rejected, and those who stand at the edges of life. Allow your love to flow through me to meet them in their place of need. Amen.

In this passage from Deuteronomy, God makes clear that life and death, blessing and curse, are set before us. Our task in this world is to choose life again and again. The heart of discernment is to recognize that life presents a call to make choices each moment and to follow the life-giving way. This way may be the most challenging work any of us can face. Life is full of ambiguities and ambivalences.

Sometimes we choose what appears to be life but which ultimately is destructive to those involved. Our world has become more complex. Choices even about what we eat each day are connected to a web of issues like pesticides, labor practices, cost to the environment.

The psalmist invites us to walk in the law of God. Walking evokes a sense of embodiment. We don't merely think about the law of God or apply its principles in the abstract. I am reminded of a line from Antonio Machado's poem where he suggests that we make the way by walking.* We follow this path step-by-step, not as a predetermined way but as a call to listen to our life and how it unfolds toward goodness. We allow every tendon and sinew to respond to God's invitation to love, and we trust that we must continue to walk in that direction.

When we look for rules to follow rather than act from love in all choices, we fall into a legalism that ultimately makes our world smaller. We are invited into the expansive messiness of life that demands discernment and listening and the risk we may be wrong.

---

*"Proverbios y cantares XXIX" in *Campos de Castilla*

Giver of Life, help me to choose love each moment of the day. Bless my footsteps so that generations to come may know the grace of life over death. Amen.

This week's passage from Matthew's Gospel makes clear that the external work of prayer does not replace the internal work required to support it. Today's warning is much like the Gospel reading for Ash Wednesday each year where Jesus warns us not to sound the trumpets when we give alms. (See Matthew 6:1-2.) Outward signs of faith have meaning only if we seek wholeness inwardly. If any place within us is divided, our prayer is to make amends, to seek reconciliation, and to allow for healing. Only then should we be showing up with our offerings at the altar.

As human beings, this journey toward reconciliation is perpetual. We all carry burdens of anger or resentment in small and large ways. I am reminded of the Jewish practice of the ten days of repentance, where our Jewish brothers and sisters seek to heal any wounds in relationships before the celebration of Yom Kippur when the New Year begins. There is great wisdom in doing this work of internal preparation before starting a new season.

The covenant of the heart asks that we show up for ourselves and for one another, do the hard work of communication and forgiveness, and remember love as our first and last motivation. This journey is ongoing; it is not a once-and-for-all task. Much like the task of choosing life that we reflected on yesterday, the covenant asks us to engage each day with what we most deeply desire for ourselves and the world we live in and to live from that place.

Beloved One, illuminate the dark places within us that carry the burdens and resentments of our lives. Help us to meet those places with compassion, and give us the courage and strength to approach those with whom we need to reconcile. Amen.

Light from Within

FEBRUARY 17–23, 2020 • STEVE GARNAAS-HOLMES

SCRIPTURE OVERVIEW: The Transfiguration is a striking manifestation of the union of humanity and divinity in Christ. In Exodus, Moses goes up the mountain to meet with God, and the divine presence on the mountain is like a consuming fire. The psalmist says that the presence of the Lord shakes the earth. In Second Peter the author declares that the truth of Christ's message is affirmed by the glory that surrounds Jesus on the mountain and the voice from heaven that confirms his authority. In Matthew's account, the revelation of the glory of the divine son of God on top of a mountain causes the disciples to fall down in fear. Moses and Elijah are present, demonstrating the continuity of Christ with the prophets and the always overwhelming splendor of God's presence.

QUESTIONS AND SUGGESTIONS FOR REFLECTION

- Read Exodus 24:12-18. When have you experienced God's cleansing and transforming fire?
- Read Psalm 99. How has God led you through darkness?
- Read 2 Peter 1:16-21. How can you be attentive to the light of God in the world around you?
- Read Matthew 17:1-9. When have you experienced God's love shining through you?

Pastor of St. Matthew's United Methodist Church, Acton, Massachusetts; author of *Unfolding Light* at unfoldinglight.net.

We long for experiences of revelation like Moses'—maybe not with all the drama and special effects, though we must admit sometimes we wish for exactly those. We want the clarity and authority of the revelation Moses receives. Wouldn't it be nice to know? Wouldn't it be nice to see God, to hear God's voice, to have Wisdom and Truth carved in stone right there in our hands?

However, the mountain isn't bathed in clear sky and sunlight; it's wrapped in a cloud. Divine revelation is shrouded in mystery. God doesn't light the way for Moses; God calls Moses to come near, and Moses enters the cloud. Sometimes the light is for our heart, not our eyes. We long for clarity and certainty, but the light of God's Word isn't subject to knowledge or understanding. As the mystical text *The Cloud of Unknowing* says, God can be loved but not thought. God seldom reveals explanations or answers. God reveals beauty, grace, and possibility. God reveals sacred blessing hidden in mystery. God's self-revelation doesn't explain the mystery; it is a mystery. God lets us see the mystery and know it is God. The result is not less mystery, but deeper mystery and deeper trust. Ultimately God's self-revelation is not a fact or a belief but a presence. It is God.

Sometimes the clearest revelation we receive is that God walks with us in the dark, and we hear God breathing next to us. God offers no words, no thoughts, no stone tablets. Just a loving presence. And even in the dark, that is enough.

Even as I seek God's light to guide me, I pray for the faith to trust the mystery of God's presence when the way is clouded and when the revelation itself is mystery. After all, when Jesus comes, Jesus doesn't light the way; he is the way.

God of mystery, help me trust your presence even in the dark. Amen.

God's glory on the mountain is "like a consuming fire" (NIV). Scripture often associates fire with God's presence. But God's fire isn't destructive. It's transforming. It consumes, yes, but to purify rather than to destroy. Glassblowers, chemists, bakers, and jewelry makers use fire to fashion beautiful, life-giving things. God's glory is not the fire of anger. It's the flame of love, the tender desire to change us by the alchemy of God's mysterious grace into something more pure, beautiful, strong, and useful.

The fire of God is not tame like a little campfire where we can make s'mores. Awesome and fierce, it burns out of our control. When we try to bend it to our own aims, it consumes us. But it burns for the sake of new creation. The furnace of God's love roars about our hearts, melts our old forms, burns away impurities, and softens us to make us new.

Whatever Moses experiences on the mountain changes him. The experience of God's presence transforms us. As frightening as it sounds to my ego, I want that. I want God to burn away all the old junk that is not really me, like gold being refined. I have to trust that God's fire won't destroy me but will cleanse me. I have to stop hanging on to my old ways. I want the warmth of God's presence to melt what is hard or brittle in me. I want the heat of God's grace to change the chemistry of my heart, to bake me into something life-giving, to mold me into a new shape. May the fire of God remake me into a vessel of love. And let that light, that new beauty, that divine glory shine in me forever.

God of light and fire, burn in me now and always. Make me into your new creation. Amen.

Yahweh is sovereign" (AP). That's relatively easy to proclaim when God is off on God's holy mountain. But what if the holy mountain is my heart? What if the cherubim God is enthroned on are my own wants and urges? What if the pillar of cloud where God speaks is my own prayer? What if God's footstool is my will? That's harder.

Here's the root of my sin: I don't entirely trust God. I don't wholly give myself over to God as my ruler, the sovereign of my heart. I want to keep a bit of the power to myself. I want to go my own way. I want to choose my path. I'm not quite ready to go wherever God leads me.

Nevertheless, God is still ruler. With infinite grace God reigns over us not by making demands or forcing us to obey but by shining light in our darkness, illuminating a life-giving way for us. We can strike off on our own and try to find our own way in the dark if we choose, but God shines light on a more life-giving way.

On a visit to a desert monastery, I went to night and morning prayers in the dark with my way lit by luminaria. We were not forced to go to the chapel, but all other paths were treacherous in the dark. Grace lit the way.

God reigns not by forceful power but in the gift of the light of beauty, mercy, justice, and grace. When we submit to God's reign of light in our hearts and let ourselves be led by God's grace, we find that God's light not only shines on our way but also shines from within into all our life and out into the world.

God of light, shine your love in my heart. Shine your grace on my path. Help me discern your light and follow. Direct my steps so that I may walk in your way. Amen.

We had been eyewitnesses. . . . We ourselves heard this voice come from heaven." What about you? What have you witnessed? What have you heard? We need not limit God's revelation to mountaintop experiences and scriptures about miraculous events. God's light shines in the everyday.

Most of the time we go through life on cruise control without really paying attention to what we see and hear. We filter our experience through our habits and preconceptions. We miss most of what we could perceive in our world—especially the miraculousness of it. We see what we expect to see. Believing is seeing. We see what we want to see, or what we think we ought to see instead of what is before us. When we do look at the world around us, we usually see just the surface—not the glory of God shining there. That is, until we open the eyes of our hearts.

Notice what you see today. Listen to what you hear. God is in the everyday elements of our lives. Even the majestic glory of the crucified and risen Christ is present in ordinary moments. Look for it there. Pay attention to Christ's everydayness, as to a lamp shining in a dark place. God's revelation comes through "men and women moved by the Holy Spirit." Reflect on what you experience through the light of the Spirit instead of mere conventional wisdom.

What do you see? What do you hear? How have you witnessed the glory of Christ shining in your life? Perhaps in the beauty of an innocent child; in the courage of someone who takes a risk for the sake of love; in a moment of forgiveness, healing, and grace; or even a simple patch of sunlight.

Let the Spirit speak to you through your senses. Pay attention to the light. God's glory may not be dramatic, but it will still be the Beloved.

God, open my eyes to your light today, so that in what I see and hear I may know the glory of Christ. Amen.

Sometimes our world seems pretty dark, cloaked in the shadow of racism, violence, greed, and hatred. When the earth is despoiled, when wars rage, when public discourse is fraught with fear and untruth, we can be discouraged. When it seems like deep night, we long for day to dawn. Where do we see light? Where do we find hope?

The darkness of evil and injustice is deep, but the light of Christ shines in that darkness. We have to pay attention to it. The more we pay attention to something, the more it fills us, captures our imagination, and colors our thoughts, until we reflect it in our whole being. If we only notice the darkness, that's all we reflect. When we pay attention to the light of God, it shines on us and in us.

The light of Christ is not a neon light God turns on at the top of a mountain. God fills us with Christ's light, which rises in our hearts. We can pay attention to the light, as to a lamp shining in a dark place, until the day dawns and the morning star rises in our hearts.

Where do you see the glory of Christ? Where do you see the light of justice and mercy? Where do you see the beauty of reconciliation, healing, and forgiveness? Where do you see the glory of God's love courageously embodied? Where do you see the power of nonviolence? Look around you. Pay attention. Keep your eyes open today for the glory of Christ shining like a lamp in the dark. Let that light fill you and shine in you.

Light of Christ, help me to see your glory and pay attention to your light. Fill my darkness. Shine in me so that I may be a source of light for others in the ways of mercy, hope, and justice. May the day dawn and the morning star rise in my heart. Amen.

Once again, as in Exodus, we are on a mountain. Once again we find Moses and the light of God. And again we experience a cloud of mystery that confounds our plans and befuddles our expectations.

Peter offers to build structures. (Has he stashed building supplies in his knapsack?) Peter's reaction reflects our inclination to try to make sense of things, to "capture" them and fit them into our way of understanding. At an art museum I watched a woman walk into a room, exclaim, "Oh, a van Gogh!" snap a photo of it, and leave. It was perhaps her only chance to see the painting in person, but she did not stop to look at it. Contemplative presence invites us to set aside our desire to control or understand, to "capture the moment," and simply, lovingly, behold what is, as it is, face-to-face.

On the mountain, Peter is still trying to make Jesus into the kind of Messiah Peter has in mind. He wants to get his picture right. But the cloud comes like an eraser to rub out that idea. We have our ideas about Jesus from church doctrines and personal convictions. But the point is not to believe certain things about Jesus; it's to listen to him.

Jesus is a living presence. We can let him speak to us and be present with us. When we set aside our expectations and let him come to us anew, the Beloved—with whom God is well pleased—may reveal himself to us. We can receive "Jesus himself alone."

As you read scripture, as you reflect on your experience moment by moment, let Jesus speak to you. Perhaps he is speaking to you right now. Ask the Spirit to help you listen to him in your heart. Listen and wonder, *What is Jesus saying to me?*

Living Christ, I open my heart to you. I listen for your voice. Help me to listen always, day by day, moment by moment. Amen.

TRANSFIGURATION

"Six days later" is an odd way to start a story. But it's not the start. The story starts six days earlier, when Jesus invites his disciples on the way of radical self-giving love, the way of the cross. At first Peter refuses to believe Jesus. Six days later (on the seventh day, a day of completion), God says, "Listen to him!"

The story of the Transfiguration is not about glory; it's about the cross. It is God's affirmation of the way of self-sacrificial love. Taken out of context it can seem like a poster of triumphalism. But it's really an affirmation of the humility, powerlessness, self-emptying, and suffering of radical love. Jesus, who has advocated such radical self-giving, appears in resurrection light.

The way of dying Jesus describes is a way of rising. The Transfiguration affirms what Jesus has said six days earlier: Lose your life in love, and you will be given life that cannot be taken from you, a life that is eternal. Love is the glory of God. Love fulfills the law (Moses) and the prophets (Elijah). The cross is the way of life. Love is the reason and heart of our faith.

When we love, we shine with the light of God. When we forgive, we have "died and gone to heaven." When we stand up for justice, we taste resurrection. The world will resist us and make us pay the cost. The world will ridicule us and call us failures. But the glory of God shines in us, and the light of eternal life radiates from within us. We can take courage, then, and give ourselves to a life of love and self-sacrifice. For love, and love alone, is the light of God.

Trusting this, we are now ready to journey with Jesus through Lent toward the cross.

Crucified and risen Christ, give me courage to follow you. May the light of your self-giving love shine in me. Amen.

The Turning

FEBRUARY 24—MARCH 1, 2020 • WENDY M. WRIGHT

SCRIPTURE OVERVIEW: In this first week of Lent, we prepare our hearts for a period of reflection. We think about areas of our lives in which we might be falling short of God's desires. The problem of sin enters the human story at the very beginning, for Adam and Eve choose to follow their own wisdom rather than guidance from God. The psalmist highlights the importance of recognizing our sin and asking for forgiveness, which God is quick to give. In Romans, Paul argues that we all partake in the broken human condition because we all have sinned as Adam did. The story of Jesus in the desert admonishes us to be on guard against the deception of our fleshly desires and our pride.

QUESTIONS AND SUGGESTIONS FOR REFLECTION

- Read Genesis 2:15-17; 3:1-7. How might this story help you turn from *superbia* to *humilitas* throughout your Lenten journey?
- Read Psalm 32. What seeming dichotomies comprise the full picture of your life of faith?
- Read Romans 5:12-19. How do you sense the differences Paul draws between Adam and Christ prompting you to turn toward God?
- Read Matthew 4:1-11. What are your own temptations? How does Jesus' response to his temptations guide you in responding to yours?

Professor Emerita of Theology, Creighton University; affiliated faculty in the Institute for Contemporary Spirituality, Oblate School of Theology; specialist in the Salesian Spiritual tradition and writer on family spirituality, women and spirituality, and the Catholic devotional traditions; author of recent books *The Lady of the Angels and Her City* and *Francis de Sales and Jane de Chantal*; parent of three and grandparent of six.

I t's a book about two trees," my student piped up in response to my query to my Classic Literature class about their first impressions of Augustine of Hippo's *Confessions*, that fabled fourth-century creation described as the first autobiography of the Western world.

"It's a book about two trees," she repeated. At first, I was taken aback by her unusual response. But in fact she had nailed it—two trees: The pear tree from which boy Augustine recklessly stole fruit simply because he could and the tree under which he heard a command to pick up the scriptures and resolved his agonized tension over embracing the Christian faith. We can use the terms *superbia* (pride) and *humilitas* (humility) to describe the two poles of Augustine's soul-life as he achingly narrated the turning, the reorientation of his entire life from self- to God-directedness. This hard-won moment of turning under the second tree may have seemed sudden for Augustine, but it ushered in a lifetime of deep probing into the mysteries of life and the ultimate mystery that is God. A life of turning again and again.

On the cusp of our Lenten journey, we find ourselves in a garden with the first man and woman, beneath a tree of knowledge of good and evil with tempting forbidden fruit. We might question some of the conclusions past Christians have drawn from this passage about ideal gender relations. Yet, taken as an insight into our shared human propensity for self-referential *superbia*, this tale of garden and tree rings true.

Further, at the end of our forty-day Lenten journey, we will find ourselves under a second tree. A cross-shaped tree on Calvary, a tree of life. In between will be our time of turning once again with growing *humilitas* in this season for reorientating our lives toward the source of life.

"Search me, O God, and know my heart; test me and know my thoughts. See if there is any wicked way in me and lead me in the way everlasting" (Ps. 139:23-24). Amen.

Our grandchildren frequently request to hear stories about when their grandfather was young, which they call "Little Grandpa stories." A favorite is the story of the printer's ink.

Decades ago, the tale begins, one Christmas when Grandpa was about your age, his parents gave him a longed-for gift: a printer's set complete with gleaming bottles of dark liquid ink. Grandpa's father sternly warned him that this gift was not to be assembled until later in the day in the basement workshop. The waiting was too hard, and when his parents were not looking, Little Grandpa opened his gift in the living room. A bottle of that dark black ink spilled onto the newly installed beige carpet. His father angrily confronted Little Grandpa: "What did I tell you not to do?" He raised his hand in a gesture that could only mean trouble. But Grandpa's mother quickly appeared between cowering Little Grandpa and that raised hand. "Dear," she gently remonstrated, "he's only a boy."

Wide-eyed, our grandchildren nod at the mental picture and its obvious moral: Do what you are told; be obedient. But they absorb a complete picture that includes merciful intervention as an essential dynamic of the story.

Here on the cusp of Lent, that most solemn of liturgical seasons, this week's readings are all about the pendulum-like swing of disobedience and obedience, sin and forgiveness, estrangement and reconciliation. But they are not simple children's stories. At a deeper, spiritual level they alert us to the process of turning. They call us to look at our life and respond once again not merely to commands but to the very desire of divine love itself, the merciful desire that we turn fully toward the love that has created and sustained us and continues to offer us fullness of life.

Reflect on these words and let them speak to you of how God thinks of you: "I have loved you with an everlasting love; I have drawn you with unfailing kindness" (Jer. 31:3, NIV).

The Turning   79

Ash Wednesday

O n Ash Wednesday as we inaugurate the Lenten season of turning, the liturgy reminds us of our mortality—"from dust to dust." We enter this season soberly, knowing that we are called once again to turn, to be cleansed, washed, purged of all that keeps us separated from God. As I write this reflection, a steady winter rain streams through the highest reaches of the coastal redwoods, soaks through the foliage, and seeps into the drought-parched earth below. For over a decade, our Southern California landscape has been dried out and thirsty. Now flows the welcome water: cleansing, healing, and nourishing.

Over and over the Psalter offers us poetry with which to express our welcome for cleansing waters. Today's psalm sings lavishly of the ways we long for water: Cleanse me from my iniquity, wash me of my sins; wash me and I will be whiter than snow; cleanse me with hyssop; create in me a pure heart. We sing of our longing to be unburdened, cleansed of the weight of our careless living and all that estranges us from our source of life.

In the center of my garden that now so gratefully welcomes the precious rainfall sits a small solar birdbath. How often I have watched with delight when some house finch or scrub jay swoops down and perches on the edge of the fountain; then, peering about, hops into the water flapping and flitting, then hops out rustling its feathers, then hops back in again for the sheer joy of the cleansing water. Pure joy. Pure delight. Psalm 51, for all its poetry that cries out our sin and our need to be cleansed, ends on a different note: "Restore me to the joy of your salvation." I like to think of those finches and jays in the water that then spread their wet wings and soar up into the air, cleansed.

In your mercy, O Lord, cleanse us and draw us toward you to soar into the joy of your love. Amen.

For years I taught a World Religions course at a Jesuit Catholic university. Most of my undergraduate students came from homes in which a faith tradition, usually Christian, had shaped them. Inevitably, when we ventured out to the local synagogue or had a Pakistani or Indonesian medical student speak in class, my students would remark admiringly on the amount of serious practice they observed in a young Jew learning the cantillations of biblical Hebrew for his Bar Mitzvah or in a Muslim observing five times daily prayer even while swamped with clinical rounds. Often, they would realize that they had considered religious observance an obligation or familiar family ritual. The concept that faith might be intensely personal, about growth or transformation, or a wild, radical, engaging adventure was not on most of their horizons.

Lent is often about variants of traditional disciplines: prayer, fasting, and almsgiving. Wednesday soup suppers. Friday fish fries. Giving up some indulgence or an addictive habit. Making donations to the poor. Setting aside time for reading scripture. These are fine practices designed to encourage our ongoing reorientation toward the source and meaning of our lives. But in their familiarity, we can easily miss the personal urgency of the biblical invitation.

As we enter the Lenten season, the ancient biblical cry rises and echoes down through the generations: "'Even now,' declares the LORD, 'return to me with all your heart, with fasting and weeping and mourning.' Rend your heart and not your garments. Return to the LORD your God, for he is gracious and compassionate, slow to anger and abounding in love" (NIV). This passage brings to our attention once again the return and the deep seriousness of the turning. May we attend to it.

Reflect on what it means to be, as Paul enjoins, "a letter from Christ . . . written not with ink but with the Spirit of the living God . . . on tablets of human hearts" (2 Cor. 3:3, NIV).

When we went with our children and grandchild for what would be our last visit to their godmother, she was confined to a hospital bed with her neck, broken in a tragic fall, supported by a cylindrical brace. Clearly in pain yet alert and attentive to us, she slowly asked every godchild about their lives and aspirations, seemingly oblivious to the precarious state of her own well-being. When we quietly left her room, each of us was absorbed in the sense that we had just been in the presence of a great soul about to pass. She always had been a faithful person, thoughtful and gracious. Yet we had just witnessed a reality beyond the sum of the parts of a lifetime, a summing up of profound goodness and attention directed at others. It was as if we had glimpsed the fullness of who God intended her to be.

In this Lenten turning, this anticipation of being washed and cleansed, of having broken hearts laid open to receive the unspeakable mercy of divine goodness, something goes well beyond what our senses can perceive: It is a slow growing into God's own intent for each of our lives. We glimpse something of this mystery of fullness in Paul's contrast between the creation account of Adam's disobedience and Jesus' obedience to God in his death. Irenaeus, Bishop of Lyon, a second-century church father, developed that Pauline insight and called Christ the "Second Adam," whose work undoes the work of sin wrought by the first man. The bishop's insight was far-reaching. In his view, the reversal of Adam's work was not merely a return to the original garden of paradise. Christ models the transformed human being, resplendent in the fullness of what God intends redeemed humanity to be. Thus we, women and men who turn toward the divine love that beckons us, gradually are remade into the unique fullness that God intends for each of us.

Reflect on this passage from Paul: "Through the Spirit we eagerly await by faith the righteousness for which we hope" (Gal. 5:5, NIV).

In his "Spiritual Exercises," sixteenth-century Basque soldier-turned-religious-seeker Ignatius of Loyola lays out a series of meditative practices focused on the life of Christ and designed to focus a person's external and internal energies to align with the ultimate desires of God. Following a program of preparatory reflections leading to a realization of oneself as a "loved sinner," Ignatius poses an exercise known as the "Two Standards."

Military man that he was, Ignatius suggests that we imagine a vast plain on which a tremendous battle is about to be waged. On one side, under one flag or standard, the terrifying troops of Satan amass. On the other, the battalions of Christ gather under the divine standard. Ignatius encourages us to put ourselves into the drama, to see the vivid details, and to let the scene play out as it will. The aim is not historical reenactment or theological rumination but present and personalized awakening to what in our life resides under each of the flags.

At the heart of the exercise we find discernment and choice, the ability to honestly distinguish what habits, desires, contexts, and forces in our lives align under each standards and to choose deliberately what is of Christ. Ignatius knew the difficulties of such a radical reorientation, no matter how earnestly (yet naively) we might participate. The rest of the exercises confirm our choices and help us contend with the inevitable external and internal oppositions, temptations, and loss of focus that accompany any real spiritual growth.

In today's reading, Paul writes to the Christian community in Corinth to plead for such a reorientation, the same turning that Ignatius struggled with sixteen centuries later and with which we continue to engage. We can be reconciled to God. Despite hardship and difficulty, we can choose that which is of Christ.

God, uncloud my eyes, open my heart, and quicken my courage to set aside that which keeps me from turning toward you. Amen.

The Turning   83

The account of Jesus' temptation in the wilderness has been proclaimed on the first Sunday of Lent in Christian communities worldwide from as early as the fourth century. It impresses on us the enduring dynamics of the reorientation central to the season. Matthew's narrative highlights the ways Satan tempts Jesus to disobedience and to rebel against his true sonship.

Over the centuries, spiritual commentators have pointed to the forms such temptations might take for Jesus' followers. Ignatius of Loyola named these temptations pride, power, and privilege. More recently, in the provocative yet insightful film *Jesus of Montreal* (1989), a rag-tag group of actors is hired to put on a Passion Play. The actor Daniel, who plays Jesus, crafts a more radical drama for the troupe than the pious script given them. Meanwhile, the actors' lives begin to mesh with the characters they play. An affluent show business lawyer takes Daniel to a penthouse apartment overlooking the glittering Quebec cityscape. If Daniel signs a contract, stardom and all of this could be his. As the troupe continues to perform the non-traditional drama, the overseers complain that their audiences don't want to be challenged but rather consoled by a familiar platitudinous message.

The film explores the temptations of religious complacency and contemporary culture: conspicuous consumption, celebrity, advertising, sexism, the quest for power, success, and fame. In characterizing Jesus' temptations through the actors' lives, the film offers novel interpretations of Jesus' true message.

On this first Sunday of the season of turning, may we be challenged to newly explore the ways in which we are co-opted by our religious complacency and our culture's false idols.

Reflect on this passage in light of your circumstances: "Choose for yourselves this day whom you will serve. . . . [A]s for me and my household, we will serve the LORD" (Josh. 24:15, NIV).

A Blessing in God's World

MARCH 2–8, 2020 • J. BARRIE SHEPHERD

SCRIPTURE OVERVIEW: The readings for this week provide an overview of the history of God's people. Genesis recounts the story of Abraham, who because of his great faith leaves his home and goes to a land that God has promised to show him. The psalmist speaks for the descendants of Abraham, who trust in the Lord to watch over them and be their helper. Paul in Romans argues against those who believe that God's grace is a result of correctly following religious law. It is Abraham's faith (for there is no law in Abraham's time) that prompts him to follow God, and for this he is commended. Both Gospel passages (John and Matthew) emphasize that the story of Jesus is the continuation of a relationship with God's faithful people that began with Abraham.

QUESTIONS AND SUGGESTIONS FOR REFLECTION

- Read Genesis 12:1-4a. Recall a major and a minor crossroads in your life. How did you listen for God's call during each time?
- Read Psalm 121. Reflect on the times in your life when this psalm has most strongly resonated with you. How do your strongest emotions point you to God's presence?
- Read Romans 4:1-5, 13-17. What motivates you to do good works? How do you balance "faith alone" and the action to which God calls you?
- Read John 3:1-17. How do you hear again the powerful words of verses so familiar they permeate culture? What makes these words fresh for you?

Minister Emeritus of historic First Presbyterian Church in the City of New York; born and raised in the UK; preached and lectured across the world; widely published author and poet; lives in retirement on the Maine coast.

The Turning Point." That's what these verses might be called. Or "The Crossroads." Until this point, things have gone steadily downhill. Our story, this scriptural history of humankind—the forbidden fruit in the garden, Cain's murder of Abel, Noah and the flood, the tower of Babel—has been one of increasing disobedience, widening and deepening rebellion against God. Scholars sometimes call the biblical narrative "the history of salvation," and this history takes a dramatic and decisive shift in today's passage as God chooses Abram and sends him on a journey. That journey will eventually lead to Egypt and Jerusalem, to Babylon, to Bethlehem and Nazareth, and on to Rome, Constantinople, Canterbury, and beyond.

God promises destination and destiny to Abram, and Abram's obedient response sets in action a chain of faithful and unfaithful descendants—folk who go forth in trust, as Abram did, to play their part in the divine plan until that plan reaches another crossroads, another decisive turning point, on a cross and in a garden tomb.

On a more intimate scale, each of our individual lives has its own turning points, its own crossroads and decisive moments when much—maybe even an entire life—hangs in the balance: the choice of a vocation or of a spouse, the birth of a child, a response to some ethical challenge or dilemma. From an even more concentrated point of view, each day can have its decisive moments, when we are called to answer God's summons to trust and obey as Abram did. In the familiar routines of daily existence and in times of testing and trial, this passage reminds us to watch for the crossroads and listen for God's call.

Make me aware, O God, of where I stand. Remind me of my spiritual roots in your working to bring renewal to creation. Then go with me as I set forth, like Abram, toward your Promised Land. Amen.

Immigrants seem to be at the center of attention these days, not only in my country but across the globe. When I read God's words to Abram, "Go from your country and your kindred and your father's house to the land that I will show you," desperate scenes from television news come to mind. Abram, of course, is not a refugee from violence as so many are today; but Jesus surely is when, as an infant, his family flees from King Herod to the safety of distant Egypt. Abram is not seeking to escape the cruel grip of endless poverty as so many now are doing, but God's promises to him include land and rich blessings.

I have long been intrigued by the nature of God's promised blessings in today's reading. The wording here suggests a fundamental link between receiving a blessing and becoming a blessing: "I will bless you and make your name great so that you will be a blessing." That's the way it seems to go in our scriptures. Jacob, Joseph, Moses, Isaiah and the prophets, and even Jonah despite his protestations are blessed by God's presence and call; they then bring blessing to those to whom they are sent. Then Jesus, visibly blessed by God at both his baptism and his transfiguration, passes along that blessing in such rich and manifold ways that we are still his living beneficiaries.

The recipient of God's blessing, it seems, must in turn become the blesser. To receive the grace of God in Jesus Christ demands that we share the gift with all we meet by living it out gratefully and gracefully in their presence and to God's glory.

Even so, bless me, Lord, as I venture forth. May that blessing overflow into the lives of all I meet today. Amen.

Now that we are retired, my wife, Mhairi, and I spend the summer months in our log cabin retreat on an island off the Maine coast. The cabin perches high above the shore looking due west; on the horizon, usually at sunrise and sunset, we catch the outline of Mount Washington, the highest peak in the northeast. When the New England weather is particularly clear, we call it a "Mount Washington Day." It is good to see it there, to glimpse its vastness, solidity, and grandeur, even at such a distance. It's reassuring somehow and makes me feel grounded and secure.

Growing up in central Scotland—right on the edge of "The Highland Line," the majestic crests of the Ochil range, and then Ben Lomond and the rest farther beyond—I knew a similar feeling. Mountains bring a sense of looming mystery too, of possibility and of wonder. So when the psalmist lifts his eyes to the hills, something within me leaps in recognition. I know what he is singing about. I've been there too.

The entire book of Psalms resonates for me from my Scottish youth. We sang hymns in church, but worship began with one of the metrical psalms, arranged with rhyming verse and meter for congregational singing. And for all their sober mien and dignified demeanor, the psalms instigated a palpably present powerful emotion and genuine faith as we sang this psalm to the tune Dundee or the beloved Twenty-Third Psalm to Crimond. Such simple yet profound piety, such basic trust in God's Word and promises, lies at the heart of the Psalms. It is a conviction that, like the eternal hills, God's promises stand firm and God's strength is everlasting.

Lead me to the mountain, Lord. Let me share its strength. Amen.

O ne of the highest privileges of my life's vocation as a minister is that of being present with people at the key moments of their lives. "Hatch, Match, and Dispatch"—an in-joke among clergy—sums up the reality that the ancient rites surrounding birth, marriage, and death mark the universal parameters of all human life. Our pastoral presence as comfort, support, and guide plays an essential role on such occasions.

Baptisms and weddings are occasions for rejoicing, whereas funerals are more somber and sad. At such times, the *Minister's Service Book* that has guided my fifty-plus years of ministry commends "the comfort of the scriptures." I have often found that the thoughtful reading of selected passages can offer fuller, deeper, and more enduring support than any words of my own.

The phrases and cadences of Psalm 121 speak powerfully at such times of loss and grief. I find the words toward the close of this psalm especially helpful. These words about going out and coming in assure us of God's unsleeping watch over our going out to school and our coming in to family and home, our going out to work and our coming in to refreshment and rest, our going out to college, to marriage, to the new experiences of parenthood, to service of God and neighbor, to retirement, and then our coming in again to the company of those we cherish. And finally, in our last going out into the unknown realms of death and the beyond, even then we will know our coming in, returning home at the last to that long-promised, well-earned rest. We may experience the joy of knowing we abide in the everlasting arms, where all we love and have loved will be reunited and fulfilled for all eternity.

May this day's going out and coming in be guarded by your presence, Lord, lived out in joyful service. Amen.

Almost thirty years ago I stood in Martin Luther's study room, high in the Wartburg Castle, in the German state of Thuringia. On the wall was the famous ink stain, said to have been caused when Luther threw his overflowing inkwell at the Devil to chase his tormentor away. A passage from Romans, including today's text about Abraham's faith in God being reckoned as righteousness, had driven Luther to that remote castle refuge. Those words became the key to the historic reformer's revolutionary doctrine of "Justification by Faith Alone," an idea that tore apart Europe and the Christian faith.

Martin Luther taught that we are justified, set right with God, not by any works but by the fundamental act of putting all our trust in God and living out of that trust—just as Abraham had done many centuries before. Absolutely nothing we can do by our own efforts, no ritual acts—circumcision for Paul, donations to the church for Luther—can set us right with God. Only faith, trust in the God revealed in the life, death, and resurrection, can save us.

We get caught up in doing things, often good things—visiting the sick, feeding the hungry—but we must never lose sight of *why* we do such things. It is not for the sake of some heavenly reward or to avoid some ultimate punishment but out of gratitude to God, in whom we place all our faith and all our trust.

Faithful God, teach us to trust you—to place our days, our lives, our eternal souls firm in your forgiving hands. Fearing for nothing, may we serve you in gladness and joy. Amen.

One summer Sunday morning, the nine-person choir moved to the center of the chancel in our Maine island Methodist chapel, and the piano sounded the opening chords of John Stainer's "God So Loved the World." I couldn't help but groan inwardly. In over fifty years of ministry, I have heard this potentially lovely piece sung poorly more times than I can remember. With such a small and relatively untrained choir, I suspected I was in for yet another disappointment. But there was something about that rendition: the voices were few but fine, the conductor worked to bring out the underlying tenderness of both the music and the words, and my own needy spirit responded to the sheer, transparent simplicity of it all. I experienced a genuine encounter with the good news of the gospel, the real presence of our risen Lord.

In today's high-speed, high-tech world oriented toward entertainment and commerce, we encounter the most famous verse from today's reading as a brand name, an advertising slogan. We meet it on a billboard beside the highway, a sign held up at a sporting event: JOHN 3:16. But this brief passage captures the essence of our faith, our unique Christian story. It cries out to be read, heard, and sung slowly, richly, and meditatively. Stainer's piece, when performed well, is powerful because it doesn't shout at you or sweep you away on a tidal wave of sound. There are times to sing the "Hallelujah Chorus," but here at the center, the heart, where the truth of all ages, the deepest secret of past and future is finally spoken, we find a time to speak and sing gently with an eternal tenderness, in a way that embraces all who hear.

Renew for me, my Savior, the grace, the wonder, and the promise of your words. I want to rest in their gentle power. Amen.

SECOND SUNDAY IN LENT

I find Nicodemus a fascinating character. John describes him as "a leader of the Jews." Judging by the three incidents in which he appears, he is a person of considerable influence. In John 7:51, we read that Nicodemus speaks out boldly against his fellow Pharisees during the confrontations of Jesus' final week in Jerusalem, contending that on the basis of Jewish law Jesus should be granted a fair hearing. Later in that same week, after the horrific events of Good Friday, Nicodemus appears again, joining Joseph of Arimathea to provide for Jesus' burial and even contributing some hundred pounds of expensive spices. (See John 19:39.) Despite what Jesus said elsewhere concerning rich men, the kingdom of heaven, and the eye of a needle (see Matthew 19:24), it seems that Nicodemus and Joseph of Arimathea, who provided the garden tomb, have become devoted followers.

But I find the scene from today's reading the most intriguing. A prominent citizen creeps through the shadows in the dead of night to seek counsel from the young teacher and healer. His questions reveal sheer confusion: "How can anyone be born after having grown old? Can one enter a second time into the mother's womb?" And then Jesus' strange teaching about the Spirit and the flesh and the nature of rebirth culminates in those simple yet immeasurably profound words that encapsulate his entire ministry and mission: "God so loved the world."

As followers of Christ, we can remember that God loved and still loves the world—not just the church. God's beloved world includes and embraces our enemies as well as our friends, our worldwide neighbors as well as our family, all fellow creatures, and every corner of creation.

Remind us, Lord, to love this world as you do, to cherish it as your irreplaceable gift. Amen.

Journeying by Stages

MARCH 9–15, 2020 • KARA LASSEN OLIVER

SCRIPTURE OVERVIEW: Three of the passages this week connect water and faith. In Exodus and the psalm, we read about the Israelites grumbling in the desert. Although they have seen God's mighty deeds in Egypt, they have begun to question God's provision for them. God provides water through Moses, but the place is remembered (and named) as a site where the faith of the people fails. In John, however, a place to draw water becomes a site of salvation for the Samaritan woman and eventually for the people in her village through her faith. The reading in Romans goes a different direction. Paul emphasizes the importance of faith in the face of trials and the fact that God brings salvation through Christ when fallen humanity has no other hope.

QUESTIONS AND SUGGESTIONS FOR REFLECTION

- Read Exodus 17:1-7. How do your memories of God's provision sustain you through tough stages of your spiritual journey?
- Read Psalm 95. What object, image, or memory serves for you as a symbol of God's faithfulness?
- Read Romans 5:1-11. How have you found hope in stages of life when God is forming your character through suffering and endurance?
- Read John 4:5-42. When has letting go of your expectations or rules allowed God to work freely in your life or in the lives of others around you?

Creates space and facilitates opportunities for people to connect with God and express their stories in words; passion for justice and spiritual formation sustained by centering prayer, yoga, and faith community; employee of The Upper Room; spouse and mother.

The week I sat down to write these meditations, a friend told me about Lauren Daigle's album *Look Up Child*. I was struck by her soulful voice, profound lyrics, and storytelling ability. As I read the scriptures for this week, I kept listening to the song "Remember" on repeat.

Moses, Aaron, and Miriam are leading the Israelites on a forty-year journey to the Promised Land. The people are tired and thirsty and complaining that they need water. As the conflict unfolds, God directs Moses and the leaders to "Go on ahead of the people, and . . . take in your hand the staff with which you struck the Nile."

Remember, the staff that became a snake.

Remember, the staff that turned the Nile into blood.

Remember, the staff that turned dust into a plague of gnats.

Remember, the staff that divided the sea.

In my mind's eye, as the leaders go ahead and Moses raises the staff, the people have flashbacks to all that the Lord has already done for them. And they begin to sing Lauren Daigle's words: "I remember, I remember/ You have always been faithful to me."

In a dramatic moment, their memory restores their hope. As the light comes back into their eyes and they stand up straight again, Moses lifts the staff and strikes the rock, and water pours forth—another memory that they can draw on the next time they begin to falter.

This week we are challenged to remember the goodness and faithfulness of God that can sustain us at every stage of our journey.

God of the journey, prompt us to lift our eyes—even in pain—and to remember that you can make a way. Amen.

Once we commit ourselves to a journey toward liberation as the Israelites did, leaving the wilderness of grief or shame or bondage of any kind, we begin our journey by stages.

At some point along the way we may wonder whether it would have been safer, more comfortable, if we had never set out. We grow tired and thirsty; doubt and fear creep in. We feel tempted to pick fights and complain with those closest to us.

Imagine these folks, free from taskmasters, the last in a line of slaves, witnesses to miracles. But forty years is a long journey, and they wonder what God has in mind; whether Moses, Aaron, and Miriam have a plan; whether the great promises will be fulfilled. Then, the straw that breaks the camel's back: There is no water. All their frustration, fear, doubt, and uncertainty spew forth, "Give us water to drink."

The Israelites' response is so human. When children are scared of the dark, they cry for someone to bring them water. When we wonder whether we have enough love to sustain our marriage, we complain about how our spouse parks the car or unpacks the groceries. In the wilderness of sin or the suburbs of Nashville, it can feel too scary to ask the deeper question, "Is the Lord among us or not?"

God knows the deep needs under our cries. God directs Moses and the leaders: "Go on ahead and get some perspective because the people aren't thirsty; they are scared. They fear I have forgotten my promises. And take the staff. Remember? The same staff that turned the Nile to blood, that parted the Red Sea. Remember. I am with you" (AP).

So God provides water from a rock. God sustains us until the next stage with exactly what we need.

Gracious God, when we cry and quarrel and blame and despair, hear the deep cries of our heart, the deep need that we are afraid to name. Remind us of your presence and sustain us. Amen.

My husband teases me that he is writing a song called, "That's Not a Question." I have a terrible habit of asking for what I want instead of stating it directly. Maybe you will recognize this pattern in a friend or family member. Instead of telling my children when and how they can be helpful, I ask them, "Do you want to carry Grandma's suitcase?" or "Would you like to clean up the kitchen before I get home?" And then I get angry when they say, "No," because, even though I phrased it as a question, it wasn't meant as a question.

There are times when I feel like I cannot state a want or need directly, so I offer it in the form of a question. Or I project my desire onto someone else in the form of a question, hoping they will hear my need. Recently I asked my husband, "Jeff, would you like to go to the beach for spring break?" But it's not an honest question.

I appreciate the conversation in today's reading between Jesus and the woman at the well because they speak directly. They ask for what they need: water. Living water. They respect each other enough to be honest, despite cultural barriers and gender expectations. They speak truthfully without feeling the need to make a moral judgment or offer a self-righteous defense.

Their interaction is refreshing and instructive for me because I tend to communicate more like the Israelites and Moses in Exodus 17. I may prompt a quarrel about something insignificant or make a dishonest request to avoid naming the thing I really need or want. I can choose to communicate indirectly and risk forty years of restlessness outside of God's promises. Or I can find the courage to ask for exactly what I need, receive it, and serve my entire community by sharing my blessings.

God, as we speak and ask questions, grant us the courage to come before you and one another in spirit and truth. Amen.

The Israelites, journeying by stages from the wilderness, seem to have lost sight of the promise of a future with hope. Their most pressing need and cry is for water to sustain them in the present moment.

I imagine if Paul could have offered them his wisdom about suffering producing endurance, which produces character, which results in hope, it may have fallen on deaf ears. Amid suffering we find it difficult to imagine any future beyond the suffering. Weariness, thirst, and fear can take all of our effort. We struggle to remember the hope that prompted us to leave the wilderness in the first place, and we are tempted to focus on mere survival rather than endurance.

The Israelites hope that they can escape slavery, that their children will live as free people in a land flowing with milk and honey, and that they can worship their God openly. But when they step out on that hope, their suffering causes them to doubt that they can endure. They lose sight of the character of God that could have been formed in them.

The process of transformation that Paul describes requires us to choose hope again and again on each stage of the journey. Through faith in Jesus Christ, with the peace of God, and in accessing the grace available to us, we can choose to hold on to hope tenaciously, to rely on God continually, and to trust that God is being formed in our character until that hope is realized.

That's no small feat. As Paul tells us, salvation comes while we are still weak. In the wilderness and sufferings of our lives, hope and salvation can feel as unlikely as water from a rock. Thank God, we have seen and we have heard that water can come from a rock, living water, a spring of eternal life.

God of endurance, may we be a people who walk together and bear witness to the times and places when endurance leads to fulfillment of hope. Amen.

Let the psalmist's words of praise and joy wash over you. Give thanks to God, to the rock of our salvation, for God's presence, faithfulness, and beautiful creation! Recall a moment when you were startled by life's goodness, when you witnessed a sunrise, rainbow, or moonrise with full attention and delight, or when you fell into bed at night content and happy. Relish that memory as a stage of your journey—no matter how brief—that was easy and joyful. This memory can serve as a touchstone for future stages that will require a reminder of God's faithfulness and a prompt to trust and look forward with hope.

In my late thirties, I entered a stage of deep depression on my journey. I feared that the crushing sadness and heaviness of every step would never end. I did everything I knew to do to find my way out of that wilderness. I returned to spiritual practices that I had neglected and sought therapy and medication. In time, regular worship and communion, journaling, and prayer led me to remember and believe in God's unconditional love. In the dark cocoon of depression, my ego and accomplishments dissolved and I saw myself as a beloved child of God, nothing more and nothing less. I felt like I grew wings as I came to know and claim my belovedness. To mark my rebirth, I had three small butterflies tattooed onto the inside of my left wrist. They are a daily reminder of the suffering that I endured, which produced character that led me to hope again. They are my response to the psalmist's warning not to let my heart harden, not to forget the love of God available to me in every moment.

We are together, people of God, sheep in God's pasture, tempted to go astray, longing for rest. But we can offer our stories of hope and fulfillment of joy to others still wandering in the wilderness.

God of creation, open our eyes to see beauty and wonder that keep our hearts soft and open, whether the journey is easy or difficult. Amen.

When my daughter was four years old, she accompanied me when I took my youth group to a Taizé worship service that included the opportunity to walk the labyrinth. Flute, violin, and cello supported the congregation's soft voices gathered around the canvas labyrinth laid at the center of the worship space as they sang the beautiful, repeating, meditative chants.

I led my daughter to the entrance of the labyrinth and, hands on her shoulders, began directing her along the curves of the path, leading to the center, the heart of God. But she kept shaking off my hands, stepping across the lines, and generally resisting my guidance. In a moment of grace, I let her go. In awe, I watched her choose one of the youth and follow closely at her heels all the way to the center. There she rested until the young woman stood to walk again; she followed her, step-by-step, retracing the path out of the labyrinth and back to me.

I had a choice that night to make her experience about a singular encounter with rules and expectations (that would have resulted in a test and quarrel) or to let that experience be a step on a larger journey of faith, marked by trust and freedom. It seems Jesus has a similar choice as he encounters the woman at the well.

Jesus needs water to quench an immediate and temporary thirst. He could wait for the disciples to return, ignore the woman, maintain decorum, and uphold cultural expectations. Or he could let go, trust a stranger, cross lines of gender to extend an invitation of living water that will quench a lifetime of thirst. The risk, the connection, extended beyond one woman's circumstance to the transformation of an entire community.

God of freedom, remind us that we never walk alone. Open our eyes to see companions along the journey who will help us find our rest in you. Amen.

THIRD SUNDAY IN LENT

On this third Sunday in Lent, we have the privilege of knowing the end of the story—that resurrection and new life are a reality. In my imagination, Easter Sunday is a day of collective exhale, a day to bask in hope, sing loud the hallelujahs, and glimpse Jesus, who calls us into a future with hope.

In the meantime, we continue the journey in stages: to the cross, to the grave, and finally to experience the resurrection. The Lenten journey is an opportunity to consider how our hearts have hardened, how our hearts have gone astray, and where we have lost our hope along the way.

Poet David Whyte commented in an interview on the program *On Being* that our younger self has done something for which our future self is thankful. He asks how we can be the ancestors of our own future happiness. Those seem appropriate questions for us as a journeying people heading toward Easter Sunday. As an observer of Lent, what fear can I release so that I will fully celebrate the joy of Easter Sunday? What can I forgive now so that my Easter self will be thankful? What am I trying to control along my journey that makes it impossible for me to be fully at peace at the end?

Like the Israelites, Moses, Jesus, the disciples, the woman at the well and her community, we walk a journey that winds in and out of wilderness and abundance. We carry burdens of fear and shame; we long to have our deepest needs known and met. The good news is that God desires for us to have soft hearts and honest encounters so that we can enter God's rest. Today, pause and notice your feet on the path. Remember God's faithfulness. Dare to look forward with hope. Your future self will thank you.

Rock of Salvation, we long to enter your presence and your promised rest with thanksgiving. Renew our hope at each stage of the journey. Amen.

The Shepherd of Light

MARCH 16–22, 2020 • DON SALIERS

SCRIPTURE OVERVIEW: The two readings from the Hebrew scriptures focus on the life of David. In First Samuel, the prophet is sent to anoint the next king of Israel. God chooses David not because of outward appearance but because of his heart. David is not perfect, nor is his life always easy. Psalm 23 declares David's trust in God in good times and bad times. Just as Samuel has anointed David with oil, so does the Lord anoint him. The New Testament readings both employ images of light and darkness. Ephesians instructs us to live as children of light, not darkness. In John, Jesus heals a blind man and brings him from darkness into light. Some religious leaders protest because although their physical eyes can see, their spiritual vision is darkened.

QUESTIONS AND SUGGESTIONS FOR REFLECTION

- Read 1 Samuel 16:1-13. How often do you judge others by outward appearances or worldly successes? How can you "look upon the heart" to judge leaders in your community?
- Read Psalm 23. When have you experienced Jesus' presence with you in the wilderness?
- Read Ephesians 5:8-14. How does God's light help you persist through struggles within yourself or in the world around you?
- Read John 9:1-41. What questions does Jesus ask you? How do your questions of Jesus help you understand him?

Theologian in Residence, Candler School of Theology; national chaplain of The American Guild of Organists.

Imagine receiving a letter that tells you that you are light and that we are all to "live as children of light." Most of the time we wander about in a kind of darkness: We resent and are suspicions of others; we lose our sense of direction; we see the world around us as confused and dwelling in falsehoods. To such a world of division and anxiety, the letter to the Ephesians is a marvel. It prays fervently for the unity of Christ's body while it speaks to our deepest personal struggles with darkness. It names our struggles and reminds us of who we are in Christ: We are to "live in love, as Christ loved us" (5:2). In the face of division and difficulty, this letter contains the central message of the gospel for our Lenten journey.

The key image in the passage for today is the light of Christ. That light exposes every human impulse toward darkness. Lent demands that we turn toward the light seen in the life and teachings of Christ. On the one hand, this means that our hidden struggles with human greed and unfruitful works become painfully visible to ourselves before God. On the other, we are invited to turn to the visible light of God's grace. Amid our struggle between truth and untruth, between our true and false selves, and between division and exclusion, Christ shines a light.

I recall being lost with three companions on an unfamiliar mountain in the darkness before dawn. Then the dawn came, and we saw where we were. This was but a small foretaste of the way our passage ends: "Sleeper, awake! Rise from the dead, and Christ will shine on you."

God of resurrection promise, grant to us a turning to your light so that we may see your way. Amen.

L ike many others, today's Old Testament story has enormous consequences. On the surface it is an account of how David is chosen to replace Saul as king of Israel. Samuel selects only one of Jesse's eight sons, and David seems the most unlikely. Even Samuel seems perplexed about God's decision—at least at first. David is a lowly shepherd; yet the image of a shepherd-king of Israel becomes one of the most beloved in Christian history. What are we to make of this story within the larger drama of God's dealings with a complicated and even unruly ancient Israel?

It turns out that the God of Abraham, Isaac, and Jacob does not judge on outward appearances. This is quite unlike our way of judging. As the story says, God does "not see as mortals see . . . the LORD looks on the heart." Suddenly I realize that I make many of my own judgments about other people based on "outward appearances." The success, power, and influence of others often shape my view of their ability and character. Recent discussions of our hidden privileges (whether of race, class, gender, or other identifier) have convinced me that our human decisions about one another rarely "look upon the heart." When making community decisions about who our leaders should be, how God sees our hearts often seems missing.

Samuel's perplexity opens us to the mystery of how God works to raise up leaders of church and society. Can we learn from God's choice of a psalm-singing shepherd to look beyond our habits of "outward appearances" to divine wisdom? Much remains hidden at this point in the story of how David will rule, but the truth of God's preference and risk in choosing the "shepherd of Israel" remains.

Christ Jesus, you looked upon the hearts of all you encountered with compassion and wisdom. Teach us to do the same in all our judgments. Amen.

Rereading and meditating on this account of the anointing of David takes us deeper than first meets the eye. Throughout the Hebrew scriptures, the continuing story of David as ruler of Israel is far more complicated than we may wish. If Samuel had known what we know about the whole history of David's reign, he may have wondered at God's choice. Yet it is the divine choice. Whatever we make of David—the Goliath-slaying, psalm-singing shepherd (one of the most cherished images in both Jewish and Christian faith)—the reality of God's gaze upon the human heart is crucial to David and to God's people.

The "Collect for Purity," a familiar prayer in my tradition, acknowledges that the Almighty God of all creation knows our hearts, our desires, and all our secrets—even before we pray. In this prayer we cry out, "Cleanse the thoughts of our hearts by the inspiration of your Holy Spirit."* Knowing that we are known by God, we ask for the in-breathing of God's Holy Spirit in our lives so that we may love and magnify the Holy Name in all we do or say or think. This prayer flows from trusting that God knows our hearts more truly than we do. As First John 3 observes, God is greater than our hearts; God sees us but does not condemn or destroy us.

The older we get, the more puzzling we are to ourselves. But as we move through the days and disciplines of Lent, we come to know that God knows us better than we know ourselves. We dare walk with Jesus toward the cross and resurrection, held fast by that unbelievable grace.

---

*Collect for Purity, The Book of Common Prayer (1979).

Pray the Collect for Purity, the Lord's Prayer, or both prayers each morning and each evening. Await what grace will be given you.

Is there any psalm as beloved as Psalm 23? Even for those who know little of the Bible, phrases from this psalm sound familiar. The beloved shepherd of whom David sings—even to unstable king Saul—speaks of the way God cares for us. God leads us to green pastures, beside still waters, and through the "valley of the shadow of death" (KJV). No wonder these words have been set to music in every generation and paraphrased in hymns and songs in every language.

Who among us does not long for quiet waters and for the restoration of our sanity in a crazy, driven world? Who among us does not hope for a banquet of plenty in the face of hunger and thirst and in the presence of danger? For those moving toward the end of life, this psalm brings promise of dwelling with God, who makes room for us in all days left to us. We find deep life and faith compressed into these few verses.

The Lenten journey takes us into the wilderness, just as the Spirit drives Jesus into the wilderness. If we pray this psalm with Jesus, in him and through him, Jesus himself prays in and through us. So, we come to imagine and to know Jesus as our shepherd. He knows us by name and will not desert us to the tangle of temptations we call life; nor will he allow us to be lost in the darkness of the world and its ways. The Gospels tell us that he will seek any sheep who are astray and without food or water. Here is the greatest mystery of all: Jesus feeds us in the banquet of his life—Holy Communion.

Please, kind Christ, shepherd us through our valleys and lead us into goodness and mercy. Amen.

We often consider John the most "theological" of the four Gospels. The Gospel begins with the incomparable words of the prologue: "In the beginning was the Word." But today we encounter one of the most utterly human episodes in the New Testament, full of irony and realism. The healing of the man blind from birth reads like a short story. Yes, it is a miracle story, but it holds a dramatic key to John's theology. I love the physical details, from the anointing with mud to the parents' honest reply to the religious authorities: "Ask him!"

This story contains a series of questions with a spiraling series of surprising answers. The healed man is asked multiple times about who has healed him. Each time we come to understand a little more about Jesus. At first the man doesn't know; then he admits that Jesus must be a prophet. Then the parents are dragged in for questioning and observe that their son is "of age." They send the inquiring religious folk back to ask him. Then we find out that the Pharisees already think Jesus is a sinner and question how on earth he could have healed the man. Then comes the man's confession, which becomes one of the most famous hymns of all time: "One thing I do know, that though I was blind, now I see." The hymn "Amazing Grace" echoes this testimony through many generations.

Could it be that we can understand who Jesus is by asking questions? This is the way of Lenten discipline. To fast and pray is like a series of questions, but now the questions are part of our own spiritual quest. Jesus will reveal his power to heal our spiritual blindness if we come in wonder.

Come to us, Lord Jesus, and restore our sight. Reveal to us who you are. Amen.

Just about the time we think we know this story, it surprises us. The second questioning of the man born blind yields his unforgettable confession: I once was blind, but now I see. But then the conversation between the religious authorities and the man heats up.

What starts as a narrative of questions and answers becomes an angry exchange. The religious authorities are offended by the sighted man's innocent question: "Do you also want to become his disciples?" We can almost hear them shout at him. "You are a sinner; you can't teach us anything about this Jesus!" (AP). The drama ends with them driving him out. But it doesn't end with the narrow view in triumph.

Jesus comes to the healed man to ask one more question, "Do you believe?" Suddenly full disclosure comes. What has been dawning slowly all the while suddenly bursts into full sight. Jesus bears divine judgment in the form of healing. Those who think they know with certainty who God and sinners are have become blind, while those who seek Jesus are given revelation to their seeing. The man sees more and more while the religious authorities see less and less—victims of their own theology. Here is John's Gospel in miniature, startled by the great theme that runs throughout it: All who yearn to understand who Jesus is are invited to "come and see!"

We are all part of this story now, both saints and sinners. In this season of spiritual discipline, Jesus comes to our world to bring sight to our blindness. His light shines in our darkness; his healing touch stretches out to us and to the whole weary world.

God of mercy and light, heal our blind souls; turn us from our narrow-minded views of others. Let us see Jesus, and grant us the light of his presence. Amen.

FOURTH SUNDAY IN LENT

Ponder the images of our week's meditations. God does not judge as we mortals do—the divine gaze is on the human heart. Shepherds become rulers, and David brings loving-kindness to how we are to live together. The great shepherd of Psalm 23 leads us in pathways of righteousness and into verdant places of life-giving water. The shepherd guides us even in the places of difficulty and death. Into our lives comes Jesus the healer. He knows our blindness and comes to us with light amid the world's wilderness. What wonderment in the course of our Lenten journeys!

We end as the week began, reading an ancient letter written to the church. Now it has our names on it. These words should be written in gold: "The fruit of the light is found in all that is good and right and true." If Jesus is truly the good shepherd who comes to us as judge and healer, then we are embraced by the grace of a Creator who will not let us perish in darkness. No wonder the letter to the Ephesians admonishes us to search and find what is pleasing to God. In these forty days we encounter difficult things about ourselves and our world. Nevertheless, we persist. This is because God in Christ will not grow weary seeking us. Through the days in our lives that fly by so rapidly, God's steady light—the light of resurrection faith—beckons us through thick and thin.

Take heart! Live in, with, and through these images. Support one another daily, for "once you were darkness, but now in the Lord you are light." Who gives us this language? It is Jesus Christ, the shepherd and Light of God speaking to you now.

Thank you, living God, for words and sight to help us see, love, and worship you. Amen.

Confessions

MARCH 23–29, 2020 • RACHEL G. HACKENBERG

SCRIPTURE OVERVIEW: Ezekiel sets the stage for the readings this week. In a vision, the prophet sees a seemingly hopeless situation, yet God restores flesh to the bones and brings them back to life by breathing into them. The psalmist calls out to God from the depths of devastation and waits confidently for God's redemption. Paul plays off the double meaning of the Greek word *pneuma*: "breath" and "spirit." Just as Ezekiel's dry bones are brought back through the breath of God, so are we raised through the Spirit of God. The Lazarus story provides a bookend resurrection story for the week. Here Jesus demonstrates in the physical realm the spiritual realities described in the other passages. These resurrection stories point us toward Jesus' resurrection and ultimately the promise of our own.

QUESTIONS AND SUGGESTIONS FOR REFLECTION

- Read Ezekiel 37:1-14. When have you heard from God directly or through others in times of devastation? How did you respond?
- Read Psalm 130. How can you listen for signs of hope and look for God's voice?
- Read Romans 8:6-11. What helps you remember that you cannot save yourself and to put your trust in God?
- Read John 11:1-45. When have you been disappointed in God's timing or response? What would be different now if God had met your expectations then?

Ordained minister in the United Church of Christ; author of *Writing to God* and *Sacred Pause*; co-author with Martha Spong of *Denial Is My Spiritual Practice*.

The situation in Ezekiel 37 seems extreme; yet many of us have experienced, witnessed, and survived such utter devastation. We have witnessed the complete disruption of life, the dismantling of everything familiar, the place from which life cannot continue as usual. What had once been the Promised Land and the seat of God—the ancient kingdom of Israel—has been torn apart by international war, shifting empires, diplomatic games, and competing religions. The people of Israel are torn apart. Prophets and politicians disagree about which empire to trust as an ally. Prominent leaders are exiled. Families are separated. Faith seems lost without a stable community to sustain it, without a Temple, without the clear presence of God. To Ezekiel and his audience, those days feel like death, like hope evaporating under a relentless sun, like dry bones scattered in the dust.

Today in our own lives these days feel like death—when life is scattered by unforeseen events, when faith can't find its breath amid the chaos, when the way forward seems impossible between a rock and a hard place. God asks Ezekiel: "Is new life possible even now when the people despair? Is renewed faith possible for people whose spirits have suffocated from despair? Can community be rebuilt among people who are separated by fear and violence?" Ezekiel replies honestly, "I don't know; but God, I believe that you know" (AP). The most faithful response Ezekiel can give is to confess that he himself cannot envision possibilities for the dry bones. But he believes that if life is possible, God is the one who can envision it and bring it about.

When nothing seems certain but chaos, when life has lost its footing and faith has lost its imagination, we can confess that our future still holds something good, even if we do not know what it is. God knows.

God of wisdom and mystery, I confess my despair, my doubt, my disappointment. Please breathe life into the possibilities that I do not yet know. Amen.

Change, whether joyful or painful or even mundane, compels us to assess what has been in the past as we make our way toward the future.

Sometimes the hardest part of change is looking at the past honestly. How does Ezekiel not faint with despair when he gazes at the valley of dry bones that the Spirit shows him as he reflects on his people's history of struggle? How does he not fall apart in grief every time his people ask, "When will we get to go home? Will God spare the Temple from destruction in this war?" Dwelling on the past can overwhelm our hearts with grief. Our desire to know what has been and why can consume us.

Other times the hardest part of change is sustaining a vision for the future. Ezekiel serves God as a prophet for more than twenty years; the Babylonian exile lasts seventy years. How does Ezekiel hold on to God's vision for the people's restoration? How does he nurture the people's curiosity for God's future? Setting our sights on the future can foment impatience: "If things will be different someday, why can't they be different sooner?" We can cling to the future so fiercely that the eyes of our hearts narrow to believe that only one vision can be true and good.

Most often, however, the hardest part of change is attending to the present, the moment when the brutal honesty of yesterday and the vague promise of tomorrow collide to ask, "What is needed right now?" Ezekiel sees yesterday's dry bones and tomorrow's revived community, but he can only act on what God gives him to do in the present: "Speak to the bones, Ezekiel. Tell them what I will do, and then I will take care of doing it. But for today, I need you to speak."

The present is the only moment when faith can take action. What does God call us to do now?

Eternal God, I confess that I am still processing yesterday and am already anxious about tomorrow. What would you have me do today? Amen.

In moments of hubris and daydream, I long to create a solution to the weights and strains and sins of the world, or at least a reasonable fix to the weights of my own worries, stresses, and shortcomings. But the psalmist requires me to confess the truth: "If sin and sorrow and evil were measured, no one could stand under the weight of them" (Ps. 130:3, AP).

Wishing to be supernaturally strong and wise and righteous so that I could manage all things gets me in trouble more often than not. I tell myself that I'm trying to be a good steward of my responsibilities to myself, my work, and my family; yet still I bite off more than I can chew, so to speak. I try to fit two days of work into one. I pile up deadlines. I don't visit the doctor. I brush off offers of assistance. I try to manage myself so that no one else notices my limitations or fatigue or disappointment, not because I mind the flaws but because I don't want to burden others. Everyone else is carrying the weight of the world too.

None of us can stand under it all.

When I was a young girl, I wanted to be either Miss Piggy or Wonder Woman; both are strong "can do" characters who take care of themselves and others (Miss Piggy with her fist, Wonder Woman with her lasso). They are larger than life, stronger than average. They could stand on their own. Yet I am not superhero nor Muppet nor deity.

When I remember to confess my humanity, I also remember the One who can save me from the weight of the world that I've been trying to lift. "You, O LORD, have the power to free us from the expectation of godly goodness, of superhuman might, of eternal restoration," praises the psalmist (AP).

I am wonderfully made by you, O God, but I am not a god. I confess that I cannot live by my own strength and cannot rescue my own soul from sin and sorrow. Amen.

The psalmist reminds me of the prophet Habakkuk, who stands at his watchpost and declares, "I will watch to see what [God] will say" (2:1). Not, "I will listen to hear what God will say." Not, "I will watch to see what God will do." The prophet watches for God's voice; he uses his eyes for listening. Similarly, the psalmist prays, "Listen to my words, and I will watch for your answer" (AP).

In both Psalm 130 and Habakkuk 2, eyes do the work of ears and ears do the work of eyes. It's a confusion of senses, an apparent reorganization of how the body works. Yet it reminds us that faith, like the body, cannot be separated into parts. Just like the eyes need the ears and the body needs the voice, prayer needs work, proclamation needs meditation, and mercy needs fellowship. Mind, body, and spirit cooperate to perceive God.

I confess that I often separate my senses and perceptions when I seek God. I ask for a sign to give me hope, and I watch for that sign so intently in the world around me that I miss the song of hope my ears receive in Sunday worship. I raise my hands and pray that God will lift me up from the depths, and I focus so much on waiting with patience for God's rescue and relief to fill my spirit that I fail to recognize the comfort of companions who travel along the same deep road. I cry to God for the long night of God's silence to end. I long so intently for any sound or sigh in God's voice that I neglect to feel the warmth of dawn on my skin as the sun rises in the east.

We often separate our minds, bodies, and spirits on the journey of faith; but God welcomes and loves us as whole people.

Help me watch for your words and listen for your actions, O God. Help me wait for you with my body, mind, and spirit together. Amen.

Writing to the church in Rome, the apostle Paul echoes the poetic truth from Psalm 130: "We cannot live by our own strength. We cannot save ourselves—who could stand if we tried? To focus on gaining salvation by our own flesh is to focus on death, but to focus on what the Spirit can accomplish is to focus on life" (AP).

Paul then references an image Jesus uses in John 15: "You are in the Spirit, because the Spirit abides in you. You belong to Christ, because Christ dwells in you. Because the Spirit is in you, life is in you, because God gives life through the Spirit just as life was given to Jesus for the resurrection" (AP). Like a vine that relies on its roots and branches to have life, God, the Spirit, and Christ work together for life. "Remember," Paul says, "that you are part of the vine and the roots and the branches—you cannot have life on your own" (AP).

Some days, I lose sight of the Root that grounds me in God's mercy. My spirit feels tossed and tumbled by self-doubt, by envy, by the rat race that says I am only good enough if I am ahead of everyone else.

Some days, I lose my perspective on the Vine that flows with Christ's love. My hope is short-tempered, my grace for others is limited, and I wonder whether people will ever stop warring with one another.

Some days, I fail to remember that I am rooted in the Branch of the Spirit's delight. My fear overthrows my faith and my heart loses its courage to fly because it sees the risk of falling.

Yet somehow the Spirit encourages me to set my mind on joy, Christ reminds me that love will never run dry, and God points out that I don't need to chase after peace.

Triune God of Root, Vine, and Branch, I confess that I lose perspective too easily and forget to love my life in you. Amen.

It's hard to believe that Jesus chooses to let someone die. Of course, it's hard to believe that Jesus raises someone from the dead too. But first it's hard to believe that Jesus knows Lazarus is dying and doesn't drop everything to go and heal him. While many of us try to spend time with loved ones when death looms, Jesus says to his disciples after he receives the news that Lazarus is sick, "Let's stay where we are for two more days" (AP).

For Jesus, death is sleep, and the time of death is like a night of sleep after which the sun will surely rise. God's time is not confined by the dance of the sun and the Earth, not limited to the cycles of mortal life and death, and not defined by the rhythms or seasons of this world. God's experience of time—*kairos*, "the right moment"—differs from our experience of time—*chronos*, "sequence."

I might have more patience with God's time if I didn't have so many opinions about how life unfolds in our time. People all around the world flee from war and drought and famine, and I wonder why we do not take better care of one another right now. Why doesn't God recognize this humanitarian crisis as a moment worthy of intervening action? Racism plagues every part of the world, so much so that the news cycle cannot keep pace in reporting its violent acts and words. I wonder when God will see fit to repair this wrong.

Lazarus dies, and Jesus isn't there to say goodbye. When Martha tells Jesus that she believes all will be well for Lazarus in *kairos*, she also admits her disappointment that Jesus was not present in *chronos*. She believes in God's power, but she misses her friend in that critical moment.

God, I confess my impatience. I want your relief to find us before our tears begin. I want your healing to find us before our hearts break. Amen.

Fifth Sunday in Lent

I keep waiting for God to do things my way. That's preposterous and I laugh aloud at the audacity of such a confession, but it's truer than I prefer to admit. I have expectations for how God works, and I'm disappointed when God doesn't act according to my plan. Today's reading reminds me that I'm not the only one who's disappointed by such expectations. "Why didn't you get here sooner, Jesus?" Mary asks. "Couldn't Jesus have prevented the death of Lazarus?" some whisper among themselves. And then, when Jesus calls Lazarus out of the tomb: "Couldn't Jesus bring Lazarus back to life without the stench of death hovering in the air?" (AP).

Many people are disappointed by Jesus and his ministry. Some want more pizzazz. Some want more quiet time. Some want Jesus to focus on teaching; others want him to focus on healing. Some think he should stick to the temple, some think he should challenge Rome, and still others want him to minister exclusively to the outcasts and fly under the radar of religious and political authorities. "Didn't I tell you to believe?" Jesus asks (AP). To Jesus, the sign of belief is not certainty but a willingness to be surprised. Believe and be surprised by life after death. Believe and be surprised by healing. Believe and be surprised by teaching. Believe and be surprised by abundance.

Given the choice between setting our own expectations and being surprised by another's, most of us will choose to set our own. When our expectations are not met, surprise can become disappointment, and disappointment can become resistance. The way someone else does it isn't good enough. I want Jesus to mourn in a certain way. I want Lazarus to be resurrected in a certain way. But Jesus doesn't do things my way. Thank God!

I confess that you do not meet my expectations, O God. You upend them and exceed them. Thank you. Amen.

Trust and Obey

MARCH 30 – APRIL 5, 2020 • AMY LYLES WILSON

SCRIPTURE OVERVIEW: The Liturgy of the Palms readings prepare us for Palm Sunday, when Jesus enters the city of Jerusalem in triumph. The psalmist celebrates the one who comes in the name of the Lord, who is celebrated with palm branches. Matthew then tells the story of Jesus, who enters Jerusalem in this way and is greeted with joy, such that the crowds quote Psalm 118. The Liturgy of the Passion points to the end of that week and the coming suffering of Jesus. Isaiah and the psalmist describe being treated with contempt, beaten, and rejected. In reciting the earliest known Christian hymn, Paul in Philippians emphasizes how Christ surrenders his glory and is subjected to humiliation and death. Matthew recounts the passion of the Messiah, who is rejected as the prophets have foretold.

QUESTIONS AND SUGGESTIONS FOR REFLECTION

- Read Psalm 118:1-2, 19-29. How has God been steadfast in your life? How do you praise God for this continual presence?
- Read Matthew 21:1-11. How would you expect a ruler to enter a city? How is Jesus' entrance the same? How is it different?
- Read Isaiah 50:4-9a. What does being a servant of God look like? How does God help you live as a servant?
- Read Philippians 2:5-11. Consider the author's suggestion that Jesus manifests his divinity by being completely obedient to God. How does this change the way you think about the divine image within you?

Spiritual director and story coach based in Nashville, Tennessee, who believes it is the sharing of our stories that saves us; Amherst Writers and Artists Affiliate and SoulCollage® Facilitator; coauthor and contributor to eight books; former student intern for *Weavings*.

The Psalms—a collection of prayers and hymns from throughout Israel's history—offer a variety of emotions, from sorrow to joy, despair to gratitude. Many of us turn to this book of the Bible when we need consolation or want to express our appreciation. This psalm is devoted to praise and thanksgiving. The psalmist celebrates the steadfastness of God's love. Using a call-and-response format, the psalmist invites others to join him in giving thanks.

To be steadfast means to be firm in belief or in place. A tall order, to be sure, but certainly one that describes the relationship God offers us. God will always be; God will not desert us or fall short.

How have you experienced God's steadfastness?

Before I go to bed on Saturday nights, I write a gratitude list for the preceding week. From family dinners to finished manuscripts, lunch with a friend to a walk around the lake, I note the sacred—in whatever form I encountered it—that graced my days. It's an evocative reminder of how God is revealed to me, over and over again, on a regular basis. And it's a nice lead-in to my attending worship on Sunday mornings.

Another practice I've adopted is to stop when I see something that brings the awesomeness of God to my attention. When I pause for a purple sunset in the mountains of western North Carolina or a middle-aged woman helping her elderly mother at the grocery store, I take a deep breath and say, "Thank you, gracious God, for this." Maybe I utter it out loud, or maybe I meditate on the words silently. Either way, it just takes a few seconds, and it grounds me in gratitude.

How might you respond to God's steadfastness today?

Gracious Lord, thank you for staying the course with me. Knowing you'll always be there, no matter what, is a great comfort. Amen.

Praise and thanksgiving continue in these latter verses of Psalm 118, and once again we are called on to express our appreciation for God's steadfast love and abiding protection.

Many of us have heard preachers open their Sunday sermons with words from today's reading: "This is the day that the LORD has made; let us rejoice and be glad in it." Any day we're with God is worthy of celebration. On this day, the psalmist is rejoicing in salvation—for himself and for Israel—that the Lord has provided.

The two verses before this one are familiar as well. Jesus quotes Psalm 118:22-23 while telling a parable in Matthew 21. As Christians, we understand the psalmist to be foretelling that God declares the One rejected by religious leaders as the One above all others—Jesus is the "chief cornerstone." You don't have to know much about construction to appreciate that the first stone set when laying a foundation is important. Without a stable, well-placed cornerstone, a building can't stand the test of time. Without a firm foundation in Jesus, people will sin and nations will fall. Likewise, without a fixed faith in something beyond himself, the psalmist would have been crushed by his enemies. Now he is granted admission into the Temple to give thanks, and he cries out for the "gate of the Lord" to be open so that the righteous may pass through it.

In addition to being words of thanksgiving, these verses can offer us a cautionary tale: Think long and hard before you cast aside something—or someone—on which you might need to rely later. Don't concern yourself with public opinion, and instead mind the ways of God—for therein lies your salvation.

Thank you, God, for the stable foundation our faith provides. Amen.

After reaching the Mount of Olives on their way to Jerusalem, Jesus instructs two disciples to get a colt and a donkey from a nearby village. They do as they are told, and soon people are gathered as Jesus enters the city. Those in attendance have spread their coats and some tree branches on the ground as an act of homage. But Jesus from Galilee is a different kind of ruler, both in appearance and in manner. Jesus concentrates on his status as servant because it has been foretold that the Messiah will come in humility.

The city is unsettled as Jesus enters, but he is undaunted by those who oppose him. Even though he knows he is journeying toward his death, he comes as the Messiah. In other words, Jesus has a job to do, and he is doing as his Father commanded.

We too are called to follow God's instructions. Even if we don't understand why we are being sent to a neighboring village for farm animals, there will be a reason. For Christians, real understanding takes place in the heart and soul. In today's culture, though, with its emphasis on forging one's own path and do-your-own-thing mentality, it can be a challenge to take the backseat, to let God drive.

I won't bore—or depress—you with how many times I've taken control when I should have just experienced the ride. Learn from my mistakes, and let God do what God does best.

Help me, O Lord, to follow your lead, even when I don't understand on an intellectual level. Blessed are those who follow your way. Amen.

THURSDAY, APRIL 2 ~ *Read Isaiah 50:4-9a*

Categorized as a "servant song," this passage introduces us to a servant who has been faithful to God to an impressive degree. Despite having been reviled by his peers for such devotion, the servant stays true. Just as God will remain committed to us, so the servant remains committed to God. He listens, hears, and responds. He warns the people of the consequences of defying God and instructs them to change their ways, the ways of the world. He encourages them with hope. There are blessings here for you if you choose to follow God instead of humanity.

Because the servant has experienced "insult and spitting" and other indignities firsthand, he will be well-situated to "sustain the weary with a word." He has been there. I suspect he is able to listen to others tell their hard stories. I believe such holy listening is one of the purest ministries we can offer our fellow pilgrims. Surely we can all recount times in which being listened to by a spiritual companion made a difference for us. Or maybe you've been that sacred container for someone else.

I think this servant might be my new hero. He does as God instructs, doesn't wimp out when he is abused, and respects the power of language—my kind of guy.

When considering this passage, I'm drawn to revisit Psalm 19:14, "Let the words of my mouth, and the meditation of my heart be acceptable to you, O Lord, my rock and my redeemer." Knowing when to speak—and what to say—and when to listen is an art we all can learn. God shows this servant how it's done, and God can show us too.

Instill in me a servant's heart, Lord, so that I listen when others turn away. Fortify me so that I can stand up to opposition, all the while turning my ears toward you. Amen.

This is not the first time we hear David cry out in the Psalms. He seems constantly to be in some sort of distress. Not only does he continue to ask God for help; he also continues to trust that God will deliver him. In short, David believes.

I hope I'm never in such a sorry state as David is here, wasting away in body and spirit, despised by those around him. I hope I never feel surrounded by that kind of terror, my life threatened with such intensity.

Certainly, though, I can relate to David in less dramatic fashion when I've felt overwhelmed by forces outside my control. When my father was dying and I wasn't sure I could get to Mississippi from Tennessee in time to say goodbye. When I was felled by a mysterious illness that defied diagnosis and landed me in the hospital for four days. Yes, I cried out to God. But I'm not sure I trusted that I would be delivered from anything. It's a weak spot in my faith. I doubt whether God will respond; or maybe I'm afraid God's answer won't match my expectations.

This passage reassures me, as I hope it does you. For even in the deepest dark, God is there for us. Even when we feel like a "broken vessel," cast aside and shattered by aspersions, God is there.

The Japanese have a practice of repairing broken pottery with a metallic compound that adds glimmer to the vessel. *Kingsugi*, which means "golden repair," turns a cracked pot into a vase veined with gold. This process honors the flaws instead of hiding them, just as God does for David in ancient times and does for us today. David trusts this promise, and we would do well to follow suit.

Lord, help me trust you as much as David trusted you to deliver him from his distress. Remind me that you can repair the cracks in my life. Amen.

Oh that we could have the same mind as Jesus! Even though it seems impossible, as Christians we are called to model ourselves after the One who was willing to die on the cross. Because we are mere humans, doing so demands a great deal of us, not the least of which are the traits of obedience and humility.

Although most of us won't be forced to die for our beliefs, we are called to live as if we are prepared to sacrifice everything for God. That kind of supplication requires that we let go of selfish intent to focus on humbling ourselves before God, just as Jesus did on our behalf. It requires that we value modesty over pretension, meekness over recognition. It requires that we trade self-will for God's plan. Jesus' gift of sacrifice is one we can participate in if we are willing. May we strive daily to have the mind, and the heart, of Christ.

Writing from prison in Rome to the Christians of Philippi, Paul points out that Jesus did not misuse or take advantage of his divinity. Jesus did "not regard equality with God as something to be exploited." Instead, he manifested it as ultimate obedience to God. In response to that emptying out, that complete and total offering, God exalted Jesus by naming him above all others.

From that day on, when the name Jesus is heard, followers are to proclaim Jesus Christ as Lord. In so doing with humility and obedience, we give the glory to God, where it belongs.

May it be so.

Lord, help me see humility as an honor, not a sacrifice, as I strive to have a mind and heart like that of Jesus. Allow me to understand that obedience does not limit, but instead deepens, my relationship with you. Amen.

PALM/PASSION SUNDAY

At this point in the story, we know Jesus will be betrayed, and we know the time is near. This is bad enough, but the fact that a disciple will betray Jesus makes it even worse. That Jesus is going to be betrayed in a manner that leads to his death is off-the-charts treacherous.

Yet there's more. Jesus has to break bread with the man who has agreed to set his death in motion. Can you imagine the restraint this must have required on Jesus' part?

When I was younger—I'm in my late fifties now—I thought I could handle just about anything as long as I knew what was coming. Whether good or bad, I used to say, just tell me how it looks. Then I'll know what to do next. Even still, I cannot imagine knowing I have to share a meal with a close companion who will soon help send me to the cross. That would be too much information for me to handle.

Thankfully, most of us won't be betrayed to such a degree that it leads to our deaths. But I bet many of us bear stories of deception that felt like they might kill us at the time they occurred. I've learned that thinking I could manipulate the outcome if I just had enough information is a spiritually immature way of being in the world. Life and God have schooled me otherwise since those early days, and for that I am grateful. It takes a lot of pressure off, not having to be in control all the time. And so, as our faith reminds us, even after the heartache, God remains.

Let me not betray you, O Lord, or those I love. Guide my ways so that I always treat others with honesty, integrity, and compassion. Amen.

The Wideness of God's Mercy

APRIL 6–12, 2020 • KATHLEEN STEPHENS

SCRIPTURE OVERVIEW: Although we anticipate the celebration of Easter, this week's readings remind us to slow down and walk through the suffering of Jesus. If we fail to understand why he has to die, then we fail to grasp fully the power of his resurrection. Monday's passage in Isaiah anticipates the Messiah, the Anointed One, coming to bring justice to the nations. Tuesday's Psalm laments that sometimes the righteous are met with scorn. The Hebrews passage for Wednesday declares that Christ knows of the suffering that awaits him, yet he endures it because of the joy to come. On Thursday, the reading in John shows us that even when facing death, Jesus continues to model selfless love. Friday brings pain and rejection, but Sunday is the greatest day in human history. He is risen indeed!

QUESTIONS AND SUGGESTIONS FOR REFLECTION

- Read John 13:1-7, 31b-35. Consider someone who has disappointed, hurt, or betrayed you whom God might be calling you to love. How could a posture of service help you act in a loving way even if you cannot feel affection for this person?
- Read Isaiah 52:13–53:12. How does this description of a suffering servant help you more fully understand Jesus' suffering on the cross?
- Read Lamentations 3:1-9, 19-24. When has grief felt like mercy? When has noticing you are alive felt like a miracle?
- Read Psalm 118:1-2, 14-24. Recall a time you forgot how to sing God's praises despite the joy around you. How did God provide the song?

Member of Christ Episcopal Church, Temple, TX; former associate editor of *Weavings*; former editor, Upper Room Books; freelance editor and writer who splits time between Colorado and Texas.

Holy Week is the most momentous time of the year for Christians. The faithful somberly recall the events leading up to Jesus' death on the cross. By now, we know them by heart—the triumphal entry into Jerusalem, Judas's betrayal, the Last Supper, Jesus' arrest, crucifixion, death, and burial. It is all so poignantly familiar to those of us who have been Christ followers for a while. But if anything about Holy Week can stop us in our tracks and capture our hearts anew, it is the mercy of it. When we pause to ponder Jesus' death on the cross, we become aware of a mercy so wide that it boggles our minds. Mercy happens when we are shown compassion we do not earn or deserve. When Jesus gives his life on the cross in our place, to atone for our own sin—that is simply mercy writ large.

As the English hymn writer Frederick Faber observed, "There's a wideness in God's mercy, like the wideness of the sea" (UMH, no. 121). In our scripture reading today, we see that God's mercy is so wide that it includes all people—Jews and Gentiles, saints and sinners, influential people and nobodies. This is good news. God provides for the needs of all people all over the world. Not only do humans receive mercy; God's providential care extends to animals too. God provides for all living things on the earth—people, wild beasts, fish, birds, bugs.

Because of God's mercy, nothing gets lost, and no one falls through the cracks. In a world that in so many ways tries to tell us that we don't matter, don't measure up, and are not "essential," God begs to differ. In God's merciful acts for all creation, every living creature is provided for, loved, and treasured.

We thank you, loving God, as we recognize just how wide is your mercy and how deep is your care for all your creation. Amen.

All humanity seems to be at odds with one another. Churches are no different. In our desire to fulfill our mission on earth, we seldom see eye-to-eye with our Christian sisters and brothers. What seems like a missional slam dunk to us may be anathema to others in Christ's body. One thing we know for sure: When two or three gather together, they are bound to disagree.

In today's reading, Paul takes to task the Corinthian church for its divisions. Like much of the ancient world, they had split into two camps over what constituted greatness. The Greeks prized wisdom. The Jews esteemed the power of miracles. Today, we likely would affirm both sides, then demonstrate how God can help each achieve their ends. That was not Paul's way. Paul astounds us by saying neither power nor wisdom is adequate for understanding how God works. Rather than siding with the Jews or the Greeks, Paul takes these two concepts of greatness and turns them on their heads. God's choice, Paul says, is the apparent foolishness and weakness of the cross.

How can we know that God's foolishness and weakness trump the wisdom and power of people? Because when we accepted the gospel message, we weren't wise or powerful. Instead we were needy and poor in spirit, and that made it possible for us to come to faith. Our own experience is proof of how radically different God's ways are from the ways of the world. In place of the power we clamor for or the wisdom we fancy, God gives us the cross as the legitimate means to greatness. Christ is the substance of everything we desire. We do not boast of any human trait, but only in the Lord Jesus Christ.

Thank you, God, for a mercy that includes all of us foolish and weak people of the world. Help us to see that true wisdom and power are found only in you. Amen.

The Hebrews are suffering under immense persecution. Many have had homes and personal property confiscated. Some have been tortured; others killed. It is no wonder that they have grown discouraged. The writer implores them to hold on to their faith in Christ by considering the example of heroes of the faith who endured to the end.

In his message of encouragement, the writer describes the Hebrews' lives as a race and then reminds them they are not alone in this race. Cheering them on are heroes of the faith who have already finished their course. Jesus is the leader of them all—the one who marked out the race, ran its course to the very end, and made it possible for us to follow. One of the basic teachings of Christianity is this: It is not how you start that matters; it is how you finish. Jesus makes it clear that those who endure to the end will receive their reward.

The finish line for us is Christlikeness, and all through our race the Creator is shaping us to be more like Jesus. When we grow weary or lose heart, we can change the trajectory of our story by considering those who have run the race before us. They give us courage to endure, to stay the course, to finish the race God has set before us. They demonstrate a life of faith that really works.

If we are to finish this race, we are to imitate Jesus Christ. He never lost sight of where he was headed. The cross, the shame— none of it could slow him down or distract him from the ultimate goal of finishing with God.

Loving God, we are grateful that your mercy includes even those who feel like giving up. When we grow discouraged, remind us of all that Christ endured on the cross so we could be saved. Amen.

MAUNDY THURSDAY

On the last night of Jesus' earthly ministry he gathers with his disciples to observe the Passover meal. But first he does something scandalous—Jesus washes the disciples' feet, a task normally reserved for servants. Jesus knows his power: God has put him in charge of all things. Yet he lays aside that power and takes on the role of a servant. Jesus is aware that in the morning he will head to Calvary, where he will die on the cross for the sins of humanity. He also is aware that Judas, Peter, and the others will fail him in his darkest hour. None of this clouds his love or his service to these men. In his mercy, he treats them all as if they already are forgiven.

Loving as Jesus loves means taking on the role of a servant by caring for the needs of others without expecting anything in return. He shows us that we are to do this service not only for those who treat us well but also for those who disappoint us, hurt us, and even betray us. Does Jesus really expect us to love and serve people who harm us? Are there no exceptions to this rule of loving servanthood? Loving one another doesn't mean we must feel affection for others. It means that we are to act in a loving way, even when we would rather not.

We may never achieve the level of God's perfect love, but we can let go of grudges and respond to hurtful behavior with kindness and gentleness. This kind of love and forgiveness is only possible because of the one who loves us fully and completely, the one who loves us to the end, even to the cross and grave and back.

O God, your will for us is that we lovingly serve others. Thank you that your mercy includes all of us who fail at this task in ways large and small and yet are forgiven to try again. Amen.

GOOD FRIDAY

A lthough today's passage is deeply revered by Christians, its meaning is far from clear. Despite the problems with interpretation—we don't even know for sure who the servant is—this passage has had a profound effect on believers. In these verses, the early Christians heard the story of the crucifixion. We also find many parallels to the Gospels' stories of Jesus' death on the cross.

What we can see in this model is that Jesus—innocent, free of guilt—took on himself the punishment for our rebellion and waywardness. There is nowhere for us to hide; we are revealed as we truly are: "All we like sheep have gone astray." We are on shaky ground as we stand before the suffering servant on this Good Friday. But incredibly, hope emerges from the horror of the crucifixion. We can see rising from the ashes the beauty of God's act of reconciliation and redemption. Even though we were sinners, Christ died for us. (See Romans 5:8.) We see the Lord in his perfection suffering for sinners like us.

Where suffering had previously been explained as the inevitable consequence of disobedience or as a test of faithfulness, this model is different. Here, suffering taken on willingly, silently, vicariously, by one doing the will of God is an act of redemption. When we see our own suffering in the same light, mourning transforms into rejoicing. In the words of Hebrews 12, it was for the joy that was set before him that Jesus endured the cross and disregarded its shame. Such love for sinners on this Good Friday stuns us and leaves us slack-jawed as we lift our hearts to the Lord.

Loving God, as we gather today to pray and reflect on Jesus' death on the cross, we are filled with gratitude that your mercy is wide enough to include every one of us who accepts your gift. Indeed, your suffering has redeemed us, and we rejoice. Amen.

HOLY SATURDAY

In the aftermath of Babylon's siege on Jerusalem (587 BCE), Jeremiah momentarily loses hope. We hear his devastation as he recounts the horrific destruction and loss of life. Perhaps even worse, though, the prophet says that when he cries out in prayer, God doesn't hear his pleas.

But a tiny ray of hope breaks through the stone-cold silence. As Jeremiah reflects on his suffering, he remembers something he learned in better times: God's steadfast love and mercies never cease. When we have eyes to see them, evidence of those tender mercies appear to us every morning. Slowly, the prophet turns from his litany of misery to praise God. "Great is your faithfulness," he declares, marking a turning point in his spiritual experience.

We may find ourselves in a state of darkness without any light. Our distress is searingly real, yet we cannot find any comfort from scripture or prayer or from others. Why do we suffer so when God could make it right? Doubt begins to creep in. But as with Jeremiah, a miracle happens. As awful as things are for us, we discover new mercies. We are still alive. Each breath we take is evidence of God's goodness to us. Our sorrow has meaning. It humbles us and teaches us to depend on God rather than on the things of the world. Even in our brokenheartedness we begin to find hope.

Every day brings its own trouble, but it also brings its mercies. We still are alive; we have not died. We may have been through hell, but we have not been destroyed by it. God allows grief, which serves a merciful purpose if we trust in God.

O God, as Jeremiah lost hope, at times we are tempted to do the same. Forgive us and restore our spirit in the light of your never-ending mercies. Amen.

EASTER

In today's reading, we hear that God is not only our strength, but also our song. *Do you hear the songs of victory in the camp of the righteous?* the psalmist seems to ask. Singing is an appropriate response to salvation. God has turned the tide. Though God tests us, we are not destroyed. In response, we gratefully sing our praise. Today Christians all across the world join in celebration of our risen Savior. The price has been paid. Our sins are forgiven. New life is ours through Jesus Christ's work on the cross. Do we find ourselves today in the joyous throng singing our praises to our Lord? Then we sing with all our heart. It is right to rejoice and give thanks.

Perhaps we find ourselves on the edges of the throng, aware that we have forgotten how to sing. There are times when through the hardness of life we lose sight of what the Lord has done for us. The days of joy and laughter, of hope and gladness all seem a strangely faint memory. If we have forgotten how to sing, we can take heart. God's mercy is wide enough for us too. The Lord is our strength, helping us do the next right thing in this long journey toward heaven. God is also our song. We were not made for lives of quiet desperation. Instead we are meant to sing a song of God's salvation and redemption from now throughout all eternity.

When we have forgotten how to sing, how do we find our voice again? We remember what we have been given through the Cross—new life with God. Then we can lift our voice in praise. Our vocal cords may be a little rusty from lack of use. No matter. Sing anyway. God provides the song.

Risen Savior, we celebrate you today. Your breathtaking gift of redemption can stir even vocal cords that have forgotten how to sing. Hallelujah! Amen.

Practicing Resurrection

APRIL 13–19, 2020 • MARK S. BURROWS

SCRIPTURE OVERVIEW: In the week following Easter, we reflect on the Resurrection. In Acts, Peter declares to his fellow Israelites that the story of Jesus is the fulfillment of promises made to their people long ago. He quotes Psalm 16, the second reading for the week, and applies it to Jesus. First Peter opens with a passage of extended praise for God's mercy, and this is rooted in the hope that comes through the resurrection of Jesus. Yes, we may suffer in this life as Jesus suffered, but just as he is glorified, we will also one day be glorified in the Lord. John recounts a post-resurrection appearance to the disciples. All except Thomas have already seen Jesus, and here is Thomas's first interaction with the risen Lord.

QUESTIONS AND SUGGESTIONS FOR REFLECTION

- Read Acts 2:14a, 22-32. How do you practice living into the "ways of life"?
- Read Psalm 16. What would change if you were to make requests for God's protection a fundamental of your faith?
- Read 1 Peter 1:3-9. How does the mystery of the Resurrection help you understand and love Jesus?
- Read John 20:19-31. What role does forgiveness play in the way you practice resurrection?

Professor of historical theology, Protestant University of Applied Sciences in Bochum, Germany; historian, theologian, and poet; recent publications include a collection of new poems, *The Chance of Home* (2018), and, with Jon M. Sweeney, *Meister Eckhart's Book of the Heart* (2017) and *Meister Eckhart's Book of Secrets* (2019); lives between Bochum and Camden, Maine.

What would it mean to "practice resurrection," as the poet Wendell Berry exhorts us to do?* The poet urges us to learn this lesson day by day in our lives. Practice beginning anew. Practice setting aside old grudges. Practice forgiveness, defiance of an unfaithful status quo. Practice joy. And here, the old adage is true: practice makes perfect, or at least better. Resurrection is not simply a long-ago event. It is a call to faith in our own lives, a call to living into resurrection day by day, year after year.

It is not enough to know about the ancient story in today's reading that recounts Jesus' resurrection. For such stories do not offer information; rather, they invite transformation. They call us to "practice" this in order to deepen our grasp of it—or its grasp on us. In this story, the apostle Thomas wants more than mere knowledge by hearsay. He wants to witness resurrection himself.

Thomas is not among the disciples gathered on the evening of that first Resurrection day, locked behind the doors of fear. He demands what any of us might have: Show me this truth, he insists; don't just tell me about it. Show me Jesus. *This demand is all well and good for Thomas,* you might be thinking, *but what about us living thousands of years later?* How can we "see" Jesus, as Thomas demands in that first Easter season? Aren't we the ones Jesus describes as "those who have not seen" and yet might come to believe?

What would it mean to live into the Resurrection story by practicing it in each act of generosity, welcome, and forgiveness by which we renew the world?

---

*"Manifesto: The Mad Farmer Liberation Front," in *Collected Poems, 1957–82* (New York: Northpoint Press, 1994), 151–52.

Revealing God, open my mind and make me spacious enough to hear this Resurrection news, and say, "Yes! This is the truth that has the power to set me free from anxiety and fear." Amen.

The Easter story presents us with the same invitation it did for those first disciples: It invites us to believe the truth of the Resurrection, to trust with our heart what our mind cannot grasp. For who can understand such a claim as Christ's resurrection, which defies our comprehension?

Among the earliest "sermons" is Peter's as recorded in today's reading from the Acts of the Apostles. Note well that this Peter is the one who has denied knowing Jesus in the hours leading up to his crucifixion. This story seems to have a shaping power in his life, and it settles on a single point: It was "impossible for [Jesus] to be held in [death's] power." Then Peter cites one of the psalms that he had come to understand as speaking of God's promise for Jesus: "I saw the Lord always before me, for he is at my right hand so that I will not be shaken; therefore my heart was glad, and my tongue rejoiced; moreover my flesh will live in hope."

The final claim is striking: "My flesh will live in hope." This claim might seem to us a strange way of thinking until we find ourselves—or someone we know—facing severe suffering. In such a case, we struggle to "live in hope," against the weight of pain. Peter reminds us that in such suffering the promise given in David's psalm is meant for us as it was for Jesus whom God "freed from death." With him, we face the pain of suffering and the shadow of death knowing, in faith, that it is as impossible for us—as it was for Jesus—to be held in its power.

Freeing God, give me the courage to believe that nothing in my life can separate me from your love in Christ Jesus, my Lord. Amen.

Sometimes, a single verse is enough for a day—if not for a whole lifetime. This is one of those verses: "You have made known to me the ways of life; you will make me full of gladness with your presence." It is a claim much like the musical scales that the pianist must continually practice, whether a beginner or an accomplished virtuoso. What are these "ways of life" that God has made known to us?

As in most cases, responses of a general nature will have little meaning for us and will do little to help us build resilience in our lives. The real question is this: What ways of life have we learned, or do we need to learn? These ways might be simple and follow the truths we learned as children: honoring others, speaking truthfully, and living humbly. Each of these postures is a way to practice resurrection. We turn from acts or habits that belittle others and open our hearts to live generously toward them—whether our friends or those who threaten us. This is the hard truth Jesus teaches again and again in the Gospels: "Love your enemies and pray for those who persecute you" (Matt. 5:44).

If the Resurrection is to mean anything in our lives, it must be this: The call to live beyond the narrow logic of fear, selfishness, and hatred, to live into the "ways of life" that constitute the generous truths of God among us.

Will this be easy for us? Rarely. Practice might not "make perfect." But it will lead us—moment by moment within our relationships—into a deepening measure of freedom and joy.

Lord, give me the courage of heart and the simplicity of mind to heed those truths that promise to lead me in the ways of life, so that I too may taste the gladness of your presence. Amen.

Poet T. S. Eliot once described the Incarnation as "[t]he hint half guessed, the gift half understood."* This description is as truthful and encouraging a description as one can find. For the claim that the "Word became flesh and lived among us" (John 1:14) is a truth beyond our mind's reach. It is one we can glimpse in part, as the poet reminds us, as a "hint half guessed" or a "gift half understood." But what a hint, and what a gift!

The psalm Peter remembers and quotes in his Jerusalem sermon is one we might take to heart this Easter week. Its message reassures us in difficult times and lifts us when we are weighted down with sorrow or fear: "Protect me, O God, for in you I take refuge."

How might you take this to heart today? Perhaps by doing something simple, if not necessarily easy, like practicing resurrection amid the sorrow or worry or suffering you face, which often feels too heavy to bear. "Protect me, O God, for in you I take refuge." Practice trusting that God will always stay "at [your] right hand"—and "[you] shall not be moved." Try practicing this today as you deal with some problem nagging at you or a worry weighing on your heart. Let go, and let God.

The best we get at understanding resurrection are "hints" of this gift in our lives. Opening ourselves to receive some glimpse of this presence will suffice. Like learning piano scales, it is an exercise we can never finally master. It is given to teach us, again and again, the fundamentals. But the practice can free us, in faith, to live into the deeper music that our lives are meant to be.

---

*"The Dry Salvages," V; in *Four Quartets* (San Diego: Harcourt Brace Jovanovich, 1971).

Protect me, O God, for in you I take refuge. Amen.

Today's text opens with praise: "Blessed be the God and Father of our Lord Jesus Christ!" This acclamation sounds straightforward enough, since it is one we hear or speak week by week, in some form, when we gather to worship. But in today's reading, it is the prelude to the story Peter is intent on telling. For Peter, this blessing opens us to God's working in our lives: We are not simply to give some report about what we believe but to live into the mysteries of faith. How do we do this? By practicing resurrection day by day, no matter what comes.

Peter follows his praise with a promise: God desires to give us nothing less than "a new birth into a living hope through the resurrection of Jesus Christ from the dead." A new birth? Really? The doubt we might feel lurking in our minds in the face of such a promise is reasonable enough, particularly when we feel overwhelmed by life and unable to find even traces of light amid our darkness. Wherever we are, God calls us to "practice resurrection"—not by verifying an ancient historical report of something that happened at a tomb two thousand years ago but by heeding the invitation to live into incarnation, that "hint half guessed" and "gift half understood."

Peter's call to meet suffering with joy might test us or strike us as indefensible. But the story of Easter is that we do not face our burdens alone because Jesus went before us, obedient all the way to death on the cross. (See Philippians 2.) As Peter reminds us, "Although [we] have not seen him, [we can] love him." What better way do we have of practicing resurrection?

Living Christ, today I seek to love you whom I cannot see and to trust in your promise that you are with me, whatever comes. Amen.

W hat does it mean to practice resurrection? Among the stories about the first encounters the disciples have with their risen Lord, John remembers Jesus' first words to his troubled and fearful disciples as being about not what has happened to him but rather what he hopes might happen among them: "Peace be with you," Jesus says. Only then does he show them the signs of his suffering and death—the wounds in his hands and his side.

As with the most important lessons we have to learn in life, learning peace takes time—and practice. And so Jesus repeats the words, as if to make it clear that his resurrection is to be grasped in their own lives, not simply as some remote testimony about his: "Peace be with *you*."

He follows with what we might read as an action plan, as if to clarify what it might mean to find this peace: "If you forgive the sins of any, they are forgiven them; if you retain the sins of any, they are retained."

We know this statement to be true in the grit and grime of our own lives: If we hold on to grudges, even if deserved because of some injury inflicted upon us, they will remain a weight—not only for those "others" but for ourselves. But if we forgive others, practicing resurrection at the places of what suffering they might have visited upon us, they will be forgiven.

How will we find our way into the deep mystery of the Resurrection? By risking forgiveness toward others, above all those who do not seem to deserve it. This brings the promise of peace—for them, of course, but also for us.

Forgiving God, let me dare today to forgive others and offer them the peace you offer me each moment in my life. Amen.

When all is said and done, what matters is not how clever we are, or even how wise. What matters is how generous we are—first of all, in receiving God's good news for ourselves and then in offering it to others. Practicing resurrection in this manner is the heart and soul of faith, the way in which God's promise comes to us, and through us to others.

We find this meaning clearly affirmed at the close of the story about the disciples' first encounter with the risen Jesus. John's Gospel is all about the "signs and wonders" that God brings about in and through Jesus of Nazareth. What signs and wonders are still to take place among us—and, more to the point, in our own lives?

John ends this story with a musing that the signs Jesus accomplishes in the presence of his first followers are only a prelude to what continues in the life of believers—then and now. For all of this comes down to one thing: That "through believing you may have life in his name." What is this but the call to "practice resurrection" in our lives, moment by moment, day by day, year in and year out? Where else should we follow this practice than in those places where we have given up—in relationships strained to the point of breaking or broken to the point of no return? Or in facing the burden of suffering—our own, and that of others—that seems to press us toward despair and perhaps to the very brink of death?

Where else but here might we seize the hints of mercy we only half guess, and receive the gift of forgiveness we often only half understand?

God of mystery and ongoing resurrection, help me believe today that you offer me nothing less than life itself, the life that nothing can overcome, not even death itself. Amen.

Exhibiting Resurrection

APRIL 20–26, 2020 • JANE HERRING

SCRIPTURE OVERVIEW: As we consider further the power of Jesus' resurrection, how should we respond? This is the question posed to Peter in the reading in Acts. Peter's first instruction is to repent, to change course in our thinking and our living to align more with God's way. The psalmist proclaims his gratitude to God because God has heard his cry, but the process began with the psalmist turning to the Lord. First Peter states that because we have turned and have faith and hope in God, we ought to love one another deeply from the heart. Luke tells the story of two men who meet Jesus on the road to Emmaus. They recognize him only as he breaks the bread, symbolizing that Christian fellowship is also part of a changed life.

QUESTIONS AND SUGGESTIONS FOR REFLECTION

- Read Acts 2:14a, 36-41. How might you allow Jesus' crucifixion and resurrection to disrupt your life or your faith? How would such a disruption change you?
- Read Psalm 116:1-4, 12-19. When have you learned of God's great joy for you? How do the Psalms remind you that you are beloved?
- Read 1 Peter 1:17-23. How can you take the author's advice to "act like someone who knows [you are] loved"?
- Read Luke 24:13-35. Recall times throughout your life when Jesus has been revealed to you. Which of these encounters have been logical? Which have been supernatural?

Author and ordained Presbyterian pastor; leads contemplative retreats on prayer, meditation, and using writing in prayer and spiritual formation.

Acts 2 finds all the believers gathered together in one place. Suddenly a noise comes from the sky, a great wind fills the house, and tongues of fire appear above the head of each person assembled. The promised gift has arrived. Everyone there is filled with the Holy Spirit. They can see and feel that something amazing is happening, but onlookers accuse them of being drunk. In today's verses, Peter stands up to speak into the excitement and confusion of the moment. He proclaims the core of our faith as Christ followers, saying that Jesus Christ crucified is, in fact, the risen Lord, the Messiah.

Peter highlights the crucifixion of Jesus Christ. Jesus is a disrupter. To those who want to maintain the status quo, he is a troublemaker. He is a threat to people who are more interested in earthly power than in God's kingdom; he is crucified accordingly, as a threat to the state. It is easy to think about those ancient rulers and their need for power that led them to crucify Jesus, but what about our own need to feel power that leads us to withhold parts of our lives from Jesus? Whatever we withhold from the Crucifixion we also withhold from the Resurrection.

To accept Jesus Christ as the Messiah is to welcome disruption in all parts of our lives, to let our own need for control be crucified so that we can make room for the gifts of the Holy Spirit and live as people who exhibit resurrection. To accept Jesus Christ is to grapple with God who is crucified, rises again, and sends the Holy Spirit to be with us.

Lord, help me not to shy away from you. Show me how to die to anything that holds me back from you, and make real to me the resurrection that comes from giving my life to you. Amen.

In today's passage, we read about the response to Peter's message on the Day of Pentecost. No one in the crowd seems to be denying Peter's claim that they are responsible for Jesus' crucifixion. Instead, it hurts them deeply. They want to know what to do.

Peter tells them first to repent. The Greek word *metanoia* can be used to mean an expression of remorse, but it can also indicate gaining new understanding. The crucifixion and resurrection of Jesus Christ require a new understanding of the Messiah. Repentance in this case may mean the willingness to see in a new way, a better way that is God's way.

Peter tells the people gathered to be baptized "in the name of Jesus Christ" so their sins can be forgiven. Forgiveness can mean the pardon of sins, but perhaps here Peter means that the people can be released from their sins. To be freed from wrong thinking and wrongdoing is to become a new person, to participate in Christ's resurrection. The cleansing waters of baptism are not only the washing away of corruption but also are symbolic of dying with Christ to be raised with Christ to a new life.

While we might be baptized only once, we may return over and over again to the cleansing power of the waters of our baptism. Repentance and baptism mark us as Christians, as people who are forgiven and free, who seek to live into our resurrection in Jesus Christ, and who are free to be in authentic relationships with God and with one another by the power of the indwelling Holy Spirit.

Lord God, make me sensitive to the indwelling of the Holy Spirit. When I see where I am wrong, help me respond like these first believers, asking, "What should I do?" Help me trust that in you there is always a better way. Help me lean into the power of repentance and the waters of my baptism so that I can see the evidence of resurrection in my own life. Amen.

Psalm 116 is a psalm of thanksgiving. It expresses gratitude to God for deliverance from distress. The word *Sheol* is used to mean a place after death or a death-like power that invades life. This psalm becomes part of the readings for the Jewish Passover meal and eventually part of the readings for the Christian sacrament of the Lord's Supper. In both instances, God is the source of salvation.

In winter, the grass looks brown and dead. Most trees have a bare, skeletal appearance. However, beneath the cold earth of winter, roots sleep and wait for rebirth. Nature seems to flow with these cycles of barrenness and apparent death into new life. A human life is full of such cycles of death and renewal. However, we rarely sense the flow of it. Phases of barrenness and loss—common to every life—come with painful feelings of being abandoned or crushed, lost to Sheol.

The psalmist knows a truth: Distressing times are part of life, and God is with us.

Amid distress we have the privilege to call out to God, who loves us. This psalm reminds us that there is deliverance for us in times of distress. This psalm also encourages us to remember the times we have been delivered in the past. Giving thanks to God for sustaining us is like adding rocket fuel to our spiritual journey. Asking God for deliverance and giving thanks for deliverance help us to become part of the evidence of Jesus' resurrection. Call out to God for help with a grateful heart. Remember the times God has seen you through into new life.

I call out to you, O God. Deliver me. Thank you for bringing me this far. Help me to be aware of your loving hand at work so that your saving power in my life makes me an example of your salvation. Lord, even in distress, make my life luminous with evidence of resurrection. Amen.

These last eight verses of Psalm 116 continue the theme of gratitude for deliverance. The psalmist's vows to the Lord and offerings of sacrifice are thankful expressions of joy.

The Hebrew word *yaqar,* often translated as "precious," can also be translated as "costly." The death of the faithful is costly to God because God works on our behalf to bring life to all parts of our existence. In mind, body, and spirit, God nurtures life in us. In our relationships, our work, and our play, God desires renewal.

Too few of us grew up in churches and families that taught about God's great joy for us. If we received a religious education, we oftentimes came away with ideas of a God who is displeased with us. We may even have been taught that our suffering is a result of God's anger or that we owe something to this resentful God and must make sacrifices to get on God's good side.

The psalmist affirms our relationship to God as cherished and beloved ones: children who are precious, costly. This psalm tells us that God yearns for a living relationship with us, not fearful sacrifices. The very act of calling to God for deliverance, resurrection, and new life is an act of thanksgiving and joy.

Perhaps today is the day to breathe in the reality that God seeks to resurrect any area of your life where death seems to have a foothold. Can you call out to God for help and believe this call is precious to God? Can you take a chance on such an act of thanksgiving? Or perhaps you have seen evidence of life renewed in you. How can you act in a way that joyously honors God's saving work?

God who cherishes my life, I call out to you for deliverance. Help me believe that you desire for me the same resurrection you gave the world through Jesus Christ. Help me act in this joy and thanksgiving today. Amen.

First Peter 1 encourages Christians to remember who and whose they are while facing the stresses of life. Verses 18, 21, and 23 make pronouncements about God's claim on our lives. We have been saved from ways that did not bring life to us. We have come into a relationship of trust with God. We have been made new. In verse 22, Peter tells us to love one another. In essence, he encourages us as a dear friend once encouraged me: "Act like someone who knows she is loved."

This letter is written to encourage Christians to persevere in the new life given them by Christ. Like us, these early Christians live in a world filled with values and habits contrary to a life of faith. In these early years of Christianity, believers look and behave very differently from their neighbors, which can cause difficulty for them. Our difficulties often arise from the fact that Christianity, politics, and culture have become greatly intermingled. When religion becomes accepted by worldly authorities, it can be difficult to differentiate between God's call and the call of a human authority. Sometimes the greatest damage to our faith life comes from sources that seem "Christian" but are not of God.

Peter's words can help us. He reminds us we have been born anew, that there is a spark within us that cannot die because the God of life has spoken it into being within us. From this new life we are called to love one another deeply and genuinely.

Today, be in conversation with God about your community. How does the seed of new and resurrected life yearn for expression through your love for others? Who of your church friends or groups share this value of genuine Christian love?

Lord of new life, lead me to act like I know I am loved. Help me to grow in community with others who seek to love genuinely and to live lives of resurrection through you. Amen.

We know that the name of one of the travelers in this passage is Cleopas. Some think his companion is his wife, Mary, mentioned in John 19:25. Others believe his fellow traveler is another believer. We know the third person they meet along the way to Emmaus is Jesus. We know it, but they do not. When Jesus questions them, they are confused about how anyone who has been in Jerusalem for any amount of time would not know what they are talking about. How could anyone have missed all the things that had recently happened to Jesus of Nazareth?

Confusion plays a major part in the disciples' story. Up until Jesus' crucifixion, they remain unclear on what will happen. At his crucifixion, they scatter in fear. These two on the road to Emmaus express their sadness, thinking that the crucifixion meant Jesus was not the Messiah for whom they had waited. They are all the more confused by the fact that the women who went to Jesus' tomb found it empty. They have heard that some angels say he was alive, but they have not yet considered that this means resurrection and the fulfillment of God's plan.

We know the story. We know Jesus is resurrected from the grave, but it is still sometimes just as hard for us to recognize the living Christ as he walks along with us. We have to be intentional about living in the presence of Jesus; we need spiritual practices that help us exhibit the resurrection in our own lives.

What are some of the practices that help you stay awake to the presence of Jesus in your life? Nature walks may refresh your mind. Keeping a prayer journal might help you connect. Singing, gardening, prayer, meditation, and meeting with friends who share your faith all have their ways of helping us recognize Jesus' presence.

Lord God, teach me about myself. Show me what I can do to respond to your grace. Show me what practices I might develop to live into the resurrection and become more sensitive to you, Immanuel, "God with us." Amen.

These travelers are grappling with stories that seem unreal: angelic visitation, Jesus' empty tomb, rumors that he is alive. When they get to the end of the trip, they ask this stranger who has tried to explain scripture to them to stay and eat. Suddenly, he reveals himself as Jesus Christ and disappears.

Do you remember when you first heard the stories of Jesus? Do you remember what your thoughts and feelings were about his miracles? his resurrection? When have you had no doubt about these events? When have you doubted them? There seems to be a schism in Christianity that runs along the lines of believing in a supernatural interpretation of the Bible or viewing the Bible logically, as a well-meaning fable.

What if Jesus meets us out beyond this divide? What if the logical view and the supernatural view are both contained in the mystery of God? Jesus remarks that the two travelers are slow to believe, but he never gives up on them. As long as they are willing to journey with him, invite him in, sit with him, and serve him, he persists in giving them the time they need to understand who he is.

What if, like Jesus in this passage, the logical and the supernatural are revealed to us in the ordinariness of our lives—talking with each other, finding the next right thing to do when all the information refuses to add up, breaking bread together with someone you care about or with someone who seems like they could use a meal. How have you seen Jesus show up?

Holy God, do not give up on me if I doubt the movement of your Spirit when it conflicts with my logical mind. When I sense your Spirit, keep me grounded in the simplicity of this life. Open my eyes to evidence of the resurrection, and make of me an exhibit of resurrection. Amen.

Holy Paradox

APRIL 27—MAY 3, 2020 • MICHAEL DOWNEY

SCRIPTURE OVERVIEW: The reading from Acts picks up the themes of mutual love and fellowship from last week's readings and records that the display of these qualities captured the attention of the people in Jerusalem. When the church displays these qualities today, they still attract people to the Lord. The psalm and First Peter are linked by the theme of suffering. In Psalm 23, David is confident that God will stay with him even through the darkest valley. Peter encourages his audience to walk through that same valley, strengthened by the knowledge that God will never abandon them and that they are following the example of Christ. In John, Jesus declares that he is the way to safety for God's sheep, so we should listen to his voice alone.

QUESTIONS AND SUGGESTIONS FOR REFLECTION

- Read Acts 2:42-47. How do you see Good Time and Bad Time coexisting in your life or in your community?
- Read Psalm 23. How do this psalm's joys and comforts change when you consider the suffering of the psalmist in Psalm 22?
- Read 1 Peter 2:19-25. When you have been caught in a struggle, how have your actions helped or worsened your situation?
- Read John 10:1-10. How have you or someone you know attempted to enter God's abundance by stealth? What does it mean for you to rectify this and enter through the gate?

Professor of theology and spirituality; schooled in the spirituality of Jean Vanier and l'Arche; an abiding concern for the wounded and marginalized; author of *The Depth of God's Reach* (2018).

In *The Gates of Ivory*, contemporary British novelist Dame Margaret Drabble tells of a circle of friends searching for one of their number who has mysteriously disappeared. With few clues about his plan or hints of his destination, the group gradually learns that their friend, award-winning author Stephen Cox, has left a comfortable life in England to get to the bottom of the story of life in Cambodia after the regime of Pol Pot and the Khmer Rouge. After stints in Thailand and Vietnam, Stephen passes through the "gates" into ravaged Cambodia, from which he never returns. In Drabble's telling, life in England is "Good Time." Life in the quagmire of Pol Pot's Cambodia is "Bad Time."

At first glance the believers described in Acts are living in Good Time. They gather together. They listen and learn from one another. They pray together. They share bread and hold in common what they have. They give to those in need. Their hearts are sincere. They are glad. There is awe. There is wonder. Their circle widens to include newcomers. It all seems too good to be true.

But the first Christians live in a world that is not friendly to them. At the outset, their number is relatively small—they are a marginal people. Even as they are looked upon kindly by their neighbors in Jerusalem, their fellowship is alien to the social structures and political forces of their day. As their numbers increase, hostility toward them intensifies. Some face the threat of persecution. Good Time? Minorities and marginalized people like the earliest fellowship of Christians do not always feel the benefits of what others consider Good Time. Far too often for the marginalized, what seems like Good Time is Bad Time.

We too live between the Times. In every time and place Good Time and Bad Time coexist.

God, we know you are gracious and loving in the darkness as well as in the light. Draw near us. Stay close in Good Time and in Bad Time. Amen.

The words of Psalm 23 come from the lips of someone who has suffered. When we read Psalm 23 in tandem with Psalm 22, we learn that the psalmist has walked through the darkest valley and has come out the other end. Psalm 23 offers words of praise only after Psalm 22 had dared to speak words of lament. Reading Psalm 23 in light of Psalm 22, we see the confidence of a people who have known deep pain and who know the care of the shepherd.

In response to the lamenting heart, Psalm 23 invites trust in God. The sadness of Psalm 22 juxtaposed with the delight of Psalm 23 reminds us that delight does not forget pain. Confidence in God's care is a balm for the hurting heart that beats in Psalm 22.

Lament can offend conventional religious sensibilities. In its most extreme form, lament is not just complaint *to* God but complaint *about* God, as in Job's lament: "I cry to you and you do not answer me" (Job 30:20), or in the words of Psalm 22 on the lips of the crucified Christ: "My God, my God, why have you forsaken me?" (Mark 15:34). Lament seems to indict God. Yet psalms of lament typically end in a confession of trust in and praise of the God who will answer. Praise arises precisely because God hears our lament and acts in response.

Psalm 23 assures us that we can trust in God. Whatever threatens us will not prevail because God is with us through suffering and joy.

Beginning and End of all my longing, embolden me so that I cry out to you even when you do not seem to answer. Hold me in the hope of the promise that you will. Amen.

Donegal is the northwestern-most county in Ireland. People from other parts of the country speak of Donegal as the hinterland, the wilds. It is the financially poorest of the twenty-six counties in the Republic of Ireland. But Donegal is rich in sheep.

One afternoon when we were children, my younger cousin Margaret took the lead as we set out to wander Donegal's rugged hills and dark mountains the color of eggplant that jut out into the forbidding black sea. As we made our way down a narrow lane, the delight of our adventure was interrupted by a bone-chilling bleating.

Coming closer to the sound—*was it bleating or pleading?*—we saw the bramble shaking. A ewe drenched in its own blood struggled to break free from the barbed wire fence in which its head was caught. Margaret whispered: "The poor creature! She's so frightened that she'll rip off her own head trying to get free."

We too lose our way, sometimes several times a day. With heads down and eyes fixed to our smartphones, we crash into others in public places. We stray in our relationships and lose sight of our commitments because we are so preoccupied and distracted. Our principles are easily compromised, our priorities forgotten, and our sense of purpose dims. And we turn our backs on what matters most and willfully march down a path that is a dead end. Suddenly we find ourselves stuck—lost with no way out. The heart bleats.

Today's scripture advises us to live with our suffering and learn from it. Unlike the bloodied ewe bleating in the bramble, we often bring our suffering upon ourselves. But like her, when we flail and panic in desperate attempts to get out of what has us bound—when we try to pull ourselves up by our own bootstraps—we will not get free.

My Shepherd, I cannot do it alone. You are not far. Draw near, stay close, especially when the hills are rugged, the waters forbidding, and the darkness of night descends. Amen.

Sheep have gotten a bum rap. Sometimes they are called "range maggots." Or "woolly locusts." Many consider sheep stupid. Without a shepherd, sheep usually cannot find pasture. They get lost and cannot make their way, knowing neither the whither nor the whence. But when sheep get lost, it is due in part to human mismanagement—bad shepherds!

Contrary to popular perception, sheep are quite intelligent and good at problem solving. They are surely as smart as cattle and nearly as bright as pigs. And they are superior to other animals in at least one way: They are able to recognize the voice of the one who cares for them. They heed the shepherd. Sheep follow no one else; they depend entirely upon and seek help from one shepherd alone. Sheep will not follow a stranger whose voice they do not know.

Part of the shepherd's job is to gather the sheep together for the night. Once the sheep are in the pen, the shepherd locks the gate to ensure that the sheep stay close together. The gate guards against all that threatens the sheep—vandals, robbers, and wolves. The next day, the shepherd opens the gate so that the sheep can set off to find pasture. They will do so by heeding the voice of their good shepherd.

We all use metaphors. Most of the time we don't even notice. If we don't pay attention to our metaphors we can mix them up as Jesus does in today's passage. He is both a gate and a shepherd at the same time. It's a bit confusing. But both the gate and the shepherd serve the good of the sheep, guarding them from harm and ensuring that they flourish.

And us? Do we recognize the voice of the one Shepherd who cares for us? Do we stay close to the Shepherd to find our way and our well-being as part of the flock? Or do we wander unaware of both the whence and the whither?

O Shepherd, tune the ear of my heart to hear your voice above all the distractions that clamor for my attention. Amen.

Holy Paradox

We are a people of the bottom line. Cut to the chase! Close the question! We want answers. Who likes living with loose ends? Who has the time or the patience to follow an argument to its logical conclusion?

Psalm 23 is the best known and loved of all the psalms. Apart from a favorite passage from the New Testament, most Christians are more familiar with the verses of Psalm 23 than any other passage in the Bible. The verses speak to the troubled heart faced with grief and loss, diminishment and death. The psalmist offers comfort and care, rest and rejuvenation, protection and peace for the troubled soul.

When we pray this psalm, we easily forget that we are in the terrain of the Israelites. Even as its words offer comfort to the praying heart, they first and foremost describe Israel's relationship with God. Echoes of the Exodus still ring in their ears; their dry throats from life-threatening desert journeys have not been slaked. The terrain of this people is marked by wandering and scarred by invasion. They have known both gain and loss, all the while struggling for peace.

While praying Psalm 23, the heart finds comfort in verdant pastures, tranquil waters, and a bountiful table with cup overflowing. How soothing to be assured of protection in those places of darkness, evil, and death! But let's not rush through these and jump to the conclusion that all is good.

Thirst lingers before still waters. The desert struggles to give way to green pastures. The people still wander as they find stability. Loss continues to come even as they gain. These are the highs and lows of a people's history—and of our own. Yet hope remains through this promise: God is closer to me than I am to myself. I shall never be abandoned to face my troubles alone.

Gracious and loving God, Shepherd and Guardian, your protection sustains me even at the very moment when things seem at their worst. In your house I find comfort. Amen.

The artist looks at his work with pride: It appears to be perfect in every way. He summons the teacher for an opinion. Inclined to encourage young artists, she gingerly opines, "It's really good. But something is missing." The student looks again carefully at his work. Quizzically he asks, "What's missing?" Without hesitation the teacher replies, "It has no life."

Jesus brings abundant life. For many of us in North America, *abundance* brings images of material prosperity: a lavish home, worldwide cruises, luxury cars, a lucrative career, surplus money in the bank, or winning the lottery. We imagine that this kind of prosperity would allow us to live life to the fullest. But for so many who enjoy "the good life," something is still missing: life.

Abundant life does not consist of an abundance of material things. If that were the case, Jesus would have kept company with the wealthy and influential. But it's just the opposite.

In today's reading, the word *abundantly* connotes excessive, beyond measure, more, superfluous—a quantity so immeasurable that it is more than what one would expect or anticipate. This is the kind of life Jesus brings. It is more than we could ever imagine.

An abundant life is not necessarily a long life, but it is a full one. We get a glimpse of this fullness, this abundance, only by looking to the One who, being in the form of God, did not exploit his equality with God, but emptied himself. (See Philippians 2:5-7.) Jesus shares wisdom hidden from the robust and the clever: The last shall be first; the least shall hold pride of place; the littlest have much to offer the big and the strong; in weakness lies strength. In emptying himself, Jesus is able to give life abundant. By learning to live with less, in emptying ourselves, we can be filled with an abundance that will truly satisfy.

Jesus, Son of the Living God, give me the will this day to make enough room for the gifts of your Spirit that hold the seeds of the abundant life you promise. Amen.

For those who sing the glories of "the land of the free and the home of the brave," of the "strong and free," the words of today's reading may ring hollow.

For most North Americans, intentionally living the Christian life is not likely to bring mistreatment, suffering, and persecution. Few of us face such threats. Perhaps the greatest threat to the Christian faith for us is apathy. We can remain unaware and unmoved by the suffering of those throughout the world who face persecution and death because of their faith.

The Christians to whom Peter writes were slaves kept in place by a political system. He does not condone mistreatment. Jesus was mistreated, endured pain, and suffered unjustly while entrusting it all to God. Peter makes it plain: The people can endure suffering because they are pursuing good—doing good deeds and glorifying God—not because they are doing evil.

The pain of Peter's readers may be juxtaposed with the present situation of many Christians who are told they are free citizens, yet are more and more restricted, indeed oppressed, by a system beyond their control that mocks the affirmation of freedom.

There is no merit in longing for some golden age of persecution and martyrdom. Good deeds by which God is glorified are within the reach of us all. They are not of epic proportions.

Verbal revenge, foul language, mockery, *ad hominem* arguments, and shrill irrational rhetoric have become part of the molecular structure of the air we breathe. When lies are told about us, when we are insulted and defamed, we can refrain from responding in kind. A disciplined silence may be the most forceful witness. When others cause us to suffer, we entrust ourselves entirely to God. "For to this you have been called."

What pressures constrain or push me to cowardly compromise my conscience? How can I stay free in relation to what I cannot change?

The Call to Trust

MAY 4–10, 2020 • ELSY ARÉVALO

SCRIPTURE OVERVIEW: The first three readings for the week contain variations on the imagery of stones or rocks. In Acts, Stephen is killed as the first Christian martyr by being stoned to death, while Saul (Paul) stands by and approves. The psalmist proclaims his confidence in the Lord, whom he describes as his rock and fortress. Peter tells the believers that they have become living stones in the household of God because of their connection to the chief Cornerstone, Christ. In John, Jesus makes an explicit claim to being the only way to God. In our current cultural context, many wonder about the spiritual status of followers of other religions. Jesus' statement in John 14:6 invites us to deep reflection on this important question.

QUESTIONS AND SUGGESTIONS FOR REFLECTION

- Read Acts 7:55-60. Recall a time when you have seen God's power in action. How was God's power different than you might have expected?
- Read Psalm 31:1-5, 15-16. Contemplate your answers to the author's questions. How do the psalmist's hope and experiences reflect your own?
- Read 1 Peter 2:2-10. When have you experienced God as a loving Mother? When has Christ been your cornerstone?
- Read John 14:1-14. How do you experience God's presence through the life or actions of others?

Assistant director of the Center for Religion and Spirituality, Loyola Marymount University.

Trusting God during times of trouble can be challenging. Even more challenging, perhaps, is trusting God while in fear of trouble to come. So often, our biggest fears are lived out only in our imaginations, though the impact they have on our physical and psychological well-being is very real. Our thoughts, if we allow them to become our center, can bring us true suffering. With so much evidence of pain all around us, it is no wonder that we often live our lives bracing ourselves for the worst.

Can I trust in God as the psalmist seems to in these verses? Can I have that type of faith? Can God truly become my rock and center?

What if instead of reading this psalm as a call to trust that God will be there for us, we read it line by line as a call to notice the ways God's grace has already been present throughout our lives?

When has God been my refuge? How has God been my rock and my fortress during times of trouble? How am I experiencing God's sustaining love today, right in this moment?

The psalmist points us toward a hope, a sustainer, a love that accompanies us through the worst parts of our lives—betrayal, persecution, suffering, and death.

We can notice and savor the times in our lives when we have experienced God's grace and can let those moments soak into our bones. In this way, we will know that God is trustworthy—not because we believe it with our minds but because we have experienced it for ourselves.

Lord, it can be hard for me to trust in your sustaining love. Fear, anxiety, and doubt keep me in a loop of worry, tension, and despair. Help me to see all the ways you have already loved me, carried me, and been there for me. Help me to notice how your grace and love are present even now. Help me to let you love me through my fears. Amen.

The disciples long to see the Father; yet they have had Jesus right in front of them the whole time. We might sigh in disbelief at the disciples' seeming cluelessness. However, we too continue to miss Jesus' powerful and life-changing revelation. "If you really know me, you will know my Father as well" (NIV), Jesus says. "I am in the Father and the Father is in me" (NIV). So, who does Jesus reveal God to be?

In the previous chapter, Jesus washes the feet of his disciples. This one simple act reveals much about God's nature. Jesus embodies a God who does not stand above and separate from us but rather seeks us, draws close to us, and humbly offers God's own self in the service of love. In Jesus, we recognize God's care and compassion for the poor, the hungry, the sick, and the outcast. He reveals a God who treats our brokenness with mercy and our humanity with compassion. He includes the excluded, reaching out to women and men, young and old, rich and poor, believer and unbeliever. Jesus shows us that the one sheep matters and reveals our worth in the eyes of God. In Jesus, we see that God is not vengeful; Jesus does not lash out against those who hurt him but chooses forgiveness until the very end.

When Jesus says that he is "the way and the truth and the life" and "no one comes to the Father except through me" (NIV), he invites us to a different way of being, perceiving, and living in the world: in communion with a merciful and loving Creator, transformed in the service of love. Jesus affirms this when he says, "Very truly I tell you, whoever believes in me will do the works I have been doing, and they will do even greater things than these" (NIV). How might our lives and the world be impacted if we truly believed and lived out the goodness of God?

Lord, "I believe; help my unbelief" (Mark 9:24). Help me to know you more deeply and to be transformed by your humility, love, and compassion. Amen.

One of the most repeated statements in the Bible is the call not to be afraid. Yet amid life's many challenges, we often struggle to heed this call.

Jesus knows the disciples are worried. When he tells them, "Do not let your hearts be troubled," he is recognizing and naming what the disciples are feeling and experiencing.

Scripture reveals time and time again a God who knows that we are afraid, acknowledges fear and worry as a part of our human experience, and offers us a way to move forward.

Jesus invites the disciples to place their trust in God's goodness. He tells them, "Anyone who has seen me has seen the Father" (John 14:9). In Jesus, we can discover more deeply that God is love, compassion, humility, forgiveness, healing, gentleness, and kindness. Jesus wants us to realize that God is a reliable, tender, and safe place to face our deepest fears.

Jesus reassures the disciples that in God's house there is enough room for everyone. God's loving nature extends not just to other people, but specifically to you and to me. So often we live worried and afraid because we see our lives through lenses of scarcity. Jesus invites us to live with an outlook of hope and abundance.

Finally, Jesus promises the disciples that he will come back to take them where he is. Our relationship with God is not a one-way journey; we are not fighting our way to God. God continually offers us generosity and abundant love. We are invited to trust more deeply that God's guidance, companionship, and love seek to find us even at this very moment.

My Creator, you know the things that trouble me at this very moment. Help me to trust in your goodness, generosity, and faithfulness. Help me to trust in your abundant love. Amen.

This passage recalls one of the fundamental challenges of Christianity: God's relationship to human suffering. The brutal murder of Stephen at the feet of Saul reminds us that following Christ is not a promise of an easy life. It is certainly not a way to escape reality. Rather, it is an invitation to live with our hearts and minds turned toward God.

In Stephen, as in Jesus, we see an example of someone who is able to turn toward trust, love, and surrender in his darkest moments. Stephen is able to find peace and even forgiveness as he faces hatred, violence, and murder. What happens in him to make this possible? Here lies our hope in this difficult passage. Stephen's example points us not toward some heavenly realm but toward a loving Sustainer who can help transform our darkest hours into hope, mercy, love, compassion, and even peace.

This passage highlights the reality that God's power, the way God deals and intervenes in human suffering, is so radically different from our own that we often miss it. Consciously or unconsciously, we expect that God will crush down the guilty and right wrongs through sheer force. Instead, God transforms human suffering from the inside out.

Today's reading not only acknowledges the reality of being a human being in a broken world, but also calls us to participate in God's plan for salvation. As we entrust our suffering to God, we will be transformed. And as instruments of God's grace, we will participate in the transformation of the world around us.

Jesus, you know that being human can be hard. You know the burdens I carry even at this very moment. Help me turn my heart and mind toward your healing love, guidance, and grace. Amen.

What is the foundation of our salvation if not the lifelong realization that God is good and that in God there is nothing to fear? God's generous offer of love, mercy, and compassion is the cornerstone of the good news of Jesus Christ. Moreover, it is the cornerstone upon which we are called to build our life.

Even though Jesus' message is good news, it is not always easy to absorb and accept. While most of us intellectually believe in God's goodness, we struggle to truly grasp the love and grace freely offered to us. Instead, we live as if we have to earn God's love. Even things that are meant to be life-giving such as religion, spirituality, prayer, and ministry can become burdensome as we add layer upon layer of things we have to do and be in order to reach God. Jesus comes to show us that God's love is pure gift and that it is not predicated upon our behavior. God is the consistent, steady, and faithful Father who joyfully runs to greet us every time we choose to return home. (See Luke 15:11-32.) God loves because God is love; we do not have the power to change God's nature.

Our ability to accept Jesus' message necessitates a lifelong process of drawing near to him. As we do so, our false and wounded notions of love are dismantled, and our deeply embedded programs of punishment and reward are uncovered. We discover that we can call God "Father" or "Mother," though the mystery of who God is always lies beyond our grasp. As we heed the invitation to taste God's goodness and mercy for ourselves, we discover that the healing the world needs most now is our own.

Jesus Christ, I want to draw near to you. I want to know you more deeply, to taste your goodness and mercy for myself. Be my living stone and show me how to build my house upon your love. Amen.

S tephen is a simple man with real fears and doubts, living in a specific historical context, who responds to the events of his life with faith, love, and compassion. Stephen's life and example remind us that even the most challenging circumstances do not have the final word on who we are.

Like Stephen, each of us is called to be a "spiritual house," a temple of the Holy Spirit, a living stone upon which the kingdom of God is built. This does not mean that we have to seek martyrdom or perform any extraordinary acts of faith. When we ache to fulfill some grand life mission, we fail to see the sacred unfolding of our lives in daily, simple, quiet, humble acts of service, love, and kindness. From where we stand, we may find it hard to see the impact and the significance of our own lives because we are not the Master Builder. But our limited vision does not diminish the value of our life.

Whether we realize it or not, we live in a delicate web of relationships and decisions that affect the whole of humanity. The lives of the martyrs and saints mattered then, they matter now, and they will matter tomorrow, as does our own life. When we open ourselves to God's grace, we can begin to awaken to this different way of seeing and being in the world. These verses remind us that we have an important place in the building of God's kingdom, and they call us to awaken to the significance and sacredness of our own life.

Lord, help me to live my life awake. Help me to see the value, dignity, and worth of my life and the lives of those around me. Grant me the courage to choose love and compassion in my current circumstances. Amen.

Babies are born with many instincts that aid their survival. One of the most remarkable abilities is their instinctive movement toward their mother's breast immediately after birth. When placed on their mother's chest, newborn babies will use their sense of smell, sight, taste, hearing, and touch to find nourishment. Stronger than a baby's own instinct toward food, however, is a loving mother's own deep need and desire to protect and nourish her child. There is nothing more disconcerting to a parent than the cry of a hungry baby. This too is a deep instinct. Loving parents will do everything in their power to make sure that their babies receive what they need. How much more is our loving Creator eager and desperate to feed us in our hour of need?

What a beautiful image! We are created with an instinct and orientation to crave, need, and move toward our source of sustenance. More importantly, our Creator and Sustainer aches to nurture and feed us.

To be like newborn babies is to acknowledge our radical dependence on the Source of our very life and to open our hearts in trusting surrender so that we will receive what we need to grow and thrive. We are invited to come to know for ourselves that there is a loving Mother awaiting us, longingly aching to feed and care for us.

This is not always easy to do. Newborn babies can get so hungry and desperate for food that they cannot settle down enough to receive the nourishment right before them. As babies learn to settle into their mother's embrace, they relax. A beautiful rhythm is established between mother and child.

These verses invite us to honestly and trustingly ask for the food we need and to allow our loving Mother to care for us.

My Creator and loving Mother, help me to let you care for me. Open my heart, my mind, my body to receive your sustaining love. Amen.

Becoming Who You Are

MAY 11–17, 2020 • L. ROGER OWENS

SCRIPTURE OVERVIEW: In Acts, Paul visits Athens and finds the people worshiping various deities. He attempts to show them the one true God not by open confrontation but by understanding where they are in their own thinking and then engaging in conversation. This model is confirmed in First Peter: We should always be prepared to give reasons for our faith, but this should be done with gentleness and respect, not confrontation. The psalmist promises to make offerings in the Temple to the Lord because God has brought the people through a period of testing. The psalm thus also ties into First Peter, where the believers are being tested. Jesus tells his disciples in John that God will send the Spirit to empower them to demonstrate their faith by keeping his commands.

QUESTIONS AND SUGGESTIONS FOR REFLECTION

- Read Acts 17:22-31. When have you searched for God? How did God's nearness surprise you?
- Read Psalm 66:8-20. What tests have you endured? How have you known God's presence through times of difficulty?
- Read 1 Peter 3:13-22. How does your faith help you determine what is right? How does it give you courage when doing what is right brings you suffering?
- Read John 14:15-21. When have you felt encompassed by the Trinity? When has your identity as part of this family felt fragile?

Associate professor of Christian spirituality and ministry, Pittsburgh Theological Seminary; ordained United Methodist pastor; loves to read, sing, listen to his children make music, and take quiet walks.

A basic tenet of the Christian faith is God's transcendence. God is utterly different from creation, a truth attested in many great hymns like "Holy, Holy, Holy" and "Immortal, Invisible, God Only Wise."

But we should never confuse transcendence with distance, a point Paul tries to make when preaching to the Athenians. Here, in the birthplace of the western philosophical tradition, the residents likely are not surprised to learn that the Divine is transcendent. But it may come as a shock to hear a preacher say that a transcendent God is not far away and desires to be known. Like skeptics and seekers today, the Athenians are searchers for wisdom and truth, seekers of the Divine. But they have not imagined that what they are searching for—the one idea that holds everything together—isn't an idea at all, but a divine Love, closer than their very breath, the nearness of which impels their very search. The point Paul makes is captured well by theologian Richard Lischer, who writes, "God is so transcendently *close* we cannot see [God], and so woven into the fiber of things that [God] remains hidden, like the key 'lost' in plain view."* Thus we need preachers like Paul to point out the truth of God's nearness.

I remember a conversation with my spiritual director not long ago. I was talking about my longing for God, my desire to become united with God's love, which at the moment seemed far away. She said, "You can't long for something you haven't already tasted, at least a little." We search for God because God has already come so near. Like the Athenians, we might find ourselves groping for God. But Paul assures us that our desire for God is driven by the sweet nearness of God's presence.

Stations of the Heart: Parting with a Son (New York: Alfred A. Knopf, 2013), 230.

Ever-near God, help us to sense your presence, closer to us than we can ever imagine. Amen.

I had a disagreement with a theologian after a sermon I preached. This seminary professor questioned my use of the phrase "children of God" to refer to all human beings. "Through baptism into God's family," he said, "we become children of God. Before we encounter God's saving grace, we are strangers to God. We must become children by grace."

I appreciated his point and recognized that scripture uses that language. But here, as Paul preaches to the Athenians, he suggests the opposite. He quotes one of the Athenians' own poets, accepting the truth of the poet's point—we are all God's offspring. The problem, it seems, for Paul is that though we are God's children, we don't know it. We haven't awakened to the deepest truth of our identity as beloved children of God. Too often we cannot see this truth, and therefore we can't live out of it. We live believing we must become something we are not.

That's why when God's son Jesus walked the earth, we didn't recognize him, and we refused to receive the gift of his presence. Through the resurrection, we are able to glimpse God's desire for us to know who we are—beloved children of God—and live out of that reality.

Hearing about it for the first time, the Athenians find the notion of resurrection difficult to believe. Christians today are in danger of making the opposite error. We've heard about the Resurrection so much that we forget what it means. But we dare not forget, for in the resurrection God's embodied Love returns and forgives, giving us the grace to become fully what we already are: children of God, offspring of divine love.

Gracious and loving God, help me to recognize the deepest truth of my identity: I am your beloved child. Give me the grace to see others that way as well. Amen.

My wife has been hospitalized twice recently with a respiratory infection that makes it hard for her to breathe. How glad I was this week when she reported how much better she was feeling! She could breathe again. She could have taken a verse from this psalm and made it her own: "[W]e went through fire and through water, yet you [God] have brought us out to a spacious place." A spacious place is a place where we can breathe.

There's a difference, however, between my wife's recent ordeal and the struggles alluded to in this psalm. The writer believes that God is testing the people; that God is behind their struggles. Some of us today might cringe to read this.

Though we might not believe that God sends us trouble, we can still view ordeals we endure as tests. How we face challenges—whether the nightly frustrations of washing dishes or more serious issues like illness or job loss—helps us to discover the truth of our character. Can we face challenges with patience and hope, or do we approach them with anger and insolence? How I face adversity can reveal or obscure my truth as a child of God.

As a seminary professor, I give students exams to test their learning. But the rest of their lives in ministry will also be a test—though not given by a professor or by God—to help them see whether they are living and loving in accordance with the truth of their deepest identity.

However we view the trying circumstances of our lives, one thing is certain: God walks with us through the fire and the water and longs to bring us to a place where we can breathe once again.

Gracious God, give me a spirit of gratitude for your presence in the difficult circumstances of my life, and help me to face my struggles with patience and hope. Amen.

When God called me to be a preacher, God used Psalm 40. I was still in high school, and when I read the beginning verses about God leaning down and lifting the psalmist out of the pit, I saw the story of my own recent conversion. So when I got to the verse that read how God "put a new song in my mouth" and that "[m]any will see and fear, and put their trust in the Lord" (v. 3), I felt I was being called to tell the story of God's gracious solicitude so that others could wake up to the truth of God's love and grace.

Psalm 66 strikes a similar note. After recounting God's gracious presence amid trials, the psalmist declares, "Come and hear, all you who fear God, and I will tell what he has done for me." What has God done? God has listened and heard the psalmist's prayer. This poet wants us to know: God listened, God heard.

So many things vie for our attention that we can't give any one thing our full attention, it seems. Psychologists describe this phenomenon as continuous partial attention. Given all the distractions, it's hard for us to focus for long on one thing; it's even harder to find another human being who will listen to us wholeheartedly without sneaking furtive glances at their phone.

In such a culture, this psalm writer's testimony resounds as good news: God listens! God hears! God is "all ears," as we sometimes say. No expression of joy, no plaintive cry of grief, no protest for aid can be lost in the attention of a mindful God who listens and responds.

Mindful God, I thank you for your gracious attention to my life. Help me to speak with you as with a friend, knowing you are listening. Amen.

I was asked to lead the youth group in a lesson about Daniel, who persevered in the ways of God and faced the lions for it. Maybe Peter has Daniel in mind when he urges the early Christians to suffer for doing what is right. Their job is to be who they are meant to be—images of Christ in a broken world. As such, they should not be surprised when the same world that has rejected Christ rejects them.

But Christ gives hope, so like Christ (and Daniel), the early Christians are called to be steadfast in serving their neighbors, persevering in peacefulness, and longsuffering in love even when living out their identity in Christ runs against the grain of the culture around them.

When I taught that youth group session, I asked if the youth could think of a time in American history when people suffered for doing what is right. I had in mind the African Americans who faced dogs and water cannons during the Civil Rights movement as they protested racial injustice deeply embedded in our nation's history. I reminded the students that Martin Luther King Jr. asked all who marched with him to meditate daily on the teachings of Jesus. As they were being transformed into the image of Jesus, they could no longer accept the blatant injustices around them. And they suffered for the stand they took.

Whether it's Daniel in the sixth century BCE, Christians in the first century CE, or us in the twenty-first century, people of faith will be at odds with the injustices that cause some to suffer while others succeed. Thankfully, we have hope that the love that raised Jesus from the dead is stronger than the hate and fear we might have to face.

Dear Jesus, you suffered because of your steadfast dedication to your mission. Help me, even today, to be willing to suffer if that's what being a faithful child of God brings. Amen.

A year after taking a position as a seminary professor, I discovered the secret fame of one of my colleagues.

For years, the hymn "Child of Blessing, Child of Promise" (UMH, no. 611) has been one of my favorites. It beautifully expresses that baptized children come from God, belong to God, and have their deepest identity in God. One Sunday morning, while we were singing this hymn, I glanced down to the bottom of the page and saw the name of a colleague, whose office is down the hall from mine, noted as the author of the hymn. The next time I saw him in the copy room, I almost asked for his autograph.

I think of that hymn now as I reflect on Peter's words, "And baptism . . . now saves you." Does that mean we have to be baptized to go to heaven? Sometimes we have a very narrow understanding of what it means to be saved. We think it's about going to heaven or not. But many strands of the Christian tradition view salvation more broadly as knowing and growing in one's identity as a child of God. To be saved is to grow into that identity, to become more like the God whose children we are.

If we think of salvation in these broader terms, then what Peter says makes sense. We are saved in baptism because in baptism God's grace marks us with our truest identity. We come to discover ourselves as God's children, children of both blessing and promise. Salvation begins when we know who we most truly are—God's children—and begin the lifelong journey of growing in love as we become more like the love revealed to us in the resurrection of Christ.

Loving God, help me to claim the truth of my baptism—that I belong to you. Help me to grow more like you in love. Amen.

Earlier in this week, we noted that Paul preaches to the Athenians to help them understand that God is transcendently close. That's good news. In this passage, Jesus is addressing his disciples on the eve of his crucifixion. He is offering them a word of comfort because he knows that after his crucifixion they will be scattered and afraid. So he promises them the gift of the Holy Spirit, which will be God's presence with them and will comfort them and lead them into truth.

Then Jesus says something that expresses the very heart of our Christian hope: "You will know that I am in my Father, and you in me, and I in you." Christians believe that God exists eternally as a trinity of persons, existing together in love as the one God. Early Christian theologians used the phrase *mutual indwelling* to describe this truth. The three persons of the Trinity live in one another. Here Jesus is making that startling and beautiful claim: We too belong in that community of love. By grace, God is taking us into our truest home, which is the very life of God.

Not only is God near to us, but also we live in God and God lives in us. We have been invited to enter into the very heart of God's life.

We come from the God of love—we are love's offspring—and we find our truest identity in relationship to God as children of God becoming who we are meant to be. Now we see in Jesus our destiny: To live forever in God's life, to live in the very heart of this Trinity of Love. Good news indeed.

God, thank you for taking me into your life and love. I long to find myself in you. May I have the grace to continue to grow as your beloved child. Amen.

Empowered by the Spirit

MAY 18–24, 2020 • STEPHANIE A. FORD

SCRIPTURE OVERVIEW: Though Jesus has taught his disciples that God's kingdom is not an earthly one, following the Resurrection some are still expecting him to set up a kingdom on earth. Instead, Jesus ascends into heaven in front of them, being taken up in the clouds. The scene recalls Psalm 68, where the Lord is described as one who rides on the clouds across the expanse of the heavens. In the Gospel reading, Jesus anticipates his coming departure and prays for his followers. Peter talks about a trial—literally a "fiery ordeal"—that is testing Christians. The reference to fire may be specific, for the Roman historian Tacitus records that Nero killed Christians in Rome by burning them alive. The author may therefore be speaking about suffering that is not just metaphorical.

QUESTIONS AND SUGGESTIONS FOR REFLECTION

- Read Acts 1:6-14. When have you experienced the power of community?
- Read Psalm 68:1-10, 32-35. Recall a time when you recognized God's power with fear and joy. How might that have been a foretaste of God's kingdom?
- Read 1 Peter 4:12-14; 5:6-11. How have you walked with faith through suffering?
- Read John 17:1-11. What does it mean for you or your congregation that Jesus prayed for unity among his followers?

Minister of Christian Formation at Binkley Baptist Church, Chapel Hill, North Carolina.

In the Psalms, as in the Beatitudes, the righteous are promised joy. Yet we know from our own and others' lives that such a promise is no formula. Godly people suffer, while those who perpetrate evil seem to get by or even prosper. Nevertheless, joy fills our hearts as we remember God's compassionate love. Goodness will overcome evil, and God is assuredly on the side of the just.

Jesus would later use *Abba*, or "Father," to speak to the Divine, but this name for God is used only twice in the Psalms. So we listen thoughtfully to the psalmist's meaning. In Psalm 68, God's nature is described as a "father to the fatherless, a defender of widows. . . . God sets the lonely in families, [God] leads out the prisoners with singing" (NIV). Thus, we see the character of God, who like a father looks with compassion on his vulnerable children.

My own family was created through adoption. I remember that first night in the hotel, with our two-year-old adopted daughter sleeping between us. I could barely sleep as I was overcome with awe and frightened by this new responsibility. And I felt unspeakable joy. I believe that this is the kind of joy the psalmist is talking about, a joy found in offering and receiving love, mercy, and justice. When we live into God's vision, when the weak are made strong, when the lonely are comforted, and when all children are welcomed and loved, we can find this kingdom of God on earth.

In just a few verses, Psalm 68 gives us a taste of the messianic vision, which, as Christians, we find realized in Jesus who blesses children, honors widows, and sets captives free. When power is used in the service of love, God is near, incarnate in this world.

God of the vulnerable, help us to recognize them and to act on their behalf. May they feel the joy of your reign in their lives. Amen.

In John 16, Jesus emboldens his disciples in his farewell speech by reassuring them with the promise of the Holy Spirit. Now in the seventeenth chapter, Jesus turns his eyes to heaven and prays for his beloved followers. Jesus is passing the torch to the disciples. And you'd better believe that the disciples, who are overhearing the prayer, are listening closely. It reminds me of visits to my grandparents' home as a child. My sister and I were supposed to be tucked into bed, but after a little while, we would silently tiptoe to the staircase and strain to overhear what our mother was saying about us to our grandmother.

Although Jesus prays openly about death being near, the tone of his prayer is almost joyous—he has fulfilled his calling, and the glory of his full return to unity with God as described in John's prologue is near. In this prayer, Jesus blesses his followers by naming their preparation for this moment. The disciples have received Jesus' words, and they are now certain of Jesus' divinity. Jesus prays for unity among his followers, "so that they may be one, as we are one."

The disciples could not have imagined the many streams and rivulets the Jesus movement would split into. Yet, even when John's Gospel is written, probably in the second century CE, there are already multiple strains: Christians rooted in Judaism and those who, like the community John writes from, have separated from the mother tree to focus on the exclusive priority of Christ. Nor could the disciples have envisioned the global church today and the complexities of church and culture that call us to deeper dialogue and prayer for one another.

How do we honor the unity Jesus envisions? How might we be healers and bridge-builders to help realize Jesus' prayer that we be one?

How is the Holy Spirit nudging you as you reflect and act upon Jesus' prayer for the unity of the church?

Mystic and philosopher Simone Weil observed that our natural human impulse is to turn away from suffering, so we tend to blame the victim. Yet the writer of First Peter challenges this view. When we encounter a "fiery ordeal," the author invites us to "rejoice insofar as you are sharing Christ's sufferings, so that [we] may also be glad and shout for joy when his glory is revealed."

Unfortunately, throughout Christian history, many believers have followed this axiom to extremes by choosing penitence as a way to move closer to Jesus and even to glorify suffering—despite what Jesus says. He declares: "I came that they might have life, and have it more abundantly" (John 10:10). Even so, the author of First Peter is not recommending a passive agreement to fate but rather bringing an expectant hope—because in trial, the presence of the "Spirit of God is resting on you."

Throughout his ministry, Jesus does not avert his eyes from those in pain—not even the tug on the hem of his garment in a big crowd. He must experience great weariness, but again and again, Jesus looks at and acts to end suffering.

First Peter invites us to cast all our anxiety upon God because God cares for us. A dear friend tells me that as she walks, she prays and offers her worries to the sky, imaging God there to receive them. I find it helpful to envision Jesus walking ahead of me preparing the path or beside me sharing the yoke. What helps you to cast your cares upon God?

First Peter 5:10 leaves us with a picture of this walk in faith amid suffering: "[T]he God of all grace, who has called you to his eternal glory in Christ . . . will restore, support, strengthen and establish you." Amen and amen.

Help me, dear Jesus, to keep my eyes open. Fill me with your compassion for the ones on my path who suffer. Help me to cast my own worries upon God. Amen.

ASCENSION DAY

On this day of Christ's ascension, we are invited to join the disciples in awe as Jesus takes his leave from earthly existence. For forty days, the resurrected Christ has been appearing with comfort and challenge. Now it is time for him to ascend to his father.

Lectio divina, the practice of reading and meditating on scripture, enables us to read even familiar passages in new ways. The practice helps us ask ourselves, *What may God be inviting me to find in this passage? What is the living word for me today?* One phrase that shimmers off the page is as simple as it is profound. Jesus tells his disciples: "You are witnesses of these things." The life of faith includes joyful and dry times. Yet 2,000 years later we too experience the risen Christ among us. We have felt Christ's presence in the grace of conversion and in hands raised in heartfelt praise. We have felt like vessels of Christ to others. Can you remember a time when the words came right through you, and you knew they were not yours but those of the Christ within you?

My father's time to leave this life caught me by surprise. We thought he had a lot more time. Rushing to his bedside, I thanked him for all that he had given our family. Then, I felt the Spirit say through my voice: "Go toward the light, Dad; go toward the light." His hand dropped, and he took his last breath. My sister, brother-in-law, and I watched in awe. These words were not planned or intended; rather, they were given. The three of us bore witness to the work of Christ among us.

And so we return to join the disciples in this moment as Jesus leads them out of Jerusalem to neighboring Bethany. We stand with them as Jesus lifts up his hands and blesses them and us before ascending to the heavenly light.

Jesus, we join generations of witnesses to your great love, forgiveness, and wisdom. Enliven us as we bear witness to you in our daily lives. Amen.

Empowered by the Spirit 177

A natural response to loss, change, or ending is to ask "What's next?" Before Jesus ascends, his disciples ask him how the messianic vision will be fulfilled now that he is gone. Jesus doesn't refer to the Father who knows all things. Rather, Jesus assures them with these prophetic words: "You will receive power when the Holy Spirit has come upon you." Jesus returns to heaven, and the disciples stare at the sky until two angelic messengers appear to send them on their way. They head back to Jerusalem to gather in the upper room along with Mary, Jesus' mother, other female followers, and Jesus' brothers. What will they do during this time of waiting? They will pray.

Waiting or words with the root *wait* appear over 140 times in the Bible. It's a word familiar to the spiritual life. Waiting upon the Spirit is a key to discernment, to speaking the right words to another, to listening well to a spouse, to loving a child wisely. It is the occupation of pregnancy; it is the calling of hospice. It is the heart of prayer.

One autumn, in a very difficult time in my life, the word *wait* came to me in countless serendipitous ways. A friend wrote to me: "I trust that you are being clearly guided by God, so wait." Another friend said: "I truly believe that already there are seeds of blessing in this that are not yet visible." Then butterflies began to appear everywhere I looked. While making a collage, I found the words "good things come to those who wait." My soul was uplifted; indeed, over the course of a year, my prayers and those of many who joined me were answered.

Like the disciples in the upper room, we are called to prayer, continuously and in times of waiting. We know what the disciples are waiting for, even as they cannot imagine what will come. Pentecost, the birth of the church, is coming.

Gracious God, it is hard not to wonder, worry, and even fear what's ahead on my path. Open my heart to trust. Guide me on the path you call me to walk. Amen.

Even if we have read the first chapter of Acts many times, we may overlook this profound moment. Here, the community of Christ followers gathers on the eve of the birth of the church. As readers, we know the story of Pentecost to come, but they do not. "They all joined together constantly in prayer" (NIV). The labor and delivery of the church—the gift of the Holy Spirit that will fall upon these first believers—begins with this simple and profound fact: A community of Jesus' followers gathered in prayer.

Connection to one another through community is written into creation. Trees were once thought to simply compete for light and nutrients. Though they do compete in some ways, trees more often assist one another. When one tree is sick, nearby trees may share nutrients through their roots to help it get well again. An intricate web of roots and fungi connect tree to tree in a forest, twice as big as the canopy overhead, which enables trees to communicate about insect predators and much more.

We too are meant to live in community. The monastic life reveals this truth. For even if one joins a monastery to flee the world, he or she will soon find that a more challenging community awaits, and it's now a 24/7 community. The difference is that the "glue" for the monastic community is prayer.

At the turn of the twentieth century, Evelyn Underhill contended that "prayer is the closest thing to absolute action." For in prayer, we join the most powerful, loving force in the world— God. And we join one another in this collective waiting upon the Divine. Electricity—power—is generated among us when we pray one for another and for our world, and our prayers open space for the Spirit to fall upon us as a community. When we are truly together in prayer, Divine love connects us.

Loving Creator, your word created a world in Genesis and your Spirit created the beginnings of Christ's church. May we awaken to your creating presence in our day. Amen.

On this Ascension Sunday, we are called to rejoice with all the company of earth and heaven in the gift of our risen Lord. Christ has ascended. Alleluia! We are not left powerless; we are promised the indwelling power of the Holy Spirit. Though Psalm 47 long predates Jesus' life and ministry, this psalm's instruction is apt for this moment: "Clap your hands, all you nations; shout to God with cries of joy" (NIV).

In my home church, many are ambivalent about clapping during a worship service. We understand worship as a sacred performance and our intention is to worship God—not to applaud certain performers like the choir, the pianist, or a child offering a litany. Yet here in Psalm 47, the psalmist invites us to go deeper, calling the congregation gathered to clap and cry out with joy to God. The psalmist also invites the body to wholeheartedly join the spirit in praise.

In our individual lives of prayer and in our prayers as a community we are called to inhabit our praise. If we are cautious about embodied expression, we can bring our bodies to worship in gentler ways. During a pastoral prayer, we might open our hands on our laps, hold the hand of a spouse, friend, or child, or even raise our hands in the silence. We may feel led to get up from our pew or chair to kneel in adoration and contrition during Communion. We might clap to the rhythms of a song of praise (even if we don't want to be first).

In my own journey, I clap my hands most often because when I feel joy, my words fail to convey the overwhelming gladness welling up in me. I am most free to embody my joy when I am driving and there is no traffic. I find myself singing to God with all of my heart and waving my right hand in praise. Remembering my first love, I long to convey that joy beyond words.

Holy Spirit, as Pentecost nears I am filled with anticipation and thanksgiving. So may I praise you with heart, mind, spirit, and body. Amen.

Spirit and Breath of Power

MAY 25–31, 2020 • ERIC H. F. LAW

SCRIPTURE OVERVIEW: Many contemporary Christians wrestle with the theology of the Holy Spirit. Some are perceived as emphasizing the Spirit too much, while others talk about the Spirit only vaguely or even not at all. Both extremes can mislead us. The Spirit is powerful and active, and we understand the role of the Spirit within larger truths about God and God's activities in the world. God empowers the disciples on Pentecost by the Spirit, and the psalmist emphasizes the role of the Spirit in creation. Paul tells the Corinthians that the Spirit enables us to recognize Jesus as Lord and serve one another. Jesus gives the power of the Spirit to his disciples. May we also seek God's help in receiving the power of the Spirit to serve and reach those far from God.

QUESTIONS AND SUGGESTIONS FOR REFLECTION

- Read Acts 2:1-21. What moments from your lifetime might you consider Pentecost moments? How have you seen the Spirit empowering God's people in these moments or movements?
- Read Psalm 104:24-34, 35b. When have you experienced God's rhythm of withholding and releasing? How can your breath remind you of your place in this rhythm of creation?
- Read 1 Corinthians 12:3b-13. How does your faith guide you to a tension between sameness and difference that might help you create a diverse unity among your family or faith community?
- Read John 20:19-23. How does your relationship with Christ help you break through fear?

Founder of the Kaleidoscope Institute for Diverse and Sustainable Communities; writes *The Sustainist* at ehflaw.typepad.com/blog/.

Breathing is powerful. Since it is an involuntary function, we don't think much about it until we are underwater, in a place with an unbearable odor, or in a dusty environment; then we realize how important breathing is.

When we don't breathe in, we suffocate. If we breathe in too much, we hyperventilate. The rhythm and balance of breathing, in and out, renews every moment of our lives.

God creates with breath: "When you send forth your spirit (or breath), they are created; and you renew the face of the ground." This psalm reminds us how God withholds and releases resources as part of life in God's creation. The same is true for ministry; the rhythm and balance of receiving and giving, holding on and letting go, helps us be good stewards of what God has given us through breath.

Every breath in is an opportunity for God's Spirit to enter our lives. Every breath out is an occasion for us to act according to God's life-giving way. Try the following breathing meditations:

Breathe slowly and mindfully, in and out, deep and slow, while saying, *When you send forth your breath, I am recreated; and you renew me.*

On the next slow and mindful breath, say, *When you send forth your breath, my community is recreated; and you renew us.*

Finally breathe slowly and mindfully and say, *When you send forth your breath, the earth is recreated; and you renew the earth.*

O God of Creation, breathe through us and help us, as we breathe in, to receive and accept your reality and your trust in us to be cocreators with you. Help us, as we breathe out, to exercise the power you have given to us to do justice, love mercy, and walk humbly with you. (See Micah 6:8.) Amen.

A small group of Jews who follow a teacher named Jesus, who had been killed like a criminal, gather in one place at Pentecost, a Jewish festival celebrated fifty days after Passover. A few days before, the resurrected Jesus had ascended and left this small group leaderless and powerless. Certainly no one would expect this group of people to be spokespersons for God. But on that Pentecost day, they prophesy.

Ever since I was a child, this text has always been interpreted to me as a miracle of tongues: the Spirit gives the followers of Jesus the power to speak in different languages in order to communicate the "mighty work of God." Then one day, Walter Wink, a New Testament scholar and great teacher asked, "Is this a miracle of the tongue or a miracle of the ear?" This simple question cracked open a persistent interpretation of this text. To understand the Pentecost event exclusively as a miracle of tongues captures only half of what happens.

Read today's passage again. Notice that starting in verse 5, listening is just as prominent as speaking in this story. The full miracle of Pentecost includes devout Jews from every nation living in Jerusalem who hear the sound and come to listen. The miracle of tongues puts out words in other languages and gives information. The miracle of the ear involves listening and receiving information.

When the Spirit comes upon us, on which side of the Pentecost miracle do you find yourself—tongue or ear? Do you respond to the Spirit by speaking and acting? Or do you respond to the Spirit by listening and receiving?

Holy Spirit of surprises, come upon us and help us discern when we should speak and when we should listen, so that your vision of the peaceable realm can be realized. Amen.

In today's reading, Peter quotes from the prophet Joel: "Your sons and your daughters shall prophesy, your old . . . shall dream dreams, and your young . . . shall see visions. Even on my servants, both men and women, I will pour out my Spirit in those days" (Joel 2:28-29, NIV).

In the biblical world, the ability to dream dreams, have visions, and prophesy is reserved for a chosen few, and they are usually powerful men—Moses, Abraham, Joseph, David, and the prophets. Of the fifty-five prophets the Hebrew scriptures identify, only seven are women.

We can appreciate the radical inclusion of Joel's prophecy by the fact that he specifically mentions both sons and daughters, old and young, men and women, and even servants (in some translations, slaves) as people who would have the abilities of a prophet, a spokesperson who conveys messages from God.

At the beginning of this story, Jesus' followers are powerless and afraid because their future is uncertain, overshadowed by the threat of persecution. Peter explains the event of Pentecost as the fulfillment of Joel's prophecy: the weak, the powerless, the ignored, and the excluded are the ones who speak for God. The disciples' speaking and the crowd's understanding at Pentecost signals the coming of the new age, when the prophetic voices will come from the powerless in society.

Who are the prophets in our society today? How do we prepare ourselves to listen to the powerless in our communities? How do we take seriously the idea that they may well be the ones appointed by God to be the prophetic voices in our time?

Breath of God, breathe on the powerless of our society to empower them to speak your truth and share your vision of the world. Breathe on us so that we can have the courage to seek them out and listen to your voice through them. Amen.

W e live in a world dominated by the voices of the powerful and rich, who use their power and money to influence our media and spread divisive information. This information polarizes people and makes us unable to communicate with one another to work together for the common good. As followers of Jesus, we sometimes feel insignificant and helpless and perhaps even powerless in sharing the good news of a compassionate and just God. At times like these, we can learn from the miraculous Pentecost story, when a small group of powerless Jews becomes so influential that 3,000 people are baptized. (See Acts 2:41.)

In every generation, Christians have used the technologies available to us to share the gospel. The early church leaders wrote down their stories so that future generations could recall the saving stories. When the printing press was invented, Christians used it to print copies of the Bible and other resources that could be distributed and shared with many more. The voiceless began to find their voices in the printing era as well.

Now, with the innovation of digital media, we can learn to use these channels to empower the prophetic voices of those with less power in our society. YouTube, for example, offers all who have access to a computer with a camera the ability to share their voice with millions. Social media allows people to network globally, which bypasses traditional information systems. The Black Lives Matter and Me Too movements are examples of the powerless finding their voice through a powerful digital network that has become a community of millions. When used faithfully, new technologies can allow us to hear and to share the experiences of the powerless, realizing a form of Pentecost.

God, help us to recognize Pentecost moments and use our technologies to network locally and globally to empower and amplify the voices of the powerless. May their dreams, visions, and prophecies be heard by your children. Amen.

Can you feel the tension between unity and diversity in this text? On the one hand, we read about the same Spirit, same Lord, same God, and common good. On the other, we recognize a variety of gifts, service, and activities. Like a string on a musical instrument, if the space between unity and diversity is wound too tight, it will break. If the bond between unity and diversity is too loose, it cannot make a sound. Only when the string is wound just right—when we find the right balance between unity and diversity—can we experience a beautiful sound.

Many of us tend to emphasize unity to the point of misinterpreting it as sameness. Others of us want to do our own thing in our own way, but only with people who are like us. Unity does not mean we all do the same thing, act the same way, sing the same song, or vote for the same political candidate. Unity does not ignore or minimize our differences for the sake of sameness. Unity operates at a deeper connection through the Spirit, which allows us to do and believe in different things and still belong to the same community. This deeper connection allows us to accept and appreciate the different gifts, skills, and talents that each person brings to the community.

We live in a world where we are so divided, especially politically, that many of us avoid diversity of opinion to the point of avoiding family holiday gatherings because we don't know what to say when politics comes up in conversations. The Spirit of God can help us wind this tension between unity and diversity just right so that we can make holy music and dance together.

Spirit of God, come upon us and help us not to be afraid of conflicts that arise from our diversity; help us find the right tension through dialogue and understanding so that together we can be activated to do the work of justice, peace, and reconciliation. Amen.

Fear is projected all around us through commercials, political ads and speeches, and polarized news reporting. Marketers and politicians figured out long ago that fear is a powerful motivator to get people to buy things that they don't need and to do things that might not be good for themselves and others. Sometimes we are so overwhelmed by the continuous triggering of our fears that we lock ourselves in emotionally and physically and hope that we will be safe. Fear becomes a prison that stops us from being able to do anything to effect change.

Before they know that Jesus has risen, Jesus' followers feel such paralyzing fear and they lock themselves in. But Jesus breaks through their prison of fear, offers them peace, and breathes on them. With his breath, Jesus invites the disciples to receive the Holy Spirit and then go out and exercise its power. He tells them that they have the power to forgive sins or to retain them. What a transformation—from a sense of total powerlessness to having the ability to forgive sins! As God's breath creates and recreates, Jesus' breath grants the power of the Holy Spirit. Through breath and through the Trinity, we—like the disciples—are empowered to break out of the prisons we have allowed our fear to build around us. Our faith can transform our fear into power.

What do you fear? Who or what triggers your fears? Who stands to benefit when you are afraid? What locks you in the prison of fear?

Jesus Christ, break into our prison of fear and empower us with your breath of peace, justice, and love so that we can be free from fear's bondage and go out to do your work of healing and reconciliation—our true security. Amen.

PENTECOST

In some cultures, it is inappropriate to speak the truth openly and in public unless the person speaking is drunk. Somehow, within the context of such cultures, a person is forgiven for speaking so directly when intoxicated. I am not promoting drunkenness for the sake of truth. I am suggesting that the people who thought that the followers of Jesus were drunk may have been saying so because they recognized the truth of what they were hearing. Since they did not really want to hear the truth, they came to the conclusion that Jesus' followers were drunk.

Acting in ways considered inappropriate could be what is required of us who follow Jesus. We might be called to speak out when it is not our place or time to speak. In the 1960s in the United States, the marchers and sit-in participants who protested and broke unjust laws were told that their behaviors were inappropriate, not the right ways to make change, or even dangerous. Today we recognize similar complaints about the recent movements that amplify the voices of the powerless and oppressed, including the Black Lives Matter and Me Too movements. As on Pentecost, God's Spirit empowers us to act in prophetic ways that may seem inappropriate to others.

I leave you with a verse I wrote to the tune of "Carry It On" by Gil Turner. Like many other songs sung at marches and protests during the Civil Rights Movement, this song lives on through modifications with new verses added to fit new contexts.

In this world, so much is broken
From the sleep we have awoken
To the truth that must be spoken
Carry it on

Breath of God, give us the strength and courage to speak the truth even if others find it inappropriate. Breathe on us, in us, and through us so that we can carry it on. Amen.

The Authority of Love

JUNE 1–7, 2020 • ROBERTA BONDI

SCRIPTURE OVERVIEW: Our first reading is arguably one of the most controversial passages in the Bible. Even among those who believe that God created the world, there is controversy. For example, should the days be understood as literal or symbolic? Much time and trouble have been spent in arguing about these things. A different approach is found in Psalm 8, where the author simply praises God for the majestic work of creation without needing to work out all the details. Perhaps this approach would lead to more love and peace among the people of God, as Paul hopes for in Second Corinthians. Matthew describes the ascension, where Jesus tells his followers to baptize in the name of the Father and the Son and the Holy Spirit, an appropriate passage in preparation for Trinity Sunday.

QUESTIONS AND SUGGESTIONS FOR REFLECTION

- Read Genesis 1:1–2:4a. When has reading the Bible in a new way or with new knowledge changed your experience of the text?
- Read Psalm 8. How do you feel called to care for the earth God has given us?
- Read 2 Corinthians 13:11-13. How does your faith community heed Paul's advice to the Corinthians? How does it fall short?
- Read Matthew 28:16-20. Recall a time of doubt. How has that experience made your faith stronger?

Professor Emerita, Candler School of Theology, Emory University.

My early childhood experience of today's reading was not a happy one. I remember sitting in a circle in Sunday school while we each took a turn stumbling through the words, verse by verse, until the end of class. I don't recall finishing the chapter, but I do recall being bored to death by the slowness of early readers and the interminable repetition as God created everything night by night and day by day, "and God saw that it was good"!

The next time I really encountered the text was the summer after I graduated college. I intended to do graduate work in English literature, and given the importance of the Bible in what I was studying, I decided to learn Hebrew. I made arrangements with a teacher at the seminary on campus and bought what I needed to get started, including a Hebrew Bible.

What a time of it I had that summer! I was given a grammar and the assignment to learn the Hebrew of this first Creation story as best I could. I was astonished and shaken to the core as I read in Hebrew this simple, marvelous description of the world emerging, bright and quivering, as God calls it out of chaos into sun, moon, and stars; out of nothing but darkness, wind, and water into dry land and oceans, fish, birds, every kind of plant, fruit tree, insects, animals and every sort of living thing—including human beings. All came bright and alive on the page before me.

I experienced the primordial wonder of the deep goodness of all God's creation. It was the first I had ever known the world in this way, and my heart filled with a joy for everything that was and is and will be. It was a glimpse of God's love. The miracle of this fact has never left me even nearly sixty years later.

God, you have made all things beautiful in your love. Help us to experience the beauty of your creation. Amen.

This first Creation story culminates in God's making of humanity in God's own image, after which we human beings are assigned our work in the world: to multiply and fill the earth and to "subdue" it. I'm afraid both of these tasks now can seem problematic in our suffering world. We have overpopulated our earth by a few billion people. We have ravaged, polluted, and subjugated the natural world almost beyond rescue. But how could such a disaster follow from these two commands?

The original context of this writing was life in a largely unpopulated and dangerous land. The world was a place where human beings were continuously at the mercy of natural events. Childbirth, broken limbs, disease, wild animals, famine, earthquakes, floods, fire—life was not a safe proposition. Raising food and hunting successfully couldn't be taken for granted.

So what can it mean to subdue the earth according to this passage? God surely did not intend for us to overpopulate it and break its back. Instead, I think it means that made in the image of God as we are, we are to "rule" as God rules: with infinite and tender love for the creation—including ourselves as human beings—that this chapter has just described for us.

Because God loves creation, when we read a scripture passage that seems to violate this love, we need to look at it again. God does not want the destruction of any thing or person that God loves. This is the principle by which we understand the Bible.

Loving God, help us learn to love as we learn to interpret scripture in a way that harms neither people nor the rest of creation. Amen.

This psalm, like the first creation story in this week's Genesis reading, is a deep call to awe and wonder as we consider what it means to be human in the face of the basic paradox of our lives. On the one hand, we need only look up outdoors to see the vastness of space, filled as it is with billions of stars and planets, in order to feel our tininess against all of this enormity. Next to such apparent limitlessness we can see that we human beings are no bigger than a swarm of gnats over a bowl of fruit. Still, as the first Creation story has already told us this week, and as our own hearts witness to us daily, God cares for us as though we have the cosmic significance of angels, going so far as to place the earth and its inhabitants "under our feet."

We have been given a similar "dominion" over it all, a responsibility to care for the world and everything in it as God continually creates and tends it with love and longing for its well-being. However, we have not fulfilled our responsibility well. Instead, we have ground creation under our feet for our own profit. We have exploited and polluted, poisoned and corrupted the goodness of the air, the water, and the land until we can barely live in it.

This psalm painfully reminds us that care for the earth is still our job. We may not be able to restore it to what it was, but nevertheless we can make healing choices if we pay attention, use our imaginations, and refuse to give in to despair.

Dear God, help us learn to love the world you have entrusted to us with something like your own love. Since we are made in your image, we know we have this capacity to learn. Amen.

In today's passage Jesus has told the disciples where to meet him for the last time. They worship him on the mountain when they see him, he passes on his authority to them, he commands them to make disciples of all nations, he tells them to baptize in the name of the Trinity, and he promises to be with them forever. All these are familiar and fundamental parts of our faith.

Before today, I had never taken in the words that come right after "they worshiped him." The crucial phrase is this: "but some doubted." Some doubted! Right here among all these orders and promises, when they are looking right at the risen Jesus for the last time, not everyone believed what they saw and heard.

We could think of "but some doubted" as an easily overlooked minor detail of the story until we remember the Resurrection appearances and the role of doubt in the very different Gospel of John. Doubting Thomas is no minor character in John 20:19-25.

So many of us have been taught that if we are to be Christian we must accept what we have been told. Many Christians' measure of faith is really a measure of our capacity to believe without questioning. I remember my terror as a child as I would pray, "Please God, make me believe so I don't go to hell."

But in the account in Matthew and the story in John, serious doubting is going on. Neither narrative condemns the doubters. This passage may comfort those of us who have been traumatized with respect to our inability to believe what we are told. Doubting is human. It is one way we grow in our ability to see the truth, and God put this capacity for doubt in us.

Thank you, God, for inviting us to bring our whole selves, doubts and all, to you. Amen.

Now we come to a greatly disputed part of this passage. Jesus says, "All authority in heaven and on earth has been given to me. Go, therefore and make disciples of all nations . . . teaching them to obey everything I have commanded you."

To understand it, we must ask two questions. First, What is this authority Jesus is passing on to his disciples? And second, What are we to do with it? Many churches hear Jesus telling them that the duly appointed leaders are to stand in for Jesus himself. They tell folks of their communities that they must not only obey the rules to be accepted by Jesus but also believe in the community's doctrines in order to be found acceptable to God. As a result, many good people are being put outside the communities of God.

Notice, however, that this is not at all what our passage is saying. It clearly says this instead: Make disciples of all people and teach them to obey my commandments. And these commandments are clear: We are to love our enemies, not to judge them. We are to understand the generosity of God's love for us and imitate the same generosity toward other people. Fred Craddock, the founder of the congregation I attend, used to say, "We only turn away those whom Jesus turned away," meaning nobody. Our job is to love God and our neighbor as ourselves, to extend God's grace everywhere. Separating the wheat from the chaff is most certainly not our job. A disciple's task is to live according to the teachings of the teacher. This is the authority Jesus holds out to us—the authority not to identify and reject the unworthy but to know that in the presence of God's love, we are all equally worthy.

Loving God, help us never to turn another person away from you by our own judgmentalism and self-righteousness. Amen.

The Bible suggests that Paul struggles to exercise authority gently and humbly but also powerfully with the church at Corinth, whose favorite sport seems to consist of serious fighting. The Corinthians are not often experiencing or expressing the love of God toward one another. After much exhortation in the rest of the letter, Paul ends with this advice:

First, try to have an orderly community. All of us, I suspect, have had the awful experience of a group where the bullies were in charge, the timid or poor were forgotten, and nothing could be counted on to happen. It is possible to have order without oppressive rules.

Second, try to agree with one another rather than live in a status quo of arguing. Paul does not say to agree on every point. But we can agree, say, that the ministry of the church is to feed the hungry. We can avoid political disagreement for the sake of encountering the lovable in one another.

Third, remember that if you live like this you will be encountered by God's peace and love. We don't need to wait for divine peace and love to hit us like a bolt of lightning. When we make a serious attempt at peace and love, God will help us on our way.

Fourth, "greet each other with a holy kiss." As most folks who practice the kiss of peace in their congregations know, there is nothing like habitually, ritually, and warmly greeting someone you don't like to bring you to a point where you begin to care for that person and can feel genuine affection and love for them.

Finally, Paul prays that the three things we need the most—the grace, love, and communion with God the Trinity—be with all of them. Let's ask for this for our churches too. I suspect we need it as much as the Corinthians.

Help us be your people, loving God, living in love, peace, and affection for one another. Amen.

The Authority of Love   195

TRINITY SUNDAY

There probably is no Christian teaching more confusing to us than the Trinity. I have heard people ask a thousand times, "Why can't we just add a fourth member to the Trinity if we want to talk about the feminine aspect of God?" The basic reason, of course, is that we are describing the God who is real, and whom we know, not the God we are constructing.

Julian of Norwich (born in 1342), in her book *Showings*, talks wonderfully and helpfully about the Trinity. She speaks familiarly of the God who creates us, the God who redeems us, and the God who preserves us; but they are not her primary names nor are they self-explanatory. She first describes God most fundamentally as Love, and she makes it entirely clear that everything else we say about God must be descriptive of that love.

She names the three persons Power, Wisdom, and the Love uniting them. "Power" and "Wisdom" are not abstract names or even separate names for these persons: the supreme power of God, the first person, whom we frequently call the Father, is not Naked Power to do anything but rather the Power of Love. The second person, incarnate in Jesus, the Son, is the Wisdom of God, which is not the brains of a huge computer but rather the Wisdom of Love. These two are not opposites. The third person is the Love between them—they are all one God, all one love.

Her other truly significant way of naming the Trinity is "God the Father," "God the Mother," and "God the Holy Spirit," who are "all one love." How easily we fall into hierarchical ways of thinking—with father on top, mother subordinate to father, and the Holy Spirit below them. But Julian emphatically says something different: The three persons of God are equal in all things. They do not operate separately. They are only one God, and they are all one love.

God, you make us in the image of your Trinity, which is love. Help us to grow into it. Amen.

Encountering God

JUNE 8–14, 2020 • LARRY PEACOCK

SCRIPTURE OVERVIEW: The readings this week lack a common theme. Genesis recounts the promise of Isaac's miraculous birth and the fulfillment of that promise—a key story in the history of God's people. The psalmist cries out with gladness to the Lord, for we are God's people and the grateful recipients of unending faithfulness. Paul rejoices because we have peace with God through our faith in Jesus Christ. This is not because of anything we have done or could do; rather, God's love sent Christ to die for us when we were distant from God. In Matthew, Jesus calls his disciples and declares that God's harvest is vast, but there are not enough workers willing to go into the fields. It is a call for us to go as the disciples did.

QUESTIONS AND SUGGESTIONS FOR REFLECTION

- Read Genesis 18:1-15; 21:1-7. How does your faith invite you to laughter?
- Read Psalm 100. How do you make a joyful noise to God? Consider trying a new practice of joyful praise.
- Read Romans 5:1-8. How has God's love for you prompted you to "the second movement of the symphony," to share God's love with others and all creation?
- Read Matthew 9:35–10:23. How are you called to participate in Christ's ministry of healing?

Retired United Methodist pastor; Director of the Franciscan Spiritual Center, Milwaukie, Oregon; author of *The Living Nativity: Preparing for Christmas with Saint Francis* and *Openings: A Day Book of Saints, Sages, Psalms and Prayer Practices.*

A braham and Sarah first appear in Genesis 12, and significant encounters with the Holy take place in nearly every following chapter. In our reading the Lord appears as three visitors in the middle of the day. Though the text alternates between the Divine as singular and plural, the visit necessitates an immediate, humble, and gracious welcome, and more than "a little bread" of hospitality; a wondrous and generous spread in true Middle Eastern fashion.

I have heard of a spirituality program called "Shade and Fresh Water," a reference to the simplest of gifts that are often offered in hospitality in many parts of the world. Hospitality is a key element in thriving churches and a constant topic in books and seminars. The message seems clear—hospitality is the hallmark of followers of Jesus. Yet too often, hospitality focuses on who is bringing snacks for fellowship hour.

Are we not called to a more radical hospitality, an offering of welcome to the stranger, the foreigner, the neighbor who may not grace the doors of a church? Can we keep in mind that the Holy One often appears when we least expect a visit, in the hottest part of the day, in the middle of a phone call, or even on Sunday morning disguised in the ordinary?

Many who read this passage will have in mind the image by Russian iconographer Andrei Rublev called *The Trinity*. It is an amazing representation of the three visitors at a table sharing one cup and pointing to the Holy as mutual relationship.

How do you see yourself in mutual relationship with the Divine as you extend hospitality to all whom you encounter?

Holy One, give us more than open doors and a few cookies on a table. Give us open minds so that we are curious. Give us open hands so that we may serve our neighbors. Give us open eyes so that we may see you in all people, including ourselves. Give us open hearts so we may receive all as a gift. Amen.

When things seem too good to be true, we doubt them; yet often we have no trouble believing that things are as bad as we are told. Sarah laughs an old-age chuckle at the message from the Lord that she will bear a child. From Old Testament Sarah to New Testament elderly Elizabeth and young Mary of Nazareth, God brings good news that seems beyond belief. New life is possible. Believe it. God is able to do something surprising, stunning, awesome, amazing, indeed, "wonderful." Or as *The Message* puts it, "Is anything too hard for God?"

God keeps promises (though sometimes it seems to take a long time); in chapter 21, Sarah bears a son, Isaac, whose name has a root meaning of "to laugh." Maybe the apple does not fall far from the tree.

In one church I served, the Sunday after Easter was Joke-and-Laughter Sunday. The Resurrection was God's biggest surprise, so we needed to laugh and remind ourselves that God is still at work in the world and that the tragedies and difficulties of the world can often have a surprising and startling turn. Laughter helps us to change our perspective, to lighten up so we can see things from a different angle.

I hoped that filling the church with laughter would point us toward God, the One who can do more than we can ask or imagine. (See Ephesians 3:20.) As Sarah moves from a doubting "ha" to joy, delight, and blessing in birthing Isaac, we too can allow laughter to show us God's working in the world.

God of wisdom and delight, fill us with open-eyed wonder to see and believe that you are working for good in our fearful, anxious, war-torn, hungry, and busy world. Keep us noticing signs of birth, and help us tend what is new and fragile to bring it to fullness. Sharpen our wit in the face of evil so that resurrection has the last word. Amen.

Though many psalms speak to our personal situation, most of the book of Psalms entered the canon as the songbook and prayer book of the community. If you imagine a procession of joyful, singing people as they stream into the gates of the Temple, you begin to catch the width and breadth and global nature of this popular psalm, often used in our churches to get us in the spirit of praise.

Psalm 100 rings out with strong verbs—*sing, worship, thank, bless*—that focus our attention and our action toward the God who made us and continues to love us. Our response is to make a joyful noise and live with praise and thanks.

Our new granddaughter was at the dinner table when we sang one of the graces we use before a meal. At the end of the song, she clapped her hands and beamed with joy. We responded with joy, and now we frequently use that same song—though we don't always get applause!

I once heard a story about a child who clapped his hands a lot. Someone asked if his parents were worried that he was being a disruption to others. They responded that they were more worried that he would stop clapping. When have we stopped clapping for the wonders of the world around us or for the kindness of strangers or the blessings of family and friends?

Today's psalm ends with the reminder that the love and faithfulness of God is more than a brief episode or a single occurrence. God goes the distance with us, from the clapping of toddlers to the dancing of the young, to the solos and duets of the adults and the wisdom of the elders. Through all generations, God is with us and offers us plenty of reasons to sing and worship and clap our hands.

Amazing God, send ripples of joy through all our days. Bring smiles and laughter. Birth hope and create opportunity. Make sweet melody in our words, and dance in our lives. Amen.

God makes us right, gives us peace, brings us into grace, and offers us hope for the future. Despite our own best efforts and mighty struggles, God is always before us offering us a hand and inviting us to take the first step toward "the wide open spaces of God's grace and glory" (THE MESSAGE).

A retreat I attended in college used an article from theologian Paul Tillich entitled, "Accept That You Are Accepted." It was a dense paper, but I still remember the title and the relief I felt that I did not have to earn, win, or beg for God's love.

After his theological welcoming statement to begin Chapter 5, Paul addresses the challenges that new Christians are facing. Paul names the suffering, our feeling "hemmed in with troubles" (THE MESSAGE). He does not deny present suffering but looks deeper and longer to see what may emerge as we face the challenges.

Can we get a new perspective on our challenges? Can we see God at work amid difficulties? Can we cultivate patience and deepen trust? Once when I was looking for new ministry, I felt God was opening doors as I had three wonderful possibilities to pursue with new applications. After all three doors closed, I began to question the confidence I had in God when the three had seemed so right and good. My spiritual director reminded me to have hope and take the long view. Sometime later, a new door opened that was an even better fit than the previous opportunities.

Behold, God is able to do a new thing, working through difficulties and troubles and strengthening our character and our hope so we are not disappointed and often are surprised.

Hold me, loving God, and steady me to keep walking with you on the paths you open. Give me patience and persistence in following your call. Amen.

"Christ arrives right on time. . . . He doesn't wait for us to get ready" (THE MESSAGE).

The first movement of the gospel symphony is that God loves us; God makes the first move to invite us and welcome us home. Christ comes to make the invitation clear and personal.

Like the childhood game of hide-and-seek, God yells through Christ, "Ready or not, here I come."

I work for a group of Franciscan Sisters who love Saint Francis, Saint Clare, and Christmas. Most scholars think Saint Francis introduced the first living nativity in the thirteenth century. He chose a cave in Greccio, Italy, gathered a manger with straw and some animals, and told the people to come for a special midnight Mass. The night was lit like day; Francis stood before the people with deep piety and wondrous joy, and the townsfolk witnessed the humble beginnings of a God who bends low to be with them (and also with the shepherds in Bethlehem), people who are totally unprepared for God to appear and to walk with them. What kind of God would choose a manger and come as a baby? Saint Francis loved Christmas and the incredible surprise of the Incarnation, God with us. The Sisters I work with have that same joy of believing they are loved, seeing evidence of God among them, and welcoming everyone with warm hospitality.

The second movement to the symphony of God's love is our response. We receive God's love, and we share God's love. One of the conversions of Saint Francis occurred when he got off his horse to give a leper a coin and ended up embracing the leper. From that experience, Francis shared God's love with all, from Popes to Muslim sultans to the birds of the air. We are loved, and we share love.

Gracious God, thank you for loving me and showing the depth of your love in Christ's life, death, and resurrection. Amen.

These verses offer a simple description of what Jesus does. He teaches, he preaches or proclaims, and he heals. All these flow out of his love of God and his compassion for people. These three roles are central to the life of a pastor and the well-being of the congregation and the surrounding community. The ministry of Jesus in these cities and towns is for those in need, and the need is great.

When I was a young pastor in my first few appointments, I spent a lot of time preparing for worship, preaching, teaching classes, and visiting the sick, but I shied away from any focus on healing during our worship. I had seen some examples on television that seemed inauthentic and overly dramatic, but I knew the stories of Jesus' healing and the community example in James 5:13-14. One Sunday, with some trepidation, I invited folks to come forward for me to anoint them with oil and offer a short prayer. I thought one or two might come. I was surprised to look up from the first person and see a long line. From that experience, whenever we celebrated Holy Communion, we invited people to come for anointing after they received the bread and cup. People in the congregation were instructed in the anointing and brief prayer and assisted me. It became a simple and profoundly moving way to practice the life of the early church. I still remember the simple prayer we often used or paraphrased, "May this oil and these words be a sign to you of our loving God at work in your body, mind, and spirit." We also invited people to come with a prayer request for someone they knew. The congregation in the pews never knew why a person came forward, but they bathed the whole sanctuary in silence and prayer.

God of compassion, speak to the hurts we carry for ourselves, for others, for the world, and for all creation. Amen.

Travel light, but travel with Christ's authority to preach the nearness of the kingdom and to heal the sick and raise the dead. These instructions to the twelve apostles follow the words in chapter 9 about needing more laborers for the compassionate work that Jesus is doing in the villages.

I don't remember the words I said, but nervously standing before the city council I spoke of the need to welcome and organize a place for the day laborers in our community. Some did not even want these workers in town, but plenty of people hired them—though some mistreated the workers or paid them unfairly. A group from the churches and community proposed a third way, and I was the spokesperson. I felt the Spirit's strength and spoke a convincing word. They recently celebrated twenty-five years of a labor center to care for the workers who provide labor for the beautiful hills and gardens of the community.

I imagine the joy of starting the mission described in today's reading is tempered by the words of Jesus that it will not always be easy. Some will not welcome the message of peace and God's love. Some institutions and structures of the status quo will turn you over to the religious authorities and local governments. There will be betrayals and rebellions and misinterpretations of the message of peace.

Many times in the Gospels, the disciples are invited not to be afraid, this time in the words "Do not worry about how you are to speak." From the Incarnation, when God bends low to be with us, to the Resurrection where love is stronger than death, the testimony of scripture is that God not only calls and sends but also is near and gives us the courage to stand firm, to speak of justice, to love kindness, and to abide in God's everlasting embrace.

Walk with us, Sustaining Spirit, as we respond to Christ's call "to kick out the evil spirits and to tenderly care for the bruised and hurt lives" (THE MESSAGE). Amen.

Seeing and Seeking

JUNE 15–21, 2020 • MELISSA TIDWELL

SCRIPTURE OVERVIEW: The story of Isaac and Ishmael resounds through human history down to today. According to Genesis, tensions between the descendants of Isaac and the descendants of Ishmael go back to the lifetime of Abraham himself. These are complex issues, and we are wise to understand them theologically, not just politically. The psalmist calls out to God from a place of desperation, yet even in desperation there is confident hope in God. Paul attacks a theology of "cheap grace" in Romans. Yes, God forgives us; but this does not give us license to do whatever we want. When we are joined to Christ, we die to ourselves. Jesus tells his disciples that following him is a sort of death. We sacrifice a life under our own control yet find something much greater.

QUESTIONS AND SUGGESTIONS FOR REFLECTION

- Read Genesis 21:8-21. Consider an action you regret or wish you'd handled differently. How might a daily examen practice help you correct or move on from your mistakes?
- Read Psalm 86:1-10, 16-17. With whom do you need to reconcile? How might this psalm help you begin that process?
- Read Romans 6:1b-11. Consider the author's question, "What does freedom from sin look like?" Allow the author's suggestions and questions to guide your searching for an answer.
- Read Matthew 10:24-39. How do you see the tension Jesus identifies between inclusion and separation in your Christian life today?

Author on metaphor, music, maps, and zombies; author of *Embodied Light: Advent Reflections on Incarnation*; former editor of *Alive Now* magazine; contributor to Companions in Christ; pastor of Westminster Presbyterian Church, Xenia, Ohio.

The story of Hagar and Ishmael being sent into the wilderness has as its backstory a great moment in biblical history gone sour. Abraham and Sarah have received a powerful, joyful promise that they will have many descendants. But what do you do when a promise from God does not seem to be fulfilled?

For Abraham and Sarah, the answer was to take matters into their own hands. Sarah sends Abraham to her maid Hagar, who bears him a son, Ishmael. This may have seemed a good solution for a while, but when Sarah conceives and bears Isaac, the relationships grow strained. Sarah perceives a rivalry between the boys and demands the first son of Abraham, Hagar's son, be sent away. Abraham's response, to send the two into the desert with scant supplies, seems rushed and cruel. The story carries a certain parallel to the story of how Abraham almost sacrifices his other son, Isaac. These stories raise the question: How do we fix the messes we make? Is repentance only a feeling of being sorry for a mistake, or should it involve action, reparations, and amends?

The spiritual practice of the daily examen helps us ask questions about where we go wrong and how we can move ahead in the knowledge of God's mercy. A simple examen reviews each day and asks, "Where did I see God at work today?" and "Where did I turn from the way of grace today?" The point is not punishment for our flawed humanity but accountability for those places that need a prayer, an apology, a shift in perspective, or a renewed commitment. However you structure your practices, the examen is a tool that can help identify patterns and deepen faithful response.

Examine our hearts, God of mercy. Assure us of your promise of presence and compassion, which we can use to amend our ways and to mend broken hearts. Amen.

If we pivot our focus in this passage from the history of Israel—the formation of the covenant family—to read it as a story about spiritual formation, the symbols and textures emerge in a slightly different way. Words of the senses emerge as significant and interrelated. Seeing and hearing are essential to survival. Hagar places her son under a bush so she does not have to see him die. She weeps, the child weeps, and God hears. God speaks to Hagar and opens her eyes. Once she knows she has been heard, she sees a well of water. Water, a symbol of life, often prompts a reflection on our spiritual journey and how the seeing of God's providential action opens up a reservoir of hope. The scene might move us to ask how being heard in our grief or pain can help us to recognize God nearby. It may also help us remember how grace has provided a means for us to not only survive, but thrive, as God promises Hagar her son will also father a nation.

As you read this passage again, ask yourself how you feel when you are not heard, when you cannot bear to see what is happening before you. Could it be that exclusion or being ignored closes us down, as it did Hagar? Does isolation or discrimination create a kind of tunnel vision where we don't see the wells that are there for our refreshment? What kind of waiting and calling on the Lord feels faithful and healthy in the place where you sojourn? What will you see when you know that your prayers have been heard?

God of the deep, living water, hear the cries of the Hagars, those cast out and struggling to survive. Send us your capacity to hear and to respond so that all your children can flourish. Amen.

When I read psalms I often try to imagine who the narrator is and why he or she composed the psalm. Sometimes I imagine the psalmist as a liturgist, rousing a congregation to praise. Sometimes I imagine the psalmist as a person like me, alone and unable to sleep, conversing with God in the wee hours.

The composer of this psalm draws on lines from many other scriptures; it is less a striking original composition and more a holy mashup. That does not mean that this prayer has less worth; it holds powerful statements that experienced persons of prayer have handed down in their hours of need.

One person I can image praying this psalm is Ishmael, the child rescued by God in the wilderness. Can you imagine this as his lament? The themes of seeing and hearing are present, as is being the child of a servant. In the reference to many nations bowing down to Yahweh, I hear a longing for the healing of the breach between the sons of Abraham. That kind of mutual worship may seem only a dream today, which makes it our lament as well.

The narrator expresses sorrow as well as certainty that God listens to our prayers, including our middle-of-the-night sighs and groans. Lament, doubt, and questioning are healthy and perhaps even necessary elements to forging a lasting faith. But our certainty that our prayers matter to God allows us to lament without bitterness, to lament with humility and power. Our spiritual formation is a long and sometimes circuitous process that seeks to make us into children of God who can pray with power.

Hear our prayer, O Lord, and the prayers of your servants and their children. Heal every division within your house, that all your children will glorify you in spirit and truth. Amen.

We refer to the writings of Paul as epistles—a literary form that uses a letter format. Paul's epistles are meant as teaching tools to be read aloud in the early church. Paul's work masterfully draws on other Greek forms, like the diatribe—a rousing speech that carries a sting of rebuke.

In this epistle, Paul adds a form of writing reminiscent of a legal argument. He begins with an impossible, outrageous question: "Should we continue in sin in order that grace may abound?" Like a great attorney or a teacher in a classroom, Paul wants to raise eyebrows in order to set up his argument. Should we sin intentionally? Well, of course not! But isn't sin inevitable? Well, yes. So how do we resolve this tension?

Now that he has our attention, Paul carefully contrasts two competing forces: sin and grace. He reminds us that death claimed Christ, but resurrection released death's hold. In the same way, sin might have a hold on our humanity; in our baptism we have new life. Can death claim Christ again? Certainly not. Can it claim you again? That question may not be as easy to answer, but it certainly provokes a useful conversation about living the resurrected life. What does freedom from sin look like? How do we know it? Carry this question with you today. Look at the forces of death and life at work in our communities, our churches, even our own bodies. Where do we feel relaxed and confident? Where do we feel anxious? Where do we see God at work? Where is God calling us to be the body of Christ, bringing resurrection power to bear on difficult circumstances?

In you alone, Lord of life, do we live and move and find our being. Empower us to choose the freedom for which you made us so that we can bear witness to your incomparable grace. Amen.

How do we experience resurrection in our earthly life? We often think of our eternal life beginning when our mortal life ends. But Paul's words in Romans 6 call us to walk in newness of life now. How do we do that?

We might begin with Paul's words in verse 9: "We know that Christ, being raised from the dead, will never die again; death no longer has dominion over him." Christ now lives free of death; death has no authority over him, or over us. In a later verse in this chapter, Paul will urge his readers not to let sin have dominion over their mortal bodies.

Dominion is often translated as "lordship" or "sovereignty." Its root is the word from which we get *domestic*, the word for home and family life. So Paul asks us who rules our home. That's a great question, and it extends beyond sin and righteousness, though those are important distinctions. Paul would likely take it further than that, to urge us not to be ruled by fear, but by trust; not by scarcity but by generosity; to live as members of our community, not in a walled-off fortress protecting us from the contagion of otherness.

Paul believes that God made us for freedom. Though doubt and fear will find their way into our hearts, as we grow more experienced in living out our faith, we can have confidence that sin has no dominion over our house. Having died with Christ to sin, we have also been raised with him and can walk in the newness of our resurrected life with joy.

O God, for the newness of life possible in Christ, we give you thanks and praise. Help us to walk in confidence of the freedom we have obtained through your infinite loving-kindness. Amen.

Sometimes reading the lectionary feels like picking up some-one else's library book by mistake and finding familiar words but an unfamiliar story. This week's Gospel lesson is like that, a chunk from the middle of the charge Jesus gives to his disciples as he sends them out to teach and heal in his name. First he recognizes that the process will not be easy: The disciples will experience rejection. They will be accused of working for the enemy, for demons like Beelzebul. But Jesus assures them that truth will endure. The kingdom of heaven is not one of the mystery cults common in the day of Jesus with special knowledge reserved only for the elite. In the kingdom of heaven, what might seem hidden, like the mysterious workings of God, will be revealed.

Jesus assures the disciples that the pain of persecution is balanced by the knowledge that their pain matters to God, who knows even when a sparrow, common as mud, falls to the ground. God is mindful of the sparrows, and God is mindful of us, knowing us well enough to number the hairs on our head.

That kind of knowing and being known might be a blessed antidote to the kind of alienation and loneliness many of us feel. While new forms of media have made us more connected to a constant flow of information, they have disconnected us from certain forms of community. A fast from shallow connection to allow room for deeper connection is a spiritual practice you might try. It could involve unhooking from social media for a week or more, or setting aside sabbath time each week in which you seek less data and more wisdom.

Send us out on your mission, Lord. Send us, in assurance of your loving attention with the good news that your eye is on the sparrows and on us. Amen.

If the beginning of today's Gospel passage offers reassurance amid difficulty, the second half of the passage reads like the fine print on a contract. It reveals some difficult information: The gospel will not always be met with acceptance; sometimes it will be met with conflict.

We usually interpret the word *sword* in this passage not as a physical weapon or threat of violence but as the opposite of harmony. Following Jesus, especially in the context of the early church, means conflict with the larger culture that expects worship of the Roman gods and within the church that contains a volatile mixture of Jewish and Gentile converts. It should always be a bracing note to modern Christians used to being in a majority that non-Jewish Christians are the outsiders to the covenant community but graciously are included by Paul's vision of a community no longer Jew or Greek, but one in Christ.

The rejection we might experience in the United States today—perhaps seeming uncool to our nonchurchy friends—is much less dangerous a situation. Still, we can observe that the love of Jesus does not grant us automatic utopia.

What, then, is our goal? Christ calls us to lose our life in order to gain it; that is, to lose our grip on the self as the center, to let go of the pursuit of personal gain, and to find instead a deeper identity forged in being authentically ourselves in service of the greater good—the kingdom's gain. The meaning felt in such a life is deeper, more profound in its scope. It grants us the relief of losing eternal neediness and gaining the lightness of being found in faithfulness, in relationship, in communion with God's very body.

Jesus, we would be one with you. Teach us daily to long for connection with the parts of your body different from our own, that together we can do your work and love as you love. Amen.

Obedience, Freedom, and Trust

JUNE 22–28, 2020 • BRUCE C. BIRCH

SCRIPTURE OVERVIEW: The passages this week highlight several different themes. Abraham is put to the ultimate test. There is no denying how terrifying God's request must have been, yet Abraham ultimately is commended for his faith. We will not face this same challenge, but are there things dear to our hearts that God is asking us to give up? The psalmist is in deep despair and weary from awaiting God's deliverance, yet even now there is confidence. Paul continues to instruct the Romans about the necessity of living a new life, no longer being slaves to the desires of the flesh. Jesus teaches that when we receive those doing his work, we receive him. When we interact with pastors, missionaries, and even nursery workers, do we treat these servants as Jesus himself?

QUESTIONS AND SUGGESTIONS FOR REFLECTION

- Read Genesis 22:1-14. What has this familiar story meant to you in your faith? How do you embody or struggle against this type of obedience and trust?
- Read Psalm 13. When has your lament allowed you to move from anger with God to praise? How long did that process take?
- Read Romans 6:12-23. How does the definition of death as a life cut off from God rather than a biological reality change your understanding of this passage? How might incorporating this definition of death change your life?
- Read Matthew 10:40-42. Who is in your wider community of witnesses? How does their example prompt you to turn to others in service?

Dean Emeritus and Professor Emeritus of Biblical Theology, Wesley Theological Seminary, Washington, D.C.

This story is one of the most meaningful and challenging stories in the Bible. It has been pondered by theologians, rabbis, pastors, and artists. Throughout this rich tradition, Jewish interpretations often emphasize Abraham while Christian interpretations focus on Isaac.

For both Jews and Christians, Abraham is presented as righteous. But here in Genesis 22, God tests Abraham's righteousness by summoning him to take his only beloved son to a distant mountain and offer him as a sacrifice. Abraham models perfect obedience and has the knife raised when God finally stays his hand and directs him to offer the ram instead. Abraham has trusted in God, and God has not abandoned him. In the long history of persecution that the Jewish community has suffered, such obedience and trust make this story extremely important.

What makes this story difficult is imagining that a loving father could entertain the thought of such a sacrifice or that a loving God would ask it. When we say we cannot imagine this situation, we are not being fully honest. Historically, many parents have allowed their children to be exposed to danger in causes they believed were righteous and in line with God's will. Parents have watched their young men and women go to war to end slavery or to oppose tyrants like Hitler; whole families have participated in the brutal moments of the civil rights and apartheid struggles. The challenge is to prayerfully discern God's will and to willingly see the hand that stays the knife. These are matters of obedience, but also of trust that God will aid our discernment and show us paths into the future.

O Lord, make us attentive to your call and the sacrifices you may require of us. Grant us the trust and discernment to seek alternative paths into the future that you may open for us. Amen.

Christian tradition tends to emphasize the role of Isaac in the story. It is notable that Isaac willingly goes with his father. Even when he notices that there is wood, fire, and knife but no sacrifice, he does not resist or struggle. He seemingly remains willing; the story does not mention a struggle as his father binds him and places him upon the wood of the altar with knife raised.

Christians often interpret Isaac as a prefiguring of Jesus and his willing sacrifice on the cross; we compare Isaac's carrying the wood to Jesus' bearing his own cross to the hill of Calvary. Christian artistic treatments of this story often portray Abraham and Isaac alongside eucharistic symbols representing the sacrifice of body and blood in the elements of bread and wine.

If Abraham models obedience in the life of faith, then Isaac suggests the role of freedom in our faithfulness. Isaac chooses to go willingly to sacrifice himself as Jesus does in the Gospel stories. And Christians are often challenged to freely choose difficult paths as willing disciples for the sake of God's mission to heal a broken world.

Thus, in Abraham and Isaac we see modeled both obedience and freedom in the service of God's will. Both postures are characterized by trust that God's grace accompanies and surrounds our obedience to God's will and our willing choices to serve the divine purpose of God's work in the world. Father and son both live in trust in this story. Whether answering God's call or making ourselves freely available to God's purposes, we trust in God's grace.

Make us willing instruments of your work, O Lord. Open us to possibilities even at the risk of sacrifice in our lives. Give us the courage to trust in your grace. Amen.

How long, O Lord?" Four times in the first two verses the psalmist cries out in distress to the Lord. He is beset by enemies. He feels that God has forgotten him. His language borders on impertinence. He implies that God is not properly coming to his aid. He even dares to instruct God in verse 3, "Consider and answer me, O Lord my God!"

This kind of candid and direct language is characteristic of lament psalms. Laments speak out of distress and anguish, and they lay it all out before the Lord. As modern people of faith, we are not accustomed to praying in this way. But in Psalms, there are more laments than any other type of psalm.

Our initial response might be to suggest that such language is disrespectful of God; but in the Hebrew and its descendant Jewish tradition, lament is an important expression of regard for a God who can receive and encompass even our most distressing experiences and reactions. The psalmist addresses a God willing to take on our distress, our impatience, and even our anger. The best-known lament psalm opens by crying out "My God, my God, why have you forsaken me?" (22:1), which becomes Jesus' cry from the cross.

Laments offer an example of a different and broader concept of prayer. Prayer is not confined to reserved and respectful address of God but includes an opening of heart and soul in honest offering of one's genuine experience before God. Prayers of lament are a vulnerable expression of trust that God cares about all of our lives, even the anguished and distressed aspects of our experience. Reading these laments challenges us to lay it all before God and to trust our entire lives to God in the confidence that God's grace can receive and transform all of our experience.

Receive our prayer, O Lord. Even in our most troubled and impatient times, encompass us in your grace. We trust that your grace will be sufficient for all aspects of our life. Amen.

We have seen the candid laying of distress before the Lord in this psalm of lament; but in the last two verses, the psalm's mood changes entirely. The psalmist may be impatient and anguished, but the psalm ends in praise.

Verses 5 and 6 speak of trust in the Lord. The psalmist calls upon and is confident of God's steadfast love and expresses hope in God's salvation. The psalmist, who seemed impatient in earlier verses, now speaks of a rejoicing heart and dares to sing to the Lord and express gratitude for God's bountiful dealing.

This psalm is not unique. The psalmist's laments give voice to every human distress imaginable, but each lament (except one, Psalm 88) moves from distress to praise. The freedom to lay one's deepest pain and distress before God is linked to the trust that God's grace will prevail. Thus the psalmist moves confidently from distress to praise.

We sometimes mistakenly reserve our praise of God for mountaintop experiences, the moments when all seems well in our lives—there are psalms of thanksgiving for such times. But praise belongs to the whole of life's experience if we trust that God is with us in every moment, the mountaintops and the valleys. Some of the most beautiful expressions of praise and trust are from the laments in the book of Psalms.

Prayer at every moment in our lives is grounded in trust that we can lay before God all of our experience. In every moment that we dare to praise God, God's grace will open new possibilities for our lives.

O God, receive all that we are, all that we experience, and all that we feel. We offer the whole of our lives in confidence that your grace can encompass it all and open new possibilities from every circumstance. For this we praise you, O God. Amen.

The apostle Paul writes to the church in Rome to try to make clear the contrast between a life governed by sin and the offer in Jesus Christ of a life lived in righteousness and grace.

Consider the life governed by sin, or as Paul puts it, enslaved to sin. Passions and desires rule a sinful life and leave one centered on oneself. Such a life leads to impurity and iniquity. Paul has preached that in Christ we are no longer bound by law but freed for grace. But apparently some have taken this to mean that freedom from the law is freedom to sin, to do what we please. No law means no rules and no limits.

But such an embracing of sin as freedom to live life by our passions, desires, and self-indulgences leads to death. Paul comes back to this theme several times in this passage. For Paul, death is more than a biological reality. Death is a life cut off from God, the source of true life and grace.

We live in a world that often celebrates self-indulgence, the freedom to live out of our passions and desires with our own gratification as the goal. Much of the advertising we see appealing to our desire for consumer comforts seems to promote our own self-fulfillment as the ultimate goal of life. But Paul warns that this is a death-dealing way of life and is ultimately governed by sin.

Lead us, O Lord, away from the path of sin that leads to death. Free us from the temptation to live out of our passions and desires and our celebration of our own pleasures as the goal of our lives. Grant us the eyes to see the path of grace offered in the gift of your son, Jesus Christ. Amen.

Paul not only warns the Romans of the dangers of sin. He has more to say about the offer of life governed by the grace of God in Jesus Christ.

We have spoken about Paul's view of being enslaved to sin, which leads to death. The contrast to this pathway is characterized in several key terms in Paul's teaching in today's reading.

Paul calls for followers of Christ to "present your members to God as instruments of righteousness." Righteousness is characterized by obedience to the teachings that brought them to recognize a path to life in Jesus Christ rather than the path to death in sin. The goal is sanctification and eternal life. Sanctification helps us realize all that we were created to be through righteousness. A sanctified life turns outward to live not for self but for God and neighbor. The final verse of this passage is the perfect summary: "For the wages of sin is death, but the free gift of God is eternal life in Christ Jesus our Lord."

Paul's language in Romans can be challenging, but he presents us with a clear alternative to the path lived for self gratification, governed by passions and desires, which is the path of sin and death. The contrasting path of life lived under the gift of God's grace in Jesus Christ is governed by obedience and righteousness, qualities that lead away from self by turning toward God and the grace of God's gift in Jesus Christ. This is the path of life.

God, give us the will to choose the path of life offered in your son Jesus Christ and the courage to turn aside from the path of sin and death that constantly appeals to our passion and self-indulgence. Open before us the gift of grace and righteousness made clear in Jesus Christ so that we may claim the gift of eternal life. Amen.

Today's brief passage from the teachings of Jesus in Matthew's Gospel contains a simple and straightforward message: In the life of discipleship we find fulfillment by turning outward from self and toward others.

When we show hospitality, welcome, and care to others, we participate in a chain of grace that extends back to Jesus and the God who sent him. When we show kindness to others, not in our own name but in the name of a disciple, a righteous person, a prophet, or Jesus himself, then we participate in the chain of grace that leads back to God as the giver of grace.

Our human tendency is to perform acts of kindness and hospitality as occasions to feel good about ourselves or to enhance our self-importance. But Jesus teaches that true discipleship is to do good not on our own behalf but in the name of the wider community of witnesses, who reach out to us and who went before us.

In this brief teaching, Jesus gives special importance to our turning toward "little ones." It is not clear exactly who is meant; perhaps those new in the faith, perhaps those who are more vulnerable in our communities. But the theme is the same: Discipleship calls us to turn outward to others not in our own name but in the name of the wider community of which we are a part.

In accordance with the theme of our texts this week, such a turning requires both obedience and freedom, grounded in our trust in God, who is the source of grace in Jesus Christ.

Lord, help us to turn away from ourselves and join in the service of others as part of a wider community of prophets, righteous witnesses, and disciples who channel your grace into our world. Strengthen us to be obedient to your will, willing to freely choose the path of your grace, and help us to trust that you will travel with us on the path of righteousness. Amen.

God's Call to Love and Our Response

JUNE 29–JULY 5, 2020 • FLORA SLOSSON WUELLNER

SCRIPTURE OVERVIEW: The reading in Genesis transitions our attention from Abraham to his son Isaac. When Isaac comes of age, Abraham sends a servant to find a wife for him. When the servant meets Rebekah, her kind hospitality convinces him that she is the one. Isaac marries her, and the readings in the psalm and Song of Solomon celebrate nuptial love as a symbol of God's love. Paul in Romans reflects on the human condition. We desire to do what is right, but we fall short over and over again. What is the solution? God delivers us through Jesus Christ. In Matthew, Jesus emphasizes his intimate relationship with God and invites all who are weary to enter into Christ's rest.

QUESTIONS AND SUGGESTIONS FOR REFLECTION

- Read Genesis 24:34-38, 42-49, 58-67. Which of these or other biblical stories model for you the relationship between God and humanity?
- Read Song of Solomon 2:8-13. How have you seen God at work in the way loving relationships have transformed you?
- Read Romans 7:15-25a. When have you refused to participate in Communion because you did not feel worthy? How might participating in Communion in times of strife or sin help you be reconciled to God and others?
- Read Matthew 11:16-19, 25-30. The life of faith holds many ironies. How do you hold together the seeming opposites of Jesus' and John's focus in their ministries? of seeking to be yoked to God when your burden is too heavy?

United Church of Christ minister; retreat leader, spiritual director, and author; lives in San Diego, California.

As this week opens near June's end, a traditional month of committed love and marriage, our first four days center on two great love stories in scripture. In this first story, Abraham and his son Isaac are in deep mourning over the death of wife and mother Sarah. Knowing they need comfort and new life, Abraham sends his trusted servant on a long trip to his old home and to Abraham's kinsfolk to ask for a bride for Isaac.

Why is this story told in such minute and fascinating detail throughout a long chapter with repetitions? It is a significant event not only describing the early beginnings of the history of a great nation but also revealing a new, great symbolic concept of how God relates to the human heart and the human community: as marriage partner.

From Genesis to Revelation, scripture uses the marriage commitment as the sacramental symbol of God's pledged love and the pledged response of God's people. This chosen mutuality is expressed by the invitation of God through the prophet Hosea, "You will call me 'my husband,' and no longer call me 'my Baal'" (which means "my master") (Hos. 2:16, ESV).

God offers a radically new concept of marriage based on mutuality rather than barter, ownership, or domination. Through this concept of mutuality, Hosea offers a radical concept of God, who comes to us not as master to submissive servant, demanding fear and obedience, but as bridegroom to bride, lover to the beloved.

God of love, as we turn to you seeking your presence and listening for your guidance, help us to respond to you not in servitude but in committed love and trust. Amen.

How does Rebekah feel about this startling encounter at the well? There, on an ordinary day, taking her ordinary trudge to fill the water jugs, suddenly she meets a travel-stained stranger who hails her as a bride and decks her in jewels. She might feel much the same way Sarah and Abraham felt when in old age they were told by strange travelers that Sarah would be giving birth.

How do we feel when God breaks into our daily routine after long waiting or amid pain and despair? A powerful story in John's Gospel shows us the traumatized disciples in a locked room after Jesus' resurrection. They are grieving his shocking death and the apparent complete failure of his mission. They themselves are in danger. Perhaps, above all, they are consumed with shame that they had abandoned him at Gethsemane. A woman has reported that she has seen him risen from death, but even if true, he will never trust them again. Their life's meaning is destroyed.

Then suddenly he is there with them in spite of the locked door. Instead of reproaches he gives them the Shalom, the peace blessing. He entrusts them with a life purpose. He breathes into them the Holy Spirit, empowering them with the gifts they need for their mission. All this is given before they have even unlocked the door! Now they are no longer drowned in frightened shame. They have become apostles. (See John 20:19-23.)

Though we may have locked ourselves in a dark room of despair, fear, or hopelessness, God is in that dark room with us, breathing on us the Spirit of renewal. Even when trapped in dull, heavy routine, God already waits by the well, offering love and the gifts that love offers.

Open our eyes, God of love, that we may know you are with us wherever we are, that your Spirit enfolds us, and new hope and life is breathed upon us. Amen.

Today's reading tells us of the fulfillment of this courtship, but the story continues in the hearts of lovers. It is the story of God's call and the human heart.

An essential aspect of this love forms the basis of all healthy love. Rebekah is given the right to choose her response. Abraham had allowed for the possibility of her refusal (v. 8). In the cultures at that time and in centuries to come, it is entirely the right of father or guardian to decide about marriage. But Rebekah's parents give her the free choice: "They called to Rebekah, and said to her, 'Will you go with this man?' She said, 'I will.'"

The freedom to choose is the cornerstone of how God relates to us. God has renounced force over us. Otherwise our consent would be without meaning. We are invited to bonding, not bondage. Love that compels is not love. It is violation.

Jesus, who carries God's heart into all his encounters, never forces consent. When the rich young man turns away from discipleship, Jesus grieves but does not pursue him demanding consent. (See Matthew 19:16-22.)

How tragic that through the centuries most branches of the Christian church have violated this spiritual freedom. We have enforced submission, through intense group pressure, fear, guilt, shame, shunning, and sometimes even threat of death. When making any commitment and within ongoing commitments, we can ask ourselves, *Am I given freedom to choose my responses?*

During the Last Supper, Jesus gives the releasing words of love to his disciples: "I do not call you servants . . . I have called you friends" (John 15:15).

Heart of God, may my choices this day rise not from compulsion but from love set free. Amen.

Today we read another love story, symbolically placed in the exact middle of the Protestant Bible with its meaning central to our life with God. This splendid anthem, sometimes called Song of Songs, is sung at weddings and at Passover feasts. When Jesus and his disciples sing a hymn together at the Last Supper (see Matthew 26:30), it may be part of this very song. It is a sacramental hymn that celebrates not only the holiness of married love but also the bonding between God and the human heart, God and the faithful community.

We are so overwhelmed by the sensory splendor of this book's imagery that we can miss the core meaning of how the human being is released and transformed within the radical power of God's love. It is essentially the story of a woman released from the autocratic domination of her older brothers, who had turned her into their vineyard laborer. She is set free by the great love of her future bridegroom, who celebrates her radiant strength as well as her beauty.

Today's verses reveal the longing of her lover seeking the release of his bride. It is also God's longing seeking us behind our walls of entrapment; seeking any open window or lattice of our being; calling for us to arise, come forth, and enter the fruitful new life offered by God's love.

Jesus' passion is transformation within God's love. I used to wonder why his first miracle is the changing of water into wine at the wedding in Cana. Surely a healing would be more appropriate! Then I began to understand the transformation as a sacramental symbol of the new life within God's love. It is thought that the early Christians had a saying about our transformation: "Jesus found us to be water and changed us into wine."

God of our life, we seek you because you first sought us. Help us to hear your call of love, which releases and empowers us. Amen.

Even amid love's fulfillment, the Song of Solomon offers a grave warning: "Catch us the foxes, the little foxes that ruin the vineyards" (2:15). Sometimes "the little foxes" erode our relationships, but often our vineyards of love are destroyed by a toxic blight. In today's passage, Paul reveals the great conflicts within us that eclipse the first bright vision of our relationship with others and with God. Paul confesses that he often feels helpless to change the destructiveness: "I can will what is right, but I cannot do it." Any of us who have ever felt trapped by fear, anger, despair, or addiction understand this anguish.

But there is a choice within this inner entrapment: We can choose to let our weakness drive us away from God because we feel so unworthy, or we can let that very weakness draw us much closer to God.

Too often, Christians turn away from partaking of the Eucharist, feeling that they will offend God's holiness. Only when they are free of sin do they dare to come to God's table. Did not Jesus tell those who came to the altar bringing a gift that they should first go and be reconciled to the neighbor? (See Matthew 5:23-24.) But when we bring a gift to God or the church, we are reminded that the real gift to God is love for one another. When we approach God in pain, need, or conflict, we are never turned away.

Sometimes the liturgical call to Communion is conditional. As pastor I used the traditional invitation: "You who are in love and charity with your neighbor and intend to lead a new life . . . draw near. . . ." Now I regret this. The less we are able to love, the less we feel able even to intend a new life; we should run, not walk to God's table, God's heart, which offers healing for us all.

Great Healer, at the very moment I feel weakest and unworthy, help me to give myself to you more fully. Amen.

There is a growing rift between Jesus and his beloved cousin John who is the first to hail Jesus as Messiah, baptizes him, and sets his feet on the path of ministry. It is not a rift of love but a vast difference in their form of ministry. John has withdrawn into the wilderness, living an ascetic, fasting way of life. His guidance to others is a stern "Repent!" "Change your ways!" "Beware the wrath to come!"

He had expected Jesus to minister in the same way. At first Jesus makes repentance his main focus. (See Matthew 3:2.) But his approach changes. He mingles with people in the villages and cities, reaches out, heals, comforts, transforms, feasts, and fellowships with "sinners." He too calls for change but within God's love, not wrath. This troubles John. He sends his disciples to ask Jesus why he is not fasting the way John does. In his reply, Jesus for the first time speaks of himself as the "bridegroom," implying that joyful abundant love and celebration is one of the main signs of a transformed life. (See Matthew 9:14-15.)

Now in prison, John has serious doubts. Is Jesus really the Messiah after all? Jesus simply reports the facts: the blind see, the deaf hear, the poor are comforted. The realm of God is at work.

Then in today's reading, Jesus reflects on the irony that John is criticized for his fasting while Jesus is criticized for feasting with outcasts.

The love of God calls us to feast with the "bridegroom" *and* to welcome the outcast into that feasting. We are called to dance with "sinners" *and* weep for their pain. These are not opposites; they are as one in the heart and realm of God.

God of love, help us this day to see through your eyes the light and the dark around us, and to hear your call to dance and also to heal. Amen.

As we read these beautiful verses we note a paradox. We are called to God when we feel weary and burdened but then are invited to put on a yoke. How will that end our weariness or lift our burden? Are we to submissively plow the field while God, the driver, shouts orders?

But a yoke usually implies not one but two working animals, a team. A marriage partner may be called a "yokefellow," a loved spouse bonded with us for the tasks of everyday life. God, who invites us as team partner, is already under the yoke. Usually a stronger is paired with a less powerful worker to share its strength and take the fuller brunt of the pull. There is no such thing as a life devoid of all burdens, but now the load is much lighter because the incarnate God carries them with us through each day's need.

Thus yoked together, we do indeed learn of our strong partner as friend and lover. Together we walk the walk, pull together, breathe together, lie down in green pastures together. And in that bonding we are transformed.

The verse in Hosea, quoted in this week's first reflection, in which the husband asks his wife no longer to call him *master*, but *husband*, continues in words of such profound love that they could be included in a marriage service, spouse to spouse. They are the voice of God directly to our hearts.

"I will make you lie down in safety. I will take you . . . forever; I will take you . . . in righteousness, in justice, in steadfast love and in mercy. I will take you . . . in faithfulness; and you shall know the Lord" (Hos. 2:18-20).

Help us this day to learn of you, God of our life, walking with us as eternal spouse and partner, yoked in love forever. Amen.

Remembering and Pondering—Then and Now

JULY 6–12, 2020 • W. PAUL JONES

SCRIPTURE OVERVIEW: Even great people in the faith have moments of imperfection. Not all biblical stories are biblical examples. Jacob should have fed his brother out of concern, but he takes advantage of the situation and robs Esau of his birthright. The psalmist asks the Lord to show him how to live. God's word is a lamp to his feet and a light to his path. Paul in Romans contrasts the life of the flesh and the life in the Spirit. Without the power of God, we are doomed to repeat our mistakes in the flesh; but the Spirit sets us free. Jesus reminds us in Matthew that the effectiveness of the gospel is not based on our efforts. We sow the seed, but we cannot control whether it takes root.

QUESTIONS AND SUGGESTIONS FOR REFLECTION

- Read Genesis 25:19-34. How do you experience God's "nevertheless"—God's grace—as you work through the baggage of your birthright?
- Read Isaiah 55:10-13. How might experiencing moments as if for the last time bring the joy of a first-time experience?
- Read Romans 8:1-11. In learning what spiritual practices strengthen you, what practices did you try that did not work? Now that you know what works, how might working on practices you once found unhelpful grow your faith?
- Read Matthew 13:1-9, 18-23. In what unexpected place might you sow seeds of God's love?

Ordained a United Methodist, now a Roman Catholic priest, Trappist Family Brother, and Resident Director of the Hermitage Spiritual Retreat Center on Lake Pomme de Terre in the Ozarks of southern Missouri; author of numerous articles and fourteen books.

Rebekah and Isaac were in love, but she was barren. Yet she was not unique; throughout scripture, key roles are played by women who are barren—Hannah the mother of Samuel the prophet, the "nameless" mother of Samson the judge, and Elizabeth, the mother of John the Baptist. Theologically, this phenomenon indicates that God can use us as God sees fit, despite any of the ways in which we might seem barren.

Every two years at our monastery, the abbot of our Mother House makes a "Visitation," working and praying alongside us and interviewing each of us privately. A "Visitation Card"—like a report card or an annual review—is the frightening result.

Scripture serves as a visitation card for all of us, and the prophets are hard graders. Do any of us make the honor roll? "Be ye therefore perfect," instructs Jesus (Matt. 5:48, KJV). In fact, "When you have done all that is commanded you, say, 'We are unworthy servants; we have only done what was our duty'" (Luke 17:10, RSV). I can manage perfection for perhaps a few hours on a sunny day.

Christianity is about the barren yet fruitful; the lost yet found; fallen yet raised; tainted yet cleansed; sick yet healed; arrogant yet humbled; guilty yet forgiven; unlovable yet loved. Grace is amazing, offered not as a "because" but as a "nevertheless." As John insists, it is "not that we loved God but that [God] loved us" (1 John 4:10). Strangely, our major undoing is the difficulty we have in accepting gifts.

On this day in 1415, John Huss was burned at the stake for his prophetic preaching.

Lord, I feel barren in speaking out for you if it upsets even one person even a little. Will you speak through me? Amen.

At the monastery, we pray all 150 psalms in a two-week cycle because they were Jesus' hymnbook. Today's psalm is terribly repetitious: Various phrases keep saying the same thing—be obedient, walk in God's ways, keep God's commandments. Yet, on another level, such repetition is like a rosary that keeps repeating, "Blessed is the fruit of thy womb Jesus." Russian spirituality features a repetition of the Jesus Prayer (e.g. "Lord, have mercy on me") at least a thousand times a day. Many of us have experienced hearing a song in the morning that we are unable to shake out of our minds as it continues to play itself over and over. "Pray without ceasing," instructs Paul (1 Thess. 5:17). But how is that possible? By choosing a sentence, phrase, or even a word—a mantra—and repeating it in the morning until it is sufficiently installed so that it echoes on its own all day, almost impossible to stop.

For this spiritual discipline, it is wise to choose a mantra that expresses best what one most urgently needs to learn if one's life is to be changed. Amid my anxieties, doubts, and wavering, I know what I most need to repeat, until belief crowds out unbelief, that nothing "will be able to separate us from the love of God in Christ Jesus our Lord" (Rom. 8:39). One's mantra is a discipline that not only can evoke God's constant presence but also aid in contemplation for halting our minds from taking weedy paths of diversion.

On this day in 1591, Ralph Milner, an elderly illiterate English farmer, was executed. Earlier, after receiving Holy Communion for the first time, he felt called to shepherd priests illegally from place to place to provide the Eucharist for others.

Lord, is Communion really that meaningful for me? Must you ask? Amen.

One of the saddest sins is boredom—taking things for granted. The cliché phrases are familiar: *If you've seen one sunset, you have seen them all. Ocean, flowers, whatever. Been there, done that. Nothing new under the sun.*

Six months ago a dear friend was told he had six months to live. We walked his terminal time together. Last week he died. We learned that experiencing things as if for the last time brings the gift of experiencing them as if for the first time. He died gratefully. Sickness, disappointment, and tragedy can trigger such mindfulness. Even aging can. The idea that one might never again see one's spouse, embrace one's children, or encounter a blooming dogwood tree—such shadows can transfigure the way we experience the world.

In today's scripture we encounter the prophet Second Isaiah, who has declared Israel's sinfulness to be terminal with a death-like exile awaiting. Yet he promises that this can bring them to encounter God's Word like rain and snow nourishing the earth with joy, birthing such peace that the mountains shall break into singing and the trees shall clap their hands.

This promise by God is not only of what shall be but also ;of what is now. Shaken by "lastness" into "firstness," we are birthed with childlike wonder. Eyes opened, ears attuned, touch sensitized, taste honed, and smell alert to the aroma of God. The hymn says it well: "Morning has broken like the first morning" that "Eden saw play!" (UMH, no. 145). Blackbirds, spring rain, dew, sunlight—now, again, still, always.

On this day in 1822, Percy Bysshe Shelley, brilliant, adventuresome, carefree, lyric poet, died at age thirty in a sailing accident.

O Holy Spirit, how can it be that a poet so much in love with your creation didn't suspect that it was you who was stirring the sails of his restless soul? Ignite us, as you did him, to the "Skylark" "Cloud," "Night," and "West Wind." Amen.

There is something disconcerting about how many persons in scripture play favorites, even God. "Isaac loved Esau . . . but Rebekah loved Jacob." God "had regard for Abel and his offering, but for Cain and his offering he had no regard" (Gen. 4:4-5). God chose David and rejected Saul. (See 1 Samuel 16:1.) God loved Israel more than all other nations, choosing them as God's "treasured possession" (Deut. 7:6).

Today's scripture deals with birthrights, the privileges bequeathed to the favored firstborn son and unavailable to all other children. Today we have something like birthrights—the baggage we carry from our relationship with our parents—and many of us receive a negative one. We dwell on a negative past in which we were unfavored or felt unwanted.

My negative birthright became clear the day I realized that all I ever wanted was to hear my mother say, "Paul, I love you." She couldn't say those words because all she really wanted was to hear the same phrase from her father, who in turn couldn't because of his negative birthright . . . and the pattern continues. We carry on the sins of our ancestors for generations.

My reconciliation with my mother came only when I could bury a note in her grave: "All we both ever wanted was to be loved. Mom, I love you." Another piece of reconciliation came through my five daughters. A precious gift came when one of them said, "Dad, you have always made each of us feel as if we were your favorite." And yet such moments are only a beginning, for it is God's love that we really need. With God, each of us is the one for whom Christ died.

On this day in 1977, Alice Paul, known for courageously authoring the Equal Rights Amendment to guarantee equality for women, died.

God, given your inclusive love, why is it so hard for us to treat as equals those different from ourselves? Forgive us. Amen.

I find it meaningful to rename some of Jesus' parables from the perspective of the giver rather than the recipient. It helps me to focus on the grace in each parable rather than works. Thus a parable is not so much about a "Prodigal Son" as about God as a "Yearning Father." Another is not so much the "Lost Sheep" as the "Passionate Shepherd." And not the "Lost Coin" but God as the "Searching Widow." Even the "Good Samaritan," already named after the giver of grace, gains added poignancy as "The Rejected Foreigner Who Cares."

So let us consider today's parable as that of the "The Extravagant Sower." The issue involved erupted for me with the new translation of the Catholic Sacramentary. At the key point in the Eucharist, the new translation reads, "This is the chalice of my blood, which will be poured out for you and for many." I yearned for the former words—that Christ's sacrificial act was "for all." In one sense, both translations are right, but which is primal—the offer or the reception, the God who says "yes" or those of us who insist on saying "no"?

Thus the focus of today's parable could be on those who are good soil, but it is far more powerful to focus on God as so hopefully in love with all of us that God extravagantly throws seed everywhere—behind the nightclub dumpsters, in the smelly landfills, on the plastic-strewn seashores—wherever there might be someone passing by. Our hope is in such a God who refuses to be limited to sowing where the investment possibilities are most promising.

On this day in 1962, the "miracle" of worldwide television transmission occurred.

Lord, we are now gifted with the power to sow truth everywhere, yet we contaminate the truth with mindless trivia. Forgive us when we seek society's noisiness instead of the quiet of your incessant presence. Amen.

The discovery of the Myers-Briggs Personality Indicator was significant for my teaching career. It provided a typology for distinguishing diverse personalities based on the polarities of introversion/extroversion, intuition/sensing, thinking/feeling, and judging/perceiving. People learn differently, experience differently—are different. For example, introverts and extroverts gain energy in opposite ways. After a day's work, the introvert needs solitary quietness, while the extrovert suggests calling friends and "going out."

Such diversity of personalities runs throughout scripture. Esau is "a man of the field," but Jacob is a "quiet man" (Gen. 25:27). The reflective Mary listens at Jesus' feet while the frenetic Martha seeks to serve from the kitchen. Peter is a doer; John a contemplative. Thus their theologies and spiritualities differ. Moses perceives God in historical events, while Elijah hears God as the whisper of "a still small voice" (1 Kings 19:12, KJV).

In today's reading, Paul declares that "fullness of life" necessitates freedom from requirements ("law") that we cannot meet. Often these are spiritual disciplines that are incompatible with who we are. When they do not work for us, we feel like a failure and we give up. The spiritual writings of John of the Cross are vastly different from those of Brother Lawrence.

Yet after finding the spirituality that fits, there comes a point when ongoing spiritual growth entails walking into one's shadow—the undeveloped side of one's personality. Thus, as an extrovert, I came to need the "forced feeding" of an introvert monastery.

On this day in 547, Saint Benedict died. He became the father of western monasticism by establishing a Rule that integrated spiritual diversity.

Lord, dare I live intentionally by creating a "rule" of which Jesus would be proud? Amen.

The book of Romans impulsed Martin Luther to reform the church. John Wesley was reading Luther's commentary on Romans when his heart was "strangely warmed." In today's reading, Paul struggles with the perennial conundrum—how Jesus, executed as a failure, can redeem the world. In it we find at least twelve analogies. Which are helpful for you?

1. In law, one must pay the penalty for crime, in our case the death penalty. Jesus paid it. Case dismissed.
2. In sacrifice, we are to offer our best to God. The "sacrificial lamb" is our best.
3. We are unable to act as we want, so Christ sends the Holy Spirit to refashion our souls into God's temple, enabling us to will and to do.
4. Our primal craving is to be loved, and no greater love is there than a God who suffers and dies for us.
5. The character of God is revealed in the actions of Jesus.
6. In banking terms, we are born with a deficit account. Jesus cancels our debt.
7. It is helpful to know someone who knows someone. Jesus knows *the* One.
8. As in the Old Testament Passover, Jesus' death is the passover lamb for us.
9. Predestination means that our reconciliation is a gift and not an achievement.
10. God is not the cause of suffering but the "fellow sufferer" with us.
11. Willingness to give oneself for another exemplifies the heart of God's marriage vows with us.
12. Adoptions are expensive. Jesus paid for ours.

Today we honor a woman named Veronica, who risked her life by wiping Jesus' face. His imprint marked her veil.

Lord, compassion marks your image on my soul. Amen.

God Is at Work—Behind the Scenes

JULY 13–19, 2020 • JAN JOHNSON

SCRIPTURE OVERVIEW: As God promised land and descendants to Abraham, in the reading from Genesis God confirms these same promises to Abraham's grandson Jacob. The psalmist meditates on and takes comfort in the fact that God knows everything and is everywhere. He asks God to search his heart and reveal if there are sins away from which he needs to turn. The Romans passage continues Paul's reflection on the life in the Spirit. Because we are children of God, we cry out with confidence that God will hear and answer. Jesus tells a parable in Matthew concerning the final judgment. He says that the wicked will be taken first, then the righteous will be gathered together.

QUESTIONS AND SUGGESTIONS FOR REFLECTION

- Read Genesis 28:10-19a. When has God quietly been at work in your life? How do these experiences help you recognize God's presence with you in ordinary days?
- Read Psalm 139:1-12, 23-24. God already knows us completely. What is holding you back from inviting God to search your heart?
- Read Romans 8:12-25. Consider the ways you already resemble God. In what ways to you need or wish to be transformed to resemble God more fully?
- Read Matthew 13:24-30, 36-43. Reflect on a time when you were frustrated by God's inaction in the face of injustice. In hindsight, how was God at work?

Author of 23 books, including *Meeting God in Scripture* and *When the Soul Listens*; retreat teacher; spiritual director.

Jacob has a strange and beautiful dream of angels going up and down a ladder reaching to heaven. Neither he nor anyone else had seen this when awake. The dream reveals that in reality, he has ready access to the heavenly places. The barriers are not there.

This idea of open access to the unseen world comes to Jacob in a dream. Amid this scene comes understanding from God that the land before Jacob will be inhabited by a group of people who will be blessed and be a blessing to the people around them, even to the entire earth. So tremendous and breathtaking is this dream that Jacob knows it has to be from God. God eagerly wants to be with Jacob and take care of him, no matter where he goes. Jacob understands that he is at the gate of heaven in the middle of a very ordinary place.

God is always at work but often behind the scenes. Often we cannot comprehend until after the fact that the wonderful things that happen to us are God's doing. Then we think, *Surely the Lord is at work, but I didn't know it!*

Maybe that surprises us because we think God would announce this divine presence with great fanfare. But God is not a show-off; wise Isaiah says, "Truly, you are a God who hides himself, O God of Israel, the Savior" (Isa. 45:15).

God may have something important to communicate to us today, even if it isn't new information. (Jacob's grandfather Abraham receives the same basic information that Jacob does.) God's word for us is often simple and wonderful: "Know that I am with you and will keep you wherever you go." If that's what you need to hear today, do not doubt that God is interested in communicating that to you.

Suggestion for Meditation: Be alert for how God is acting behind the scenes today to guide you, comfort you, and help you move forward. Ask God to show you!

I remember a television drama in which a young man explained to his family why he liked a certain woman whom they did not like. He said, "Very few people really understand me, but she truly 'gets' me." Many of us feel as though few people "get"—understand and value—us. It's a wonderful feeling to be known and have someone who knows us think we're terrific. The psalmist says something similar about God: There isn't one thing about me that God doesn't "get." There isn't one piece of our logic that God does not understand.

God knows what to expect from us. Think of how you grin when you know someone so well that when you overhear them in a conversation you already know what they're going to say next. God is like that with us. "Even before a word is on my tongue, O LORD, you know it completely." That last phrase, "you know it completely," may refer to how God not only knows what we're about to say but also knows the motives and perhaps the pain behind it. No one on earth knows us like that. Because no human knows us like that, we don't really comprehend God's understanding of us. We haven't experienced it here on earth. So we're amazed and almost puzzled. "Such knowledge is too wonderful for me; it is so high that I cannot attain it." It makes perfect sense that we don't grasp this concept. Who am I to think I can understand God? God works behind the scenes, within the layers of our reality, days in advance of us and yet resounding in words said to us yesterday.

Suggestion for Meditation: Picture the phrase "lay your hand upon me." Is it a hand of comfort or a hand of caution or simply a hand of caring?

When I was ten, I took swimming lessons at the YWCA. On the day of the final session when parents came to watch, my dad's car broke down in the parking lot of the Y. He needed to stay with the car to wait for help to come, so I knew he wouldn't be watching me from behind the glass with the other parents. I was a little overwhelmed by the deep water maneuvers, but I still did my best.

Much to my surprise, my dad later described to me everything I did. He had run up and down the stairs between the parking lot and the viewing mezzanine many times so that he would not miss seeing my performance. He was there and he was smiling, but I didn't know it.

In the same way, even when we do not know it, God is with us and is eager to be with us. We cannot chase away God as we may have chased away others. God remains a steady presence, almost like the beating of our heart. Scripture calls God's love *steadfast*—unwavering and unfailing. God sticks with us, no matter what.

We live a with-God life, and the more we embrace this reality, the more confidence in God—that is, faith—we will have in everyday life. In that confidence, we practice awareness of God's presence and let God guide us as never before. We can sense God's hand leading us in the most ordinary things and holding us no matter what.

Thank you, God, for never leaving me or letting go of me. I am never truly alone. Help me to sense your guiding hand leading me forward, and help me to be eager to go with you. Amen.

If someone comes to our house with a search warrant, we may feel guarded. Can we trust this person to be fair? What if they've fabricated evidence? Certainly we don't trust the person to be kind.

Think of how much the psalmist must trust God to invite God to search his heart! With whom would we be willing to have our deepest motives revealed, to be tested to see if any bit of sharp or cutting thought existed? The psalmist must trust that God does not try to catch us doing something wrong or seek to "teach us a lesson." He must feel completely safe with God.

Many of us don't feel safe with God, especially if we've experienced a lot of darkness. But God is a creator of light, and God works behind the scenes to help us shed darkness.

A friend once told me that God had put him out on a ledge and made him dangle there in panic. My other friend turned to him and said, "Don't think anything bad about God" as if God would punish him for saying or even thinking such a thing about God. God is good and God is love—patient and kind, firm in truth but doing what is best for us. As we settle into that realization, we can trust God enough to invite God to examine us and learn what's really going on below the surface.

Best of all, the search ends with God guiding us in the way forward—"the way everlasting"—from darkness to light. If something is found to be wrong or if nothing is found to be wrong, there's a next step toward moving into union with God.

Prayer Suggestion: Invite God to search you and know you, to sift your motives and thoughts. If that's too scary, ask God to help you trust God enough to be willing to allow God to search your heart in the future.

At the church I grew up in, I was as likely to be called "Kay" (my mother's name) as to be called by my own name. I resemble my mother with our dark hair, but not so much in other ways. She was outgoing and kind; I was a self-conscious, self-absorbed teen. I answered when church members called me "Kay" because my mother cast a long, positive shadow, which I was happy to live in. They recognized me as Kay's daughter because I resembled her.

Now and then we are noted as "children of God" because some glimmer of God's goodness makes its way through us, and we resemble God for a minute or two. We're glad to see ourselves as God's children because God makes a good parent. As God's children, we can be led by the Spirit of God and can put to death our self-absorbed tendencies to live according to the flesh.

Being specially chosen by God as children, we can move away from our fears and learn to love well. Once again, God works behind the scenes to make us joint heirs with Christ so that we receive the flow of goodness from God. We learn to trust in what we cannot see rather than in what everyone else says.

That flow of God's goodness can transform us into the person we've always wished we might become. We learn to wait on God with patience because the transformation into the "freedom of the glory of the children of God" is slow. In fact, it's normally so gradual that we don't notice it; but the people who live with us may well notice the changes in us that indicate our growing oneness with God.

Thank you, God, for the Spirit that takes away fear and helps us cry out, "Abba! Father!" because we are children of God. Thank you for creating us as coworkers with Christ, who suffer with and are lifted up with him. Amen.

When I work hard to do something right and it gets spoiled, I feel surprised at first, then perturbed, and finally sad. The householder-master in this parable responds to the malevolent tampering with his hard work of sowing good seed with an objective response: "Somebody else did this." I am like the servants in the story: Let me pull those weeds. Let me fix this now. Isn't that how most of us would respond?

But the householder does nothing. At least that's how it appears. He delays the clean-up. We often see God this way, as one who doesn't care if justice is done or one who tolerates evil to avoid the trouble of confrontation. We wonder if God likes the troublemakers better.

Our problem with God is that God is patient and we are not. God waits and has a good reason to wait. God's highest concern is not for removing the weeds but for protecting the wheat at all costs. Uprooting the weeds would cost the life of some of the wheat. What seems like inaction is God acting wisely in the interest of the ones who are productive and will grow into what they were created to be. In this way God seems to be "flying under the radar," doing magnificent work that isn't always recognized.

Doing something makes me feel better. But waiting on God isn't doing nothing. Waiting can mean that we are discerning the situation, asking God what our part is and to nudge us when the timing is right. Waiting on God can be quite active—full of conversation and concern for others. Especially in the Psalms, the words *wait* and *hope* appear together (39:7; 62:5; 130:5) because they are two parts of the same thing. Sometimes hope looks like expectant waiting.

Patient God, when a quick fix will not solve my problems, help me to wait patiently for solutions by asking you for next steps and listening for your nudges of direction. Amen.

Imagine a world leader who delivers a speech that includes a story that doesn't make a lot of sense to listeners. Then behind closed doors comes the meeting of the cabinet or diplomats or generals who ask the leader, "What did you really mean?"

That's how it is with the disciples. They are Jesus' coworkers in building a beloved community, the family of God on this earth. "I'm the householder," Jesus implies. "While I—even we—plant seeds all over the territory, the opposing side is doing the same. For now, I'm not going to call them out, even though you may want me to do so" (AP).

Imagine the disciples' agitation. If they are like most of us, they already have a list of names of people who aren't authentic, genuine, bona fide followers of Christ. What about these "weed people?" Does it help them to hear Jesus say that he will send his angels to collect out of his kingdom all causes of sin and all evildoers at the right time? All will be taken care of. Everyone will be known by the fruit they produce—love, joy, and peace or selfishness, crabbiness, and chaos. (See Galatians 5:22.)

In the meantime, the "wheat" will grow steadily toward an enormous benefit to others. In fact, those in right relationship to Jesus will come to shine "like the sun in the kingdom of their Father." As always, God will continue to work behind the scenes as the wheat matures and grows. The impatience of the rest of us can be put on hold as God keeps working.

O God, I trust you to do the work of separating the wheat from the weeds. Keep me from harming any wheat, but help me to nurture others in their growth in you. Amen.

Faithfulness, Grace, and Growth

JULY 20–26, 2020 • ROBERT MORRIS

SCRIPTURE OVERVIEW: Jacob has tricked his brother out of his birthright and has tricked his blind father into blessing him instead of his older brother. This week the trickster is tricked, and his desire to marry Rachel will cost him dearly. The psalmist reflects on the faithfulness of God. God has made a covenant with Abraham, Isaac, and Jacob, and the author is confident that God will honor that covenant. Paul builds upon his argument to the Romans about the power of the Spirit. The Spirit helps us pray to connect with God, and nothing can separate us from the love of God. Jesus continues to teach about the kingdom of God using parables. Finding our way into the kingdom is worth far more than anything else.

QUESTIONS AND SUGGESTIONS FOR REFLECTION

- Read Genesis 29:15-28. How does a wise faith help you discern between differing loves?
- Read Psalm 105:1-11, 45b. How is your faith journey an extension of God's covenants with Abraham, Isaac, and Jacob?
- Read Romans 8:26-39. How have you experienced prayer as an opening of yourself to God's Spirit rather than a petition for yourself or others?
- Read Matthew 13:31-33, 44-52. How are you growing in Christ? If your faith has become stagnant, what "sorting" might help you to continue to grow toward proficiency in being Christlike?

Episcopal priest, spiritual director, and founder of Interweave, an ecumenical and interfaith adult education ministry; regular contributor to *Weavings*; author of three books: *Wrestling with Grace, Provocative Grace,* and *Suffering and the Courage of God.*

The saga of Jacob, Laban, and Laban's daughters revels in a clash of wits. Laban, with possible collusion by the two sisters, outwits Jacob (who has just outwitted his brother Esau).

Jacob's heart is so captured by the beautiful Rachel that he agrees to work seven years to win her hand. Laban's love, however, is centered on the well-being of both his daughters. So the bride Jacob assumes is Rachel turns out to be her elder sister, Leah. Just as Jacob had dressed as Esau to deceive Isaac, so Leah dressed as Rachel, the rabbis say.

"That's just the way we do things around here," Laban seems to explain. Jacob the deceiver has been outfoxed. Yet Jacob's love is so great that he works another seven years for the hand of Rachel, whom the rabbis imagine helped her sister Leah with the disguise.

Thus cleverness serves conflicting loves. Jacob loves Rachel; Laban loves his daughters; Rachel loves her father and her sister. How can all of these different and possibly conflicting loves come to a successful conclusion? Jacob will continue to be challenged to use his wits to love his newly formed family.

Likewise, our lives are filled with conflicts between legitimate but differing loves. How do we allot time and energy between spouse and children, family and career, personal commitments and the church? These conflicts all challenge us to develop skill and discernment in giving each love its rightful due. Our love must become "wise as serpents" (Matt. 10:16)—ever more deft and fair. Jesus cautions us to let such wisdom always be in the service of *agape*—loving consideration of the other.

Lord, grant me the wisdom to love wisely and well. Amen.

We've all known those who say they love the "whole human race" but seem to have difficulty interacting with individuals in front of them. Enduring relationships are specific, relational, and intentional.

The God who loves the world gets specific about relationships by entering into covenants with individuals and nations to work for the well-being of all humanity. Psalm 105 is one of many psalms that celebrate God's covenant with Israel through Abraham, Isaac, and Jacob—a covenant that Paul insists includes any who "share the faith of Abraham" (Rom. 4:16).

As Christians, we understand God's choosing of Israel as neither arbitrary favoritism nor the disenfranchising of the world. Rather, it is part of the divine strategy for the salvation of the world. God chooses Abraham and his clan as a pilot project for all humanity, a "light to the nations" (Isa. 49:6) to show a real people struggling to grow into the love, justice, mercy, and kindness God knows we all need to survive and thrive.

God knows and chooses all of us to be included in a covenant designed to bring blessing to the world. God has a destiny for us if we will cooperate with it. As Israel's destiny was to learn how to walk God's path of human flourishing, so our destiny is to learn the steps that help us grow as reflections of God's character revealed in Christ. As the acorn grows into the oak, so we are called to the fullness of Christ.

Destiny is not fate, but a destination to walk toward. Each of us will bring into play our different abilities and choices as we move toward the goal. As we face difficult choices, just as Israel did, even our distresses help us find blessing and help.

Your special love for me, O God, is exactly what you offer to all you love. Help me see everyone I meet with your eye of love. Amen.

You're reading the paper or watching TV. You see or read something terrible that lands with an impact. You give a deep sigh; you groan or grieve inside yourself. Paul tells us that when we groan like that, we may actually be participating in the Spirit's groaning over sin and evil in the world, for the Spirit prays for us in "sighs too deep for words." Or perhaps you're dealing with a really frustrating situation, and you go to bed discouraged but having turned over your situation to God. The next morning you feel renewed resilience, maybe even a new idea. "The Spirit helps us in our weakness," declares Paul.

Prayer begins in the heart of God, not with us. When we truly pray, the wings of our prayers catch the wind of the Spirit's flow, filled with God's desires for the world. We join Christ's constant intercession for humanity.

Paul speaks frankly about the fact that we don't really know how to pray "as we ought." So why pray? Regular prayer, even in our ignorance, can open us to those deeper sighs and yearnings that get buried in our daily busyness.

Prayer serves to put us in the flow of the Spirit, not to find satisfaction for our superficial desires. Prayer is time with God, openness to God, a time for relationship, a regular connection. Spirit-life flows from that relationship.

As we bring our gratitude, thanksgiving, honest confession of our needs, and frank assessment of both our mistakes and our successes into the flow, the Spirit can begin to shape our desires for ourselves and the world. God can awaken and stir up yearnings for goodness and justice, humility and courage, patience and self-control, kindness and compassion, which are the many faces of love and the many faces of Christ.

Help my prayers catch the wind of your Spirit, O God. Amen.

There's a big difference between "all things work together for good for those who love God" and "in everything God works for good with those who love him" (rsv). The Greek text can mean either. Is everything willed by an all-controlling God? Or does God weave meaning, purpose, and blessing even out of mistakes and random accidents?

Whatever the answer, we can claim this promise: God's Spirit hovers within every event, working "for us," to shape Christ in us amid any circumstance. Claiming God as a companion on the journey can make the difference between feeling trapped by circumstances and being challenged by them. Trapped, our imagination easily closes down and our inventiveness can be stunted. Faced with a challenge, however, a cleverness may awaken that shows us new ways to cope.

On a deeper level, difficulty can strengthen and open us to the God who reaches out to "justify" us and embraces us in a love that claims us as we are—warts, wonders, and all. This same divine love then wants to sanctify us, to link every thought and deed to the flow of the Spirit. The result of both of these activities will be to "glorify" us, to make us "partakers of the divine nature" (2 Pet. 1:4, rsv), fully able to breathe the atmosphere of heaven.

Our personal ups and downs, likes and dislikes, loves and hates, careers and pastimes are part of a much bigger story. God wants to make us partners in God's own purposes for the world. Our first taste of salvation is the beginning of a lifelong training in service. The story is not about us; we are about the larger story of God's love for all of creation, which "groans" in a birthing of which each of us has a part.

Create in me, O God, the desire and determination to become your partner. Amen.

After all our efforts to reach adulthood, we may be surprised to realize at some point well into our adulthood that we still need to grow up. Perhaps our patience or self-control is still immature, or our capacity to forgive or the courage to take a stand needs growing. Different aspects of our soul mature at different rates, depending on which challenges present themselves to us and how willing we are to respond.

Each of our capacities reflects an aspect of the image of God in us and our ability to reflect God's character as seen in Christ. This *imago dei* is like a seed, capable of slow and steady growth until the Spirit of Christ pervades our whole self, just as leaven suffuses the whole loaf of rising bread.

The images of growth Jesus uses to describe the presence of God's rule among us point to both inner soul and outer community. The kingdom is "within" and "in your midst" (Luke 17:21, KJV, NIV). The seed of Christ develops organically, nurtured by our choices for the good and the gift of God's grace rather than by rigid rule-keeping. Christ's "commandments" are challenges to live into, not rules to live up to. Discipleship is an adventure of discovery about ourselves as partners with Christ in the world.

Even "love your neighbor as yourself" contains a lifetime program of learning because there are so many kinds of neighbors, including the outcast, the stranger, and even the opponent. Seen as a gradual process rather than a pass/fail test, even our sinful mistakes can become grist for the mill, chances to learn. These parables are invitations to trust that grace can help us grow up, all the way to our capacity to be Christlike.

Lord Jesus, help me to trust your slow growth within me. Give me eyes to see my immaturities and mistakes as opportunities. Amen.

Have you ever been with friends, family, or some large group where the goodwill seemed to overflow and the love radiate without conscious effort? You may have been very near "the treasure."

The kingdom of God is the zone of unhindered grace, yet to come fully among us, but always appearing when human beings are willing to do justly, love mercy, and walk humbly. (See Micah 6:8.) The slow process of discipleship involves learning through trial and error to live into these better angels of our nature.

The same gift of God's love that embraces us completely as we are calls us to change if we want to possess the treasure fully. Both plower and merchant must sell all they have to purchase their precious finds. Just so, Jesus tells us to "strive to enter" the zone of more fully realized grace (Luke 13:24). The Greek word for *strive* implies a struggle, a dealing with opposition and hindrance. The next parable in today's passage (vv. 47-50) offers an image of sorting through that which is of the kingdom of heaven and that which is not.

Jesus, in another passage, says that where our treasure is "there will your hearts be also" (Matt. 6:21). But so many attachments set down roots in our hearts. Do I enjoy the adrenalin rush of argument? Do I find self-justification in criticizing others' faults? What in me resists truly life-giving, reciprocal relationships of mutual help and service? All such attachments are like the unsuitable fish that must be sorted through in the parable.

Practice may not make perfect, but it can make proficient. *Agape*—loving care, consideration, and compassion—can be practiced. This is the treasure buried in the field of all our hearts, waiting to be released and developed by grace.

"Create in me a clean heart, O God, and put a new and right spirit within me" (Ps. 51:10). Amen.

Jesus Christ may be "the same yesterday today and forever" (Heb. 13:8), but that requires us to keep changing and growing rather than holding tight to our unchanging past. Human souls, churches, and the world have a long way to go to catch up with Christ. Perhaps this is why Jesus says that those who are "trained" in the ways of God's rule are able to "bring out . . . what is new and what is old" in themselves and the world at large.

Healthy human psyches and groups maintain a good balance between the need to conserve and the impulse to change. Too much change too fast can unsettle and unbalance us in matters both great and small. On a long trip, while enjoying exquisite Italian food in Rome, I suddenly found myself making a beeline to a McDonald's restaurant for three consecutive meals in one day. The new and different was suddenly too much. I needed familiar American fare. Social systems experiencing too much change eventually face resistance and backlash. Conversely, holding on to the security of the familiar can blind us to what needs to change in family, social, or religious life.

Make no mistake: The grace of God in Christ is out to change us, to expose and heal the ways we resist goodness, to challenge the ways our hearts are closed to compassion, and to upend the injustices we take for granted. The Jesus of the Gospels is far from meek and mild. While he affirms the best in the Judaism of his day, he forthrightly challenges the parts of ritual law he sees as barriers to love and justice. His keen eye sees both the potential in those he loves and the baggage they must give up to grow to full stature. Creative change, rooted in the good practices of the past, honors both old and new.

God of all growth, root me in time-tested good and show me the best of the new. Amen.

Painful Blessings, Bewildering Abundance

JULY 27–AUGUST 2, 2020 • DEBORAH SMITH DOUGLAS

SCRIPTURE OVERVIEW: Jacob is attacked one night by an unknown assailant and wrestles with him until morning. We discover that the assailant comes from God, so Jacob is given a new name, Israel. The psalmist is feeling unjustly accused and cries out to God. He is confident that he would be vindicated if all the facts were known. In Romans, Paul deals with difficult theological issues. He states that he would sacrifice his own soul if his fellow Israelites would accept Christ. Jesus teaches a crowd that is growing hungry, and his disciples are trying to figure out how to feed them. They see only what they lack, while Jesus asks them what they have. This story is a lesson about offering God what we have and trusting God to multiply it.

QUESTIONS AND SUGGESTIONS FOR REFLECTION

- Read Genesis 32:22-31. When have you been forced to wrestle with yourself or your self-identity? How did this struggle reveal a blessing?
- Read Psalm 17:1-7, 15. When have you felt the need to serve as your own advocate before God? How has this experience affirmed your trust in God?
- Read Romans 9:1-5. When have you experienced Paul's anguish that others do not accept what you have come to know in your faith, whether by conversion, denominational change, education, or encounter with God? How do you continue to be in relationship with such family or friends?
- Read Matthew 14:13-21. When have you witnessed small acts of sharing that have led to great abundance?

Member, The Episcopal Church USA; writer, spiritual director, and retreat leader in Santa Fe, New Mexico.

Jacob is returning to his ancestral home in Canaan after twenty years of exile. He is rightly uncertain of his welcome. The last time he saw his brother Esau, he cheated him out of their father's blessing. Now he hears that Esau is coming to meet him with an army of 400 men. After crossing the river Jabbok with his wives and children and servants and flocks, he sends them ahead of him and stays behind.

Alone in the dark, he wrestles with a mysterious stranger all night long. Jacob demands, and receives, a blessing as the new day dawns—a blessing that is also a wounding.

This is not the first time Jacob has demanded and obtained a blessing: He received his father's by treachery and deceit years earlier after cheating his twin brother Esau of his rightful blessing as the firstborn.

But this blessing is wholly different. It comes suddenly. Jacob obtains it not by cold-blooded cunning but by means of a violent, intimate, prolonged struggle with an unseen stranger sent by God.

This strange blessing grants Jacob a new name: He is no longer to be called Jacob (the "grabber"), but Israel ("may God prevail"). Somehow newly born with an identity far beyond himself, Jacob has been given a second chance.

Jacob sees the dawn of a new day and continues on the journey that seemed too much for him the night before. Now he is ready to seek reconciliation with the brother he has wronged, but he limps as he goes. Jacob, the "grabber," the schemer, the winner, has been undeniably and painfully reminded that God is God.

Mysterious holy God, may we be willing to accept your blessing and your plans for us even when they cause us pain. As we limp toward forgiveness, may you meet us there and be with us on the way. Amen.

In this passage, Jacob fords the River Jabbok with his whole family and everything he owns, and he sends them on ahead of him. We do not know why he stays behind alone.

But we know something about the river: The Jabbok is no shallow, meandering stream. A tributary of the Jordan, its bed is a deep gorge with steep, often precipitous banks. Its rushing waters cut a great cleft that splits the land of Gilead in two. Like most rivers in the ancient world, the Jabbok is a great divide, a serious obstacle, an important boundary, a dangerous place.

Jacob has sent all he loves and all he owns across to the other side of the river to meet an uncertain future. And now he seems unable to go any farther.

It is poignant to remember that Jacob is an old man. He was young when he last saw his brother Esau and cheated him out of their father's blessing; Jacob has been in exile ever since. Now he is old and alone, and night is coming. He may be weary; he is almost certainly afraid. Perhaps he is at the edge of his strength.

Jacob's strength and cunning have been formidable. He (the "grabber") has worked hard and practiced all kinds of deception to win his wives and sire his sons and build up his flocks and his fortunes. But now he seems to have come to a halt, a great divide within himself. In this decisive moment he can't proceed.

Perhaps it is only now, weary of himself with his past catching up with him, that he is ready to wrestle with himself and with God—to receive a blessing, a wound, and a new name.

Dear Lord, when all our scheming has brought us to the limit of our own strength, when we are weary and afraid, meet us by the river and do not let us go ahead without your blessing. Amen.

This psalm of David is a tough one to read. And it seems a dangerous one to pray. The psalmist is sure of his own righteousness, convinced that his personal enemies are enemies of God and thirsting for savage vengeance (especially in the verses of the psalm omitted from the lectionary reading for today).

I have done nothing wrong, he declares: My feet have not slipped; my mouth does not transgress; I have avoided the ways of the violent. (This claim of innocence is an interesting one for David to make, given the accounts of his life in First and Second Samuel in the Hebrew scriptures.)

Surrounded and threatened by those who wish us ill, any of us, like David, may be tempted to protest that we don't deserve such enmity and to demand protection. It's a passionate prayer, but not a pretty one. Considering its merits and temporarily overlooking its faults, this psalm is worth a closer look.

David serves as his own advocate, presents his case to his Lord, the judge, and cries for vindication against his adversaries. To his credit, he does not seek authorization to take his own vengeance against his foes but calls upon God to save him. Regardless of the self-righteous tone, he trusts God to deliver him.

The prayer reflects a journey from embittered fear and anger toward confidence in God's saving presence. Having vented his spleen, David seems by the end of the psalm to be able to rest in the hope of deliverance and to express a simple faith that God will help him.

As trusting as a child, the troubled king is sure that when he wakes he will behold God's face and "be satisfied."

Gracious God, deliver us from self-righteous anger, and "wondrously show your steadfast love" to those who put their trust in you. Amen.

This passage from Paul's letter to the Romans reveals a deeply personal side of him. He confesses his "great sorrow and unceasing anguish" that his "own people," his fellow Jews, have rejected the gospel. They seem unable to see Jesus as the Christ, the fulfillment of the ancient promises, the culmination of all history and prophecy. And they may well see Paul's conversion as a betrayal or repudiation of his heritage.

That Jesus is the fulfillment of all Jewish history and law and prophecy is so clear to Paul that it breaks his heart that his kindred, the elect of God through the ages, don't seem to see it. The Jews are the rightful heirs of those promises: "To them belong the adoption, the glory, the covenants, the giving of the law, the worship, and the promises." In the strongest language imaginable, Paul confesses that he "could wish himself accursed and cut off from Christ" for the sake of his own people.

For any of us who grieve that some of our own kindred do not share our faith in Christ, this "sorrow and anguish" can ring all too true. Even those of us who have left the denomination in which we were raised for the sake of another faith tradition that feels more authentic to us can relate to Paul's pain. What seems a natural, reasonable, and organic choice to us can feel to our own families like a repudiation of our heritage.

Paul's grief is real, but his anguish is generous, not angry. He does not cast off those who cannot follow where he would lead. Through it all, his conviction that Jesus is the promised one of Israel, the "Messiah who is over all, God blessed forever," remains unshaken.

Dear God of all, help us to love those who do not share our faith. May we love as you love all that you have made. Amen.

Paul is agonized over Israel's failure to recognize Jesus as the long-awaited Messiah. It breaks his heart that they cannot share his conviction that Jesus is the fulfillment of the ancient promises. But even amid his sorrow, he is becoming aware that God's purposes will not be thwarted. Paul realizes that perhaps salvation history is beginning to move beyond the Jews. Perhaps the ancient promises will be not just for the elect, the chosen people, but for all people. The Messiah comes from the Jews, but the Messiah is "over all, God blessed forever."

In the rest of this section of Paul's letter to the Romans, he affirms his assurance that God's mercy will not and cannot be constrained: The mysterious abundance of grace will flow where it will. Paul seems to be on the cusp of his world-shaking understanding that what God has done in Jesus is good news for all creation. But first he has to come to the dead end to which his expectations and assumptions have led him.

Sometimes what seems to us like a dead end will, if we follow it as far as we can, turn out to be a threshold rather than a wall—an opening, not a closing.

Often in hiking, the trail seems to end in a blank wall of impassable stone. But if one follows the way closer to the impasse, what seems an impenetrable barrier discloses a hidden cleft in the rock, a passage not visible from afar. We must persevere to the apparent end to see it and be willing to relinquish our own expectations of what lies ahead and our own assumptions about what God has in mind.

Sometimes, Lord, your grace is so abundant, your purposes so large, that we don't see them at first. Help us to trust that you are the way and to follow where you lead us. Amen.

When this story begins, Jesus has just learned of the murder of his cousin John at the order of Herod. He wants to be alone for a while. But, as always, the needs of the broken world intrude upon his solitude. Great crowds pour out of the towns and follow him to the isolated place to which he has withdrawn. Instead of sending them away, he has compassion on them and moves among them, healing the sick.

At the end of that long day, the disciples want him to dismiss the crowds, but Jesus, in his boundless mercy, wants not only to heal them but also to feed them. The miracle by which he accomplishes this is, as usual, so quiet and achieved by such indirection that it's possible the crowds themselves don't notice it anymore than the guests at the wedding at Cana knew that he had turned water into wine.

"Not counting women and children," about five thousand men ate of the mysteriously multiplied loaves and fishes. "And all ate and were filled," with twelve basketfuls left over. Even the "no-account" women and children had plenty. Jesus fed them all.

A woman likely had prepared and sent the five loaves and two fishes, probably as lunch for a child. The miraculous abundance begins with a humble, small, ridiculously inadequate offering from among the "discounted" for whom Jesus always has compassion: women, children, the poor, sick, blind, lame.

If we too offer Jesus all that we have, however humble, small, ridiculously inadequate it seems, he will work wonders with it. In divine humility, God uses us—"you give them something to eat," Jesus tells the disciples—and uses created things— even barley loaves and little fish—to accomplish redemptive purposes.

Grant us, God of compassion, the courage and humility to offer all that we are and have to you, that you may accomplish blessing beyond our imagining. Amen.

This chapter of Matthew's Gospel invites us to compare two banquets: Herod's decadent feast of excess, arrogance, scheming, and murder in a royal palace and, in this passage, Jesus' impromptu feast of healing, compassion, community, and miraculous plenty under the open sky.

Matthew's first readers likely also would have heard in this passage an echo of the story in Second Kings 4:42-44, in which the prophet Elisha, in a time of famine, orders that a gift brought to him of twenty barley loaves be set before a hundred hungry men. When his servant asks (reasonably enough) how twenty small loaves could meet so great a need, Elisha says again, "Give them to the men, that they may eat, for thus says the Lord, 'They shall eat and have some left'" (v. 43, RSV). And so it happens. The faithful providence of God does not fail.

Jesus' feeding of the much greater number with a much smaller offering reveals the same promise: The abundance of God's mercy writ large. But perhaps most of all we are invited to hear in this story of the feeding of the five thousand a foreshadowing of the Last Supper. On the last night of his earthly life, Jesus once again takes and blesses and breaks a loaf of ordinary bread and gives it to his disciples. This is a sacred meal we remember every time we share Holy Communion, itself a foretaste of the greatest gift, Jesus' world-changing self-offering on the cross.

God sustains us in many ways, all the time. Scripture and our own experience are full of examples of God's faithful providence—unfailingly incarnational, sacramental, and astoundingly abundant.

Faithful and generous God of all, thank you for all the quiet miracles in our lives, all the ways you feed and heal and love us. We thank you above all for the gift of your Son, our Savior, who is the bread of life. Amen.

Faithful Presence within the Abyss

AUGUST 3–9, 2020 • FRANK ROGERS JR.

SCRIPTURE OVERVIEW: The strange dynamics in the history of Abraham's family continue in Genesis. This week his great-grandson Joseph is sold into slavery by his jealous brothers. God will ultimately use this for good, as we read in Psalm 105, but in Joseph's time there clearly is significant dysfunction. Perhaps the story brings encouragement to those of us who also have challenging family dynamics. Paul emphasizes in Romans that every person is welcome to call on the name of the Lord and be saved, but it falls to us to offer them the good news. How can they believe if they never hear? In the Gospel reading, Peter learns a valuable lesson about trust. He initially shows great faith, but he falters when he allows himself to be distracted by the waves.

QUESTIONS AND SUGGESTIONS FOR REFLECTION

- Read Genesis 37:1-4, 12-28. In the face of cruelty, how do you continue to believe in God's dream of unity for us all?
- Read Psalm 105:1-6, 16-22, 45b. When has a glimpse of God absorbed your pain?
- Read Romans 10:5-15. When have you witnessed Christian violence against persons of other faiths? How does your faith compel you to proclaim God's love for all—"no exceptions"? What does this look like for you?
- Read Matthew 14:22-33. When have you struggled to trust Jesus through life's trials? How has Jesus revealed his presence and companionship anyway?

Muriel Bernice Roberts Professor of Spiritual Formation and Narrative Pedagogy and co-director of the Center for Engaged Compassion, Claremont School of Theology; author of *Practicing Compassion* and *Compassion in Practice*.

Beaten and left for dead in a dried up well; sold into slavery by your own family; tossed about by tempest winds within a stormy sea. Life can be brutal. Sometimes, we find ourselves battered and abandoned, swallowed alone in a pitch-black emptiness. Where is God in the abyss of our lives? What is faith when we feel forsaken and forgotten?

This is the theme of each text this week.

Today, we start with Joseph. Ultimately, Joseph's story testifies to God's faithfulness. It is the prelude to Exodus. God will hear the cries of God's people; God will liberate them from the horrors of slavery in Egypt. Joseph's story tells how God's people got there in the first place. And the story begins with the lead character left to die in an empty pit.

Truth be told, the family from which God's chosen people—the twelve tribes of Israel—are formed, is ravaged with dysfunction. A father spoiling a favorite child who parades, robed, around his brothers; the favored one informing on his brothers then flaunting his dreams of lording over them all; the brothers, so seething with jealousy and spite, scheming to murder the favored child then crushing their father with their deception. Their crime is deterred only in part. They rip the robe off their brother, cast him in a barren well, then ponder how to be rid of him. God promises to be faithful. That promise, however, is made with our hope stripped and abandoned within a pit.

For God to meet us in the abyss, we must first speak truthfully about how empty and alone the abyss really is. The waterless cisterns in which we sometimes find ourselves are dark—abuse, abandonment, betrayal, enslavement, the murder of a sibling, the death of a child. Where is God when we are beaten down by life's cruelty?

Within the abyss that swallows us, please, O God, come. Amen.

So the brothers sold Joseph to some traveling merchants who promptly took Joseph to Egypt" (AP). We know what that means. As sure as if Joseph had been taken to the Deep South through the Middle Passage or to the death camps of Nazi Germany, Joseph is gone now. He is lost within the capricious system where bodies are property bought and sold, wrung of all labor and then summarily disposed of. Swallowed into an abyss of human cruelty, he will never be seen again.

The story of Joseph is the story of how God's chosen people are formed—how God transforms the clans of twelve brothers into a single people, the twelve tribes of Israel, with whom God's covenant with Abraham, Isaac, and Jacob will be fulfilled. Unifying these twelve tribes, God creates a people to whom God will always be faithful, whom God will always companion, and whom God will lead into a Promised Land of peace and prosperity for all.

As God's covenant extends through the generations, this part of the story is unique. God is not choosing between brothers. The covenant is no longer for Isaac or Ishmael, Jacob or Esau, Joseph or the eleven other brothers. God's covenant extends to all twelve brothers. All are included; no one is excluded.

Yet human frailty threatens to sabotage God's dream. The father chooses Joseph. The brothers choose themselves. Joseph disappears into the wasteland of slavery. Nevertheless, God still chooses them all. God dreams of the day when all twelve will be reconciled, living in peace as one. Can God's dream endure the death camps of Egypt? Can the exiled one survive and still desire reunion with the ones who cast him away? Can the eleven come to grieve their transgression and embrace the one they banished? Can the dream for reconciled unity endure when hope disappears into cruelty's abyss? Can ours?

God, within our tendency to exclude and oppress, reconcile us into a single human family. Amen.

Faithful Presence within the Abyss   263

Joseph survives the abyss of slavery. In fact, incomprehensibly, he not only survives, he thrives—becoming the ruler over all of Pharaoh's possessions, even lord over the entire land of Egypt. Joseph's rise within an oppressive land is hardly cavalier. Each step is a test of his faith and fortitude. Today's psalm reminds us of the story. It begins in brutality. His feet lacerated with chains, his neck choked by a collar of iron, Joseph enters Egypt in shackles.

Purchased by Potiphar, the captain of Pharaoh's guard, Joseph quickly proves his worth. He becomes Potiphar's personal assistant, in charge of the entire household. Potiphar's wife takes notice and tries to seduce him. When rebuffed for the final time, she accuses Joseph, who is sent to prison. Once more, Joseph's forbearance prevails. Placed in charge of the prison, he interprets a dream for Pharaoh's cupbearer on the promise that he will be remembered favorably to Pharaoh. When the cupbearer is freed, Joseph is forgotten. For two more years, he remains falsely imprisoned. Only when Pharaoh has some dreams of his own does the cupbearer remember Joseph. Joseph is brought to Pharaoh, where once more he demonstrates his value—he interprets the dreams that reveal how to survive an upcoming famine and is placed in charge of Pharaoh's house, ruler of all the land.

Today's psalm is a historical one. It retells the story of God's faithfulness, reminding the Jewish people that God is true to God's covenant even when all looks hopeless. Joseph is faithful as well. He does not let slavery crush his spirit; he does not succumb to seduction's temptations; he does not slip into paralyzing despair even when imprisoned, disgraced, and forgotten. God will not abandon God's people. Liberation is on the horizon. Our invitation is to stay true to our faith, persevere, and hope.

You have been faithful before, God; you will be faithful again. Keep our hope alive. Amen.

Years ago, I made a pilgrimage to Saint Peter's cathedral in Rome. My core intention was to see Michelangelo's *Pieta.* Mired in grief at the tragic death of a sibling, I longed to behold firsthand Mary cradling her son's broken body.

Walking up, I anticipated a reverential, quiet cathedral. Instead, I entered a cacophony. Mass was being shouted; tour guides were yelling anecdotes; hundreds of pilgrims gawked about in a noisy throng. A crowd surrounded the *Pieta.* Over the crowd's shoulders, I glimpsed the white marble. The maternal face of God gazed upon the lifeless body in her lap. The tenderness, however, was lost in the noise.

Roaming to find a quiet respite, I slipped through a hallway door into a tiny chapel. It was pitch-dark but for a few candles up front. I sat in a pew, my eyes adjusting, the silence palpable. Then I heard it. From the back corner. Sniffles. A young woman pressed a tattered baby's blanket against her chest, dabbing her eyes with one corner. After a while, she walked to the front, laid the blanket before a Madonna statue, kissed her fingers, crossed the blanket, then left. In that moment, I knew that God's infinite compassion held that young mother's grief. Mine too. As sure as the maternal presence that enveloped us in that room, the *Pieta* held our bodies too.

Today's psalm invites us to remember God's wonderful works, to meditate upon the various times God has been present to us, absorbing into our tissues the healing grace of our grief. As a people, Israel experience God's presence; they paused to remember even while in exile. We have glimpsed God's face as well. In ocean sunrises, sleeping children, strangers' kindnesses, and in cathedrals' back chapels. Remembering such moments is restorative. When in exile—in grief or in heartache—such moments keep us alive.

Remember a moment when you glimpsed God's presence. Savor it and absorb its grace.

Faithful Presence within the Abyss   265

My son lives on a boat. He says that a storm at sea—the world pitch-black, the rudder a plaything, crashing waves tossing the boat at will—can drive him below deck balled up and crying out for relief.

Biblical scholars understand Matthew's story as a word of encouragement for the early church. As it was written in the years after Jesus' death and ascension into heaven, the earliest hearers would certainly have recognized the themes. Jesus sends the disciples out into the waters of the world without him. After all the transformative teaching, the miraculous healings, the inspired proclamation of the reign of God, Jesus is no longer with them. He has sent them, commissioned them, but he has stayed back. The church—the disciples in the boat—are out at sea alone.

They know what it is like to be battered by the waves, to lose one's bearings far from land, to have headwinds constantly against them. They must feel terrified. They must feel abandoned. Perhaps they feel abandoned by Jesus himself.

But Jesus has not abandoned them. Amid the soul-numbing tempest, defying all odds, Jesus walks into the storm to be with them. He echoes the self-authenticating words of Yahweh to Moses. "It is I," Jesus says. "Be not afraid."

We too are in the boat with the disciples. We seek to be faithful followers; we strive to live the gospel; we give ourselves to love and good works. Sometimes the storm batters us as well. But Jesus is in the center of the storm. No matter how thrashing the waves, how ferocious the winds, Jesus walks through them. He meets us, even if we are cowering in the cabin below deck. "Take heart," he says. "I am with you."

Help us remember the truth, Jesus: No matter how stormy the sea, you are—and always will be—with us. Amen.

On the last Thanksgiving I spent with my little sister, Linda, she was all smiles. Her son was home from the Marines; her first grandchild was due that summer. Unfortunately, she would not live to see the birth. A brain disease erupted within her. We tried everything to no avail. She died before summer came. We all have been there. We are sailing along the seas of life when, seemingly out of nowhere, a tempest descends. A cancer diagnosis; a vocation terminated; a relationship ruptured; a loved one dies before our eyes. Life brings storms. Sometimes they are brutal.

Today's story reminds us that within whatever storm we find ourselves, Jesus is with us. He comes as a compassionate companion. He understands our terrors; he grieves for our suffering; he sustains our spirit even as the storm continues to rage.

Peter finds himself within a storm. And, as promised, Jesus comes. But Peter does not trust. "If it is really you," Peter says, "command me to walk on water" (AP). Peter can't. He sinks. His lack of faith is exposed. Peter's lack of faith is not that he cannot walk on water. It is that he does not trust that Jesus is with him in the storm. He demands proof. He demands the extraordinary.

The truth is, oftentimes, the storms endure. Cancer has its way; the relationship dissolves; our loved one succumbs to disease. Our faith cannot prevent it. Jesus does not promise to help us walk on water. He promises to be a compassionate companion within the boat navigating the rough seas. While such compassionate presence may not defy the laws of physics, it has the power to calm the storms of terror and anxiety swirling within us.

When the waves of despair threaten to swallow us, Jesus, be our calm. Amen.

A bumper sticker compassionately proclaims, "God bless the whole world. No exceptions." The sentiment echoes that of Paul in today's reading. Paul is writing to Gentile Christians who are suffering from an insidious form of Christian exclusivism. These Gentiles believe that God's new covenant made through Christ extending to Gentiles now no longer includes Jews. A few years earlier, at the first church council, people argue the other way: that one has to be Jewish—even circumcised if male—to be Christian. The council is clear—God's covenantal love, revealed in Jesus, extends beyond Jews to include Gentiles as well. Now, Gentile Christians are arguing the reverse. They suggest that the covenants God has made with Abraham, Isaac, Jacob, and with the twelve tribes of Israel are now voided altogether. Jews are no longer God's chosen people—only Gentile Christians are.

Paul rebukes this exclusion. He implores the Gentile Christians to recognize that the God Abraham knew is the same God Jesus knew, that the covenant God creates in Christ includes all persons—Jews, Greeks, Romans, barbarians. In Christ, God has reconciled all of humanity to God. The God who loves one is the God who loves all.

Christianity carries a tragic history of exclusivism. Through the centuries, Christians have waged violence against Muslims, Jews, pagans, witches, and hosts of persons deemed infidel. This is an abysmal violation of Paul's gospel message. To proclaim that Jesus is Lord is to proclaim that a God of love and compassion governs and sustains our universe. The inclusive love that moves Jesus to dine with sinners, befriend outcasts, embrace untouchables, and pray for persecutors has beaten the powers of hatred and exclusion. In a world where divisiveness threatens us anew, this is our faith: No more in-groups, no more out-groups. God blesses the whole world. No exceptions.

May our hearts be as big as yours, God—big enough to embrace the entire world. Amen.

Come Closer

AUGUST 10–16, 2020 • RACHEL M. SRUBAS

SCRIPTURE OVERVIEW: Joseph has risen to a high position in Egypt, and now his brothers come searching for food in a time of famine. He reveals his true identity and reinterprets their evil intentions as being part of God's plan. Sometimes we too are granted perspective to see God's working in difficult times. The psalmist rejoices when God's people are living in unity, as Joseph and his brothers were after their reunion. In Romans, Paul declares that his people are not rejected by the merciful God, for God's promises are unchanging. In Matthew, Jesus teaches that God looks on the inside, not the outside. Thus, what you take into your body is less important than what comes from your heart, and God does not favor one ethnic group over another.

QUESTIONS AND SUGGESTIONS FOR REFLECTION

- Read Genesis 45:1-15. When have you experienced God's grace in forgiving or being forgiven? How were those needing forgiveness still held responsible for their actions?
- Read Psalm 133. How has God called you to live in unity with those different from you? How do you receive God's abundant blessing through such unity?
- Read Romans 11:1-2a, 29-32. How does the eternal mercy of God's gifts and callings sustain you when it seems like God has rejected God's people?
- Read Matthew 15:10-28. When have you, like the Canaanite woman, felt like you had to insist that Jesus come closer? How did your faith change or grow from this experience?

Author of four books on Christian life, most recently *Benedictine Promises for Everyday People*; Presbyterian Church (USA) pastor serving the Mountain Shadows congregation in Tucson, Arizona; oblate (non-monastic associate) of the Order of St. Benedict; teaches on the faculty of the Hesychia School of Spiritual Direction; www.tucsonspiritualdirection.org.

Today's reading from Genesis has a backstory: Joseph, one of Jacob's twelve sons, is his father's favorite. Joseph is self-confident, imaginative, clever, and insightful. But his resentful brothers see him as spoiled and self-aggrandizing, so they plot to kill him. Instead, they sell Joseph into the hands of Egyptian spice traders. The ensuing years in Egypt bring Joseph both suffering and success, and through it all, spiritual growth. By the time Genesis 45 begins, Joseph is about forty years of age, prosperous, powerful, and finally ready to reconcile with the brothers who once viciously abused him.

Unrecognizing, they stand before him now. Sorrow shot through with joy, hope, and fear overcomes Joseph, who cries for privacy. Emotionally naked, he weeps and shows his brothers the human being he truly is—their own flesh and blood, who, despite betrayal and injury on all sides, loves them still and loves their father. Shocked beyond words by Joseph's self-disclosure, the brothers can't respond until he speaks the invitation that dissolves two decades of estrangement: Come closer.

Come closer is God's invitation not only to Jacob's sons but also to all humankind—to you and me. If the words *come closer* had another name it would be Jesus Christ. God comes close to us in Jesus because God yearns to heal the wounds of separation; undo the trauma of exile; reconcile all broken, distanced souls, families, and communities to Godself; and make human beings whole again. Our wholeness develops not in splendid isolation but in right relationship with others. Young Joseph once dreamed of reigning supreme over his brothers and even over heaven's stars. Through the wreckage and reconciliation of his relationships, Joseph learns that no power is preferable to love.

Humbly, may we come closer to you, O God, and be reconciled to you through Jesus Christ. Embolden us to reveal our true selves, to forgive and be forgiven, and to be reconciled with the ones we love. Amen.

Joseph stands before the brothers who once drove him into exile. He not only forgives them but also affirms God's gracious initiative shining through their past vicious behavior: "And now do not be distressed, or angry with yourselves, because you sold me here; for God sent me before you to preserve life. . . . So it was not you who sent me here, but God."

While Joseph celebrates God's sovereignty, his brothers retain responsibility for having harmed him. Likewise, the good that God brings about—even through the stupid, sinful things we do—does not exempt us from personal accountability for our hurtful actions. The sure and certain grace of God is not a moral loophole but a gift that gives us courage to face ourselves and those who need us to make humble amends.

Joseph's anguish surges into the present. He needs desperately to live toward a future with his family, unencumbered by their terrible former behavior. He understands that only God can move him and his relations together in peace. In order to become whole human beings, the brothers need to face, full-on, the ways they wounded Joseph and then receive the love he offers them despite their hateful history.

Which is harder—to stand in Joseph's shoes, or the brothers'? To forgive the ones who sinned against you, or admit you sinned against another and accept that person's forgiveness? It's unavoidable: Christian life entails both forgiving and being forgiven. Joseph's raw reckoning with his brothers shows us to ourselves as we stand before our God.

Until we acknowledge the depth of the meanness and violence of which we are capable, the grace and forgiveness of Jesus remain theoretical for us. But when God's love overcomes us, we are mended, our relationships are restored, and we are sent out as messengers of the mercy that has saved us.

Help us come closer to knowing our need for you, O God. Amen.

Psalm 133 is a song of ascents, an ancient liturgical lyric of the children of Israel. They would climb a mountain to come closer to the Most High God in a high and holy place—the Jerusalem Temple—and offer their sacrifice of praise. How wonderful it is, the people's hearts would sing, how happy we become when we, the family of faith, meet as one with the Holy One. This psalm calls all Israel to join their lives together in the kinship created by faith. In other words, as Joseph and his reconciled brothers might have said to one another, "Blest be the tie that binds" (UMH, no. 557).

Those ties connect the people to the priesthood signified in the psalm by Aaron and the oil of ordination. This connection confers a blessing not only on Aaron but by extension on all who assemble together in God's presence. The fragrant anointing of God's Spirit in worship flows as fresh snowmelt runs down a mountainside, renewing the earth and the creatures below. As dew freely falls on the descending terrain, so God pours goodness on the faithful congregation. The people's joy multiplies when they share their blessings with one another in a harmony of worship, a song of ascents.

The "kindred [who] live together in unity" are not only Israel, but the whole, hallowed network of humankind unified by God's far-reaching and inclusive love. How good it still is, how pleasant, when present-day people of faith together come closer to God in worship. The prayers we pray and songs we sing were always meant to be not solos but ensemble pieces offered to the One who gathers us from north and south, east and west, to make us one community, the body of Christ.

Gathering God, may we never forget how we need one another. When we come closer to each other in worship, refresh our faith and anoint us with your presence. Amen.

Psalm 133 opens on an idyllic note that carries through to the end. The family of faith that worships together ascends to heights of happiness. God's protective favor streams over the people like soothing oil and refreshing water.

To present-day migrants, refugees, and asylum-seekers surging across national borders, Psalm 133 may read like fantasy fiction. At the time of this writing, a record-setting crush of people from Honduras, Guatemala, and El Salvador is surging into the southwestern United States. They are fleeing gang violence in their homelands, domestic abuse, and the poverty that causes it all. Desperate pilgrims looking for work in construction, food service, landscaping, and housekeeping, many traveling with children, are housed for seventy-two hours in Immigration and Customs Enforcement holding facilities. Then, by law, they are transferred into immigration detention facilities.

When detention centers exceed capacity, migrants are released into the care of churches equipped to shelter guests. Christians who are determined to come closer to the psalm's imagery of kindred living together in unity assemble at their houses of worship. They inflate air mattresses, loan mobile shower units, and collect hefty sacks of *frijoles rojo de seda*, the ruddy little legumes (red silk beans) essential to Central American cuisine. Donated corn tortillas stack up by the dozens. Onion-studded rice steams in a stockpot, offering its savory aroma to all comers, regardless of their national origin or family name. Everyone's hungry—visitors and volunteers alike. Everyone, deep down, is looking for home.

Governments and gang leaders may exploit human need to gain social control. But God uses our humanity to put us to the holy work of welcoming strangers and of being welcomed by people who, it turns out, are our sisters and brothers, our children, our mothers and fathers.

Gather and unify your people, O God. Shelter us all. Amen.

In some eras, the daily news is so bad it seems to eclipse the gospel's good news. The people wring their hands or stare morosely at their screens and wonder if all hope is lost. A question, inarticulate perhaps but haunting, underlies their fear: Has God rejected us?

Paul deals such despairing doubt a swift, decisive blow: "By no means!" Paul's conviction comes not in reaction to a string of faith-damaging events but in passionate response to the world-redeeming power of the risen Christ. Through the death and resurrection of the Anointed One, God fulfills the promise made to Israel and expands that promise to include all believers. *All* is Paul's clear and universal term for both the Hebrew people of the covenant and their now equally summoned and saved Gentile neighbors.

By no means does the gospel's all-welcoming reach terminate God's commitment to Abraham and Sarah's descendants, of whom Paul is one. Rather, Paul explains, Jews who do not follow Christ are nevertheless subject to mercy, which is the sign of gifts and a calling never to be revoked.

When injustice, violence, and suffering bring us to our knees and press us to wonder whether God's back is turned, we can draw courage from the ancient, unbreakable bond between Israel and the Lord. Encouraged by eternal ties that bind, we can come closer to the One whose voice carries on in the hearts of all generations and nations, calling the people to faith. We can listen inwardly and know God is faithful always. We can recall the ways we have been helped by divine mercy and trust that it reaches through us and beyond us to liberate prisoners of disbelief and wrap even those who reject Jesus Christ in the blessed ties that bind all humankind to God.

Thank you, God, for embracing people of every time and place, for showing mercy to all, through Christ. Amen.

*D*efile is not a word we often use in ordinary conversation. But it's a word central to Jesus' teaching. He contradicts the Pharisees' conviction that eating foods deemed unclean makes people ritually impure. What defiles people, according to Jesus, is not the food they eat but the hurtful words they speak—lies, curses, condemnations. The English word *defile* is rooted in the French *defouler*, which means "trample down." This definition comes close to home. We're living in a time when powerful public officials trample down vulnerable populations with aggressive and degrading speech.

In the Gospel, *defile* is a translation of the Greek term *koinoi*, meaning "common, ordinary, mundane, profaned." Usually, when a version of the term *koinoi* occurs in the New Testament, it carries negative connotations. One notable exception, however, occurs in Jude 1:3, which refers to "the salvation we share," or as a literal translation of the original Greek, "our common salvation." To be *koinoi* or common in this case is to belong to God's beloved community. The first thing Jesus does in Matthew 15:10 is to gather the community. He calls the crowd of ordinary, mundane people to come closer to him and listen to his teaching, which is essentially this: breaking traditional dietary laws will not distance you from God, but hate speech will. To tell lies, issue threats, or verbally abuse another is to desecrate yourself and trample your own relationship with God.

The spiritual work that matters, then, is inner work, or what the 12-step community calls "a searching and fearless moral inventory of yourself." Jesus instructs the people, including you and me, to come closer to our own hearts. That's where desecrating sin begins, and it's in the examined and repentant heart that we can shut down destructive talk before it ever comes out of our mouths and harms another soul.

Help us know our hearts, O God. Teach us to renounce verbal violence and speak only words of peace. Amen.

Have you ever been insulted by a powerful religious leader? Has your child been denied life-saving healthcare because of gender, ethnicity, or faith? If you have ever been reduced to begging for help, or been sent away by people who couldn't be bothered to give it, you may identify with the Canaanite woman. She shouts after Jesus, imploring him for mercy on behalf of her suffering daughter. An insurmountable barrier built of history and mistrust separates the desperate mother from the one she calls "Lord, Son of David." By conventional standards, the woman is unclean and untouchable. Her child is downright deadly.

Think of your gravest apprehension—the lethal contagion, the threat you pray never draws near to you or your loved ones. Now you may understand the dread and revulsion Jesus' disciples feel when the Canaanite woman won't stop shouting after him. Patriarchal tribalism has taught them to fear and revile this "other" and the evil they believe her sick daughter embodies. To come closer to her would be to kiss death. Jesus' initial silence suggests he's assessing the risk. His metaphor of food unfit for dogs conveys, if not outright contempt for a neighbor in need, then tradition-bound prejudice against "her kind." Is this the Jesus we know and love?

This is Jesus, human and filtered through Matthew's literary lens. But this is not ultimately a story of healthcare denied, nor of the divide between chosen children and filthy animals. The Canaanite woman's shout penetrates the barricade of ethnic exclusivism. Her chutzpah and rationality change Jesus' mind. He no longer treats her as an impure nuisance but as a human being of dignity and deep faith. Through Jesus' transformed perception of the woman, mercy extends to her daughter and heals her. Thanks to her, all "outsiders" can now come closer to God and to those who once sent them away.

Thank you, Jesus, for coming close to us and making us whole. Amen.

The Priesthood of Believers

AUGUST 17–23, 2020 • BRAD SARTOR

SCRIPTURE OVERVIEW: Genesis now introduces a painful turn in the story of God's people. The Israelites are forced into slavery; yet amid this dark time, a baby boy, Moses, is born. God has already begun the story of their deliverance. The psalmist recognizes that the Israelites would be overwhelmed and swept away without the help of the Maker of heaven and earth. Paul gives the Romans two specific instructions: First, they should be changed so that they follow God's ways, not the world's. Second, they must understand that they all need one another. Each child of God has a part to play in the overall body of Christ. In a famous passage in Matthew, Peter makes the basic Christian confession: Jesus is the Messiah, the Christ, the Son of God.

QUESTIONS AND SUGGESTIONS FOR REFLECTION

- Read Exodus 1:8–2:10. How can you serve in a priestly role?
- Read Psalm 124. Reflect on the many ways God has blessed you and your community. Consider writing your own song of ascent.
- Read Romans 12:1-8. What part of yourself are you holding back from God? How can you bring your whole self to your faith?
- Read Matthew 16:13-20. Why do you think it is important to fully understand Christ's identity before witnessing to Christ's mission?

Pastor and nursing student in Mississippi; spouse and father.

One who mediates between the Divine and the human is called a *priest*; in Christendom the title refers to a ranking official who participates in rites of worship. This week, however, we will reflect on the more basic understanding of the priestly role and reflect on Christ as a priest and his followers as a kingdom of priests.

In the sixteenth century, developments in Europe began to change the world, mainly because those developments turned human power toward democracy. Spiritually speaking, though, this did not change anything, for power in the hands of the people or a monarch or even clergy remains power that may oppose God and God's purposes.

In approaching the Hebrew midwives, Pharaoh naturally assumes these women must serve him and his purposes. But he is mistaken. While Pharaoh works to suppress and oppress a group of subjects, the God of Shiphrah and Puah works quietly to deliver those subjects. In spite of the obvious dangers involved in doing so, the midwives act on faith and are blessed.

Shiphrah and Puah believe deeply in the God of Genesis, so their characters are timelessly written into Exodus. They serve as trailblazers in a very important capacity before Moses ever enters the scene. They stand courageously and compassionately between humans and the Divine. Shiphrah and Puah's hands mediate life and salvation by delivering the Hebrew male infants Pharaoh would have killed. Equally importantly, their bold actions communicate to Pharaoh that a mightier power exists. The women serve the Hebrews as God-fearing midwives. They serve as priests.

O God, write me into your salvation story today. Let my hands also serve you and your purposes as your kingdom continues to come into the world. Amen.

Brother Ron was a big man—and hugely wise. He once told me about his experience of leading weekly worship services. As he stood before the congregation with arms outstretched, he imagined that he was lifting up the congregation from the nave and then turning around to place the people gently inside the chancel to receive God's mercy. This is an image that I have recalled often: a priest in the priestly office bridging the space between God and people.

As prescribed at Sinai, the Levites attended to matters of Israel's worship throughout Israel's history. Incidentally in today's passage, which is prior to the event at Sinai, a Levite household produces the central leading figure of the Old Testament. The Levite baby placed into a basket on the edge of the Nile is Moses, who later becomes a mediating leader for Israel. Moses serves as a communicator between God and the people on Mount Sinai and in the tent of meeting.

The enslaved Levite mother trustingly hides her baby from Pharaoh in the reeds, and years later the man the baby grows to be encounters God at the burning bush. In the Exodus story, all of this leads directly to God's people being led to freedom. This Levite baby is "drawn out of water" and named by a foreigner, yet he is lovingly raised by his own mother—a beaming, wage-earning, royal nursemaid handing down to her "fine child" his Hebrew heritage. Poetic justice and prevenient grace meet beautifully well in this story.

God, I thank you today for the priestly role of Moses. Amen.

Just a little ways north of Galilee lies a cultural and religious crossroads. There the waters from Mount Hermon spring so gloriously from a cliff into a moist, lush valley below that early local worshipers of Baal-gad exalt the god of ground waters as their deity. Later the Greeks and Romans erect shrines so travelers can worship there: one to Pan, a mythological god of the earth, and one to Caesar, the emperor. The shrine to Caesar is erected by Herod the Great, a Jew. Later, Phillip, the Jewish tetrarch, maintains his father's allegiance to Caesar by adopting this place as his own. He called it Caesarea Philippi—a disheartening place to visit for any devoted worshiper of Yahweh.

Jesus—true Deity incarnate—stands in that place and asks a preliminary question of his disciples. "Who do people say that the Son of Man is?" The waters gushing from the cliffs nearby are known to be the headwaters of the Jordan River, and so the entire history of Israel and the mighty prophets of old are on the minds of the disciples already. Those prophets' names being given to identify Jesus might be flattering if Jesus were anyone else. So Jesus asks them the main question: "But who do you say that I am?"

The answer springs from Peter's lips just like water from the cliff. Jesus is the Christ, the Anointed One. He is the Living Water; Baal-gad is not. In Jesus all things hold together; not in Pan. And Jesus, rather than Caesar, is Lord.

Jesus' identity as Christ marks him as the central figure of all history who mediates between God and creation as High Priest. He alone is the Son of the Living God.

Lord, may popular opinion not alter my personal conviction that you are the Christ. Amen.

To be strictly silent about Christ is not very evangelistic. Why, then, does Jesus instruct his disciples to keep quiet regarding his identity? The disciples will eventually be Christ's witnesses to the whole world, but they have not yet fully witnessed Christ, so they don't understand that he must die. Even today as Christ's witnesses we must at times silently live a Christlike life so God can show the world the meaning of the Messiah. Jesus is about to do just that. Talk is always cheap by comparison.

Jesus is to be crucified on a Roman cross, a public event the Jewish leaders would not have wanted to happen during Passover. Yet the Messiah willingly offers himself as a sacrifice for humanity, as the ultimate Passover Lamb. In this case, not telling people that Jesus is the Messiah helps avoid awakening death-dealing forces before their appointed time.

Still, we wonder about all the gates-of-hell and keys and binding-and-loosing language. Yet Jesus clearly says, "I will build my church." The context of Peter's confession reveals that this passage unveils Christ's messianic mission. The complete and utter victory of heaven over hell is at hand, and Christ's church will be on the front lines.

God shares God's all-important kingdom building work with faith-filled humans professing Jesus as Christ. Peter later takes up the idea in his letter: "You yourselves . . . are being built up . . . to be a holy priesthood" (1 Pet. 2:5, ESV).

The messianic mission might not be announced in your Sunday bulletin or talked about at your church fellowship dinner this week, but it is nonetheless a reality—one that hinges on Peter's confession: "You are the Christ."

Jesus, I want to stand with Peter and your holy church today and always. Amen.

In Romans 12 Paul is taking a breath. He has written to inform the Christian Jews and other Christians in Rome of the glorious mercies of God (chapters 1–11), and now he will instruct them in the worship of God (chapters 12–16). Although the Jews have previously worshiped God and the Romans have not, both groups need instruction and encouragement for engaging in appropriate Christian worship. The instruction is clear: "Present your bodies as a living sacrifice."

Both pagan and Jewish worshipers in the ancient world are familiar with the language of sacrifice to deities. In this universally practiced ritual, offerings such as grains and other produce are burned or consumed in worship and living animals are presented and even killed as part of the ritual. The sacrifices vary, however; a Jewish or Roman worshiper would never be expected to volunteer his or her own body (whole self) as the sacrifice. Why then does Paul prescribe this approach for Christian worshipers?

I once knew a teen who, amid supportive family and friends, assumed positive public roles at school and church. He enjoyed baseball, playing guitar, fishing, and attending worship; he was an all-around great kid with a seemingly happy life. But inwardly he was haunted by shame. He prayed and worshiped often but could never find more than temporary relief from his persistent and intense loneliness. This almost drove him to despair, until one day he found the courage to present his inner struggles to a trusted counselor. The experience of total acceptance by the counselor illuminated his mind to the mercies of God. Suddenly, Paul's instruction for Christian worship to "present your [whole selves] . . . to God" begins to make sense.

Lord, your desire is that I worship you and experience transformation in my life, both private and public. Take all of me, I pray. Amen.

Within the kingdom of priests that is the church, every Christian is a mirror of grace. We each are the very image of God mediating Christ: first to one another, then to the rest of the world. In today's passage, this enormous and foundational grace is contextualized within functional limits: each of us can live according to our individually assigned faith.

But what is the meaning of this assigned faith? Whatever it is, unless we experience it in the light of true faith and true humility, we will be tempted to jealousy.

As we grow in the worship of God with our whole selves, we realize that God transforms each of us in a unique way. God magnifies us in Christ, and the very transformation of our character is the result, much like the physical transformation of a caterpillar in a chrysalis. And—just as every butterfly knows—transformation is challenging. We have to adjust. We must learn to live with our wings.

Apart from faith, the wings of our uniqueness tempt us to become proud of our own wings and say, "I'm glad I'm me and not you!" or to become jealous of others' wings and say, "I wish I were you instead of me."

But each person's giftedness is a unique grace. Since we are one body with many parts, not individual Christians competing for glory, we are free to cooperate in our uniqueness. So Paul's call to "sober judgment" is answered in us only as we realize that we are a kingdom of priests for one another.

Lord, grant me humility to avoid both aspects of the comparison trap: pride and jealousy. Advance your kingdom in my church by instilling a sober judgment in us about such things. Amen.

Psalm 124 is part of a group of psalms that are songs of ascent, or praise songs used by ancient Jewish worshipers traveling to Jerusalem for various feasts. The following could be our own "song of ascent" taken from our journey of this week's readings:

Let us go up to Jerusalem together and give God credit for being so great! It is time to worship!

In the early days we were being worked cruelly by Pharaoh, and he wanted to kill our male children. Our God was working through the hands of two midwives to save us. Shiphrah and Puah—we will never forget those names!—mediated life to Israel. Their boldness made us want to believe.

And when the Nile was being filled with our children—Oh the horror of the thought!—that river was a graveyard for our future. God protected a certain baby from Pharaoh's evil hand. That was Moses. He was preserved for the time that God would raise him up and prepare him to lead us. God raised up Moses to lead us!

God raised up a whole nation. We are a kingdom of priests whose presence in the world among nations has proved to be an eternal blessing to all people. God has done all this! Humanity will be restored. Let us go up to Jerusalem all together!

Pharaoh may have once dominated us in Egypt, but that was temporary. God called us out of Egypt. And at the same time, God called God's Son out of Egypt. Who is the Son of Israel? He is the Messiah. He is the Chosen One who will rule the nations with an iron scepter. Our Messiah leads the mission. He will lead a new humanity.

Let us go! God has done all this. Why would we not go up to Jerusalem and worship God?

God, who made heaven and earth, you are the One we worship. Amen.

Divine Action, Human Response

AUGUST 24–30, 2020 • ANNE BROYLES

SCRIPTURE OVERVIEW: Moses has fled Egypt and is living in the desert, where God calls him to return and free the Israelites. Moses resists, but God does not relent. In many of the Psalms, the psalmist reviews God's record of faithfulness. Psalm 105 is no different and highlights the calling of Moses. In Romans, Paul addresses practical ethical concerns. How should we treat those who treat us poorly? We should never repay evil for evil, but instead should bless those who harm us. This goes against our natural instincts, yet the gospel is countercultural and calls us to a higher standard. In Matthew, Peter has just had a tremendous moment in declaring his faith in Christ. Now he stumbles in failing to understand that Jesus' path to glory will pass through suffering.

QUESTIONS AND SUGGESTIONS FOR REFLECTION

- Read Exodus 3:1-15. What sacred encounter might have been your burning bush? How did you know God's presence was with you in the encounter?
- Read Psalm 105:1-6, 23-26, 45b. How does obedience to God shape your life? Recall an instance where your obedience to God's call or teachings made a difference.
- Read Romans 12:9-21. When has working toward a common goal helped you better love your family, friends, or community?
- Read Matthew 16:21-28. When have you had to trust God and accept that you "have no idea how God works"? How did your trust help you through the situation?

Served on *Weavings* Advisory Board all the years of its publication; retired from the United Methodist ministry to write children's books; for more information, visit www.annebroyles.com.

My childhood family vacations alternated between driving 1,600 miles east to visit my paternal grandmother one summer, then 1,200 miles north to see my maternal grandmother the following summer. I loved reconnecting with various family members, but the biggest treat was riding in the back seat of our family car with my mother. We sang hymns and church camp songs, shared family stories, and rehearsed genealogy so I would remember how everyone was related.

This "Hallelujah Psalm" invites us to do the same on a grander scale: to sing praises to God, remember what God has done in history and in our own lives, and to rehearse the history of those who have gone before us. Like our ancestors in faith, we are called to

Thank GOD! Pray to [GOD] by name!
Tell everyone you meet what [GOD] has done!
Sing [GOD] songs, belt out hymns,
translate [GOD's] wonders into music!
Honor [GOD's] holy name with Hallelujahs,
you who seek GOD. Live a happy life!
Keep your eyes open for GOD, watch for [GOD's] works;
be alert for signs of [GOD's] presence. (THE MESSAGE)

We each have our own ways of acting out our faith. How do you thank God, pray, tell, and sing about God's work and wonders? What do you do to honor God's name? To seek God and be alert to God's presence? Choose a focus for your week from this psalm.

For instance, if you decide to "Keep your eyes open for GOD," you might take time each day to name how you have seen and experienced God. This could be written, shared with a friend, or a silent prayer of thanksgiving. If you want to sing to God, make time to belt out old hymns or new songs.

Hallelujah, God! Thank you for all you've done for me. I want to be mindful of your great works. Amen.

Moses' ordinary life as a shepherd is interrupted and upended when he spies "a flame of fire out of a bush" that "was blazing, yet it was not consumed." As most of us would if we saw such a sight, Moses wants a closer look. Once he has changed direction to check it out, God calls him by name. "Moses, Moses!" And Moses answers, "Here I am." When God has Moses' attention, God instructs the shepherd and soon-to-be leader to keep a distance and show reverence by taking off his sandals.

Perhaps you yearn for your own burning bush moment—something dramatic, a clear sign that God knows you and has a plan for your life. But God comes to humanity in many ways. Our burning bush may be words of challenge or comfort spoken by an honest friend, a sudden realization about a necessary action, or a moment of clarity about an important decision.

A man fell into a mountain cave and wondered if anyone would ever find him. Alone in the deep darkness, he was gifted with the sure sense that he would be rescued. "God didn't exactly call my name, but I felt a deep peace in my core that helped me stay calm for fourteen hours until I was found." When a woman observed a particularly vivid sunrise, she felt a sense of the Holy that led her to volunteer with a nature conservancy that eventually led to a career change.

No matter what our burning bush might look like, Moses' divine interaction in the desert reminds us that God knows us by name. God meets us where we are. God comes to each of us in a way that touches us deeply. Where we are in each present moment is sacred.

God, help me recognize that where I am standing, right now and in each moment, is holy ground so that I will be ready to hear you call my name. Amen.

In the burning-bush encounter with Moses, God says, "I have observed the misery of my people who are in Egypt; I have heard their cry on account of their taskmasters. Indeed, I know their sufferings." God invites Moses to work to alleviate those sufferings: "So come, I will send you to Pharaoh to bring my people, the Israelites, out of Egypt." Moses responds to God's invitation by protesting four times: "I am not your guy!"

God knows that, years before, when Moses saw an Egyptian beating a Hebrew, he was angry enough to murder the Egyptian. God calls Moses to a different way of righting wrongs: Work with God to deliver the Hebrew people from Egypt. "I will be with you; and this shall be the sign for you that it is I who sent you: When you have brought the people out of Egypt, you shall worship God on this mountain."

"I will be with you." God's promise to Moses gives him the strength to become a leader who brings his people out of suffering. That same promise is ours. Just as God pays attention to the suffering of all the world's people, we are called to pay attention even when we feel overwhelmed by the pain of opioid abuse, school shootings, ethnic wars, or starving children. After paying attention, we are called to action just as God called Moses. Even when we don't feel up to the task or know where to start, we can find a small, specific action to take in our community.

Knowing you are with me gives me strength, God. I don't need to be Moses or Miriam or Jesus. With you, I can take action, make a difference, and respond to the suffering I see around me. Help me find my unique strengths and learn where my efforts can make a difference. Amen.

*M*y *oncologist.* I never expected to use these words in daily speech, along with *breast cancer* and *mastectomy.* After a routine mammogram recently set my life spinning, I found my language had shifted, as had my perception of what really mattered. I made a quick life review and felt deep thanksgiving at all I had. I also fell into the arms of God and the support of people who loved me.

The Message labels today's verses "You're Not in the Driver's Seat." Cancer reminds us of that fact, as do failure, broken relationships, job loss, and myriad other aspects of human life.

Jesus calls ordinary people to be his disciples, and by the time of today's scripture conversations, those chosen ones must be feeling pretty good. Sure, Jesus is "in the driver's seat," but they have witnessed healings and been instruments of healing themselves. They've been commissioned to "proclaim the good news, 'The kingdom of heaven has come near' " (Matt. 10:7). Sometimes Jesus says things that confuse them, but he walks on water and feeds five thousand.

When Jesus explains how his earthly story will end, the disciples balk. "God forbid it, Lord! This must never happen to you," says Peter. Jesus responds, "You have no idea how God works" (THE MESSAGE).

Jesus asks us to set our mind on "divine things." How do we lift ourselves above the human and find the divine? I suggest we keep our eyes on Jesus, heed his example and words, and remember that we are not in the driver's seat. No matter what life throws our way, trust God.

Gracious God, I am along for the ride and trust in you to guide me, wherever life takes me. Help me get out of the way so you can work in me. May I keep my mind set on your divine ways. Amen.

What does love look like? Television commercials and magazines show starry-eyed love between romantic partners; sweet, cuddly love between parents and children; and "I've got your back" love between friends. If only love were as simple and uncomplicated as those images. In reality, whether it's connecting individuals or groups, love can be hard work.

In the preceding verses, Paul reminds his listeners that we are one in Christ. Today's verses detail how we live out our connectedness. It starts when we "love from the center of who [we] are" (THE MESSAGE). Paul's words to the faithful in Rome are specific. He offers no "just be nice" platitude but rather a series of exhortations that apply today as much as they did thousands of years ago. Ultimately, "we love because [God] first loved us" (1 John 4:19). Although some of Paul's ideas echo Jesus' teachings, he very specifically lists behaviors of how to show genuine love.

Read these verses slowly and pause after each suggestion. Which of these feel easy? Which ones do you still need to work on? Think of specific persons or situations that fit. You might also name individuals you know or know of who exemplify genuine love or perseverance in prayer. It may be someone famous like Nelson Mandela, Dorothy Day, or Malala Yousafzai. It may be an honored elder in your congregation or a young adult whose work with the church youth inspires you to deeper love.

As you read, listen for that place deep within where God nudges you. Does one of Paul's admonitions jump out at you? Perhaps you have had a falling out with a friend or your faith community is experiencing division. One of these verses might be a fitting breath prayer of focus as you work through conflict by "loving from the center of who you are."

God of Love, may my love be genuine so that I serve you in all things. Amen.

For most of my adult life, I have belonged to a non-geographic covenant community, Sisbros, in which we live by a series of practices that govern our spiritual, economic, and political lives. We come together for a yearly gathering of study, reflection, deep listening, recreation, and caring for each other and the world.

I have known some of the people in the group for over forty years. In the beginning, I felt more comfortable with some individuals than with others, as I'm sure was the case for everyone. Our commitment bound us together even when we were not all best friends. In that long span of time, I have grown to sincerely love each person in Sisbros. Today's words from Paul detail much of what keeps Sisbros united. We live in harmony because we prioritize the work of our community and our call to bring change to the world.

Paul's letter to the Romans goes to a church that has a diverse community: Jews and Gentiles, enslaved and free people, women and men. His words speak to any group of people who are trying to live in Christian community. He speaks generally ("live in harmony with one another," "live peaceably with all") with pointed specifics such as "bless those who persecute you" and "never avenge yourselves." He covers many of the human emotions that get in the way of deep, loving relationships. Instead of coming across as judgmental, Paul lifts positive examples of how we might walk the earth in obedience to Christ's call.

Reread Romans 12:9-21, considering what's currently happening in your interactions with loved ones, friends, and the wider community. Are there any rough edges in your relationships that might need smoothing out? Choose one phrase or action from this passage that jumps out at you. Is there a specific situation or action to which God might be calling you?

Loving God, help me love in the ways you call me to love. Amen.

We live in an intergenerational household that includes a toddler. From the adults' example, she learns what behaviors our family considers important, whether in showing love through hugs, respectful conversation, and kisses, or practical applications like using her words, saying "please" and "thank you," or putting away her toys. She is developing into an independent, compassionate human being who fits into and adds to our family dynamic. Research shows that children do best when adults set limits and provide clear expectations of appropriate behavior. This not only keeps kids safe ("We hold hands when we cross the street") but also teaches kids self-discipline. Similarly, God has given us a series of limits and appropriate behavior.

Today's verse names Moses and Aaron as chosen by God "that they might keep [GOD's] statutes and observe [GOD's] laws." In Deuteronomy 4:40, Moses tells his people, "Obediently live by [GOD's] rules and commands which I'm giving you today so that you'll live well and your children after you—oh, you'll live a long time in the land that GOD, your God, is giving you" (THE MESSAGE). Jesus says that the greatest commandment is "'Love the Lord your God with all your passion and prayer and intelligence.' This is the most important, the first on any list. But there is a second to set alongside it: 'Love others as well as you love yourself.' These two commands are pegs; everything in God's Law and the Prophets hangs from them" (Matt. 22:37-40, THE MESSAGE). Christians and faith communities throughout the centuries have followed the Great Commandment, the Ten Commandments, Jesus' teachings, and other specific guiding principles. Saint Benedict of Nursia encouraged "keeping every rule for the love of Christ." John Wesley offered these three rules: Do no harm, do good, stay in love with God. What are the rules and principles that guide your life?

Gracious God, help me follow the statutes and laws you have given me. Amen.

Remember!

AUGUST 31—SEPTEMBER 6, 2020 • WILLIE S. TEAGUE

SCRIPTURE OVERVIEW: We move forward in the story of Moses to the climax in Egypt, the tenth plague. God tells the Israelites to prepare for the terrible night to come and establishes the feast of Passover. It is to be an eternal reminder of what God has done for the people. The psalmist praises God for faithfulness and victory, including overthrowing those who would oppress them. Egypt is not mentioned specifically, yet the Passover represents just such a situation. Paul echoes Jesus in summarizing much of the Law in one simple commandment: Love your neighbor as yourself. Jesus provides practical teaching on handling disagreements. Our first responsibility is to go to the other party privately and then include others only as necessary. Gossip and social media are not the ways to handle our disputes.

QUESTIONS AND SUGGESTIONS FOR REFLECTION

- Read Exodus 12:1-14. How has the story of Passover shaped your faith?
- Read Psalm 149. How has God called you to seek freedom from oppression for yourself or others through praise and through action?
- Read Romans 13:8-14. What does it mean to consider love a driving force rather than a warm feeling? How does this understanding change the way you act toward yourself and your neighbors?
- Read Matthew 18:15-20. When have you participated in or witnessed true reconciliation? How did you see compassion at work?

Retired United Methodist pastor, South Carolina Annual Conference; interim pastor, Cross Road Presbyterian Church (USA).

A professor of mine liked to tell the story of his first blind date. He said as they left the house the mother said to her daughter, "Now remember who you are." That is good advice. The memory of who we are can shape our actions and relationships. In our lesson from Exodus, the Lord tells Israel to "observe . . . a perpetual ordinance" to remember God's saving act in Passover. The life of the people of Israel has always been shaped by the degree to which they remember God's continuing covenant of salvation with them. That memory also has shaped their relationships with other nations. Now their exile as slaves in Egypt is to end. The Lord is about to pass over their oppression and lead them into the Promised Land. The Passover meal will become central to Israel's ritual life and thereby shape her actions and relationships.

The story of humanity is filled with oppressed people who have identified with Israel's story of freedom from oppression. That can be observed in the spirituals of African Americans and in the central place of the Lord's Supper in the worship life of many African American churches. Indeed as Christians, Communion has become our observance of "a perpetual ordinance." We believe that Christ has become our Passover Lamb. We know that through Jesus, God has passed over us to free us from those powers that oppress and bind us. Like the Israelites, we have been set free to claim the covenant of love that comes to us as we remember our identity in Christ. So the issue for us remains: How do we remember our Passover? Does it shape our lives?

Lord, you have freed us from all that would enslave us. You have passed over our sin and set us free to be your children. Help us to remember who we are and whose we are. Remembering our Passover, may we praise you, serve you, and graciously care for our neighbors. Amen.

The psalmist calls the Israelites to learn a new song. They are very familiar with the songs of sorrow and suffering. But the psalmist reminds them that as "children of Zion" they have a new song to sing, a song of joy and praise of God who has saved them more than once. God has been faithful despite their unfaithfulness. They can sing this new song because they remember the mighty power of God. They remember that "the Lord takes pleasure in his people." They remember that God has adorned them with victory over their oppressors. The new song of joy and praise is to be the heart of their worship.

But a new song is difficult to learn. I have never served a congregation that learned new hymns with much grace. It is easier if the tune is familiar and there is strong accompaniment; easier still if the words are simple and speak of familiar ideas. The psalmist is calling us to sing a new song. The words are simple, faithful, and joyful. The tune is familiar. It's the tune to which our hearts sing of love and peace. The accompaniment is strong. It is those saints who taught us the faith and those who daily support us in our journey. It is also the Holy Spirit gracefully keeping the vision of the Lord of our life ever before us. That vision reminds us of God's faithfulness that frees us from all that oppresses us. It is that vision that fills us with joy and calls us to sing our new song.

Lord, help me remember the many times you have set me free from evil, fear, pain, sorrow, and indifference. By your Holy Spirit, help me more clearly see the vision of your grace in Christ Jesus and feel anew the joy of my salvation. Lord, I praise you, and I will try to sing my new song and to dance with joy. Amen.

The second half of our psalm takes a sharp turn from praising God with a new song and dancing to executing vengeance, punishment, and judgment. Verse 6 tells us to have praise of God in our throats and a two-edged sword in our hands. The vengeance, punishment, and judgment we are to execute are God's, not ours. The phrase translated "two-edged sword" is literally "sword with two mouths."* Could that mean that we are to use two words or forms of praise to realize God's ultimate victory over the powers of evil?

Perhaps it is praise that remembers God's grace and praise that proclaims the hope of God's continuing grace. Such a sword with two mouths can pierce the human heart as a two-edged sword can pierce the human body. While the first half of the psalm is a call to praise, the second is a call to action. The psalmist urges us that as we praise God's grace, we also proclaim grace to all who "are weary and are carrying a heavy burden" (Matt. 11:28).

---

*James L. Mays, ed., *Harper's Bible Commentary* (San Francisco: Harper & Row, 1988), 494.

A Guided Meditation: Get comfortable and relax. Take several deep breaths, and rest between each of these suggestions: Remember when God has been gracious to you. Remember the saints that showed you the way of faith. Remember when you have found rest from the weariness of life. How often do you praise God with a loud voice and dance in God's presence? Who in your life needs to hear Jesus' offer of rest? To whom do you need to show the way to faith? Give thanks to God for your "sword with two mouths."

Paul reminds us that love is central to our lives as Christians. We are to "owe no one anything, except to love one another." He reminds us that love is the fulfillment of all that God requires of us. Love is not a warm feeling or a deep longing. Love is the energy that drives our actions in response to the love God shows us. We do not believe that God loves us because of some warm feeling God has toward us. We believe God loves us because of the way God has acted in our lives through Christ. Here Paul tells us who and how we are to love. We are to love our neighbor as we love ourselves; that is, we are to work for our neighbor's good. Jesus reminds us who our neighbor is: even our enemy is our neighbor. Working for the good of our neighbor is one thing, but to work for the good of our enemies?

When we understand love as acting for good on behalf of others, then love truly can fulfill all that God requires of us. Acting for good on behalf of those we love keeps us from breaking our vows to them. Acting for good on behalf of our neighbors keeps us from harming them. Often we speak of love as if it is sweet and easy, but it is often anything but easy. So the issue Paul presents to us is: Are we willing to do the hard work of action for the good of others? What might our families be like if we love this way? our relationships? our church family? our relationships with "them"?

A Guided Meditation: Get comfortable and relax. Take several deep breaths, and rest between each of these suggestions: Remember how God has acted in your life. Ponder how you might act for good in your neighbor's life. Seek God's help in loving others.

Paul believes that Christ will return before he dies. He urges Christ's followers to remember "what time it is." Two thousand years later, we are not so certain that Christ's return is imminent. Nevertheless, Paul's reminder calls us to live as if Christ were coming tomorrow. Paul tells us that we are closer to God now than when we first believed. With that comes an urgency to "lay aside the works of darkness" to live as people of the light. Paul believes that living as people of the light requires more than loving our neighbor as ourselves. It requires us to live honorable lives. Note that he defines honorable as living free of reveling, drunkenness, debauchery, quarreling, and jealousy. I find it interesting that he puts quarreling and jealousy on the same level as things we often think of as immoral.

Is this what Paul means by loving ourselves? Do we love ourselves by living free of excesses to work for good in our own lives? "Make no provision for the flesh, to gratify its desires." We are not to neglect our own needs, but neither are we to obsess over them. They can easily take control of our lives. That is not loving one's self. When we are self-absorbed, how can we find time to love our neighbor?

A Guided Meditation: Get comfortable and relax. Take several deep breaths, and rest between each of these suggestions: Remember and give thanks for when you first believed. Remember how urgent the moment is. Ask yourself what obsessions you have. Ask for help in regaining control. Ask yourself if you are jealous and quarrelsome. Ask the Holy Spirit to strengthen your love for yourself and your neighbor. Come, Lord Jesus, come and make us more holy. Amen.

As Christians we are called to be reconciled to one another. This issue is very real in most of our Christian fellowships. What am I to do if a sister or brother sins against me? According to Jesus, we are to go to that person and have an honest, loving conversation about the brokenness of our relationship while remembering that the purpose is reconciliation, not judgment or punishment. If that fails, take one or two fellow Christians in order to broaden the conversation but not to overpower the sister or brother. If all else fails, then involve the Christian fellowship. Remember that the emphasis is upon reconciliation rather than browbeating or overpowering.

If all fails, today's reading tells us to let them be to us as a Gentile or a tax collector. Is this a call for shunning? That sounds harsh coming from Jesus until we remember that Jesus tells us to love as he loved. How does Jesus speak of outcasts and tax collectors? He shows compassion and extends love to them. He often is accused of associating more with tax collectors and sinners than with the righteous. That leads us to remember that Jesus never gives up on or shuns anyone. When Peter asks Jesus how many times he is to forgive, Jesus says seventy-seven times. If we are to pray for our enemies, how much more should we continually pray for reconciliation?

A Guided Meditation: Get comfortable and relax. Take several deep breaths, and rest between each of these suggestions: Remember and give thanks for God's reconciling love. Give thanks for friends. Are there people with whom you need to be reconciled? Name them. Give thanks and pray for them. Are there those from whom you need forgiveness? Give thanks and pray for them.

This week's scripture lessons have focused on the importance of remembering God's gracious acts in Jesus Christ; our need to praise God, to have a sword with two mouths, and to love our neighbors as we love ourselves; and the call to be reconciled with those who sin against us. Now we are reminded of the efficacy of prayer, the importance of Christian fellowship, and the sustaining presence of God. Jesus calls us to begin and end our efforts in prayer. Our prayer seeks reunion not victory, and that requires God's assistance. Does prayer ensure reconciliation? As the text says, "It will be done for you, by my Father in heaven."

If we are gathered in Jesus' name, he is among us. This second verse reminds us that the efficacy and power of prayer are realized when we are gathered in Christ's name. To gather in Jesus' name requires more than invoking the name of Jesus. To gather in his name is to be aware of Jesus' teachings and ministry as we consider our prayer request. Finally, we are assured that Jesus will be present to encourage and assist us in our efforts. With that comes the assurance that God is present to sustain us with or without reconciliation.

A Guided Meditation: Get comfortable and relax. Take several deep breaths, and rest between each of these suggestions: Give thanks for God's reconciling love shown to you in Christ. Give thanks for your Christian fellowship. Take time to name two or three people and pray for them. Are there those from whom you need forgiveness? Name them and pray for them. End as you began, giving thanks for God's reconciling love and continuing presence in your life.

Repairing the Story

SEPTEMBER 7–13, 2020 • REGINA M. LAROCHE

SCRIPTURE OVERVIEW: Again this week, Exodus tells a story about Moses that is retold in the psalm. The angel of the Lord protects the Israelites and allows them to cross the sea on dry ground, but their enemies are swept away. The psalmist recalls this glorious event. The forces of nature tremble and bow before the presence of God, and the people are delivered. Paul recognizes that there are matters of personal preference or conscience that are not hard and fast rules. Some will feel freedom in areas that others do not, and we are not to judge each other for these differences. Jesus tells a parable in Matthew that highlights the danger of hypocrisy. We who have been forgiven so generously by God have no right to judge others for minor offenses.

QUESTIONS AND SUGGESTIONS FOR REFLECTION

- Read Exodus 14:19-31. When has the path of faith seemed risky? How have you trusted God and others' wisdom along the way?
- Read Psalm 114. How do you listen and act to repair the story of God's love for the whole world?
- Read Romans 14:1-12. When have you recognized something as more important than your being right? How has that recognition shaped your faith?
- Read Matthew 18:21-35. How do you recognize your own wounds—or those you have inflicted on others—in this parable? How might this parable help you to repair these wounds or the relationships attached to the wounds?

Ecumenical farmer, storyteller, dancer, retreat leader, spiritual director, and worship artist; living in family and community on the edge of Lake Superior; www.DiasporaOnMadeline.com.

A few hardy souls live year-round on an island in Lake Superior. It is often icebound in the northern hemisphere winter.

When the ferry boat can no longer push through the thickening ice, residents pray for an ice road. Usually County Road H is plowed to the mainland across the iced-over water.

Stepping or driving onto the ice road when the GPS is crying "Warning—no road! Turn back now!" can be unsettling. But there are many reasons to cross the water: grocery and supply runs, family emergencies, work, or to escape the cabin fever of being trapped in a beautiful but tiny frozen island world—a privileged run for freedom.

The Israelites have a powerful reason to step into the uncertainty of a road through water: to escape centuries of enslavement and for a chance to repair their history and destiny as God's people. Pharaoh also has reasons, perhaps related to repairing his own sense of destiny.

What plays through the imaginations of Israelite mothers clutching their children, walking a pathway with waters bearing in on either side? Do some Egyptian soldiers pause at the tenuousness of the situation and then choose to follow orders?

As a resident of the Lake Superior Island, I am asked how I dare to venture onto the ice road. I venture onto the ice road not because there is no risk involved with a skin of ice over deep, cold water, but because I trust the ones who tend the road with their generations of experience.

Perhaps some of the Israelites understand the tides and winds. But most likely they take the risky steps into that waterway in a desperate bid for freedom and because of trust in their leader and their God.

God of the risky road to freedom, teach us to trust and walk for the freedom of all. Amen.

The fleeing Israelites praise, dance, and sing as the waters close behind them and rescue them from the pursuit of soldiers intent on re-enslaving them.

Many of us have a story of waters closing behind us. It dwells deep in our bones, in our genetics, in the hidden folds of our souls, in the lyrics of our spirituals, or on thin paper stored carefully in attic trunks. We recognize ourselves in the Israelites: their resistance, fear, anxiety, and complaints along their freedom walk. So we acknowledge the likely sinking of their hearts as waters flood or seep back after their crossing to eliminate the way back and force them on into the unknown. Perhaps this dread coexists with their relief and joy, or perhaps it surfaces later.

Part of the power of the story of God and beloved Creation as recorded in the Bible is how that story intersects with, informs, and is informed by our experiences. As we are called to repair the jagged breaks in God's whole-world family, part of our work is to call forth and recognize the many pieces of God's story in Creation. This touching and piecing together of each bit heals the silenced ones and repairs the whole.

So we invite other pieces of the story. We wonder about the men and horses submerged by miracle waters; the Africans kidnapped and borne away on great waters; the European immigrants crossing starting-over waters; the modern-day migrants tossed on dangerous waters. And we wonder how the image of the bodies of African men washing up on the shore connects to today's disproportionate incarceration, disease, and death rates for brown and black bodies in North America.

Perhaps these wonderings, these invitations, help deepen and repair God's story for the healing of the world.

Creator of the story of life, open our hearts to the stories, questions, pain, love, and healing of this whole world. Amen.

Repairing the Story

Psalm 114 is a praise song of remembrance to be sung at Passover. Passover itself is a festival of lived remembrance, embodied for several days. This holy day is memory experienced through careful preparation, story, song, prayer, blessing, feast table, and children.

Today's psalm sings the story of freedom gifted through miracles, presence, and power of a promise-keeping God. Eight short verses cannot depict every detail of the freedom story. Scrolls, chapters, and books overflow with portrayals of fear and faith, shameful and shining moments, years and yearnings—all significant pieces in the liberation journey of the Israelites. But this song offers powerful images that dive deep into individual and communal history. These images enliven the pieces of the story that repair a people's ability to believe, to step forward with strength and faith, and to look beyond the particularities of their sometimes anguishing circumstances with hope.

This idea of sea, river, mountain—the immovable, the impassable, the impossible—giving way, making way, becoming the way serves time and time again. Thousands of years after this story, Israel's descendants needed this memory in the face of Nazi genocide campaigns and death camps.

This song of surviving the impossibility of enslavement and slaughter, of being in relationship with One who declares people "free at last, free at last" serves many. It touches in deep places the fervor and faith within African heritage people, within indigenous people, within diverse marginalized people. The history of surviving repairs the vision of the world, the vision of ourselves so that it sings in old spirituals, in freedom songs, in liberation theology, in justice movements. It sings, repairing us and all creation in big and small ways.

Promise-keeping God, may your freeing spirit sing in our remembrance and in our day-to-day living. Amen.

Years ago Trevor Hudson, a South African preacher, invited some North American Christians to consider how we build stories, how we choose some elements out of countless events and possibilities as markers to frame the story we will tell ourselves and the world over and over again.

In a world full of faulty, silenced, and damaging stories, we are invited to repair—to make whole the stories by considering the pieces left out, unheard, or unexamined. As the psalmist asks questions of the waters and the hills, we can ask a few questions.

What if we soften our defenses, our sense of already knowing the answers, our fear of doing something wrong, and open our caring curiosity?

What if we open ourselves to a strange language? Perhaps the language is strange because it has unfamiliar sounds or an unfamiliar alphabet. Perhaps the language is strange because the perspective of the story is framed by the ways skin color, culture, gender, or access to food and health affect history and the way events play out. Or perhaps the language is strange because we have little practice listening to the voice, the story of rock, sea, earth, and sky. Our biblical faith ancestors testify to nonhuman creation telling a story of God and responding to or becoming part of the story of human pain and ignorance.

What if we patiently listened for the strange language to become intelligible? We might sense all of creation as "all our relations,"*—part of the body of God. How might this begin the repair of the story, to create a hospitality space that could become a holy refuge or a sanctuary for God?

---

*Translation of the Lakota phrase "Mitakuye Oyasin"

Renewing Creator, allow our lives to listen to the strange languages around us so that we can become tender repairing sanctuary spaces. Amen.

I enter this text as a vegetarian. My spouse, whom I typically adore and highly respect, is an omnivore—an eater of all foods. For almost thirty years we've practiced living, hosting, cooking, praying, and raising children together. We've had to practice Paul's challenge of nonjudgmental welcome to each other around our diets as well as our differences in gender, race, and culture.

At the time of this writing, The United Methodist Church is struggling mightily in excruciating ways about how or if to welcome sisters and brothers of varied sexual orientations into different parts of the life of the church. Judgment abounds amid the disagreement. In the ruckus and heartbreak it's hard to hear Paul's and Jesus' calls and prayers for radical welcome of one another—mutual upbuilding and righteousness, peace and joy in the Holy Spirit (see Romans 14:17, 19) and unity (see John 17:20-21).

So I return to lessons I'm still learning in our small family. Outrage and shock have at times flashed through me at the contrasting ways my spouse and I maneuver and view life with our different races, genders, histories, and more. More often I have been irritated by tiny misunderstandings and perceived minute acts of disrespect. That's when an observant friend who lost her cherished spouse quietly reminds me, "Some things are more important than being right." *Really!*

Perhaps her point is Paul's as well. So I turn gratefully to welcome my beloved and the life we share. I am grateful that our imperfect unity in some way repairs the story we pass on to our children and offers welcome in a world marked by acts of terror, destruction, and separation.

> *Unifying God, may we practice small unconditional welcomes until we gather as one united community—vegetarian and omnivores alike!—around your feast table. Amen.*

In different parts of Africa, you will find a Palaver tree. It's usually large with spreading branches to shelter and shade those who gather below it, making it a tree central to village life. A Palaver tree can be a fig tree, an acacia tree, or— famously—the massive baobab tree. (The baobab is often referred to as the tree of life because it supports myriad life forms in many ways.)

At the Palaver tree, people gather for remembrance and celebration in drum, dance, song, and history; for teaching and envisioning; and to request advice and help. It is also where people gather to negotiate, discuss, and resolve their differences. The welcome of the space is such that anyone may speak and all are viewed equally. In a dispute, the words of a chief and those of a low-ranking citizen are regarded equally: No one is weaker or stronger than his or her opponent. There is no guarantee that a winner will be declared because what happens beneath the reaching arms of the Palaver tree is beyond and outside of the interests of the disagreeing individuals. Those who gather to listen, discuss, and resolve conflict know that the priority is the continued communal life of a people united and at peace.

The reparative truth and reconciliation talks in South Africa, Rwanda, Canada, and other places have risen from this and similar models.

Paul advises us to live our convictions to the honor of God and reminds us that we live and die not to ourselves but to something much bigger. Paul's reminders empower us to welcome others without judgment. Perhaps the invitation is to gather beneath the outstretched sheltering arms of God with time enough to welcome one another and our own selves without condemnation. Perhaps we will be repaired, and perhaps we will repair.

Tree of life God, may we gather in your Spirit to dance peace, healing, and unity. Amen.

I do not know the back story of the characters in this parable. However, key words and phrases catch me: *slave* (which is *servant* or *bondsman* in other translations), *ten thousand talents, seizing him by the throat.*

I am a descendant of enslaved persons impacted by immeasurable wounds from the United States' history of slavery. The slavery in this parable differs from the centuries of slavery in North America. But any form of slavery cuts deep.

The enslaved man in this story owes a debt of ten thousand talents. Some scholars estimate that this debt could be translated into wages from fifteen years to multiple lifetimes. I am a descendant of share croppers—a system in which it was impossible to get out of debt. The hopelessness and harm of this scenario only built upon the scars remaining from enslavement.

"Seizing him by the throat." I am a daughter of a political exile, a refugee who was granted asylum in the United States after he was smuggled away from his would-be killers. My father arrived bearing torture scars on his body and soul. Deeply grateful for his new life, he still unexpectedly spewed violent words and actions from unhealed traumas. These seemed contradictory to his faith ministry and his gratitude for deliverance.

Survivors of trauma manifest disease in their cells, thoughts, and behaviors. How do we outrun the demons within us? But survivors of trauma also manifest incredible resilience, light, and grace. Repair after the tangle of years and generations of damage takes far more than one act of love and forgiveness for the wounded and the wounder. We both are broken.

So perhaps the parable of non-forgiveness and punishment is the story of our woundedness. But perhaps we can repair it and be healed by the invitation in the first verses to forgive again and again: seven, seventy-seven, seventy times seven.

God of many chances, may we practice forgiveness so deep and continuing that we become repaired and repairers. Amen.

Worthy of the Gospel

SEPTEMBER 14–20, 2020 • DAVID RENSBERGER

SCRIPTURE OVERVIEW: The psalmist recounts many of God's glorious deeds. The escape from Egypt features prominently, including the Exodus story we are reading this week. God knows that the people need food and provides both meat and bread. Unfortunately, the people do not have the perspective of the psalmist, so God's miraculous provision does not stop their grumbling. In Philippians, Paul reflects on Christian suffering. Although he would rather be with the Lord, he endures suffering so that he may help others. Other believers should expect to suffer as well. Jesus tells a parable about a landowner. No matter what time the workers go out, they are all equally paid. Likewise, those who follow Jesus their entire lives and those who meet the Lord late in life will partake equally in glory.

QUESTIONS AND SUGGESTIONS FOR REFLECTION

- Read Exodus 16:2-15. When have you been confident of God's love and presence? When have you been uncertain?
- Read Psalm 105:1-6, 37-45. When do you smooth over the "bumps" in the stories of your family, your church, or your faith? When is it important to recount the complaining or mistakes along the way?
- Read Philippians 1:21-30. When has the "good news to the poor" challenged you? When you feel challenged by it, how do you seek to live "worthy of the gospel"?
- Read Matthew 20:1-16. How does Jesus' idea of equality surprise you? How might a posture of generosity change your concept of fairness?

Retired seminary professor; scholar and writer on the Bible and on Christian spirituality; workshop and retreat leader; member of Atlanta Mennonite Fellowship and Oakhurst Baptist Church, Decatur, Georgia.

"Live your life in a manner worthy of the gospel of Christ," Paul exhorts his Philippian readers. He encourages them to live in a way that reflects the good news of God's love, mercy, and empowerment for new life. "Living worthily" does not mean following a strict set of rules but rather embodying the message of liberating divine love seen in Jesus Christ.

This love made itself known particularly in Jesus' offering of himself for humanity. In Philippians 2, Paul quotes an early Christian hymn that celebrates how Jesus abandons his "equality with God" and empties himself to become "obedient to the point of death." This is the mind-set that the Philippians are to take up.

This mind-set will hold the Philippians together in unity and enable them, in a time and place where their faith is peculiar and contested, to endure suffering for Christ as Christ has suffered for them. Such endurance is not all there is to live "worthy of the gospel," but it is an inescapable part.

Because God's love is embodied in the poor, outcast, and condemned Messiah, Jesus, those who enjoy affluence, power, and security in a well-established system may hear the "good news to the poor" (Luke 4:18) as a challenge. Those who accept this good news must be prepared to give of themselves for the well-being of others and be prepared for the backlash that may come.

The Philippians share in this privilege of suffering for Christ alongside Paul. The life worthy of the gospel is not restricted to a few; it is for all who have received it in faith.

Christ, who accepted human life and its sufferings on our behalf, grant us faith and courage to bear our share of the gospel life for the good of all those created in the image of God. Amen.

The parable of the workers in the vineyard appears to take place in the familiar world of workers, bosses, and paychecks—including the perhaps all-too-familiar world of subsistence wages. But don't let appearances fool you! Rather than reflecting ordinary everyday life, this story is a strange one—like the parable of the mustard seed that impossibly becomes a tree or the ludicrous shepherd who leaves ninety-nine sheep to seek one. (See Luke 13:18-19; 15:3-7.)

This parable seems to make no earthly sense. We may feel that the workers who started early in the day are *right* to be aggrieved. We wonder whether any employer would act like this landowner—certainly none who ever wanted to get a full day's work from anyone again!

We can see in the landowner's strange behavior a representation of the unearned grace of God that Jesus preaches. His mission accepts many who appear to repent only at the very last minute. Yesterday they were prostitutes and tax collectors; today Jesus opens the door to the reign of God to them. Why should they get equal treatment with the faithful and diligent, with those who have spent long lives "seeking the reign of God and God's justice" (Matt. 6:33, AP)?

Yet Jesus tells these faithful ones (could they be you and me?): "Relax. Be glad that the God you have served so well is generous" (AP). Like the prodigal son (see Luke 15:11-32), this parable is addressed not to sinners to urge them to repentance but to good people to urge them to join with God in joyous generosity. Jesus' message of unmerited kindness is the gospel Paul urges us to live worthily of.

Generous God, whether over a long life or starting just now, we are grateful that we are able to serve you alongside others whom you love. Amen.

If the parable of the workers presents God's grace in a story with surprising social contours, it fits well with what precedes it. In Matthew 19, Jesus overturns expectations about family and property, reducing the absolute rights of men and elevating vulnerable children to be proprietors of God's reign. He advises a successful young man seeking eternal life to sell his goods and follow him, since wealth is an obstacle to God's reign. His disciples protest repeatedly, but the final verse says it all: "Many who are first will be last, and the last will be first" (Matt. 19:30).

The parable of the workers embodies this drastic proverb but probes deeper still into the nature of justice and equity. The landowner promises the workers hired first, "I will pay you whatever is right," and when they complain replies, "I am doing you no wrong." It may feel unfair. Yet for Jesus, what is right is what is generous, not what balances out.

The first-hired also complain, "You have made them equal to us who have borne the burden of the day." Perhaps the landowner knows that the workers hired later have also borne a burden: anxiety over whether they will find work to feed their families. The landowner then addresses a complaining worker as "friend," implying that they are socially comparable, something a landowner and a day laborer never could be.

Those who labored long are treated as equal both to those who were hired last and to their rich employer. This strange justice reflects God's enormous grace. We are not merely servants but *friends*, companions of God—and we are all friends, on an equal footing, whatever our spiritual and moral achievements.

Loving God, your generosity goes beyond what we expect or desire. Help us rejoice that you call us friends, and help us act as friends to all. Amen.

If only we had died . . . in the land of Egypt, when we . . . ate our fill of bread." When we go through liberating change, we may feel that the grass is greener not only on the other side but also in the fenced-in yard where we used to live.

The Israelites' long journey through the wilderness is fraught with peril; we can't blame them for wanting to be assured of resources. The manna story fits into a pattern of anxious questioning. Just before and after it, the complaint is about water: the bitter water of Marah and the waterless waste of Massah and Meribah. (See Exodus 15:22-27; 17:1-7.) In the first case, God shows Moses wood to sweeten the water; in the second, God has Moses bring water out of a rock.

In Exodus, the Israelites suffer lack, complain, and have their needs supplied by God. They "test" God (17:2, 7), who also "tests" them (15:25; 16:4; 20:20). When they arrive at Sinai, they are ready to make a covenant of obedience (19:8). Later, though, they still longingly remember the abundance of Egypt: "there is nothing at all except this manna" (Num. 11:6).

Do we fail to "live worthily of the gospel" by complaining that there's nothing to live on but miracles? A life bounded by rules and regulations seems safer and more predictable than the freedom of the gospel. A life bounded by nothing at all seems more gratifying than the way of the cross. The gospel life, formidable in its self-emptying yet shot through with the liberating presence of God, may leave us wishing for remembered or imagined alternatives. "If only we had died in Egypt!"

God of redemption, we have heard that you stand ready to meet our needs. Open our hearts to complete faith, so that we may always rely on you. Amen.

Read Exodus 16:12 a few times. How do you hear God's voice? Aggravated, almost threatening? "I heard that! Here, take this and keep quiet!" Or gentle and promising? "Yes, children, I hear you. You'll be all right. It's me—I've got this!"

I admit that I've always heard God's voice as exasperated in this passage. But in working on this meditation, I began to hear something different. Our ways of reading the Bible are often conditioned by remembering the scariest passages or by things we were taught that seemed simple but had hidden biases. Perhaps the God we are afraid to complain to is more patient than we imagine.

Like the parable of Jesus we looked at earlier this week, the actions of both the Israelites and God in these stories may be more complex than they seem. As we learned yesterday, God and the people keep testing one another, probing one another's faithfulness. The people express their uncertainty and complain about water and food. Yet mingled with this mistrustful grumbling is obedience and ultimately firm commitment: "Everything that the Lord has spoken we will do" (Exod. 19:8).

God's complex behavior toward the Israelites is represented in the ambiguity in Exodus 16:12. God is committed to rescuing them and supplying their needs along the lengthy road to freedom. Yet there is that note of annoyance mixed in, almost browbeating the people with abundance until they recognize the Lord as their God. This mix of divine patience and aggravation persists throughout the stories of the Exodus wanderings.

Our spiritual journeys are likely to be complex. Our motives are mixed, our relationship with God is . . . complicated. All relationships are. Growth in trust and growth in love take place through stretches of both confidence and uncertainty.

As a meditation exercise, chart some times in your life when you have wondered about God's care and times when you have felt confident of it.

This selection from Psalm 105 includes the story of "bread from heaven" that we read in Exodus. When comparing this psalm to the version of the story in Exodus, the differences are striking: In the psalm the Israelites do not grumble about food and water; they only "ask," and God provides.

Psalm 105:7-36, the portion omitted from today's reading, sings of the covenant with the patriarchs, God's protection of them, and the Exodus. Narrative psalms like this are not just recitations of historical events. They are hymns for use in worship, in this case probably in celebration after the people of Judah return from exile in Babylon in the late sixth century BCE.

Exodus motifs are important for postexilic returners to the Promised Land. Psalm 105 focuses on God's care for Israel, especially protection from foreign powers, and on God's gift of the land to them. The covenant made by the God who rules all the earth (see vv. 7-11) is a promise of continued protection for those who have returned to the land.

For this psalm, it is in the land rather than during the Exodus that the people keep God's statutes. As in Ezra and Nehemiah, returning to the land means keeping the Torah. (See Nehemiah 8–9.) There is no point recounting the people's complaining during the Exodus, since the period of rebellion is over.

People often tell stories of their families, churches, and communities that level out the bumps in the road and straighten the twists and turns. Sometimes we need to create a milder story, especially when we are starting over with new hopes. "Inconsistencies" in the Bible reflect the normal inconsistencies in human life. Sometimes we need to hear sharp truths; sometimes brighter reminiscences serve a specific need.

God of truth, help us to discern with clear but gentle insight the time to confess our faults, to you and to ourselves, and the time to remember your faithfulness and our desire to respond in faith. Amen.

Living worthily of the gospel includes Christlike self-giving and God's joyful generosity; friendship with God and equality with others; abandoning fantasies of security and accepting complexity; discerning God's correction and God's encouragement. The good news is that we don't have to do it all on our own.

Earlier in Philippians, Paul expresses confidence "that the one who began a good work among you will bring it to completion by the day of Jesus Christ," and prays that their love may abound in insight "to determine what is best," and so produce "the harvest of righteousness that comes through Jesus Christ" (1:6, 10-11). Later he urges them, since he can't be with them, "to work out your salvation with fear and trembling, for it is God who works in you to will and to act in order to fulfill his good purpose" (2:12-13, NIV).

The Philippians don't need Paul's presence for guidance. Nor do they generate lives "worthy of the gospel" on their own. They don't have to be anxious about whether they are doing enough or doing it right. The righteousness (or justice) God desires, even the will to do justice, is created by divine purpose and action among them, created by God's activity through Christ in them.

The life Paul envisions as "worthy of the gospel" calls for discernment, determining what is best, by attending to the guidance and movement of the Spirit within the believer and the believing community. Our spiritual and moral lives are not just a matter of our personal growth. They are part and parcel of God's overarching plan for humanity and all creation. God is active in us, works hand-in-hand with us, to accomplish what needs to be accomplished for the sake of justice and righteousness.

Through prayer or meditation, offer your openness to the Spirit to work from within you to move the good purpose of God toward completion.

Remember Who and Whose We Are

SEPTEMBER 21–27, 2020 • MARIA A. KANE

SCRIPTURE OVERVIEW: For the second time this year, we read the story of the Israelites complaining in the desert about water, only to see God provide a miraculous spring. The psalmist reminds the people of the many powerful deeds performed by the Lord, including leading them through the sea out of Egypt and providing them water from the rock. Paul emphasizes to the Philippians the need for humility and unity. In quoting the earliest known Christian hymn, Paul encourages them with the example of Christ, who gives up all his rights for the sake of others. In back-to-back encounters with religious leaders, Jesus evades an attempt to trap him in his words and then teaches that true obedience is shown not by our speech but by our actions.

QUESTIONS AND SUGGESTIONS FOR REFLECTION

- Read Exodus 17:1-7. When have you tried to "do it all"? How can admitting your limitations help you lead?
- Read Psalm 78:1-4, 12-16. Recall times when you have known God's presence. How might remembering and retelling these stories shape your faith?
- Read Philippians 2:1-13. How does your life speak of God's love for you and for all humanity?
- Read Matthew 21:23-32. How have you created your idea of Jesus in your own image? What would change if you found your identity in Jesus rather than creating Jesus' identity from your own?

Episcopal priest; historian; proud godmother; Texan residing in Maryland.

As a child, whenever I found myself complaining, hurt, or wishing ill-will on someone who had wronged me, my grandmother would say to me: "Always remember who you are and whose you are." If I was in the wrong, her words reminded me to treat others better. If I was on the receiving end of someone else's meanness, her words reassured me that I couldn't be reduced to petty spats and arguments. Nearly forty years later, her words are a balm of strength and comfort in the face of darkness and doubt. To remember who we are as baptized children of God is to remember that in life and in death, we remain captive to God's tender yet fierce love and devotion. No matter what we do or don't do, God will not abandon us. Above all, to remember who we are is to know that we are not called to settle for simply getting by in life; God yearns for us to thrive as whole beings.

It can be hard to remember this all-encompassing love. Amid the barren wilderness and the weariness of the long journey to the Promised Land, all the Israelites want is immediate relief, even if that means a return to slavery. However, as God's chosen people, they were not created for enslavement—no one is. They, and we, are called to know and experience the richness of God's abundance and creation.

When circumstances leave us overwhelmed and feeling forsaken, it's easy to retreat and yearn for what was familiar and guaranteed. But we aren't called to settle for the status quo. We are called to the greatness of children who know who and whose we are.

God, when circumstances lead me to forget, help me to remember what matters most. Amen.

The Temple leaders are flummoxed. For once, instead of having all the answers, they are at a loss for words. When they ask Jesus to account for his authority as God's son, he in turn asks them to explain whom they believe John the Baptist to be. If they acknowledge John's authority as coming from God, then they know Jesus will question them for failing to heed John's message to change their hearts and lives. They don't want to look stubborn or hard-hearted in the eyes of the people they lead. On the other hand, if they deny that John is a prophet, they run the risk of stirring the ire of the crowds of people who heeded John's words and are now following the way of Jesus.

No matter how they answer, the Temple leaders know that their reputation, authority, and future as leaders are at stake. Because the chief priests and elders cannot imagine themselves outside of their role as experts and leaders on whom others are dependent, Jesus' question is more than a true/false question. It's a question about meaning, purpose, and authority.

What should they do?

What would you do in their situation?

From whence do you draw your identity and purpose? Do you see yourself only in relation to your profession or lack thereof? Are you most comfortable identifying who you are in accordance with your relationship to others—perhaps as the "responsible" older sibling, the aimless and mellow middle child, or the parent who can fix anything?

Amid the varying expectations and responsibilities placed upon us, our purpose and authority can be found in how we receive and respond to the love and grace poured into our lives through Jesus' life, death, and resurrection.

By whose authority will you live your life today?

God, help me to derive my purpose and identity from you and not the expectations of others. Amen.

Several years ago, I began a new job thousands of miles from family and friends. Not long after settling in, the peculiar rhythms and challenges of the position left me lonely, regretful, and in despair. After a particularly hard day I confessed to a friend that I had no idea how I would make it through the remainder of my contract. She listened, prayed with me, and promised to keep believing and trusting in God's goodness toward me even if I struggled to do so. A week later, she sent me a few words of encouragement she had scribbled on the back of a napkin. She continued sending similar notes every week for the next several months until I found myself on stronger ground. Her messages rarely said much beyond a few words of scripture or a reminder of some event in the past in which God's presence had been palpable in my life. Over time, I found myself more attuned to the presence of God around me. Above all, the notes reminded me of the ways in which God has always made a way out of seemingly no way—from the dawn of creation until now. When I couldn't remember, she did it for me.

The act of remembering has long been a foundation for God's people, especially amid slavery, exile, or oppression. Psalm 78, which speaks to this tradition, is an act of remembrance and a call to hope. When circumstances suggest otherwise, recounting God's faithfulness helps the Israelites see beyond their despair into the truth of their faith, even when they struggle to believe. Perhaps, most *especially* when they cannot believe. Don't give up. You are in good company—the company of the saints in light.

Meditate on a word or phrase in today's psalm. Write it on a slip of paper, and keep it with you throughout the day.

Remember Who and Whose We Are

Sometimes our greatest threat is not from what others do to us but what we do to ourselves. When I first began serving as a solo pastor, I was eager to quiet comments about my age and fitness by leading in whatever way I could. If people expected me to serve for forty hours a week, I'd serve fifty. If they wanted me to stop by the ladies' lunch, I'd arrive early and be the last to leave. If someone presented a question at Bible study for which I had no answer, I'd stay up late scouring for one. It didn't take long for a case of burnout to reveal that much of what I thought was proof of my dedication and leadership was actually a case of pride and fear—fear of letting people down, of not being who I thought others expected me to be, of not being enough. In short, I was afraid to acknowledge the limitation of being human.

Moses, on the other hand, is quick to admit his fears and limitations and reveals the making of a true leader. Faithful leadership isn't about having all the answers, being the loudest in the room, or not making mistakes. Faithful leaders look to God for guidance and slow down long enough to recognize the ways that God provides direction, support, and strength. Letting go of the illusion of control can be hard; but the more we do it, the more we begin to see that God's grace and mercy—not our efforts—have been sustaining and will sustain us.

May we, like Moses, come to see that surrender is not a sign of weakness but the path that leads to freedom.

God, help me to see my limitations not as a sign of weakness but as an opportunity to place my strength and trust in your loving faithfulness throughout the ages. Amen.

Don't do anything for selfish purposes, but with humility think of others as better than yourselves" (CEB). The truth of the matter is that Jesus is better than everyone else, but he refuses to brag about it! Considering that he is God's son, Jesus has every reason to put people in their place whenever they challenge his authority or question his judgment. Vindication or being "right" is never on Jesus' mind, only love.

Instead, he lets the way he lives his life speak for itself. That's why he loves, serves, prays, and teaches with abandon—even with the people who most question his worthiness and presence. This isn't simply an act of willpower for Jesus. By not worrying about getting ahead or cementing his reputation and future, Jesus is able to continue setting the stage for the world's redemption.

Jesus is confident in his identity and therefore his purpose and mission. Can we say the same? I know that far too often I am more concerned with being right and making sure that others know it than I am with listening, letting go, and seeking harmony with others.

Paul reminds us that our highest aim is not to win, succeed, or be right. God calls us to offer ourselves in humble service and love to others. In doing so we prove to the world that the only love and validation that matter are God's. Through Jesus' death and resurrection, such affirmation is eternal for us. Today, can you slow down? Think before speaking. Listen before answering. Love before judging. Love is the only thing worth proving.

Loving God, you poured out your love in the form of Jesus. In doing so you proved once and for all that what matters most is not power and might but sacrificial, life-giving love. Help me to embrace the humility that Jesus embraced. Amen.

"L isten, my people, to my teaching; tilt your ears toward the words of my mouth" (CEB).

So many things clamor for our attention that it can be hard to know what's most important. Between social media and the twenty-four-hour news cycle, we're conditioned to believe that we must stay on top of things in order to be relevant and ready. This rush to know, however, can lead us to drown out the wisdom and perspective that time, stillness, and prayer can bring. Today's psalm invites us to consider what we're listening to. What gives us a sense of purpose and meaning? What shapes our decisions and choices? To whom do we give most of our attention and allegiance?

As much as I'd like to think I'm focused only on doing God's will, I must admit that I'm sometimes tempted to seek the approval of others or hop on to the latest trend. Other times, I look to my work to shore up my sense of purpose and meaning. But if we only hear what's wrong or how to cut corners, we'll probably be inclined to do the same. If we are constantly attuned to our society's obvious and not-so-obvious messages about success, striving, achievement, and acquisition, we will be unable to hear the truth about ourselves and one another—that we are beloved. But if we hear of God's faithfulness, we may find that we have an anchor amid life's turbulence. Indeed, when we stop to be still in God's presence, we can recognize that all that we need is not on TV or our smartphones but in the cross of Christ, calling us to a life of forgiveness, beauty, and grace.

Ever-present God, you are always among us, speaking to us in the most unexpected ways. Help us to have eyes to see and ears to hear your truth and hearts courageous enough to follow you. Amen.

Remember Who and Whose We Are

If the popularity of superhero comic books, action movies, and comic conventions are any indication, our society is desperate for someone who will sweep in at just the right moment to save the day. Christians aren't immune to this yearning either. A few years ago, I saw an advertisement for an action figure called Superhero Jesus. Superhero Jesus had strong muscles positioned for a fight. I originally laughed at the idea because most depictions of Jesus portray someone of rather average build with an otherwise forgettable frame. But the more I thought about it the more I realized that we all have the tendency to make Jesus in our own image at times—be it meek Jesus, superhero Jesus, or helpless baby Jesus. Like some of the religious leaders, we can find ourselves believing and insisting that what we think and feel must be exactly what Jesus thinks and feels.

For the religious leaders, Jesus is exactly who they didn't want. They are expecting someone who will vanquish all their political enemies in battle, a first-century superhero. Instead, they get someone who came as a baby from the "wrong side of the tracks." Jesus is prone to the same hunger, sleepless nights, and fears that we have. He does not use pithy one-liners to silence his foes. Nor does he seek revenge. He only seeks to make us one with himself and with God. Jesus does not wield a sword to shed the blood of others; rather, his hands, his feet, his side become instruments of love as his own blood is shed on the cross.

It's more than anyone could have imagined. It's all any one of us will ever need.

God, when I'm tempted to make Jesus in my own image, help me to see Jesus as he really is—meek, passionate, humble, committed, merciful, and more than enough. Amen.

It's time to order

The Upper Room Disciplines 2021

Regular edition: 978-0-8358-1924-4

Enlarged-print: 978-0-8358-1925-1

Kindle: 978-0-8358-1926-8

eBook: 978-0-8358-1927-5

Bookstore.UpperRoom.org

or

800.972.0433

Disciplines App Now Available

Read *The Upper Room Disciplines* on the go with your mobile device. Download the app through your smartphone app store.

Did you know that you can enjoy

The Upper Room Disciplines

in multiple ways? Digital or print?

The Upper Room Disciplines is available in both regular and enlarged print, but are you aware that it is also available in digital format? Read a copy on your phone, computer, or e-reader. Whatever your preference, we have it for you today.

Visit Bookstore.UpperRoom.org or call 800.972.0433 to learn more about digital and print combo subscriptions.

What is a standing order option?

This option allows you to automatically receive your copy of *The Upper Room Disciplines* each year as soon as it is available. Take the worry out of remembering to place your order.

Need to make changes to your account?

Call Customer Service at 800.972.0433 or e-mail us at

CustomerAssistance@upperroom.org.

Our staff is available to help you with any updates.

Stop, Look, Listen

SEPTEMBER 28–OCTOBER 4, 2020 • AUTUMN DENNIS

SCRIPTURE OVERVIEW: A common theme this week is the danger of self-absorption. When we are young, we may struggle to understand the importance of rules because we think that our individual freedom is the highest good. God gives the Israelites commandments to guide their relationships with God and others. These laws will help them thrive because God knows what is best for us. The psalmist understands this: The laws of the Lord are good and sweet. Self-absorption might also lead to pride. Paul shows that a true understanding of the gospel means laying aside our rights in the knowledge that God will reward us. In a parable about the rejection of the prophets and Jesus, servants seek to seize a vineyard for themselves, unwisely ignoring that the owner will eventually reclaim what is his.

QUESTIONS AND SUGGESTIONS FOR REFLECTION

- Read Exodus 20:1-4, 7-9, 12-20. Recall your earliest experiences with the Ten Commandments. How do they continue to shape your understanding of God's expectations?
- Read Psalm 19. How does the natural world call you to follow God?
- Read Philippians 3:4b-14. Whom do you emulate? What would it mean for you to emulate Christ in life and in death?
- Read Matthew 21:33-46. When have you participated in or witnessed the rejection of one who could be God in disguise? How might things be different if you had recognized that person as a potential cornerstone of your community?

Director of Missions, Manchester UMC in greater St. Louis, Missouri; native of Nashville; graduate of Vanderbilt Divinity School and Eden Theological Seminary; ordained through the Catholic Worker Movement.

In this passage, we witness Moses delivering the Ten Commandments to the nation of Israel. When we think of the Ten Commandments, we may remember memorizing them in Vacation Bible School or seeing them displayed in front of courthouses as symbols in political battles. For many of us, they've lost their meaning.

But the people of ancient Israel are hungry to hear a word from God spoken through Moses as they wander in the wilderness toward what God has promised them. The first commandment in today's reading is a declaration of who God is—the God who delivers captives from slavery. God cannot be replicated, replaced, or compared. God's name in the scriptures, often written as "Yahweh," is unpronounceable and cannot be spoken. Many in the Jewish tradition today will spell the word God as "G-d" to remember this holy, unspeakable name. In not saying God's sacred name carelessly, we remember how set apart God is.

The last commandment of our readings today is the commandment to keep the sabbath day holy and to rest from work on this day. I once heard a rabbi speak who was asked about why orthodox Jews refuse even to turn on lights or cook food on the sabbath day. He said that in essence, keeping sabbath is not only about working but also about taking a break from "creating" in order to remember our Creator. In not turning on lights, we remember the One who said, "Let there be light." In not working the earth, we remember the One who created the earth.

Loving God, help me remember that you are God and I am not. Help me to rest from my creations to recenter on you. Amen.

Today we read more of the commandments God gives the people of Israel through Moses on the mountain. We recognize the familiar "thou shalt nots," and the passage ends with a scene of thunder, lightning, a trembling mountain, and people cowering in fear. They say, "Don't let God speak to us, or we will die!" Moses assures them that they do not need to be afraid of God, but the fearsome image remains.

We can be turned off by long lists of "do not do this" or streams of negative statements, no matter how good the ideas may be for our well-being. When it comes to scripture, sometimes our avoidance of "not to-dos" is paired with religious guilt—does this mean I'm a bad person? How can we connect with passages when we personally do not struggle not to murder or not to steal? Perhaps this is an opportunity to reimagine these scriptures in their "positive" versions. Such a rewriting might help us dig deeper into the heart of what the commandment is saying to us across the ages.

"You shall not murder": Work to pursue life-giving things; advocate for those being crushed under oppression; uphold peace and love.

"You shall not commit adultery": Uphold yourself with fidelity, honor, and trustworthiness.

"You shall not steal": Be satisfied with all you have, and give generously.

"You shall not bear false witness against your neighbor": Speak with truth, integrity, justice, and joy.

"You shall not covet": Instead of seeking the next new thing, thank God for what you have.

Loving God, help us to be centered in gratitude, love, hope, joy—life-giving things. Help us to engage more fully with you and your words. Help us to pause and reflect more deeply on how you are speaking to us today. Amen.

Many of us are constantly inundated with busyness. Email inboxes demand our attention. Our calendars are full with appointments. Our sabbath days often become full of chores—the exact opposite of the point! We find it hard to rest, and even when we do, we are plagued with the sense of "I should be doing something right now. What am I forgetting?"

Recently, I was sitting in a seminary class next to an open window. While my mind was racing with papers I had to write, sermons I needed to prepare for church, and the endless stream of projects waiting for me after class was over, I noticed a spider spinning a web on a bush covered in dew. While I am not a fan of eight-legged creatures, I was in awe of how this spider seemed to tell me that her agenda for the day consisted of finding food and making this web. This web, while small, was mighty and beautiful.

Later that week, I decided to walk to a local coffee shop to do some sermon writing. Even though it is only two blocks away, I often drive to this coffee shop because I am impatient and feel rushed to complete my tasks. As I walked through my neighborhood, I noticed the changing of the leaves, the slight crispness of the air, and my neighbor's garden. I heard laughter from the local playground and the whispering and chirps of birds and squirrels. How might our sense of busyness change if we slowed down enough to notice and take stock of the beauty around us?

Loving God, you have made the beauty of the world with tender care. Open our eyes to recognize your beautiful works so that we can be more present to you. Amen.

Paul reflects on how he was raised to honor the letter of the Jewish law as best he could. For Paul, being a member of the tribe of Benjamin is an honor; they have a reputation for being strong leaders and good warriors. He hails from Tarsus, a large trading post, so he is familiar with many different cultures. He comes from a devout Pharisee family, so he is well-versed in the law. In this passage, he describes how he had lived the letter of the law as closely as he could, yet still it was not enough. He describes that all of his accomplishments, reputation, and law-keeping paled in comparison to the joy of knowing Christ. Paul states that he is now "found" in Christ and that his righteousness comes from faith in Christ.

We often hold ourselves to high standards that can feel like a never-ending checklist we must maintain to feel worthy: go to church, read the Bible, pray frequently, volunteer with the youth group, sign up for service projects, make a casserole for the potluck, listen to a spiritual podcast, read the book everyone keeps recommending, quit gossiping and complaining, don't forget to order altar flowers this year. When we get home, we can be constantly pressured to take care of our families and pets, do what we need to do to stay healthy, be a good employee, be a good friend, and somehow take time to do self-care as well. If only we could be . . . perfect!

Paul knows this struggle. He tells us that even if we did get it all right every time, it still wouldn't be enough. That's okay. Through the grace of God, we can find ourselves in Christ. Through the empowerment of the Spirit, we can grow in the practice of letting go, of learning self-compassion, of knowing that everything we are and everything we have—even our checklists—belong to God. We can rest knowing that God's grace is sufficient.

Loving God, thank you for your grace. Help me to understand how to let go and rest in your presence and power. Amen.

Stop, Look, Listen

When I was younger, I looked up to a lot of people. I wanted to be just like them—I would wear the same clothes as certain celebrities or watch the same shows and listen to the same music as my friends. I wanted to emulate the things that I liked the most about those people. When I became a Christian as a teenager, my desires changed. I wanted to be more like Christ, and I tried to figure out what that meant by reading scripture.

I read passages such as this one, where Paul's fervor and zeal for Christ is especially palpable. He asserts how deeply he wants to know Christ. For him, one way of knowing Christ is emulating Christ. One of the things Paul names is "becoming like him in his death" with the hope that he would also be able to attain resurrection. He sees attaining this as a future goal that Christ will secure for him. In the time that these letters were written, this resurrection was seen as happening imminently.

It's important for us to remember that Jesus' death was strongly political. Crucifixion was a means of death reserved for political insurrectionists and criminals and was meant to be an especially humiliating and public way to die. When Paul says, "I want to die like him," he is saying he too wants to have a life and a cause worth dying for—a cause rooted in grace and inclusion of the marginalized.

Let us slow down as we read Paul's words so we can really absorb the depth of what he is saying. What would it look like for us to press on toward this goal, to be so radically rooted in love that we are willing to die for it?

Loving God, help me to be brave and bold in my love for you and for my neighbor. Empower me to be more like Christ, willing to risk all for the cause of love. Amen.

This parable is sometimes called the parable of the wicked tenants. It is often interpreted as an allegory where Jesus is foretelling how he will be rejected by the Jews. To understand this parable, however, it is important for us to read it in the context of the other parables Jesus is telling at the time. On the day Jesus tells this parable, he begins his teaching by cursing the fig tree for not bearing fruit. Then the Pharisees question his authority because he does not resemble or represent familiar sources of authority, such as rigorous interpretations of the law. Jesus responds with the parable of the two sons, which asks the essential question: "Who understood the heart of the father's will?" This is followed by our passage for today, where the wicked tenants seek to disrespect the vineyard owner by doing whatever they can to usurp his resources. After this passage, the parable of the wedding banquet demonstrates the radically inclusive love of God.

The author of this Gospel is writing to a Jewish audience and is set on showing them that Jesus is the fulfillment of Jewish prophecy, which has foretold that the Messiah would be rejected. However, when we listen to the other stories being told in these chapters, we can hear the deeper story of what was so offensive to the Pharisees. The overall theme of these parables is that God's heart is not centered in rigorous pursuit of the law but bends toward justice and radical inclusion of all people. In welcoming others, we are respecting God and bearing fruit. How can we choose to reject having greedy, cold hearts like the tenants and instead move toward celebrating the abundance of God's resources and seeking to welcome all those who come to us as God-in-disguise?

Loving God, help me to recognize the truth of your radical love that is all around me. Help me to see you in my neighbor. Amen.

Yesterday, we read about the parable of the wicked tenants. Jesus follows this parable by quoting Hebrew scripture: "The stone that the builders rejected has become the cornerstone." The Pharisees hear this and are offended by Jesus' implication that not only will Jesus be the cornerstone but those with whom he associates—tax collectors, prostitutes, those who are considered sinners—will be the first to enter God's kingdom. The Pharisees are offended to hear yet again that these marginalized people will inherit the kingdom of God ahead of them and the religious elite.

What is the importance of a cornerstone? In architecture, the cornerstone was the first stone the builders laid when erecting a building; every other stone would be laid in reference to the cornerstone. If the stone was placed off-center, the entire building would be off-center. A well-founded cornerstone would ensure the building's stability and guarantee that it would not collapse. For Jesus to imply that the kingdom of God will be built upon himself is risky enough. But by including those whom the religious elite reject as unworthy, Jesus places himself squarely at odds with them.

Throughout the Bible, God frequently comes disguised in those we least expect. We frequently affirm that God's ways are not our ways, and we should show kindness to all we meet because we may be meeting angels. Whenever we meet someone whom we struggle to love, we can stop, open our eyes, and consider that God may be meeting us through them. Consider that there are things we can learn from them about God's love. We may be surprised.

Loving God, help me to have the courage to love those whom society casts out. Open my eyes to how you are present with them and what I can learn from them. Amen.

God's People Can Be Wrong

OCTOBER 5–11, 2020 • STEVE HARPER

SCRIPTURE OVERVIEW: The texts this week remind us of how quickly we can turn away from God. Even while Moses is on the mountain receiving the Ten Commandments—the first of which is not to worship any other gods—the people fashion an idol and begin to worship it. The psalmist refers to this story as evidence of how often the Israelites have gone astray, and yet God repeatedly has restored them. The parable in Matthew speaks of many who are invited to a banquet, yet they reject the invitation of the king. It is often read as a warning about turning our backs on God's gracious invitation. Paul encourages the Philippians to seek God with confidence in difficult situations and to focus their thoughts in ways that lead them closer to God.

QUESTIONS AND SUGGESTIONS FOR REFLECTION

- Read Exodus 32:1-14. When have you or your faith community gotten it wrong? When have you interceded with God on others' behalf?
- Read Psalm 106:1-6, 19-23. How has forgetting that you can be wrong hurt you or your faith community? How has admitting that you were wrong strengthened you or your faith community?
- Read Philippians 4:1-9. What issue or conflict has divided your faith community? How might Paul's urging to "be of the same mind in the Lord" help you work toward peace?
- Read Matthew 22:1-14. What work might you need to do to open your heart so you can resolve a conflict?

Retired seminary professor and retired elder in the Florida Annual Conference of The United Methodist Church.

We are never in more danger of getting things wrong than when we are certain we have them right. The saints of the ages warn us against seeking certainty in our faith and remind us that even the people of God can be wrong. Each reading this week offers an example of our ability to be wrong, along with related insights regarding how we might avoid the problem.

We begin with the people of God in the wilderness. When Moses does not return from Mount Sinai when they expect him, they turn to Aaron. Strangely enough, he asks the people to take off their golden earrings and give them to him. He then melts the gold and refashions it into a golden calf. When the people see the calf they declare, "These are your gods, Israel, who brought you up out of the land of Egypt." At first glance, their exclamation seems blatantly false, almost unbelievable. But then they turn the occasion into a hedonistic display.

The Israelites get it wrong when Moses and God do not meet their expectations. They are not the last ones to do so. All the way up to the present day, we are tempted to turn to new leaders who will make us "golden calves" when our accustomed ones do not say and do what we expect. There are always leaders and golden calves to substitute for the real thing. We get it wrong when we live by a "my way or the highway" view of life.

O God, help me to understand what to expect of you so that your will takes center stage. Amen.

By the time Moses makes it back to camp, the people of God are under the spell of the golden calf. God says they "are ruining everything." And God makes it clear that divine fury will soon burn and devour them.

But for reasons not given in the passage, Moses does not take God's decision as the last word on the subject. Instead, he pleads with the Lord to change his mind and not carry out the intention to destroy the people. Amazingly, Moses' intercession prevails, and "the Lord changed his mind about the terrible things he said he would do to his people" (CEB).

Fast forward to Jesus' time. A woman has been caught in the act of adultery. The law is clear: She must die. *Bona fide* religious leaders gather around her to make sure she gets what is prescribed. But Jesus is there too, and like Moses he intervenes and prevents her stoning. (See John 8:2-11.)

Whenever the people of God get it wrong because of their expectations, it's easy to think in terms of consequences: "They made their bed, let them lie in it" or some other version of, "They get what they deserve." From the lesson today, it seems God has felt that way too. But however the mind of God changes, the story in Exodus ends where the story of the woman ends: with mercy. When we read the Psalm lesson tomorrow, we will discover the pivot. Today, it is enough to be amazed at how things turned out. If, for a moment, we put ourselves into Moses' or Jesus' shoes, we may discover times when we must go and do likewise, so that grace is the last word—even when the people of God get it wrong.

Dear God, I am quick to cry out for mercy when I am wrong. Give me the vision and will to cry out for mercy when others get it wrong. Amen.

God's People Can Be Wrong

Perhaps as many as 500 years have gone by between the time the people of God get it wrong in the wilderness and the psalmist writes about it in today's lesson. This tells us that the people of God take their historic sinfulness with dead seriousness, so much so that the psalmist writes, "We have sinned—right along with our ancestors" (CEB). With force equal to the original moment, the people of God are once again getting it wrong.

This time around their rebellion does not seem to be so much that of expectations but of failed understanding. The psalmist means more than forgetfulness, although that is surely a factor. The writer more nearly means that the people of God do not realize that they have not moved beyond being susceptible to the things that resulted in the defeats and downfalls of their predecessors. The scene shifts in today's reading to reveal that the people of God get it wrong through presumptions.

We share a similar history. The church has gotten it wrong before. When we fail to acknowledge this part of our history, we turn susceptibility to being wrong into self-declared certainty that we are right. When we purport certainty, we repeat the mistake of the Israelites in the psalm-period of their history. What we take for correctness is once again arrogance. We allege a certainty about our views apart from the humility to ever call them into question. The psalm names the problem and, as in the wilderness, gives us hope—the hope found in God's steadfast love. We claim mercy not by touting our "correctness" but by making the confession, "We could be wrong"—just as the people of God have been before.

Dear God, I confess—I could be wrong. Keep my heart open and my mind tender through this confession. Amen.

Euodia and Syntyche are at odds with each other, so much so that news of their conflict reaches Paul in Rome. Clearly, their disagreement is not minor, and apparently it has been unresolved for some time. Fellow Christians in Philippi have contacted Paul, asking him to intervene even from a distance. In his letter to the Philippians, he includes the problem in his writing and exhorts his two coworkers in ministry to "come to an agreement in the Lord" and recruit a loyal friend in Philippi to be a mediator toward that end.

God's people can get it wrong in ways that rupture relationships among us and erode the common life of the Christian community. Paul knows this firsthand. He and Barnabas have separated over their sharp disagreement about John Mark's usefulness. (See Acts 15:36-41.) From what little we know, it seems that Paul comes to realize he is mistaken: He later asks Timothy to have Mark visit him because he had been a big help to him in the ministry. (See 2 Timothy 4:11.) Paul's exhortation to Euodia and Syntyche carries not only a note of urgency but also his belief that reconciliation can happen.

We live in a day when God's people get it wrong in our disagreements and need to be reconciled to each other. Sadly, we often stay in our bunkers and settle for animosity and division. When we do this, we weaken our life together, and we diminish our witness in the world. Just as Paul knows the problems have to be addressed, we can pray for a similar conviction when believers are unable to get along with one another.

Dear God, keep me from escalating my disagreement with other Christians to the point where animosity wins over agape. As you see fit, help me be a reconciler when there are divisions in the body of Christ. Amen.

Just as God uses Moses and the psalmist to bring the people of God back to their senses, God uses Paul to effect reconciliation in the Philippian church. We do not know for sure whether Euodia and Syntyche restore their relationship, but we can see the basis Paul uses for exhorting them to do so. His twofold appeal can be useful today when fellow Christians need to be reconciled.

First, Paul counsels the believers to work for emotional stability. He commends a renewal of gladness and gentleness and an elimination of anxiety brought about through earnest prayer. He knows that very little is changed when we live in the whirlwind of negativity. We don't think straight. We don't respond well when we are engulfed by deformative feelings. Paul points to the big Bible word *peace* as the goal for which to aim in reconciliation.

Second, he exhorts the Christians at Philippi to seek edifying soundness. He tells them to think of things that are excellent and admirable. Often, reconciliation occurs not by coming to complete agreement but by deciding that the things that unite us are more important than those that divide us. We come together along the lines of common commitments. Paul names good places for common ground: truth, holiness, justice, purity, loveliness—"all that is worthy of praise." When we get it wrong through disagreements, we are often reunited through our core convictions and common pursuits.

God, give me the will to share in fellowship with other believers, not on the basis of uniformity but on the basis of unity. Teach me the difference between agreeing on things and being in agreement about the things that matter more than disagreements. Amen.

Our Gospel lesson is among the most difficult to interpret of all the teachings of Jesus. If we admit this up front, maybe we have some hope of gleaning something of value from a complex and confusing story.

Context helps. It's the day after Jesus' triumphal entry into Jerusalem. It's also the time when the religious leaders are laying trap after trap to justify their plan to eliminate him. In every respect, the chips are down. Jesus' teachings are more pointed than ever and aimed at those who use religion as a cover-up for all sorts of hypocrisy and sin. Today's reading is the second of two parables linked together (the first being Matthew 21:33-46) to show that the people of God can get it wrong through presumption—in this case, by trying to convince people they should attend the party when, in fact, they have not properly dressed for the occasion.

The story has nothing to do with actual clothing but rather with giving an appearance that doesn't exist. The man in the story has an invitation; otherwise, he would not have gotten inside the door. But he uses his invitation as an excuse for not taking the occasion or his condition seriously. He thinks having an invitation is enough. The religious leaders know Jesus is talking about them (see Matthew 21:45), and they know he is condemning their presumption. Stripped of their outward appearance (represented in the parable by a wedding robe), their hypocrisy is revealed.

The people of God get it wrong whenever we show up alleging to be "clothed" when we are not. Others may be fooled, but God is not. If faith means anything at all, it must be genuine.

Dear God, deliver me from appearing to be someone I am not. Keep me from using my faith as a way to make impressions that are not genuine. Save me from presumption. Amen.

W e come to the end of our readings this week in a strange place. The Gospel lesson puts us there. Unlike the other readings, the parable from Matthew offers no deliverance, no repentance, no resolution. We find no positive outcome. There is no Moses to intercede, no psalmist to call for confession, no Paul to commend reconciliation. The person in Jesus' parable is thrown out of the party—"into the farthest darkness" (CEB).

What are we to make of this? Is this where we are to end up this week? Apparently so, at least from the ordering of the lectionary texts. But why? Keeping in mind that we are in confusing territory in our Gospel lesson, I am nevertheless willing to surmise that Jesus tells the story—at least in part—to remind us that there are times when the only one who can bring us to our senses is ourselves. As the people of God, there are times when we get it wrong, and unless we recognize our error and do something about it, things will not end well. The religious leaders are unwilling to admit they might be wrong, and they never get out of that trap. Perhaps Jesus is telling us that the prerequisite for a changed heart is an open one.

I think this is what Paul means when he writes, "Carry out your own salvation with fear and trembling" (Phil. 2:12, CEB). As Oswald Chambers put it, "You have to work out with concentration and care what God works in."* The man lacked this concentration and care. Rather than gloss over it, Jesus leaves us to see that such presumption is not a good place to be.

---

*Oswald Chambers, *My Utmost for His Highest*, June 6. Chambers's book is available in multiple editions.

God, the sobering end to this week's readings and to today's Gospel lesson leaves me to take seriously the fact that even as your beloved child, I can still get it wrong. Give me grace to do something about it when I am. Open my heart to the humility necessary for change. Amen.

We Belong to God

OCTOBER 12–18, 2020 • BETH A. RICHARDSON

SCRIPTURE OVERVIEW: Popular images often portray God as a passive grandfather figure. However, this is not the picture scripture provides. God's presence has a profound impact on the physical world. In Exodus, Moses feels insecure about the calling on his life and asks to see God's glory. God in part grants this request, but no one can experience the presence of God completely and live. The psalmist describes how God is exalted and how God's holiness shakes the earth itself. The New Testament readings explore different themes. Paul opens his letter to the Thessalonians by commending them for their faith and partnership in the spreading of the gospel. In Matthew, the Pharisees attempt to trap Jesus in his words, yet he confounds their efforts.

QUESTIONS AND SUGGESTIONS FOR REFLECTION

- Read Exodus 33:12-23. When have you struggled to believe that God is with you? How did you find a sign of God's presence?
- Read Psalm 99. How has God heard your cry? How can you listen with God for the cries of others?
- Read 1 Thessalonians 1:1-10. When does your faith call you to live in a countercultural way? How do you show the world how to live?
- Read Matthew 22:15-22. You belong to God. How do you feel God's call on your life?

Director of Prayer and Upper Room Worship Life; worked with *Weavings* 2014–2017.

Thanksgiving Day, Canada

In today's reading, the people of Israel are nearing the end of their wandering in the wilderness. Moses is proclaiming God's word to the people who have journeyed together from the chains of captivity in Egypt through forty years of wandering. Soon the people will enter the Promised Land, "a land where you may eat bread without scarcity, where you will lack nothing."

And yet, the people are reminded, never forget that God is the one who brought you out of slavery. "Take care that you do not forget the LORD your God." God is the one who fed you as you wandered in the wilderness. God is the one who will bring you into "a land of wheat and barley, of vines and fig trees and pomegranates, a land of olive trees and honey." This God is the source of all that is. And you belong to this God.

On this day of Thanksgiving, we recall with gratitude the small and the mighty works of God in our lives and in the world. This God who liberated the people of Israel, who created the stars, the earth, and all that is in it; this same God knelt down on earth, lovingly formed humans from dust, and breathed into them the breath of life.

We belong to this God of all creation, who pushed up the mountains and filled the oceans with life. We belong to this God of all creation who flung the stars to the farthest corners of the night and crafted the most delicate of flowers. We belong to this God who created us and covenanted with us to be partners in creation.

What are the places that you see the small and mighty works of God in your life? In the community around you? In the world? Make a list of the things for which you are grateful today.

Who is this God to whom we belong? In today's reading, this God is proclaimed as the sovereign of the universe, "enthroned upon the cherubim." This enthronement psalm recognizes God as the King of Israel, ruling from the heavens.

Yet, this mighty ruler is active and present in the world, in our lives. God does not sit on a heavenly throne watching over the creation. God is present with us, caring about the least and smallest of God's creation. God is incarnate with us in love.

God is a lover—of wrens and humpback whales, of orchids and redwoods, of candle flames and galaxies, of tender newborns and wise old ones. God, creator of the universe, sovereign of our hearts, is present in every breath, every moment, every heartbeat.

Our response to this God is praise and gratitude. Holy are you, God of the universe, creator of 200 billion galaxies. We praise you, source of all. You loved creation into being, flinging stars across the darkness, forming the earth and its creatures with tender care. You knit us together in our mother's womb. (See Psalm 139:13.) Before we were ever imagined, you knew us and loved us.

This God to whom we belong is a lover of justice, a fierce protector of the vulnerable. "Strong king who loves justice, you are the one who established what is fair" (CEB). Our response to this lover of justice is action. Holy are you, God of the universe, lover of justice, protector of the weak. We praise you, source of all, and we commit ourselves to be justice-seekers in this world that you created. You created us in your image and breathed into us life, love, and passion. May we, your beloved children, join with you as lovers of justice, working for good in the world in our thoughts, actions, and intentions.

What is my response to God, the lover of creation, the lover of justice?

Who is this God to whom we belong? God, the sovereign of the universe, enthroned in heaven upon the cherubim, is not a distant God. This God listens to us and hears our cries.

This sovereign God is present to the people of Israel, calling Moses and Aaron to free the people from captivity in Egypt, leading them into the wilderness, and guiding them in the pillar of cloud by day and fire by night. Even though they grumble and complain and doubt, the Holy One remains faithful to them, leading them to the Promised Land.

In these days of turmoil in our world, it often seems that no one is listening. Who will comfort us when all around us seems to be turned upside down? Who will guide us when we do not know the way to go? Who will listen to our cries of sadness, grief, and despair?

The God to whom we belong hears our cries. God hears the moans of a wounded world in the turmoil of a warming planet. God hears the keening of those who have lost loved ones in disasters, in war, in acts of terrorism, in instances of gun violence. God hears the anger and pain of the victims of sexual assault and discrimination. God hears the prayers of those who suffer because of the color of their skin, the country in which they were born, or their immigration status. God hears the despair of LGBTQ youth who struggle, wondering if it is worth continuing in this world.

God hears the cries of our hearts. Some of these desires we can name. And some of these yearnings are hidden even from ourselves. God hears our cries, spoken and unspoken, known and unknown.

Take time to list the cries of the universe, the world, the nation, your community, your family, your heart. Offer these cries, those known and unknown to you, to the God to whom you belong.

In today's reading the people of Israel are in a time of crisis. They have broken their covenant with God by making golden idols. God has called the people of Israel "stiff-necked" and is considering sending them into the Promised Land alone. (See 33:3, 5.)

But Moses argues with God on behalf of the people. "Don't send us alone," Moses pleads. "If your presence is not with us, how will others know who we are?" (AP). Moses acknowledges that we are indeed a stiff-necked people. And we will probably mess up again. So send your presence as a mark upon us so that others will know that you are our God and we are your people.

God hears the pleas of Moses on behalf of the people and agrees to what Moses has asked. And then, Moses, emboldened, asks to see God. Moses cannot see God's face and live, but God will put Moses in a cleft of rock, cover Moses while God goes by, and then let Moses see God's back.

In this story we're invited to reflect on the ways that we are stiff-necked, stubborn, and hard to control. We are a people who think that our way is the right way. If we suspect that God is not keeping up God's end of the bargain, we are likely to strike out on our own, making it up as we go along.

Yet we have this yearning to be able to see God—if not God's face, how about a peek at God's back? We travel through a wilderness in our own homes, communities, and nations. We long to see glimpses of God's good work in the world. We hunger for signs of God's presence with us.

Reflect on the places in your life where you feel you are in a wilderness. Where are you seeing glimpses of God's good work in the world? Write a prayer of yearning and gratitude.

This passage from Matthew's Gospel finds Jesus back in Jerusalem in the last week of his life. He has cleansed the Temple (21:12-17), cursed a fig tree (21:18-22), confronted those who questioned his authority (21:23-27), and recounted parables (21:28-33; 22:1-14). He is then confronted by Pharisees who attempt to entrap him with the question, "Is it lawful to pay taxes to the emperor, or not?"

Jesus asks to see the coin used to pay the tax, and when a denarius is produced, he asks whose head is on the coin. It is the emperor's, and Jesus says to them, "Give therefore to the emperor the things that are the emperor's, and to God the things that are God's."

Through this statement, we are invited to take a closer look at our own "coins"—the things we place value on through our commitments of time, attention, resources, and energy. What are the parts of our lives that belong to the culture versus those that belong to God? And do those "coins" reflect the values that we want to hold? What image is written on our hearts?

As those who belong to God, we can ask ourselves, *What does it mean for me to give to God the things that belong to God? What parts of my life do I hold back from surrendering to God?* We might hold back our relationships, finances, jobs, churches, or political views. What would it mean for us to give to God all of ourselves—our hopes, fears, dreams, grief, disappointments, and regrets?

Spend some time today examining the ways you live out your values. To what do you give the greatest commitment of time? money? attention? worry? Based on these commitments, what image is written on your heart? What are the things you are holding that need to be surrendered to God? What would it mean if you gave to God all of yourself?

Our passage today is from Paul's letter to the Christian converts in Thessalonica—one of his earliest missionary journeys. Paul affirms the people: "You became imitators of us and of the Lord, for in spite of persecution you received the word with joy inspired by the Holy Spirit."

It's hard for us to imagine the experience of this community, which holds the message of a new faith in a community that has never experienced Christians before. Paul visits for a time, living with, teaching, and orienting people to the new faith. And then they are left on their own, holding on to what has been given to them. Living, as most of us do, in a predominantly Christian culture, we have no frame of reference for the experience of these early Christians.

Yet we can identify with their experience of having been called to live a life that is countercultural. As Christ followers, we are called "to do justice, and to love kindness, and to walk humbly with [our] God" (Mic. 6:8).

When we follow Jesus, we are called to Christ's ministry to the poor, the sick, the prisoners, the hungry, and the stranger. We are commanded to welcome the refugee among us. To provide for those who are hungry and homeless. To work for justice for the LGBTQ members of our communities. To hear and respond to the cries of those who have been assaulted or abused by persons they had trusted. To break down systems that oppress and imprison a greater proportion of black and brown bodies. These "Christian values" are often in conflict with the prevailing actions of our societal and political leaders. May we follow in the steps of the Christ who marked and named us, that we may "[show] all the Christians in the countries of Macedonia and Greece [and the United States and Canada and all the world] how to live" (NLT).

God of love, guide our steps so that we may follow the Christ who claims us. Amen.

In this passage, Jesus asks to see the coin used to pay the taxes to the emperor. He asks what image is on the coin and counsels to "Give . . . to the emperor the things that are the emperor's, and to God the things that are God's." Earlier in this week we examined our "coins" and the things on which we place value through our time, attention, resources, and energy.

As those who belong to God, let us consider that it is our human image that is written on God's "coin." Created in God's image in the womb of creation, God forever marked us as beloved. God carries our image stamped on God's heart, cherished, cared for, loved, and nurtured. God holds us in great value.

Like the children of Israel in Exodus 33, we have been selfish and "stiff-necked." We often make decisions that do not offer life to one another or to the world that God has created. We spend our lives seeking the treasures of the earth and losing our way in a culture that values riches over relationships. We cannot recognize our own selfishness and greed. Yet God continues to woo us and to love us. This God of creation, the one to whom we belong, holds us in love and invites us into a new commandment, that we should love God and love our neighbors.

Holy One, creator of the universe, creator of us, you lovingly formed us in your image at the dawn of creation. We are beloved children of yours, and you love us more than we can imagine. We are astounded at the possibility that you carry our picture written on your heart. We are beloved children of yours, the one who created us and loves us no matter who we are or what we have done. Create in us desire to serve you, to love you with all our hearts, and to love our neighbor as we love ourselves. Amen.

Dwelling with God

OCTOBER 19–25, 2020 • MARILYN MCENTYRE

SCRIPTURE OVERVIEW: The end of Deuteronomy completes the story of the life of Moses. Although he led the people out of Egypt, he is not allowed to enter the Promised Land because he lost his temper in the desert. The difficult task of leading the people back to the land will fall to Joshua. The psalmist calls out to God for mercy because the people have been suffering as a result of their disobedience. Paul defends himself against the charge that he has been preaching out of a desire for fame or money. The approval he seeks comes only from God. Jesus has yet another confrontation with religious leaders attempting to trick him. He avoids their schemes and emphasizes that love of God and love of neighbor summarize the entire law.

QUESTIONS AND SUGGESTIONS FOR REFLECTION

- Read Deuteronomy 34:1-12. When has a leadership transition in your faith community been difficult for you? When has it been sacred?
- Read Psalm 90:1-6, 13-17. How do you make God your dwelling place?
- Read 1 Thessalonians 2:1-8. How can you strive to love those whom you have never met? How can you meet new people with love as siblings?
- Read Matthew 22:34-46. How do you wrestle with the Bible? When have your questions strengthened your faith or revealed something new?

Professor of English; author.

Each of us is irreplaceable; each of us can be replaced. Both these statements are true, and both are important for us to remember as we look around at those we love. We know that they, and we, are mortal.

When Moses dies, the people mourn for thirty days. "Then the days of weeping and mourning for Moses were ended" (ESV). No doubt they miss him for the remainder of their lives. No doubt some find fault with Joshua, though he too is "full of the spirit of wisdom." The Israelites have to learn what each of us has to learn again and again: Every death is final. The power and unique effect of Moses' presence will not happen again.

Thirty days are given for mourning and then, though sorrow remains, it is time for the Israelites to turn their energies to tasks at hand. A harvest has to be gathered; babies are born; young people marry; old people need care. This, for some, is the hardest phase in a season of loss—return of "ordinary" life when ceremonies of commemoration give way to obligations, even those that may seem dreary and unrewarding.

"Behold, I will do a new thing," (KJV) we read in Isaiah 43:19. We often read Isaiah's words as an exuberant promise, but we do not always welcome a "new thing." New things, new leaders, new relationships upset our routines, require new learning, and sometimes disappoint us in ways that compound grief. Faith that is "new every morning" is faith that nevertheless makes ready for the new thing to come and commits the old things to God even while weeping endures. Faith in God's promises turns us toward what God gives, trusting that God provides what we need most even as our hearts still ache.

God who makes all things new, renew us today, even in the midst of our losses. Help us to entrust all things, past and present, to your tender mercies and your boundless love. Amen.

Wendell Berry's story "Pray Without Ceasing" begins with the narrator's memory of his grandfather, who would sit beside him when they met, clap him lightly on the leg, and greet him by name: "Hello, Andy." The shape of the old man's hand remains with him "as vividly as a birthmark." "This man who was my grandfather," he muses, "is present in me."* The passage reminded me of how our children's grandfather laid his hand on their heads to bless them and how my mother would lay her hand on my shoulder as she listened to me read aloud.

Laying on of hands is a ritual that imparts blessing. In some churches deacons lay hands on the sick. In some, a bishop touches those being confirmed to ratify their commitment. In some, elders lay hands on those leaving for mission trips. In many, ordination is marked by laying on of hands. We need this sacred contact. While not all touch is healthy, sacred touch imparts blessing and has power.

Joshua was "filled with the spirit of wisdom because Moses had laid his hands on him." Something charged with the grandeur of God** was transmitted in that gesture. It ordained and empowered Joshua and assured the community's stability. We need this from one another—the touch that says, "We stand behind you. God's own blessing comes to you through us, who love and care for you." We have no way of measuring what such a touch may mean in another's life, but we know from stories like this how a touch can connect us not only with one another but also with God.

---

*Wendell Berry, "Pray Without Ceasing," *Fidelity: Five Stories* (New York: Pantheon Books, 1992), 4.

**Gerard Manley Hopkins, "God's Grandeur," *Gerard Manley Hopkins: Poems and Prose* (London: Penguin Classics, 1985), 27.

Source of all blessing, we ask that those we touch may be comforted, encouraged, and blessed. Amen.

I love the word *dwelling*. It invites and it implies resting, enjoying, pausing, pondering, and making oneself at home. My own history of packing and moving, relocating, and making homes in new places has sometimes made me envy those who dwell in one place for many years and their sense of knowing, being known, and belonging in that place. My envy was assuaged when a beloved mentor pointed out that there have always been those who settle and those who roam. The two ways of life, she reminded me, are different callings. Those who move about may learn valuable resilience, that change need not be merely loss, and that God, more than any place on earth, is our dwelling place.

That conversation helped me consider my moves and changes in a new light and with a larger perspective. Though "uprooting" myself and my family has had its costs, over time it has deepened my dependence on this truth: God is our dwelling place. The words of two different psalms stay with me: "Though I take the wings of the morning and dwell in the uttermost parts of the sea, even there thy right hand shall hold me" (Ps. 139:9-10, AP). Wherever I go, God meets me there. In today's passage, the psalmist writes, "Satisfy us in the morning with your steadfast love." Every day we awake in God's light. Even if we wake up in strange places in our travels, in new apartments, or in provisional accommodations, among all that is temporary the love that surrounds us is "steadfast." It is our dwelling place. We are held there, found and familiar and at home.

Loving God, you are our home. Teach us and remind us of that truth as we go our ways, some winding and wandering and uncertain. Help us to dwell in your steadfast love and to seek our security not in our own plans and devices but in you. Amen.

The history most of us learn in school takes us from war to war, from conqueror to king, and shows us how governments and empires rise and fall. It is an important narrative, but it is generally told from the point of view of the privileged victors. To trace the hand of God in history is to understand the events of the past in very different terms. It is to consider the great mystery of creation and forgiveness, intervention, and loving provision that continues in all that grow and die, mutate, and emerge and blossom and erupt—to recognize the Source of all human achievement without whom there would be nothing.

When the psalmist prays, "May your deeds be shown to your servants, your splendor to their children" (NIV), perhaps the psalmist is asking God to open our eyes to see more truly those things we think we know. It takes trained, prayerful awareness to recognize the thread of grace in failure, suffering, and tedium. Quakers learn to ask what is "of God" in any event they encounter. A pastor I know asks himself in any new situation what God may be "up to." My spiritual director has taught me to watch expectantly each day for what comes from God for learning and healing.

Though I still fret about my frustrations, I have found that when I watch for God and remember that God is "more present than we think," I more often recognize God's surprising deeds for what they are. As we learn to practice the presence of God in this way, it may be that our children will grow more readily aware of the splendor that lovingly abounds in the light and darkness that enfolds us.

Creator God, help us to recognize the wisdom of your deeds and the splendor of your divine imagination in nature, in human stories, and even in the hardest of times. Amen.

I sometimes find Paul's writings less appealing than other parts of scripture; he doesn't hesitate to challenge or complain, and some of his admonishments are hard to grasp outside their ancient context. But then I come upon moments of tenderness that remind me of the urgent love that drives him from one place to another.

Today's passage ends on one such note of tenderness: "We are determined to share with you not only the gospel of God but also our own selves, because you have become very dear to us." Even before they arrive, Paul and his companions anticipate a joyful meeting of brothers and sisters.

I realized not long ago how easily the phrase "brothers and sisters in Christ" can dwindle into cliché. But those we are given to love—those to whom we are sent—are "our people," bound to us by ties deeper than blood, as cells in the same body, working together in ways we can never fully fathom toward God's mysterious purposes.

I remember traveling to North Carolina to meet a sprawling clan of cousins I had heard of but never met. A wide, warm welcome greeted me just because I belonged to "Uncle Jack" or "Aunt Effie." They loved me before they knew me. A place was prepared for me because I belonged to them.

Though there is a dark side to clan culture, that experience helped me imagine more fully what it might mean to greet those we don't yet know as brothers and sisters: Whoever you are, I come to you in love because we are loved by the One who made us for each other. So we can meet in hope with open hearts and confident curiosity about what gifts may come in our meeting.

Loving God, you made us for your own delight and for one another. Help me to recognize in each encounter your invitation to extend and receive grace. Amen.

I love when Jesus is smart and edgy—when he trips up the Pharisees, puzzles them, mystifies them. They know the scriptures, but he knows God. They're well schooled; he's subtle and deft and wise. They live by the letter; he lives by the Spirit.

Too many Christians have weaponized the Bible, using it to defeat and exclude, sometimes to destroy. Too many have driven honest seekers away from faith by making its sacred stories into traps or tests.

After being subjected to some of those tests and caught in a few of those traps, I have come to see the great legacy we have in the Bible as an invitation: Dwell in these stories. Explore them. Wrestle with them. Imagine your way into them. Talk about them with one another. Seek the wisdom of scholars, and let the words speak to you across the ages in your own language, in your own heart. Listen for the word or phrase that stops you. Let the Spirit breathe in the sentences and the spaces between them. Carry the stories in your heart. Remember the tax collectors and sinners, the wise virgins and the sheep, the ravens and the angels. Treasure them and let them teach you. Never use them to browbeat others. Don't reduce poetry to pious pronouncements or parables to rules. Let them mystify, invite, unnerve, and delight you. It's all yours to enter—this many-roomed mansion—but not to own or control. All may enter and dwell and learn by going.

When I read the Bible in that spirit, the passages can enliven me. I find what I need and sometimes what I didn't know I needed: bread and breath and song.

Loving God, teach me to treasure your Word and to read it with generosity, holy curiosity, and humility. Open my eyes and ears and heart to your mysterious, living Word. Amen.

Despite years of listening to sermons, reading spiritual texts, learning prayer practices, and attending retreats, I still manage now and then to mire myself in anxiety, confusion, guilt, shame, and restlessness. When that happens, I find great comfort in Jesus' clear, challenging answer to the Pharisees who asked him to identify the greatest commandment. *Comfort* may seem an odd word here: Jesus appears to be answering a straightforward question about the law by quoting the first two commandments given to Moses. But I've come to see that those two "laws" are not merely laws; they are much more complex, challenging, and liberating.

Jesus' interrogators want law, but he gives them love without which all laws become either meaningless or dangerous. The implications of his reminder—that love is the first and greatest commandment—disrupt their governing misapprehension that the law is what saves us. Love trumps law, Jesus insists. It doesn't discount it, but it overrules it. Where law divides, love unites. Where law assigns priority, love equalizes. Where law excludes, love includes. Where law mires in argument, love fosters gratitude and generous discernment. Where the law leads to guilt, shame, and judgment of self and others, love leads to forgiveness and repentance—relational and rooted in trust.

I am comforted by Jesus' clarity about the primacy of love over law because it allows me to look at the harm I've done, my failures of faith, my own versions of the seven deadly sins with compassion. Freed from debilitating self-judgment, I can return to gratitude and trust, receive grace, and even find my way to an appreciation of the rich guidance the commandments offer. I find myself joining with the psalmist in his surprising and exuberant cry: "Oh, how I love your law!" (Ps. 119:97).

God of love, release me from the letter that kills and help me to dwell trustingly in the Spirit who gives life. Amen.

Our Strength and Portion

OCTOBER 26—NOVEMBER 1, 2020 • ELIZABETH CANHAM

SCRIPTURE OVERVIEW: The book of Joshua tells the story of the return of the Israelites to the land promised to Abraham. They have escaped captivity in Egypt by a miraculous crossing, and now they enter the land in a similar way. Psalm 107 speaks of God gathering the people from distant lands and bringing them out of the desert into a land of plenty. It is a poetic reflection on the experience of the Israelites. Paul often experiences resistance from various sources. In a defense of his integrity, he points to his actions as proof of his virtue. Jesus reminds us that we can do the right thing for the wrong reasons. If we act in order to draw attention to ourselves, then even good deeds lose their luster in God's eyes.

QUESTIONS AND SUGGESTIONS FOR REFLECTION

- Read Joshua 3:7-17. When have you had to trust leaders for the good of your community?
- Read Psalm 107:1-7, 33-37. Recall difficult times in your faith journey. How did you experience God's steadfast love through these times?
- Read 1 Thessalonians 2:9-13. What daily practices give you insight into God's Word? How do you encourage others in their life of faith?
- Read Matthew 23:1-12. Do your leaders live what they preach? If you are a leader, how do you strive to live the gospel?

Priest in the Episcopal Church; "retired"; retreat leader, spiritual director, writer.

Every morning I am reminded of the great turning point in Hebrew history when Moses led the people across the Red Sea. My coffee cup depicts the event. The people stand fearfully on the edge of the rolled-back waters as Moses cries, "What do you mean 'it's a bit muddy'?!" Clearly the artist uses humor and imagination to guess at the type of response the Hebrews might have made. This week's readings all challenge us to trust in God's strength and presence to carry us through every difficulty.

Since the time of Moses, a long struggle for freedom and a place to call home has kept the people going as they endured some hard times in wilderness conditions. The writer of Joshua offers a new story that also reflects liberation through water. After Moses' death, Joshua brings the journeying people across the Jordan. The community now has a priesthood and the ark of the covenant as a symbol of God's dwelling among them. The levitical priests have carried the ark ahead of the ragtag group for days until they all finally come to the edge of the Jordan. On the other side stands the fortified city of Jericho; they need a strong faith to believe that God will protect them while they cross and after their crossing. The priests, representing the twelve tribes, go into the Jordan first and stand in the middle as long as the people cross. Their risky action and steadfastness surely encourage others to trust that God will sustain the company as the future unfolds.

We all journey in faith and sometimes encounter big challenges that can keep us from getting our toes wet. Who stands in the middle to encourage us? How do we thank God for safe crossings?

"O Most High, when I am afraid, I put my trust in you" (Ps. 56:3). Amen.

The Psalms offer us a model for honest prayer that addresses every part of our lives. Whether we are rejoicing in God's goodness or struggling through fear and brokenness, these ancient songs offer words to name our present state. I was blessed to spend six years in an Episcopal Benedictine Monastery where the Psalms were recited or sung morning, noon, and night. I came to love them and to find myself identifying with the celebrations and the struggles, the teaching and songs of praise, the doubts and hopes that gave voice to ancient Israel.

Psalm 107 is a song of "Thanksgiving for Deliverance from Many Troubles" according to the title in the New Revised Standard Version. For many years people have come from every direction seeking safety and a community. They have known hardship, hunger, thirst, and lostness as they have wandered through desert places and have cried out to God. Now it is time to return thanks to God for the steadfast love that has never left them. God leads them on a "straight way" that brings them to an inhabited town.

This psalm reflects the experience of struggle considered in yesterday's scripture reading. It reminds me of some rough patches in my own journey of faith. Taking time to reflect and to write a daily journal entry clarifies where I am and how I choose to act. It also challenges me to think again and to celebrate all the moments of deliverance from fear, loneliness, and anxiety. I thank God for leading me to the USA where many struggles awaited me along with great joy and blessing. I give thanks to God who is good and whose steadfast love endures forever. And I need to be reminded to do this often.

Recall specific times when you became aware of God setting you free from difficulty and suffering. Try composing a list of those times using the opening verse of the psalm as a prayer of gratitude.

The opening verse of Psalm 107 is repeated as a refrain many times in the text: "O give thanks to the LORD for he is good; for his steadfast love endures forever." No matter our struggles and deficiencies, God's *hesed*—steadfast love, loving-kindness— never comes to an end. In the Hebrew scriptures the word *hesed* occurs 248 times. Most of those occurrences are in the Psalms, where prayers and songs describe the relationship between God and people. God's people do not escape the hard times that others suffer, but their trust lies deeper than catastrophe. Through it all, God's steadfast love remains present.

Recently, hurricanes have destroyed thousands of homes and countless possessions in my state—North Carolina—and fires in California have ravaged thousands more. Natural disasters do not differentiate between good, faithful people and those who do not have faith in God. But those who trust in God's loving-kindness have a perspective of hope. The prophet Habakkuk bears witness to where his hope lies: "Though the fig tree does not blossom, and no fruit is on the vines; though the produce of the olive fails and the fields yield no food . . . yet I will rejoice in the LORD; I will exult in the God of my salvation" (Hab. 3:17-18).

Thanksgiving plays a huge part in the worship of Israel, especially in the Psalms, which were sung and often accompanied by musical instruments, marching, and dramatic presentations of events. So it is appropriate that the refrain keeps repeating in various forms: "Let them thank the LORD for his steadfast love, for his wonderful works to humankind" (v. 21). Despite our sufferings from violence and natural disaster, God's love remains steadfast, and we can offer the same refrain: "Thank you. Thank you. Thank you."

Loving God, thank you, thank you, thank you. Amen.

After a very difficult time preaching the gospel in Philippi, Paul, accompanied by Silvanus and Timothy, moves on to Thessalonica. Here too are challenges. Paul then moves on to another city but writes to the Thessalonians to address some issues of behavior and to encourage the believers to live the gospel faithfully. Today's passage reveals how Paul and other leaders live and preach among Jesus' followers. Paul and his associates work tirelessly, and their behavior is "pure, upright, and blameless." Paul and his friends live what they preach.

What does this passage of scripture have to say to us today? How do we live a life worthy of the God who has invited us into the kingdom of grace? Daily reading of scripture and time for prayer and reflection have greatly enriched my life. I also belong to a small group that meets weekly to share our faith journey with Christ and to do *lectio divina* together. Following this model from the Benedictine tradition, we read a passage of scripture, enter into a time of silent reflection, and then share what we have gleaned from the Bible passage. We need one another to encourage, support, challenge, and love us ever deeper into grace.

It is a good idea sometimes to revisit the effectiveness of the daily disciplines we have chosen. Lately I am finding that poetry, music, and art are also rich sources for meditation; a walk in the woods opens my eyes to the awesome presence of the Creator who is always faithful. In today's passage, Paul reminds us that when we recognize God's Word coming to us in any form, God's Word is at work in us.

Faithfulness is one of the nine fruits of the Spirit. (See Galatians 5:22-23.) Read this passage at the end of the day to help you reflect on how fruitful your work, relationships, and prayer have been today.

Jesus uses strong words to caution his disciples about some of the religious leaders among them. The scribes and Pharisees teach and interpret the law of Moses, just as Jesus does. But there is a problem: These religious leaders teach one thing and live another. They have made following the law burdensome for others and enjoy the benefits of their social status. But Jesus' words condemn hypocrisy—saying one thing while living another.

This passage comes toward the end of Matthew's Gospel. Jesus has spent three years teaching his followers about the nature of the kingdom of God as a way of life that begins now. It is founded on love rather than rigid rules. It is a way of life that honors and responds to our Creator and to one another by living with compassion for the poor, outcast, and needy persons that we meet on our journey of faith. Jesus rebukes the religious leaders because they are looking out for themselves. At a time when Rome is all-powerful and the emperor appoints a Jewish high priest who will best accomplish his political ends, those appointed as teachers and leaders of the people find it convenient to compromise their truth-telling and way of life.

This passage invites me to look at how I relate to the life and teaching of Jesus. Is what I say in conflict with the way I live? Am I following Christian leaders who live in conflict with the gospel of love and grace they teach? Jesus gives wise counsel about how to relate to those who are like the scribes and Pharisees: "Do whatever they teach you . . . but do not do as they do."

Loving Creator, wake me up to pride and pretense, and help me to live the gospel way of love. Amen.

Bishop Colin Winter was a dear friend whom I met when I was teaching at a seminary in London. Colin had been the Anglican Bishop of South West Africa, now Namibia, but he was thrown out of the country because he refused to separate people from each other during the apartheid years and repeatedly held events that brought black and white Christians together. He wore out his body as he continued the fight against apartheid through his prophetic ministry in the United Kingdom and the United States. In his exile, Colin turned down ministry in a comfortable Oxford Church and spent his time among the poor in London's East End.

I remember Colin as I read Matthew 23 where Jesus opts to directly address those guilty of promoting inequity and oppression. To the scribes and Pharisees he cries, "Woe to you . . . hypocrites" (v. 13) and accuses them of turning people away from God's kingdom and failing to enter it themselves.

It is one thing for Jesus to warn his disciples about their religious leaders, albeit within their hearing; but it is another to address them directly. There is no subtlety in his confrontation and no smooth talking about their behavior. My friend Colin was like this; and his church hierarchy, which was protecting huge investments in South Africa, did not like it.

Jesus' courage becomes clear throughout this chapter as over and over he pronounces woe to the Pharisees and scribes. No wonder they look for a way to silence him, and all too soon the political and religious authorities come together to plan his crucifixion. It makes me wonder, *What acts of injustice might I protest today? Is my faith community a place where all are affirmed and accepted?*

Reflect on 1 Corinthians 16:13-14: "Keep alert, stand firm in your faith, be courageous, be strong. Let all that you do be done in love."

ALL SAINTS' DAY

In this passage, commonly known as the Beatitudes, Jesus tells us what it means to be blessed. He does not mention winning the lottery, being elected to high office, or buying a new model car each year. Blessing comes to those who are poor, humble, merciful, hungry, working for peace, and accepting persecution. So who wants to sign up? Jesus speaks these words to the disciples apart from the crowds with whom he is popular and by whom they, by association, might be respected. Jesus seems to be asking his followers, "Do you really want to be a disciple? Then here is what to expect!"

In 1 Corinthians 1:2, Paul reminds his readers that they are "called to be saints"—those who strive to follow the teaching of Jesus and to live like him. The Greek word *hagios* refers to those who are sanctified or set apart by or for God. Saints look like ordinary people; they are known not by holy clothes or a halo but by their faithfulness to the Christian gospel. Over the course of time, the Roman Catholic Church begins to name persons of exceptional holiness as "saints." November 1 was established as All Saints' Day, when all Christians come together to remember those who have gone before us on the journey.

Most of us can recall saint-like people we have known: persons of patience, love, and service who were also great listeners and encouragers. On All Saints' Day, we can include them in our thanksgiving. Their memories remind us that we are "called to be saints" each day. Even when we stumble, maybe even fall, the grace of God is always there to lift us up.

Loving God, thank you for the cloud of witnesses who encourage and strengthen us to follow Jesus, the pioneer and perfecter of our faith. Amen.

Choose, Now!

NOVEMBER 2–8, 2020 • GERRIT DAWSON

SCRIPTURE OVERVIEW: Although God miraculously has brought the Israelites into the Promised Land, some continue to worship foreign gods. Joshua tells them that they must choose whom they will serve and warns of the dangers of unfaithfulness. After they declare that they will follow God, Joshua reminds them of the laws given by God. The psalmist affirms the importance of this kind of reminder; telling the story of God's faithfulness in the past encourages us in the present. The New Testament readings address Christ's return. The Thessalonians are concerned that those who have died might miss the final resurrection, but Paul assures them that this will not be the case. Jesus tells a parable to highlight the fact that his return will be unexpected, so we should always be ready.

QUESTIONS AND SUGGESTIONS FOR REFLECTION

- Read Joshua 24:1-3a, 14-25. We are prone to wander. When have you failed to keep promises you have made to God?
- Read Psalm 78:1-7. How do you put your hope in God? What are you doing to awaken faith in the next generation?
- Read 1 Thessalonians 4:13-18. How does the promise of the "coming of the Lord" provide hope when present authorities seem to have a stranglehold? How does the notion that the coming Lord will hold us all accountable encourage you?
- Read Matthew 25:1-13. How do you daily choose your faith? How do you keep awake?

Pastor, First Presbyterian Church of Baton Rouge, Louisiana; author of *Raising Adam*.

You might want to skip this week's readings. They won't be easy—way too much truth-telling for my comfort. But if you've had a feeling that lately your idea of God has become too sweet to account for the cauldron of contradictions bubbling just under the surface of your daily life, it might be worth sticking around.

This week's passages are all about choices. They focus on the contrast between fidelity and failure arising from how we respond to God. In today's introduction to Psalm 78, the psalmist prepares to recall "the glorious deeds of the LORD" so that "the next generation might know them" (ESV). Learning God's mighty deeds of redemption is not some idle academic exercise. It is the path to living in hope even when everything around us is a mess.

Earlier generations were "stubborn and rebellious" (ESV). In heart and action, they were "not faithful to God" (ESV). Disastrous consequences followed their failure to respond to God's work and way. When our wills buck up against God's reality, we cannot flourish.

The psalmist yearns to teach the next generation "so that they should set their hope in God" (ESV). These stories fuel a life of trust. The psalmist wants to save us from the despair of a world that has forgotten God. He wants to awaken faith.

But hope is not the final goal. We learn and remember what the Lord has done in order that we will "keep his commandments" (ESV). The point is to live according to the way things really are. God exists. God has acted to redeem a particular people as part of a plan to bless the entire world. God has shown us a way to live that leads to flourishing—by responding in worship to God's redemption and in obedience to God's commands.

Triune God, remind us of your works, teach us your will, and enable us to worship and to obey. Amen.

"The LORD, the God of Israel" has worked redemptively for centuries on behalf of this particular people. Joshua has led the people across the Jordan and into the Promised Land. Near the end of his life, peace at last reigns. But Joshua does not want them to forget all that God has done for them and the great work the Lord has for them to do in the world. So he gathers the people for a ceremony of covenant renewal. He begins by recalling the great history from Abraham and Sarah to Moses and Aaron to the present day. Then Joshua challenges the people to a faithful response.

They have to choose afresh: "Fear the LORD and serve him in sincerity and in faithfulness. Put away the gods your fathers served . . . choose this day whom you will serve" (ESV). Is this really necessary? Surely everyone worships only the God who has done so much for them.

Have you ever thought, *If only I lived in Bible times, it would be so much easier to believe*? Not so! Even so close to the miracles of the Exodus, the people constantly feel a tug toward the local gods. Even when Moses is delayed briefly on the mountain, they smelt their jewelry into a golden calf and worship it. (See Exodus 32.) Serving God requires constant choices of fidelity.

We are prone to want easier gods—less demanding, less exclusive, more manageable, more fashionable. Gods who promise a more appealing path where we can be ourselves instead of dying to ourselves. Gods who say they want to help us have a life more like our dreams.

Oh, we are prone to wander. Joshua knows it. He demands that the people choose once again. He leads by declaring his intention first: "As for me and my house, we will serve the LORD" (ESV).

Dear Lord, make us bold to choose you first, last, and always. Amen.

Joshua challenges the people to make a decision that moment and declare it publicly. But before anyone can reply, Joshua takes a bold stand in declaring his allegiance to the Lord. It works. All the people cry out their loyalty. A great celebration should follow.

But Joshua doesn't buy it. In effect, he says, "You can't do it. You won't stay faithful, and it will be worse because you broke another promise. If you stand here swearing faithfulness and then go after other gods, the Lord will turn against you." Imagine your preacher responding like that on commitment Sunday. I think I'd look for another church.

But I also know that Joshua's critique is true. I have made sincere promises to God and broken them before the day is out. I've repented of sins with contrition and then committed them in my mind before I even finished praying. We're pathetic.

At this point, we each may want to say just what the people said, "No, but . . ." (ESV). No, but what about grace? No, but doesn't God understand? No, but I really mean it, and hey, we're good people. God's got to take us! We join them in their demands to declare their loyalty.

So Joshua lets them pledge. He reminds them, "You are witnesses against yourselves" (ESV). Choice has to be made. They will fail in that choice. But in all their naiveté, pride, hope, yearning, and hubris, they swear they will serve the Lord alone. The burden is heavy. The consequences are frightening.

Our God acts to save. Our redeeming Lord requires response. God calls us to choose daily. We say "Yes" even as we know during the day we will say "No." And like the text, I will leave you to stay in that contradiction.

Great Lord I Am, we choose you. We leave you. We fail you.
But we still choose again this day. Help us to stay true. Amen.

Choose, Now!

Are you ready for some good news? We get a breather today and some words of encouragement.

God's people have always suffered the awkwardness, and sometimes even persecution, of not being like everyone else. The God of Abraham comes with strict rules and a more defined revelation of who God is than other gods have. Jesus said the way we follow is "narrow" (Matt. 7:14, NIV).

But we also have treasures not available to those who aren't in conscious relationship with God. We have hope for the life to come. Paul writes to the Thessalonians about the future of Jesus with his people, "that you may not grieve as others do who have no hope" (ESV).

Our hope is based on what Jesus has done on our behalf and on what Jesus will do in the future. Paul explains, "For since we believe that Jesus died and rose again, even so, through Jesus, God will bring with him those who have fallen asleep" (ESV).

Jesus, who comes to us in the flesh, who dies, rises, and ascends, is Jesus who will return. The "coming of the Lord" (ESV) is a key part of our hope.

I once asked a Christian from an officially atheist country about living there. He told me that he could talk about Jesus as long as it was about the past. Jesus the great teacher was no threat. But he could not proclaim openly the return of Jesus because a returning king threatens present claims to authority. No nation or ruler will last when the Son returns to establish his reign. Even death will give way.

This is the hope we have, no matter who seems to hold power in the present. For the dead in Christ will be raised. And "so we will always be with the Lord" (ESV).

Even so, come Lord Jesus! Amen.

The good news of Jesus' return fills our sails with winds of hope that propel us forward into even the most difficult days. Those who have died are not gone forever. Present sufferings will not last. Jesus is coming to clean up all the mess—including our broken promises to God. We don't have to solve everything. It doesn't all depend on us. We have the freedom of relying on the hope of Jesus' coming again.

At the same time, the promise of Christ's return applies a pressure to our lives. This restoring of all justice and peace involves calling the world to account. Paul describes an act of irresistible authority: "For the Lord himself will descend from heaven with a cry of command, with the voice of an archangel, and with the sound of the trumpet of God" (ESV). Christ's dominion is so thorough that even the dead must obey the summons. The great adjustment of creation back to harmony means revealing everything for what it is. And that includes us.

So like the Old Testament passages we studied, the context of this magnificent hope urges us to readiness and right choices. Earlier in chapter four, Paul has "solemnly warned" (v. 6, ESV) the Thessalonians away from impurity and into holiness. In chapter five, Paul will remind them that when Jesus returns, "The day . . . will come like a thief in the night" (5:2, ESV). Our choices matter. They don't vanish into a past that can't be recalled. They reverberate in God's eternity. So we want to be found going about the Lord's business. We want to expect Christ's return. We want to live ready each moment for Christ to shine full light into our lives.

Lord Jesus, give us grace to ride the current of both the accountability and the hope of your return. Amen.

The passages this week have made me squirm. I want more grace and less accountability. I've thought, *Well, that's the Old Testament. Give me Jesus.* Or, *Paul sometimes speaks abruptly; Jesus must have a kinder word.* Oh my! He's the hardest of all.

Today's parable is set in a first-century Jewish marriage. Great ceremony precedes the wedding feast. The groom and his friends set out for the bride's home. Her bridesmaids are to be on the lookout. When the bridegroom gets close, they will light torches to welcome him. The marriage will occur at the bride's house. Then the whole wedding party will process back by torchlight to the groom's house for the banquet.

In Jesus' story, the groom is delayed. Perhaps the negotiations with the bride's father over the bride price have gotten sticky. In any case, it is midnight before he arrives. Five of the bridesmaids have brought extra flasks of oil to replenish their lamps. Five have not. They have to go wake up a merchant to get the fuel. By the time they get to the party, the door is closed, and the master of the house will not let them in.

Jesus says this scene is what the kingdom of heaven is like. We can miss it if we are not prepared and awake. "Watch therefore, for you know neither the day nor the hour" (ESV).

The door can be closed. Calling "Lord" can fail to gain us entry. We can miss the banquet of Jesus. Is it really so severe? Before we address that question tomorrow, let's pause to consider the emotional impact of Jesus' parable. What does this story make you want to do? I want to stay awake. I want to be ready. I don't want to miss the wedding. I am urgent, desperate to move from the foolish group to the wise.

Jesus, keep me awake. Prepare me with your Spirit to receive you joyfully. Amen.

Is God really so severe as our week's passages imply? Are we shocked, even outraged, to entertain that the answer might be "Yes"? Perhaps we have domesticated the "consuming fire" of our living God (Heb. 12:29, ESV) into the warmth of a space heater. God gives us extra heat when our own efforts leave our lives a bit chilly. So we may think God's function is to help us live better the life that we have chosen for ourselves. Thus, we remain the measure of what matters. We are the autonomous who find it offensive to submit to anyone.

Jesus' parable pretty much slaps us out of that worldview. His parable revolves around the bridegroom. The story of the world is foremost about the Triune God revealed as Creator, Redeemer, and Holy Spirit. Not us. We are not self-generated; we are created. We are not the lords of our lives; Jesus is Lord. We are not the center of reality. The fundamental human choice is whether to acknowledge moment by moment that everything begins and ends with God. God's reality is as inflexible as gravity, as necessary as oxygen, and as dangerous and life-giving as the sun.

But Jesus doesn't tell this or any of his other frightening parables to condemn us. He comes to save us. Scripture declares that "the fear of the LORD is the beginning of wisdom" (Ps. 111:10, ESV). That's so we can live fruitfully now and live eternally.

Over and over Jesus is an inflexible brick wall to the self-righteous who admit no need of him. Yet to the sinners and the broken he superabounds in mercy.

This week we have been called to readiness and steady, unqualified choice for God. In Jesus' words, "Repent and believe in the gospel" (Mark 1:15, ESV). Such a daily choice leads us to the ocean of God's mercy.

Lord Jesus Christ, have mercy on this sinner, and enable me to choose you wholeheartedly day by day. Amen.

Growing in Faith the Hard Way

NOVEMBER 9–15, 2020 • LORETTA ROSS-GOTTA

SCRIPTURE OVERVIEW: Like us, the Israelites struggle to be consistently faithful to God. God therefore allows a foreign king to rule them until the people come to their senses and cry out for help. The prophet Deborah gives instructions for the battle that will begin the deliverance of the people. The readings from Psalms and Zechariah demonstrate that this pattern of unfaithfulness and restoration has occurred frequently in the history of God's people. In Thessalonians, Paul echoes what Jesus says in last week's Gospel reading: We must always be prepared for the return of Christ because we do not know when it will occur. God gives us resources to use for the kingdom, and in Matthew Jesus indicates that God will ask for an account of how well we have used them.

QUESTIONS AND SUGGESTIONS FOR REFLECTION

- Read Judges 4:1-7. Who has been a judge—someone who helps you discern—in your life? How can you help others discern the way?
- Read Psalm 123. How do you focus on God through conflict and struggle?
- Read 1 Thessalonians 5:1-11. When have you encouraged someone in a time of darkness? When have you been the one in need of encouragement?
- Read Matthew 25:14-30. What would change if you considered your dreams and desires as from God? What first step can you take to enact your desires?

Presbyterian clergy; Director of The Sanctuary Center for Prayer; author and spiritual director; assistant pastor at Crestview United Methodist Church, Topeka, Kansas.

Not Again!

Y ou are slumped on the stairs, head in your hands, going over in your mind what she said, what you said. You feel that hard knot of anger tightening in your stomach. *Here we go again,* you think. *Why do I keep getting myself into the same messes over and over?* You feel the hurt and frustration wash over you as you pray, "Jesus, do something! I can't stand this anymore."

God has a way of giving us opportunities to learn something until we get it right. Our actions, attitudes, and life circumstances bring us up against impasses that invite us to face our failure and sin and to find the courage to grow beyond our limitations and the faith to trust God more totally in our lives.

At such moments, backed up against the wall with "the same old, same old," we feel defeated. Israel had many such moments. We read in Judges, "The Israelites again did what was evil in the sight of the LORD." The book of Judges tells the story of Israel's crooked road to obedience. Over and over the people wander from God and experience oppression. Then they repent and are renewed and delivered, only to wander again away from God.

God is determined that we live in the fullness of redemptive love, no matter how many times we ignore that saving power.

Suggestion for Meditation: What has you sitting with your head in your hands? Where do you see a repetitive pattern in your life that leads to frustration and broken relationships? What lesson might God want you to learn?

What Are You Looking At?

You are still sitting on the steps. You hear the dryer buzz, but you can't make yourself get up to go fold the laundry. You have gone over and over the problem. God has been silent. "It really isn't my fault," you tell the Lord. "If she would just see what she is doing." Tears well up in your eyes.

It is easy to give in to the temptation to blame others or indulge in self-pity. "O Lord, have mercy upon us, for we have had more than enough of contempt," writes the psalmist. "I'll say," you comfort yourself. The humiliating scorn of others is a bitter experience.

At any given moment the spiritual journey presents us with a kaleidoscope of options for action and attitude. Which options come from God or lead to God? Which lure us away from obedience and the way of love?

In the Bible the wise person stops worrying about what to do, stops placing blame or trying to figure things out. The wise person simply looks to God. Wisdom has a lot to do with where we look, what we give our attention to. The psalmist is backed in a corner, an object of scorn and derision. Is his focus on the persecutor? No. "To you I lift up my eyes," he proclaims. My attention, my focus, is on God—not on my enemy or my wounds. I trust in God's mercy. I fix my gaze on God while I await the mercy that I am absolutely certain will come my way.

Merciful God, help me lift my eyes from my predicament and frustrations to fix my attention wholly on you. You will not fail to bring me comfort and help. I will trust in you alone with all my heart and not rely solely on my own insight. Amen.

In the Meantime . . .

Much in our lives is ambiguous, uncertain, unresolved, and conflicted. What do we do while waiting for clarity and resolution? Paul advises that we keep awake. Be sober. Wear the breastplate of faith and love and the helmet of the hope of salvation.

The peace that passes understanding doesn't have to wait for us to have all the answers before it enters our lives. Christ's peace grows with our faith. The integration of our faith into every nook and cranny of our lives is a lifelong process.

To check your progress in this area ask yourself: How does my prayer, as I pray it, reflect my life as I live it? And conversely, How does my life, as I live it, reflect my prayer as I pray it? Do I root what I bring to God in prayer in the truth of my life and not pious fluff? Am I walking the talk?

Most of us have areas in our lives that evidence discontinuity, lack of congruence or integrity. Such internal conflict may obstruct the full and free movement of grace through us into the world.

Paul admonishes the Thessalonians not to be in the dark about obstructions to grace. He says in effect, "You are Christians. Act like it. Be who you are all the way down to your toes. Don't let your actions or thoughts cancel or hide the truth of Christ's power in your life. Quit moping about and feeling sorry for yourself. Get back up on your feet. Live in the light."

Suggestion for Meditation: In what ways do you sit in the dark? What is your pattern as you wait for Christ to break in to your need? Dare to wait with absolute confidence on your Savior. Be bold to claim God's power and goodness, even when there is no outward sign of them.

Get Help

Perhaps Christ gave us the church because it is too hard to follow him alone. Sometimes pride prevents us from reaching out to others for help. We may be ashamed of our vulnerability. We may tell ourselves no one else can understand or help. Yet the community of faith supports and nourishes individual wisdom. "Encourage one another and build up each other," writes Paul. The dark is seductive, offering many temptations that encourage us to rely on ourselves, to nurse grudges, to feel sorry for ourselves, to find fault, and to rationalize behavior and thoughts that lead us away from the light of Christ.

Reach out to the wise spiritual leaders in your life. Make a phone call. Send an email. Ask for prayer. Hang out with people who live in the light.

Sometimes when our faith is in a growth crisis, we have to allow the faith of others to carry us for a while. We may go to church, pray, and read the Bible, but we feel like we're just going through the motions. We may feel that we are losing our faith, but we hang on because others have faith in God and faith in us to persevere.

The church in all its variety, scattered throughout time and space, is there in part to help us persevere. We need not walk this journey alone.

God of light, I cannot find you in my darkness. I sink into despair instead of standing in faith. I am afraid to hope and too wounded to love. Send your angels and saints to strengthen and build me up. Encourage me with the witness of others who believe when I cannot believe. I claim refuge in your church, the living body of Christ. Amen.

Untie the Knots

Deborah, prophet and judge, was a woman of heroic stature who had the courage to lay her inner leading on the line of fire. She spurred military leader Barak on to victory and served as his constant inspiration.

Part of spiritual maturity is developing good judgment, the ability to discern good from evil, as one becomes ever more finely tuned to the will of God. Sometimes we need to consult a person of mature spirituality for help in making decisions, finding peace, settling conflicts. Such a spiritual guide willingly lends his or her heart and mind to God on our behalf.

The biblical understanding of judge includes the notion of sifting and separating and contains discernment in its meaning. Discernment is like someone who carefully unknots a wad of necklace chains in the bottom of a jewelry box or painstakingly sifts sand and dirt from grains of wheat. Discernment can be a tedious process that requires patience and the desire to get to the heart of things.

A spiritual friend is someone who won't become frustrated by the process, who will respect the separate strands of your life and motivations, who will be free to listen, and who will not take advantage of your need to get his or her own needs met. A Deborah can be present to God for you when you feel confused or overwhelmed.

Maybe you feel called to be a judge in this sense—to offer another your intimacy with God and to help the person notice and name God's footprints in his or her life experience.

Thank you, Holy One, for Deborah and for the other Deborahs in my life. Thank you for those whose faith and encouragement have inspired me to take risks and reap victory for your glory. May I bring your love and wisdom to those you send to me. Amen.

So I Was Afraid

Fear may be seen as having faith in the enemy. Fear can hold us enthralled, imprisoned. Paralyzed by the "what-ifs" and "maybes," we decide we would rather be safe than sorry and shrink from challenge and the opinions of others. With the gift of life comes responsibility and risk. To accept that responsibility moves us from a comfortable but unimaginative existence to the great adventure of the Christian life.

The diaries of Etty Hillesum, the young Dutch woman who died in Auschwitz, tell the story of her deepening faith and courage. Once, when she received an exemption from being sent to a concentration camp, she wrote, "I want to be sent to every one of the camps that lie scattered all over Europe, I want to be at every front, I don't ever want to be what they call 'safe.' "

Do you have a buried talent? Do you have an idea for a song, a painting, a project? How about a recurring notion to start a food pantry? Sometimes we see our talents, longings, and desires as wishful thinking, mere fantasy. Yet our desire may be God's desire for us as well.

What would it be like to trust that the thing you long to do is what God wants you to do as well? What would it be like to stop thinking of your heart's desire as impossible but rather as totally possible through God's power? What if you believed that God put the notion in your head in the first place? What then?

Ah, what fun we would all have! How the angels would laugh! How the realm of God would rush in like a sky full of geese winging their way into the morning sun!

God, give me the courage to be all you have created me to be.
Teach me to love you more than my own comfort. Amen.

There Will Be Consequences

Whatever. . . . Been there, done that. I don't care. . . ." A jaded callous attitude seems to pervade popular culture. I wonder if what appears as cynicism may be a mask for the pain and disappointment of promises not kept, authority figures who betrayed our trust, and the duplicity and deceit of many of the institutions of government, education, business, and, yes, even religion.

The good news about judgment is that what we do matters. We are responsible to God and to creation to bear good fruit. We are held accountable for our lives. The image of the servant hunched over in the outer darkness, excluded and isolated, weeping and gnashing his teeth stands in strong contrast to the postmodern individual shrugging casually over the latest scandal, "Whatever. . . ."

Our woeful servant reminds us that things matter. Things matter a lot. When Israel repeatedly shrugs its shoulders saying, "How's a little idolatry going to hurt anyone?" God does not reply, "What idolatry?" The truth is that each of us is important and unique. I have God-given talents the whole universe depends on my sharing. God has destined us not for wrath but for salvation through Jesus Christ.

Do not let fear impede the full release of your gifts or hobble your service to Christ. Christ's victory on the cross destroyed the demon of fear; you can stand forgiven and reconciled. You see, there is no way you can go wrong because whatever happens, this God of ours will not say to you, "Whatever. . . ." You are loved with a love that will not let you go.

God of miracles, give me the courage to live the adventure of faith. Give me the faith that allows you to bring joy and healing through me into your creation. And thank you, amazing God, for forgiving and loving me even when my courage shrivels and my faith shrinks. Amen.

The Promises of God

NOVEMBER 16–22, 2020 • CLAIRE K. MCKEEVER-BURGETT

SCRIPTURE OVERVIEW: The Bible uses metaphors meaningful in its time, and the image of a shepherd and sheep evokes protection, care, and safety. Through the prophet Ezekiel, God declares that all the scattered sheep will be joined together again. The weak and oppressed will receive special protection and justice from God. The psalmist says that the Israelites are the sheep of God's pasture. In the Gospel reading, Jesus describes the final judgment as separating the sheep (those who are his) from the goats (those who are not). The distinction is made in part based upon how they treated the weakest among them. Although the epistle does not use the imagery of sheep, it describes the promises of a glorious inheritance reserved for those in God's flock.

QUESTIONS AND SUGGESTIONS FOR REFLECTION

- Read Ezekiel 34:11-16, 20-24. What does it mean for you that God seeks you as an individual and as part of your faith community?
- Read Psalm 100. In times of trial or pain, how do you gather with others to praise God?
- Read Ephesians 1:15-23. How do you express gratitude to God and for your faith community?
- Read Matthew 25:31-46. How do you sit with unresolved questions of faith? How does asking questions of the Bible strengthen your faith or your comfort in not having answers to your questions?

Hails from the dry plains of West Texas; graduate of Baylor University and Vanderbilt Divinity School; ordained clergy; Associate Director, The Academy for Spiritual Formation; pastor, spiritual leader, writer, teacher, poet, mother, spouse, certified yoga, dance, and movement instructor, and birth and postpartum doula.

As a child, I was terrified of being lost. I understood "being lost" as being separated from my parents. When I was five, I tried to spend the night away from home with a friend for the first time ever. Around nine o'clock, I asked my friend's parents to call my parents so that they could come and pick me up. I longed for the safety of my own bed, which was only steps from my mom and dad.

As a teenager longing for a boy to kiss me; as a college student wondering if the God of my childhood could still love me; as a new pastor questioning if I could sustain this work forever; as a mother in need of silence and space, rest and renewal, I also felt lost, disconnected, sick, tired, and alone.

In all these times, I could hear the distant promise of Ezekiel's prophecy during Israel's exile in Babylon: "I will seek out my sheep. I will rescue them from all the places to which they have been scattered."

An active God who searches, rescues, gathers, heals, nurtures, and shows up for an entire people is the promise Ezekiel offers in today's reading. It promises that the Creator of life longs to be with God's people and is willing to act in order to make it so.

We need not choose between individual or communal disorientation in Ezekiel. Rather, both reveal themselves as part of what God seeks to make whole. God offers goodness, mercy, and healing to the individual sheep and to the collective herd. These offerings come with a promise that our hearts, our spirits, our minds, and our bodies will not be exiled forever.

Holy One, help us hear your promise of healing, rescue, and mercy; help us know that we will not be lost forever. Amen.

Take a moment to picture divisive politics ruling the land, military alliances and violent crimes taking place at alarming rates, policies privileging the wealthy, and a society ruled by its greed. This is the world in which Ezekiel, instructed by God, is to prophesy.

Hence, Ezekiel's message to the people takes a turn in today's reading to focus on the ruling class and their treatment of others. God, speaking through Ezekiel, is clear: Judgment will come for those who ignore the weak, discard the poor, and ravage the sick. God will return for the lost, forgotten, and lonely.

This is good news for those who find themselves scattered, devastated, and weak; for those who do not feel represented; for those whose voices go unheard. This is good news for any person or group of people who long to be gathered in by the One who promises justice, mercy, and love.

In our own world of division, violence, wealth, and greed, might Ezekiel have a message for us? Might we have ears to hear it?

For, says the Lord, a shepherd is coming to feed the hungry, to make right that which is wrong, to heal the sick, to rescue the brokenhearted, to find the lost, to carry the weary. Hearing the proclamation of the actions the Lord will take to restore wholeness to the land and to a people invites those who have ears to hear and eyes to see and hearts to open to join in the restorative actions of God.

Come to us, O Shepherd. Invite us to be part of your actions for peace, for justice, for love. Lead us in the way everlasting. Amen.

Irecently heard Rabbi David Horowitz describe the Kaddish, an ancient prayer recited regularly in Jewish worship services and originally known as the Mourner's Prayer, as a prayer for those who proclaim, "In my hurt, I am willing to praise God."

When he said these words, I saw in my mind's eye all those throughout the ages who, amid their oppression, abuse, exile, discrimination, and pain, stand and stumble to say, "In my hurt, I am willing to praise God."

If we need further evidence that these people and these prayers exist, we need look no further than Psalm 100. A song of thanksgiving and praise to the Shepherd who leads and guides, rescues and restores, Psalm 100 testifies to God's great love for God's people.

Psalm 100 is a communal hymn that offers straightforward instruction for the congregation: Make a joyful noise; be glad; give thanks; know that the Lord is God; know that the Lord is good. Amid all sorrow, heartache, grief, and pain, gather with the community and praise God.

Though straightforward, these instructions are not easy for those who know the pains this life can bring. Therefore, when singing this psalm and praying this prayer, we never stand or sing alone. The Mourner's Prayer or Kaddish is communal, meant to be recited in the presence of a person's community of faith, just as this psalm is meant to be sung with all people who know of God's goodness and love.

Holy God, we come into your presence with singing; we will make a joyful noise as a witness to your goodness and love. Amen.

A master letter writer, Paul offers a heartfelt and inspiring introduction to the church at Ephesus in today's reading. Suggesting that he does not know them personally with the phrase "I have heard," Paul is not prohibited from encouraging them in their faith, recognizing their love, and offering them the hope that faith in Jesus gives.

In an introduction to the book of Ephesians, a biblical commentator reminds readers that the main theme of the letter is "God's plan to reconcile Jews and Gentiles, which was accomplished through the death and resurrection of Jesus."* Through Jesus, then, a world reconciled and made whole is not only possible but also on its way and made real through the love, devotion, and faith of followers of Christ.

Thanksgiving is the appropriate response both of the letter writer and of the people receiving the letter. Paul is grateful for the Ephesian church's witness of love and faithfulness; in turn, Paul implicitly invites the Ephesian church to offer thanksgiving for the "hope to which he has called you . . . the immeasurable greatness of his power for us who believe, according to the working of his great power."

Gratitude begets gratitude, and in the presence of a faithful God is a faithful people, who are open, ready, and willing to continue Christ's church for the sake of the world. This is our inheritance as followers of Christ today. Thanks be to God.

The New Interpreter's Study Bible (Abingdon: Nashville, Tennessee, 2003), 2090.

God of faithfulness and love, we are grateful for your presence throughout the ages, for your love shown to us, your hope given to us through Christ Jesus. May we be a people of gratitude and loving sustainers of your church. Amen.

In today's scripture reading, we find Jesus echoing Ezekiel's prophecy to the Hebrew people. Jesus offers his disciples and us warnings of judgment and a call to righteousness. There is a right way to live, and it has everything to do with feeding the hungry, caring for the stranger, clothing the naked, and being present with the prisoner.

Returning to a favorite biblical metaphor of sheep and goats, Jesus is clear that those who do the will of God will live with Jesus in the kingdom of heaven. At first glance, it seems this scripture passage is all about who's in and who's out, which can be a bit terrifying for those of us trying to follow the way of Christ.

Today's passage may tempt us to begin to make a checklist of all the ways we've cared for God and God's people, ensuring our place in heaven and alleviating our fears of judgment and condemnation. And it is easy to worry and wonder, "Are we doing enough to get in?"

But what if we read this scripture passage differently? What if, instead of being about whether we are in or out, the focus shifts to our love and care of others? Perhaps, in offering this dramatic and fearsome proclamation, Jesus means to convey just how passionate he is about the least, the last, the lonely, and the lost.

What if it's not about us at all? Perhaps shifting the lens from our own worry and fear to the ways we live and love in the world, and thereby offering ourselves to others, is the way of eternal life. How does living in this way change you? How does it change everything?

Jesus, your words shake us to our core, and we thank you. Help us love and serve others as you command; help us trust that what we offer to the least of these, we offer to you. Amen.

One of the gifts the Jewish tradition offers is the practice of midrash, a way of reading a biblical text with a question mark instead of a period. The practice of midrash grapples and wrestles with what the text lays forth and helps us understand the story beyond the story, the meaning beyond the meaning.

When presented with the troubling realities of Jesus' teachings in today's reading, midrash can be a helpful guide. Upon first reading, Jesus is the ultimate judge, who condemns those who do not feed, satiate, care for, clothe, or visit those who are in need. The chapter ends saying that "these will go away into eternal punishment, but the righteous into eternal life."

Are we to understand this passage to mean there is, indeed, a hell; that God's punishment is certain for those who do not follow the way of Jesus; that fire and brimstone await the unrighteous? Furthermore, how do we read this harsh judgment in conversation with God's mercy found elsewhere in scripture?

Remembering the context in which Jesus proclaims his message is vital. Often preaching in opposition to the Roman empire, offering an alternative to power, corruption, greed, and violence, Jesus turns everything on its head. Thus, a dramatic message helps his disciples and other followers truly understand how radically different his way is.

As followers of Jesus today, we might have to sit with our discomfort regarding hell and trust that unresolved questions are the gift of midrash and part of the call of being followers of Jesus. Reading in this way keeps us from jumping to conclusions; rather we can let the text sink deep into us and form us in our faith. It was countercultural then. It is countercultural now.

With our questions, wonders, doubts, and fears, we come, O God. We trust you hear us, hold us, guide us, and form us in Christ. We give thanks for the path of formation in you. Amen.

REIGN OF CHRIST

We have been walking through some tenuous scriptural ground this week, grappling with hell and judgment, salvation and righteousness, empire and God's kingdom. It is no easy terrain, no simple way to follow. Yet, as the questions arise, as confusion settles, and as wonder returns, we can hear the faint, far-off song of the creation of God. Through all and in all is God. God claims us. God loves us. God is good. The right response, then, is to praise, to sing, to gather with others both near and far, and to make a joyful noise, all the earth. Tambourines shake. Drums beat. Feet stomp. Hands clap. Trees dance. Moon pulses. Sun shines. Rivers flow. Seas rise. Voices of all sing God's praise not because it's easy but because it's true.

We might consider Psalm 100 among the most honest of all the psalms as it testifies to what we and all creation know: God's love endures forever, and God's faithfulness extends to all generations. A song of promise, a song of faithfulness, a song of hope, a song of truth reminds us that amid loss, worry, pain, and regret; amid evil empires, violence, and greed; amid hopelessness and hate, we are never alone.

Our praise of God, however, never excuses us from our praise of others. We enter the sanctuary to find the renewal and strength we need to return to the world Jesus commands us to serve and love. Finally we understand doxology; we understand praise as an integrated flow of song and service offered to God for the sake of the world God so loves. In our singing, in our living, in our praising, and in our serving, may we "enter his gates with thanksgiving" and leave God's gates buoyed to feed, clothe, and companion those we are called to serve.

Holy and Gracious God, you are good and your love endures forever. Thank you for promising to be with us in all and through all. Thank you for the gift of song that lifts our spirits and encourages us to share your love in the world. Amen.

Trusting God's Love Even in Bad Times

NOVEMBER 23–29, 2020 • KEITH BEASLEY-TOPLIFFE

SCRIPTURE OVERVIEW: The readings from the Hebrew scriptures have a common theme: The people have sinned and turned away from God, and now they cry out for God to forgive them. Even though they have created the separation from God, the authors are confident that God will restore them. These images of longing for God are appropriate as we begin the season of Advent, and the expressions of thankfulness coincide with the celebration of Thanksgiving in the United States. Paul opens First Corinthians with thanksgiving for the Christians in Corinth. They have been richly blessed by God (although the rest of the letter shows that they, like us, are far from perfect). Again this week, the Gospel reading refers to the return of Christ, a day known only to God.

QUESTIONS AND SUGGESTIONS FOR REFLECTION

- Read Isaiah 64:1-9. When have you treated God as a vending machine and held a grudge against God? What restored your faith or changed your perspective?
- Read Psalm 80:1-7, 17-19. When have you been frustrated by others' praises of God's blessings? When have you cried out to God, "Restore us"?
- Read 1 Corinthians 1:3-9. How do you ignore your spiritual gifts? What might your faith community look like if everyone employed their spiritual gifts?
- Read Mark 13:24-37. What is your job in the household of God? How do you stay alert?

Retired United Methodist pastor; writer; editor; barbershop singer.

The Israelites experience God not as an abstract set of attributes but through stories of saving power. Yes, God is described as holy, powerful, just, steadfast in love. But mostly God is the one who has chosen Abraham and his descendants, has brought them out of slavery, has provided food and water in the desert, has led them to the Promised Land, and has defeated their enemies, even down to the days of King Hezekiah and his prophet Isaiah when God destroys the Assyrian army besieging Jerusalem. But after Hezekiah's day, kings turn away from God and the nation is taken into exile in Babylon. There, a prophet arises in the tradition of Isaiah to promise divine comfort and a triumphant return home. This prophet, whose words appear in Isaiah 40–55, is sometimes called Second Isaiah.

The return comes not as a triumphant march but as a sporadic trickle facing constant opposition from people who have occupied the territory of Judah in the interim. (See the book of Nehemiah.) In this unsettled situation, a new prophet speaks new words of encouragement along with paraphrases and expansions of the words of First and Second Isaiah. This Third Isaiah's words are in Isaiah 56–66. Against Nehemiah's calls for great strictness and racial purity, Third Isaiah invites all to come to the feast of God's people and looks for a day when the entire world will answer that call. Still the prophet laments the unending opposition: "If only you would tear open the heavens and come down! Mountains would quake before you like fire igniting brushwood or making water boil" (CEB). Taking care of God's people—that's what God (and no other "god") does. "You look after those who gladly do right; they will praise you for your ways" (CEB). The prophet expects those days to come again.

God, come to us. Inspire us to speak your words of comfort and hope. Strengthen us to work for their fulfillment. Amen.

The prophet speaking for and to the returned exiles pleads for God to blast their enemies. But that doesn't happen. It is time for a sort-of confession. "But you were angry when we sinned; you hid yourself when we did wrong" (CEB). Yes, they've sinned. But isn't God supposed to fix everything when they ask? If not, then who needs God? "No one calls on your name; no one bothers to hold on to you, for you have hidden yourself from us" (CEB).

That's the vending machine response. You know what I mean, don't you? You put your money into the machine, push the button, and nothing comes out. So what do you do? You pound on the machine, shake it, maybe even give it a swift kick. Then you walk away and hold on to your anger. Long ago, when I was a kid, I put my dime (I said it was a long time ago) into a machine for a pack of chewing gum. Nothing came out. I pulled on the knob. Still nothing. My mom was ready to go, so I had to leave. I swore off chewing gum—for the next sixty years or so. That's how some folks treat God when they don't get their heart's desire.

The prophet pleads once more: "Lord, you are our father. We are the clay and you are our potter. All of us are the work of your hand" (CEB). Is that really the way to move God to action: by blaming God for our sins, criticizing God for making defective people, and then abandoning us?

God, we are broken, bent out of shape. Remold us so that we can be closer to your dream for us. Please help us. Amen.

Do you ever get distressed when others are praising God for the blessings they've received? Do you feel left out in the dark while others are in the sunshine of God's love? Perhaps you want to shout with the psalmist, "Restore us, God! Make your face shine so that we can be saved!" (CEB). Restore me! Renovate me! Save me!

Then come the recriminations, the accusations against God. God has given us "bread made of tears" (CEB) and more tears to drink "three times over!" (CEB). God has incited neighbors against us and enemies to laugh at us. God has broken us. So it's up to God to fix us. The refrain comes again, "Restore us, God of heavenly forces! Make your face shine so that we can be saved!" (CEB).

The lectionary skips the next bit of the psalm, but it is worth a look. It's a parable: the history of Israel as the story of a vine. God brings the vine from Egypt, clears the land, and plants it. It grows to fill the land, covering the mountains and even the tallest trees. And then God tears down the walls so that boars and bugs can devour the vine. The beloved root God planted has been burned and chopped down. Unless God does something quickly, it may disappear completely. "Restore us, God! Make your face shine so that we can be saved!"

There's a story about a monk who asks his teacher, "When will I see God?" The teacher takes him to a pond and holds his head down until bubbles come up, then pulls him out. As the monk lies gasping, the teacher asks how he feels. "I thought I was going to die. I'd have given anything for a breath of air." His teacher responds, "When you feel like that about God, that's when you'll see God."

"Restore us, LORD God of heavenly forces! Make your face shine so that we can be saved!" (CEB). *Amen.*

THANKSGIVING DAY, USA

Deuteronomy is written as a farewell address by Moses. For forty years he has led the Israelites around and around in the desert. Most of the folks who came out of Egypt have died. A new, tougher generation has grown up. Now they are about to enter the Promised Land. Moses knows he can't go with them. But before he dies, there are a few things he wants to remind them about: They are going into a land where they will "eat food without any shortage." There will be abundant water, grains, vines, fruit trees, rocks for building, metal for weapons and tools. "You will eat, you will be satisfied, and you will bless the LORD your God in the wonderful land that [God has] given you" (CEB).

But what if they forget that it was God's gift? What if they become arrogant and think, *My own strength and abilities have produced all this prosperity for me*? Think of the old New England farmer who got a visit from the new preacher. The preacher looked at the field full of corn between firm stone walls, at the snug house and barn, and enthused, "What a wonderful farm you and the Lord have made here!" "Ayuh," said the farmer, "but you shoulda seen it when the Lord was working it by himself!"

Thanksgiving can be hard; it can be hard to squeeze out any thanks in bad times, hard not to forget about God as we congratulate ourselves in good times. "Remember the LORD your God . . .who gives you the strength to be prosperous" (CEB).

God, we thank you for all your blessings: for health and strength and daily food; for people who have entered our lives and blessed us with their presence; for all who have long been part of our lives; and for love and grace you have poured out on us so we can be a blessing to others. Amen.

Jesus and the disciples are leaving Jerusalem after a long day of teaching in the Temple, when one of the disciples gushes about how awesome the stones and buildings are. Jesus says they'll all be demolished soon enough. When they get back to the Mount of Olives, the disciples start asking when that's going to happen. What sign should they look for?

Jesus responds with promises of deception and destruction, persecution, beatings, and death. And then things will get really bad, with stars falling from the sky. But then the Human One will appear in splendor and all of God's people will be gathered into everlasting glory! None of the disciples works up the nerve to ask, "Teacher, couldn't we just skip all the pain and darkness and go straight to the glory?" That may be their greatest display of restraint in all of Mark's Gospel.

Then Jesus says, "Learn this parable from the fig tree." What fig tree? The one Jesus cursed the day before because it didn't have any figs? What did he expect in springtime? But that tree was withered and dead when they passed it this morning. Now he claims that was all a parable about the foolishness of not recognizing the time. Tell it to the tree! When things get bad, he says, that's not the sign of the end—only when things get horrible. Only then can we tell each other, "He's standing just off stage, behind that door, ready to make his big entrance."

Jesus, we often get caught up in looking for signs that your coming is near. Some see hope in earthquakes, floods, and wars, as if they could force you to make a glorious re-entrance to our world. Keep us mindful that you are with us always, to the end of the world and beyond. Amen.

Paul addresses this first letter to the church in Corinth to the "saints." He writes for the people who have been set apart as God's people by their baptism. But when Paul begins the letter with thanksgiving, it's not for their holiness or their good deeds. In fact, it's not about anything they've done. Paul is thankful for what God is doing in the people of Corinth, how God has made them rich in spiritual gifts and spiritual knowledge. They have everything they need to stand firm in their faith and be blameless in their testimony and conduct until "the day of our Lord Jesus Christ." God has called them, and God is faithful.

Have you ever seen a church like that? Where everyone is Spirit-gifted, filled with wisdom, and blameless? I've known some individuals who seem to meet such a description, but I know I fall short. Even among the folks in Corinth, despite all that God is doing in their lives, Paul complains a lot about divisions, lawsuits, sexual immorality, and spiritual one-upmanship. It's almost as if God continues to pour out gifts on them, but some of them have put up umbrellas to keep dry. There are legends about mass baptisms where armies marched through a blessed river but held their swords out of the water because they still had to fight and kill.

We still try to ignore any spiritual gifts or fruits we find inconvenient. I once bought a banner headed "Ingredients for a Happy Home." Below that title was the list of the fruit of the Spirit from Galatians 5:22-23, all except for the last one: self-control. Apparently whoever made the banner thought that one wasn't really needed for domestic bliss.

Holy Spirit, keep on pouring your grace on us. Give us the courage to accept your gifts and to bear your fruit. Amen.

FIRST SUNDAY OF ADVENT

Ionce saw a bumper sticker that read, "BE ALERT! THE WORLD NEEDS MORE LERTS." Jesus tells his disciples not only to be alert but to stay alert until the end comes. "I assure you," he says, "that this generation won't pass away until all these things happen" (CEB). Well, it's been nearly 2,000 years, Lord, and we're still here. That's a long time to sustain eager expectation. Of course, Jesus admits that he doesn't really know. "Only the Father knows" (CEB). So what's a lert to do?

Once again, Jesus tells a helpful parable: He says the situation is like when a householder goes away leaving the servants in charge, giving each one a job to do, then telling the doorkeeper to stay alert. So the doorkeeper has the special job of staying alert, of watching and warning. The rest of the staff have their own jobs. If they all do their jobs, then the house will be ready whenever the householder returns.

So, what's your job to help the household of Jesus be ready? Is it to make disciples of Jesus Christ for the transformation of the world? Or is it more generally to be a disciple of Jesus Christ and take actions that transform the world around you? Maybe it's encouraging others or teaching or interceding in prayer or any of the other jobs that sustain the household of faith. Maybe it's being a doorkeeper. You can find your job, learn how to do it, and then get to it. Do all the good you can in all the ways you can as long as you can.* Don't just be a lert. Stay alert!

---

*Attributed to John Wesley

Lord Jesus, on this first Sunday in Advent we think about your comings: to Bethlehem long ago, into our hearts, in glory. Teach us to find our jobs and fulfill your plan for us, so that your people will be ready to recognize you and welcome you when you come. Amen.

Turning to a Radical New Way

NOVEMBER 30–DECEMBER 6, 2020 • JANE M. THIBAULT

SCRIPTURE OVERVIEW: Prepare the way of the Lord! This is the theme for the second week of Advent. Isaiah cries out from the wilderness that the people should prepare for the arrival of the Lord. This will be met with shouts of praise and rejoicing. The psalmist tells his audience to prepare the way of the Lord by living rightly, namely by showing love and faithfulness to each other. Second Peter restates that we do not know the day of the Lord's ultimate return, but we know that the delay is a result of God's patience and desire for all to come to repentance. Matthew opens his Gospel with a quotation from this week's Isaiah passage. Here John the Baptist is presented as the one preparing the way of the Lord.

QUESTIONS AND SUGGESTIONS FOR REFLECTION

- Read Isaiah 40:1-11. When have you profoundly experienced God's guidance or protection? How did this experience change you?
- Read Psalm 85:1-2, 8-13. Consider the author's questions. How can you and your faith community return to God to "dwell in God's land"?
- Read 2 Peter 3:8-15a. How might considering God's time alter your perspective on your daily rush and prompt you toward a greater experience of peace?
- Read Mark 1:1-8. When have you reached a spiritual dead end? How did the working of the Holy Spirit help you turn around or move forward in a new way?

Clinical gerontologist and professor emerita, University of Louisville School of Medicine; spiritual companion, retreat leader, transformational aging consultant; member of Shiloh United Methodist Church, Prospect, Kentucky.

Ilived in California's Mojave Desert before GPS and cell phones, and I often hosted friends who were novice hikers but eager to explore the rugged area. They occasionally ventured into the wilderness without a map, ignoring my warning about its dangers. Sometimes they wandered into a box canyon—a dead end and a treacherous place with its intense heat and steep canyon walls. Hikers must quickly turn around to find a safer path.

The throngs following John the Baptist are stuck in a spiritual box canyon. Their lives have come to a dead end, and they seek a different way of living. In John's message they recognize a path to a new beginning as he exhorts them to turn from their sins, ask for forgiveness, and have their sins washed away. But beyond this traditional rite for remission of sins, John offers something different. He prepares his followers for a prophet greater than he, who will bring them a new message and who will be the message. John prophesies that what they have been waiting for—the time when God will pour out God's Spirit on all of Israel—is imminent. The baptism with the Holy Spirit that Jesus offers will remit past sins and empower his followers to enter into a radically new way of living that he will teach and demonstrate.

When we're trapped in our own box canyons, the way out is to admit that we can't save ourselves. In recognizing that our path leads nowhere, we can turn to God and seek forgiveness from God and from those we've hurt. We can ask the Holy Spirit to motivate us to change and empower us to grow in our love of God, others, and ourselves.

Spirit of God, we know that refusal to follow Jesus and his teaching leads us away from your life-giving path. Grant us wisdom to ask you for help. Enable us to recognize and respond to the guidance you offer. Amen.

In this portion of the earliest Gospel, Mark introduces the good news of Jesus Christ, the Son of God, and validates John as the messenger prophesied by Isaiah who will prepare the way of the Lord.

Vast crowds follow John's call to turn away from sin, confess publicly, and be baptized. But John announces that one greater than he is coming who will not baptize with water but with the Holy Spirit. Hearing this, John's followers likely take this announcement to mean that he is prophesying the beginning of the long-anticipated messianic age, when God would pour out God's Spirit on all of Israel.

Fast forward to the present. The gift of the Holy Spirit empowers us to follow Jesus' teaching to love God and all our neighbors—even our enemies. By our own efforts we may be able to love our families and friends reasonably well, but rarely our enemies and those who hurt us intentionally.

The Amish community near Nickel Mines, Pennsylvania, showed the world how, empowered by the Spirit of Christ, they were able to love their enemy. In October 2007 their regular, non-Amish milk delivery man entered the schoolhouse and shot ten children, killing five. Instead of responding with revenge, community members—including parents of the children killed—visited the family of the shooter, attended his burial, and donated money to his widow and children. The Amish believe in demonstrating their faith in the goodness of God by the way they live their daily lives. Responding with forgiveness didn't remove their grief, but their decision to refrain from revenge enabled them to grieve and to begin healing and not get stuck in anger and hatred. Their example demonstrated what love looks like in action.

Holy Spirit, it is hard to love people who hurt us. Help us understand that we are all your children. Enable us to see one another through your eyes and to love with your love. Amen.

Turning to a Radical New Way

Scholars believe that Second Peter is among the last of the New Testament documents, written by a person who lived a generation after Peter and identified with his tradition. The author is trying to defend and reenergize belief in the second coming of Christ—the *parousia*. Because Christ hasn't arrived, some followers are becoming impatient, and others have begun to question and ridicule the belief. The writer reminds them that Christ could come at any time and encourages them to spend their days growing in faith with behaviors of goodness and love so that they might hasten "the coming of the day of God."

While impatience for the second coming may not be high on our agenda of concerns, perhaps it should be. What if the Second Coming requires—or actually is—the spiritual transformation of those of us who call ourselves followers of Christ, members of the Body of Christ? What if we are to be Christ—present in love to one another?

Jesus, you have called us to follow, watch, and learn from you, act as you do, and share your life with others. We are to participate with you in creating your kingdom here on earth, as it is in heaven. We know it will take time, and we grow impatient as we see wars and refusal to love all over the world. Help us not become scoffers. Help us not to give up hope. At every moment of every day, help us to see, hear, taste, smell, touch, think, feel, care, and love as you do. Transform our lives into your life so that together we may love, serve, help, and heal the world with you. Let all those whose lives we touch feel your loving presence reaching out to them through us. Be in our lives until we all see you face to face. Amen.

Responsible in some way for the second-generation followers of Jesus, the author of Second Peter seems worried about them. Since Jesus' death, his return has been believed to be imminent. But as years have passed and the resurrected Christ hasn't come back, his followers' fear of final judgment and hope of everlasting life has lessened. Strong anticipation of the Second Coming once kept believers on the straight and narrow. Now those who hadn't benefited from knowing Jesus in the flesh are straying from the good news and returning to sinful ways, influenced by "scoffers" who ridicule their belief. One can almost hear the author of Second Peter thinking, *How can I convince them to hang in there?*

He addresses clearly and firmly the subject of timing. He reminds all Christians that God's time and human time are entirely different. In God's time one day is like a thousand years and a thousand days are like one day. He warns us not to be upset by how long Christ's return is taking because God is patient and does not want any to perish. On the other hand, Christ could arrive at any moment, so the author encourages Christians to use whatever time we have to grow in holiness and godliness.

We live in an increasingly time-obsessed, fast-paced culture. We demand things on time and fear not having enough time. If computers aren't fast enough, we're agitated. If someone interferes with our tightly-budgeted time line, we're inhospitable to them. Road rage is increasing. Even today we need to be reminded that God's time is different from ours. Preoccupation with time affects our spiritual lives just as negatively as concern about the lateness of the *parousia* affects the early followers: We are straying from the gospel's call to peacefulness and loving behavior.

God, please help us now—Oops! Correct that—please help us in your own time. Amen.

In this portion of Second Isaiah, Cyrus of Persia has promised release of the Jews from Babylon back to Palestine after their exile. The author begins with the voice of God calling for Israel to be tenderly comforted with the news that the Exile is to end. Jerusalem has paid for her sins, and the way must be prepared for the Lord to return in victory. Miraculously, all manner of things will be healed and renewed to show God's glory. No matter how fickle people may be in the future, God will prevail. God will come with a gentle might and respond to human need as the good shepherd does: feeding, protecting, and guiding the flock.

How helpful to you is the image of God as shepherd? For a long time, I was unable to relate to God or Jesus as the Good Shepherd and dismissed the image as anachronistic. But thirty years ago, my husband and I visited the Scottish Highlands and hiked into the hills of Glen Lyon, where a herd of sheep grazed without a shepherd. The view was glorious until we stumbled upon a deep hole under an uprooted tree. The hole was filled with a decaying adult ewe that had strayed and fallen into the hole. Without the help of a shepherd to crawl out, she had perished.

As I gazed at the dead ewe, the reality of God as Good Shepherd became apparent. I realized that all my life, especially through the death of both parents when I was a teenager, God had been tending to my needs. Without the care and guidance of the Good Shepherd, I might not have survived.

God, help us to honor the Bible's context by recognizing that biblical images were created to help your children know you. May we never let old images be a barrier to our relationship. You are beyond all images, and someday we will know you as I AM. Amen.

This passage represents another assurance: that no matter how many times we turn away from God as individuals or nations, we always will be God's beloved children, and God will welcome back repentant hearts. As powerful king and gentle shepherd, God will guide and protect us—not just one generation or group but all of us. As promised, all people shall see God's glory together. Though this passage speaks of the renewal of a nation, we often witness examples of God's joyous welcome home in individual lives. If you or anyone you love has ever been released from imprisonment of any kind, whether virtual imprisonment in addiction or behind the locked bars of a building, this passage offers hope.

A few years ago Jim,* a friend's teenaged son, stole $1,500 from the fast-food restaurant where he worked. In his state, theft of that amount is a felony. A frightened teenager was sentenced to a year of incarceration in a juvenile detention center. Hope for a "normal" life of high school sports, prom, graduation, and college were gone—at least in our eyes—because reports of the results of adolescent detention are dismal. Yet by the grace of God, who sent one of God's messengers to care for and encourage Jim, he earned his GED and was awarded a scholarship to a state university. Because he hadn't reached the age of eighteen, his prison record was expunged. He emerged from prison free from the bondage of a lifelong record and went straight to his college dorm. Four years later he walked triumphantly down the walkway to receive his diploma, and our hearts were filled with awe and joy. This is the glory of God manifested in the salvation of one of God's beloved children.

*Name changed

God of the imprisoned and the free, help us be your messengers to bring hope to those imprisoned by addiction or shame or by state institutions. Amen.

SECOND SUNDAY OF ADVENT

A plaintive cry for forgiveness and restoration of God's presence seeps like tears through Psalm 85. The psalmist begins by remembering and acknowledging God's material and spiritual goodness in the past, especially the forgiveness and pardoning of the sins of the people. (It seems they need both again. How many similar pleas have been made since the Covenant began?) Then, in a burst of hopefulness and confidence in God's mercy, the psalmist offers a vision of salvation—what life can be like when the relationship with God is healed and restored. The congruence of love and faithfulness, righteousness and peace will prevail.

Though composed long ago, Psalm 85 could easily be written today as the cry of the whole modern world, of a nation, a specific community, or an individual. Examining our personal and public lives we can all ask: How have we turned away from God and deliberately acted against God's ways? How have I experienced misery because of decisions I've made that were not life-giving for me or proved destructive for others? How have we resisted asking for forgiveness from God or those we've hurt? How have we been complicit in excluding or marginalizing God's children? How often have I turned back, repentant, to receive God's grace-filled pardon?

Each time we return to God, we receive the gift of emotional and spiritual healing. Our relationship with God is restored, and we enable God's glory to "dwell in our land."

God, we are citizens of a nation, but more importantly we're siblings of 7.7 billion humans created in your image. Help us look beyond our personal needs and biases. Empower us as individuals and with others to promote the flourishing of love and faithfulness, righteousness and peace so that your glory will "dwell in our land"—planet Earth. Amen.

Justice and Hope

DECEMBER 7–13, 2020 • BENJAMIN HOWARD

SCRIPTURE OVERVIEW: Isaiah speaks of the day in which God's Anointed One (Messiah) will bring good news to the poor and hope to the oppressed. Jesus will later read this passage and declare it to be about himself (Luke 4), so we read Isaiah's prophecy during Advent. The psalmist rejoices that God has restored the fortunes of the people. They have come through a period of difficulty, but God has brought them into a place of joy. Throughout Advent, we also look forward to such rejoicing. Paul encourages the Thessalonians to pray continually with an attitude of gratitude and rejoicing, and the God of peace will sustain them. In the Gospel reading, John the Baptist repeats the theme from last week—that he is merely the messenger to prepare the way for the Lord.

QUESTIONS AND SUGGESTIONS FOR REFLECTION

- Read Isaiah 6:1-4, 8-11. God is coming. How do Isaiah's words of praise and justice inspire you to act in response?
- Read Psalm 126. How do you celebrate the justice that you have seen come to fruition while hoping for future justice? How does your anticipation of the fullness of justice affect your faith?
- Read 1 Thessalonians 5:16-24. How can you return to the basics of faith during this Advent season?
- Read John 1:6-8, 19-28. How is this Advent season both familiar and new for you? How might simple announcements of Jesus' coming change your experience of the season?

Master of Theological Studies, Lipscomb University; writer and editor in Nashville, Tennessee, focusing on youth and intersection of theology and pop culture.

There's a certain kind of poetry in the repetition and simplicity of John 1 as the Gospel writer lays the groundwork for the world-bending story to follow. In today's passage, we're told directly that John was sent from God. There are no frills, no extra bits of information; nothing needs to be inferred or extrapolated. It's direct and no-nonsense. But John wasn't just sent from God. John was sent with a mission: to tell everyone that the light is coming. Each word works together to build anticipation for the coming of Jesus, which is a key characteristic of the Advent story.

However, the story of Advent and Jesus' birth are familiar for many of us—so familiar that we often spend our time trying to make them more exotic to remind ourselves of the profound nature of the Incarnation. We create works of art and elaborate reworkings of these stories to remind ourselves that Jesus' birth is not normal; it is paradigm-shattering.

The plain, understated way John's Gospel opens up the story of Jesus might surprise us. The direct nature of the Gospel's words are almost bracing; their simplicity prepares us to encounter the familiarity of God, who is always with us, and the profundity that God would become human and come to live among us.

John's use of light as the symbol for Jesus further reveals this dichotomy. Like air or water, light is an ever-present aspect of our life. It's so fundamental to our existence that we rarely contemplate its power or our inability to live our lives without it. John's Gospel reminds us that Jesus is both entirely familiar and profoundly essential to our lives.

God, allow us to hear the sharp, clear call of the Advent story and to encounter Jesus again, as if for the first time. Amen.

Today's passage is one of those where it can be hard to place ourselves in the mind-set of the people who first heard it. We can try our best, but it's nearly impossible for most of us to recreate the physical, emotional, and spiritual distress of an entire nation that has been sent into exile. The people of Israel haven't just lost their homes; they have lost their sense of safety, their sense of control over their own lives, and for some, even their sense of identity as God's chosen people. It must have been devastating on every level.

And then Isaiah offers them today's reading. These words must feel like drinking deeply from cold water when you're dying of thirst. Isaiah tells the people that God has neither abandoned them nor forgotten them. Far from it. God is coming and will bring relief from all the pain and suffering that has afflicted them for so long. They will be comforted, they will be freed, they will be healed, and perhaps most importantly, they will be vindicated.

Where John's Gospel talks about the light, here Isaiah addresses the darkness. Everything that has been taken away will be not only restored but also renewed. Life will spring again from places that were marked with death. You can almost feel the rising passion as Isaiah's words build.

It's important to note that God is not the only one acting here. Yes, God will free the people, and God will heal them. But it is the people, those who have been powerless, who will rebuild the ruins and restore the places deserted by past generations. God doesn't just act on our behalf; God empowers us to act.

God, you bring relief to our pain and justice to our suffering. Restore us and support us as we work to bring your will to the world. Amen.

Advent is a time of reflection, but it's also a time of tensions and uncertainty. In its quiet and dark, hope and expectation for new life begin to rise. Amid this swirl of emotions and conflicting feelings, today's passage reminds us of the basics of our faith. No matter what is happening to us or around us or even inside us, we can follow these simple directions. Rejoice always. Pray continually. Give thanks. Listen to the Spirit. Avoid evil.

Life is hard. At some point, everyone has felt that way—not only because of the things that happen to us but because of the uncertainty that permeates our existence. Today's passage provides us with calm in the middle of a sometimes chaotic world.

It's also illuminating that the writer of First Thessalonians refers to the "God of peace." God and God's Spirit provide us with peace. God desires for us to be healthy and whole, even when situations and circumstances would cause us to feel otherwise. No matter the situation, the Spirit is with us. We're told that God is faithful.

Finally, we are reminded multiple times in this passage to be alert to the work of the Spirit. The writer tells us not to "suppress the Spirit" (CEB) and not to "brush off Spirit-inspired messages" (CEB). Instead, we should "examine everything carefully and hang on to what is good" (CEB). God is not just present with us; God is speaking to us and working within us. In Advent, we are invited to use this time of quiet and reflection to listen for the words of the Spirit and to cling to what we hear.

Spirit, we pray that you will help us calm our hearts and quiet our minds so that we can listen for your words. We pray for wisdom to understand them and for boldness so that we can put them into practice. Amen.

It can be easy, especially when we live in comfortable sur-roundings, to let the words of the prophets become discon-nected from our tangible, grounded realities. That's why this passage from Isaiah is so powerful. It's straightforward, physical, and gritty. It's what politicians might call a "kitchen-table issue." The Lord loves justice. The Lord hates robbery and dishonesty. The Lord will pay fair wages and keep the promises the Lord has made.

These words must feel so liberating to a people who have been in exile, who likely have been struggling to make ends meet for years as they fight against the oppression of a foreign nation who has taken them from their home. The Lord is with them. That doesn't just mean that God is on their side in some abstract way; God is on their side with regard to economics, fair-ness, and their place in society. They are not powerless anymore because God is in charge and God will be fair.

The second half of this passage adds even more weight to this point. God is not only with them now but will continue to be with them, providing justice for generations to come. What more comforting words can you give to a parent than to say that your child is safe, will continue to be blessed, and will thrive even after you are gone.

The hope that we find in Advent is a hope not only for our-selves but also for our community and for our families. This hope alleviates our most mundane anxieties by telling us that God is present and working to provide us with justice and a future. We may not know what the future holds, but we know that the future is not something to be feared.

God, you are good, you are just, and you are our hope. Help us invite others to experience the same hope we have in you. Amen.

It was like we had been dreaming" (CEB). Sit with this phrase for a moment. We see dreams throughout the Bible, most prominently in Joseph's interaction with Pharaoh, but they are also mentioned throughout the prophets. Dreams even come up in Peter's sermon on Pentecost when he recites the prophecy from Joel that "your elders will dream dreams" (Acts 2:17, CEB). Dreams are usually so abstract that they are hard to decipher, but the content of dreams isn't as important here. The truly important thing is the feeling of dreams, the euphoria of the unexpected and the unimagined coming into existence. The people were so shocked that things could get better that it was no longer a hope, it was a dream.

And then God does it. God changes things and saves the people. In verse 3 the psalmist says, "Yes, the Lord has done great things for us" (CEB). God sees the people in trouble and saves them. The people could never have hoped for such a thing even during their waking hours.

Yet, when we read Psalm 126 more closely, it appears that this salvation has happened in the past; once again the people of God find themselves in dire circumstances. In fact, this is a psalm of lament most likely written after the people have returned to Israel from exile. They have been saved, yet they still need God for more. Their salvation has come in part, but not in full. They celebrate the justice they have received and hope for justice to come.

As we've seen throughout this week's readings, Advent reminds us that the salvation we have received is only a glimpse of the fullness of God's story. There are more and greater things to come in the person of Jesus, and our salvation will be made complete.

Lord, change our circumstances for the better, like dry streams in the desert waste. Continue your work within us, and lead us to give thanks for your glorious deeds. Amen.

These two verses serve as a crescendo to the verses of Isaiah we have examined earlier this week. Isaiah 61 tells of God's mighty work among the people and the justice that has come at the hand of the Lord. It recounts how the Lord breaks the chains of oppression and suffering that so often hold us down and keep us disconnected from God.

Isaiah's words swell and expand our understanding of God's vision for the new creation that we know will come when Jesus walks among us. We look back with excitement and forward with anticipation for the coming of the Lord.

Then Isaiah's words begin to crash in on us and ring out with joy about the coming of the Lord and the victory that God has given us as God's people. We are the bride. Despite all that humanity has suffered and all the pain that God's people have been through, we are loved. God sees us as the beautiful creation that God has always intended for us to be.

While things may be difficult, we can look forward with joy and anticipation because we know that God's presence and God's will have overtaken the forces of evil and pain. "The LORD God will grow righteousness and praise before all the nations" (CEB).

The ecstasy of Isaiah's words reminds us that we are waiting for a singular moment in the history of the world. God, the one who created the universe and imbued it with life, is coming to us. God, who understands and has power over all things, cares for us. In this passage, all of that is bundled together and crashes over us in waves. God is coming.

Lord God, our words cannot express the joy we feel in our hearts. Listen to our hearts, speak to our souls, and help us embrace the love and joy you so freely offer us. Amen.

THIRD SUNDAY OF ADVENT

The religious leaders ask John the same question three times. "Who are you?" They say it over and over again. It's clear that the priests and Levites sent by Jewish rulers know that there is something special about John's message even if they are skeptical of it.

The mystery is part of the story, and though the priests and Levites ask John the same question three times, he never really answers them. He first responds by telling them who he is not: "I'm not the Christ" (CEB). It's interesting to note that the Gospel writer adds that John "didn't deny but confessed" (CEB) that he is not the Christ. John does not want there to be any confusion. He knows he is not the Christ, and he wants everyone to know that he should not be mistaken for the Christ.

The priests and Levites ask him again. They ask him whether he is Elijah. John says no. They ask him whether he is a prophet. John says no. Finally, they press him even harder. They have to receive an answer for the people who have sent them.

In John's response we discover that the priests and Levites have been asking the wrong question all along. It does not matter who John is because John is the messenger preparing the way for the one who is to come. John is the herald. He is not the king. John then doubles down when responding to the question about baptism. If we read further, we learn that even John does not yet know who Jesus is, but he does know that "someone greater" is coming and that he, John, is not even worthy to perform the lowest of tasks for this mysterious person. But we know it is Jesus. We know God in the flesh is about to arrive and the world will change forever.

God, we praise you and we serve you in worship and adoration. Help us to ask the right questions and know you when we meet you. Amen.

Promises Fulfilled

DECEMBER 14–20, 2020 • BONNIE BOWMAN THURSTON

SCRIPTURE OVERVIEW: In the fourth week of Advent, we focus on prophecies of the arrival of the Messiah. When David commits to build a temple for God, God promises to build a house for David as well. This is the line of David that will rule forever, and Jesus comes from this line. In the first reading from Luke, Mary rejoices after her visit to Elizabeth, for she understands that her child will play a key role in God's redemption. Paul reminds the Romans that his message about Christ did not begin with him. Instead, it is the fulfillment of promises made through the prophets. The second reading from Luke might more logically have come first this week, for it describes how Mary reveals the importance of this child in her song of rejoicing.

QUESTIONS AND SUGGESTIONS FOR REFLECTION

- Read 2 Samuel 7:1-11, 16. When have you thought you were participating in God's plans and later realized you had misunderstood God's desire or instruction?
- Read Luke 1:47-55. Consider how you magnify the Lord. How do you pass on your faith to future generations?
- Read Romans 16:25-27. Remember the carols you have been singing this Advent and have sung throughout your life. How do they help you proclaim the mystery of the Incarnation?
- Read Luke 1:26-38. In this season of giving and receiving, how do you remember that God is the giver of all good gifts? How do you return your God-given gifts to God?

Former university and seminary professor, pastor, author, and poet; now lives quietly in West Virginia; ordained in the Christian Church (Disciples of Christ) and a licensed lay preacher in the Episcopal Church; enjoys classical music (and sings with a community and college choir) and is an avid walker, gardener, reader, and cook.

This week's Bible readings seem haphazard: David and Nathan (not *that* story), blessings on Roman Christians, Gabriel's annunciation to Mary, and Mary's song. And the Mary stories aren't even in chronological order! But careful reading reveals two "golden threads" running through them: God's benevolent action in fulfilling divine promises and the widening inclusiveness of beneficiaries of God's benevolence.

In 2 Samuel 7, King David wants to build God a "house." God doesn't want one and tells Nathan to tell David, "The Lord will make *you* a house," a dynasty (v. 11). Remember that when you hear Christmas references to "house and lineage of David." In Romans 16, Paul reminds Roman Christians of God's mysterious inclusion of the Gentiles "made known through the prophetic writings" (v. 26). God expands promises to people to whom they weren't originally made.

Gabriel announces that Mary's son will have "the throne of his ancestor David" and "will reign . . . forever" (Luke 1:32-33). The promise to David is to be fulfilled in Jesus of Nazareth. (Nazareth!?) Mary greets Elizabeth, who confirms Gabriel's promise saying, "Blessed is she who believed that there would be a fulfillment of what was spoken to her by the Lord" (Luke 1:45). In response, Mary sings the Magnificat, which closes by affirming that all it describes is "according to the promise [God] made to our ancestors, to Abraham and his descendants forever."

These texts disclose God's faithfulness in fulfilling promises—some made generations ago—not only to those to whom they were made and *their* descendants but to everyone. God's *hesed* (loving-kindness) includes David, Mary, Paul's church in Rome, Gentiles, and us. We are challenged to accept with Mary's faithful hope the promises God announces which, in the fullness of God's time, will be fulfilled.

What promises to you has God fulfilled? What divine promises await fulfillment?

At this juncture, David is a big winner: king of Israel and Judah, conqueror of the mighty Philistines, with the captured city of Jerusalem his capital. Living in "a house of cedar"—not local stone, but expensive wood, a tribute gift from King Hiram of Tyre (see 2 Samuel 5:11)—David, perhaps out of guilt, has a great idea: *I'll build God, who resides in the ark in a tent, a house to live in.* He checks this out with Nathan, who thinks it's a splendid plan. But God doesn't. God comes to Nathan that night with a message reminding David of all God has done for him in the past and previewing what God will do for him in the future. God's got other building plans in mind.

Especially from a place of strength, it's easy to get inspired about what to do for God before consulting God. Unfortunately, good intentions sometimes get ahead of God's plans, which can seem slow to become evident. But as the hymn says, "God is working his purpose out as year succeeds to year."* God has eternity to accomplish God's plans. Getting results (like building houses) may not be the point.

As Advent draws to a close, what does God want you to do before God comes, not in mighty Jerusalem but down the road in sleepy little Bethlehem? Sometimes adults must do what we admonish children to do: Stop. Look. Listen. We should be cautious about our Nathan-like haste to jump on our latest project's bandwagon. Before we order lumber and get out the tools (or the shopping list, baking pans, or wrapping paper), we should listen in the night for God's desire and directives.

———————

*"God Is Working His Purpose Out," Arthur Campbell Ainger (1894).

God, help me put aside my good ideas for your gracious plans. Amen.

I love puns, especially those based on a *double entendre*, a word with more than one meaning (one often risqué!). These exchanges among David, Nathan, and God are based on a pun on *house*, which occurs seven times in twelve verses. The first five refer to a building; the other two a dynasty. David tells Nathan he wants to build God a house. God tells Nathan that God is going to build David a house. David wants to build an edifice (like all human creations, only temporary). God wants to give David a lineage, a divine creation, "forever."

David's house idea is iffy: gods who live in houses or temples are geographically limited, gods of a particular place. Israel's God is the God of time, of history, and therefore is mobile. "I have moved about among all the people of Israel," God reminds Nathan. "I have been with you wherever you went." (Is this God's oblique warning against sacralizing real estate?) Binding God to a location limits God. What God builds is not static; it is living, a people descended from David. "The Lord will make you a house," a lineage, declares Nathan.

Matthew's Gospel begins with a genealogy. Luke states that Joseph "was descended from the house and family of David" (2:4; Rom. 1:3). Through Jesus, whose birth we await, Christians are grafted into David's family tree. This fact shocks Paul, who nevertheless makes it focal in his preaching. Peter declares that Christians "are a chosen race, a royal priesthood, a holy nation, God's own people. . . . Once you were not a people, but now you are God's people" (1 Pet. 2:9-10). God builds an enormous house. We are it.

How do we settle for less than what God wants to give? Why do we build temporal houses instead of eternal lineages? How do we limit God?

Luke is Christianity's first historian. Scholars note his use of Greco-Roman history's literary models. We too use cultural forms to convey Christian content. It's good evangelism: Something new in something familiar. Luke opens many stories by situating them in historical times and places. "Gabriel was sent by God to a town in Galilee called Nazareth."

Galilee first appears in Joshua (20:7; 21:32) and First Chronicles (6:76). Isaiah 9:1 describes it as a place of foreigners, "the nations." Galilee is conquered by Alexander the Great in 332 BCE, captured by the Romans in 63 BCE, and thereafter subject to occupying forces. (See Luke 3:1.) How does the angelic promise of a new house and reign sound to this daughter of a subjugated people? Nazareth is a village, perhaps an outpost of Sepphoris, the expanding Roman administrative center three miles northwest where a *tekton* (carpenter, craftsman) might find work. Hearing Jesus is from there, Nathanael asks, "Can anything good come out of Nazareth?" (See John 1:46.) Well, yes, something can.

Luke emphasizes that Jesus comes from real places. Their history culminates when God's promises are fulfilled in them. "Throne of . . . David," and "reign over the house of Jacob" introduce Mary's yet-to-be son as fulfillment of God's dynastic promise to David. (See 2 Samuel 7:11-16.) The "house" Jesus establishes fulfills Isaiah's prophecy of "a house of prayer for all peoples" (Isa. 56:7; Mark 11:17). Like David's, Jesus' "house" isn't a place. It is a person. Mary's "yes" facilitates prophecies of salvation history. As Paul later explains, "In [Jesus] every one of God's promises is a 'Yes' " (2 Cor. 1:20).

Lord, as Mary did, we accept your goodness and mercy and ask to dwell in your house forever. Amen.

Elizabeth blesses Mary who "believed that there would be a fulfillment of what was spoken to her by the Lord" (Luke 1:45). Mary's response is now a great liturgical canticle, the Magnificat. Mary interprets and then praises God for what is happening. She magnifies and rejoices about what God has done for her. She describes God's action on behalf of others. The verbs highlight divine activity and preference: God has mercy, shows strength, scatters, brings down, lifts up, fills, sends away, and helps the marginalized, downtrodden, and suffering. We could relate many biblical narratives that exemplify each action, each "according to the promises [God] made." The Magnificat is introduced and concludes with promises fulfilled. "From now on all generations will call [Mary] blessed."

"The apple never falls far from the tree." "Like mother, like son." In Luke, these adages hold true: The essence of Jesus' preaching in Luke's Gospel originates in Mary's song. It echoes in The Sermon on the Plain. (See 6:20-26.) Jesus declares that God blesses the poor, hungry, weeping, and reviled; he foretells woe to the rich, full, laughing, and apparently laudatory. Had Jesus learned these promises of God at his mother's knee? They echo again in Paul's letter to Corinthian Christians: "Not many were powerful, not many were of noble birth," but "God chose what is foolish . . . what is weak . . . what is low and despised" (1 Cor. 1:27-28).

Do Mary, Jesus, and Paul think God chooses those the world considers the wrong people? Or do they profoundly understand the divine heart in light of a suffering world? Who are we in view of God's activity? It is sobering to remember that Mary sings about divine promises she believes are being fulfilled.

By word and action, what are we teaching our children about God's favor?

Romans 16 contains scholarly puzzles. First, Paul knows twenty-nine people in a church he hasn't visited. (Have you a similar conundrum in your Christmas card list?) Greetings to friends, final instructions, and a blessing signal the conclusion of Paul's epistle. Verses 17-20 are typical Pauline directives, including a warning to preserve the received teachings and a promise that Satan will be crushed. Our text today is an extended benedictory wish that foreshadows a major theme of Paul's last letters: "the revelation of the mystery . . . made known to all the Gentiles."

The mystery is that "the Gentiles have become fellow heirs, members of the same body, sharers in the promise in Christ Jesus" (Eph. 3:6). Erudite Paul never recovers from amazement that God's promises are extended to Gentiles, which is precisely what the risen Christ charges him to do: "Bring about the obedience of faith among all the Gentiles" (Rom. 1:5). The final verses of Romans from today's reading summarize salvation history and rehearse the epistle's great themes. But how does one proclaim a mystery, something which, by definition, is unknown and at least partially unknowable? Paul proclaims no doctrinal statements with which we must agree, but an action: God's inclusion of the Gentiles by means of a *person*, Jesus Christ. As we know, people are always mysterious. When we proclaim *this* mystery, the best rhetorical strategy is doxology.

Christmas carols reflect this strategy. We don't sing dogmatic statements about the Trinity or the meaning of the Atonement, though both are important. We join the "multitude of the heavenly host," singing "Glory to God in the highest." The proclamation of the Christian mystery begins with doxology. Glorifying God is the point of proclamation and the basis of Christian spirituality.

Do your favorite carols include glorifying? What do your Christmas traditions proclaim?

Fourth Sunday of Advent

Scripture's characteristic word from heaven to earth is "Do not be afraid." When an angel announces this to a human, the human is usually "in for it." To understand Mary's response, we must understand Gabriel's announcement. It isn't evident in English, but three crucial words in verses 28 and 30 contain the same Greek root: *charis.* Its changes in form reveal an important aspect of Mary's response.

Charis can be translated as "grace," "mercy," or "good," understood as manifesting divine presence, activity, and power. Gabriel's *greetings, "chaire,"* implies "rejoice, be glad." He calls Mary "favored one," "*kecharitomene,*" from the verb *charitoo,* "to bestow or endow with grace." It is in the perfect tense, which signifies an act completed in the past with continuing effects. It is also in the passive voice, which indicates that something is done *to* the subject; one doesn't act but receives. To avoid saying the Sacred Name, some biblical writers use the passive voice when God is the actor. Mary was and continues to be favored or graced by God. She has been given something that she has maintained.

Gabriel's declaration "you have found favor" can be translated as "you have discovered, come upon, or received *charin.*" If you find something, are you the source of it? Mary's response, "Let it be with me" (allow it to happen), beautifully expresses her acceptance of God's plan. Previous occurrences of *grace* suggest that she is giving back something she has received. Her fiat returns a gift to its giver. In Episcopal liturgy as the offerings are presented, the congregation says, "All things come of thee, O Lord, and of thine own have we given thee." Mary has done so perfectly. Our challenge is to go and do likewise.

God of promises and grace fulfilled, in obedience to your will and purposes, we will recognize and return the gifts you have given us. Amen.

Portraits of the Immeasurable Gift

DECEMBER 21–27, 2020 • STEVE DOUGHTY

SCRIPTURE OVERVIEW: As we celebrate the birth of our Savior, we do so with cries of praise to God. Isaiah delights and rejoices in God, who will bring reconciliation to all nations. Psalm 148 declares that all of creation praises the Lord, for creation knows who formed and sustains it. Paul explains to the Galatians that God sent Jesus to redeem us, and as a result we may now call out to God as God's children. In the Gospel reading, Luke sets the story of Jesus within the history of the Israelites. Both Simeon and Anna are devout people, filled with the Holy Spirit. They have been praying for God to send the Redeemer, and God gives them insight to recognize him as Jesus. Praise be to God for this indescribable gift!

QUESTIONS AND SUGGESTIONS FOR REFLECTION

- Read Isaiah 61:10–62:3. How do you yearn for righteousness? How do the prophet's words give you hope?
- Read Psalm 148. Pause and consider the joy of God's coming salvation for the whole world.
- Read Galatians 4:4-7. Consider your identity as a child of God through Christ. What joy does this identity bring you?
- Read Luke 2:22-40. How can you, like Anna, joyously proclaim the freedom and redemption Christ brings all of humanity?

Retired minister of the Presbyterian Church (USA); author, retreat leader, spiritual director; lives in Greenville, SC, with wife, Jean.

I am always grateful when another person sees something in scripture I have missed. Biblical scholar Artur Weiser worked for years on his commentary on the book of Psalms. A man of keen intelligence and deep piety, he produced a work that reads as if he prayed every paragraph he wrote. When he came to Psalm 148, he wrote exactly what I expected he would. In spare, stunning language he highlighted the all-encompassing *Praise the Lord* surging through this psalm (*Alleluia!* in the magnificently energetic Hebrew tongue). Line by line, Weiser gradually assembled a whole thundering cosmos of praise.

To my surprise, he then did more. Weiser turned to a single phrase near the psalm's end as cause for all the praise: "He has raised up a horn for his people." This, he wrote, was the horn of salvation. The Hebrew listeners would have understood instantly. Why all this praise? Because the Lord God is giving salvation, a gift that reaches all realms of creation. And at its deepest level, Weiser noted, the psalm points far beyond itself to the salvation the heavenly host announced to the entire world at the birth of Jesus.

The Bible offers multiple portraits of the immeasurable gift we receive at Christmas. No single image can contain it. In coming days, we will look at several biblical portraits. Most are tightly focused. Today's calls for our widest vision: A prayerful scholar looked at Psalm 148, and he saw all heaven and earth break into praise at the coming of Jesus. I ponder this. As I do, and as Christmas now approaches, I hear a gentle invitation for us all to pause and consider the immensity of the gift that is coming.

Loving Lord, open our eyes today so that we may see the people, landscapes, and realms you seek to bless by your saving presence among us. Amen.

If we consider today's reading in its original context, we recognize a portrait of a people yearning for righteousness and receiving God's response to that yearning. The first Israelites to hear today's passage ache for righteousness. They have returned from captivity in Babylon filled with joy, but their homeland lies desolate. As they labor to restore it, overlords seize the fruit of their harvests and leave them barely enough for survival. This situation drags on. Even God seems distant. Suddenly the prophet moves among them speaking words of joy. This is no naive joy. The prophet does not claim all is well, but he notes that God is beginning to break out garments of righteousness. God will cause righteousness to spring up even more. One day this righteousness will shine before all the nations. The prophet's listeners take hope.

In our era we too yearn for righteousness. For some of us this yearning comes as we see the increasing chasm between those with more than enough of the world's abundance and those straining for a crust of bread. Or it comes as we watch fear turn away mounting tides of refugees. For some of us, the yearning surges as unfairness pervades our workplace or hurts someone we love or smothers a cherished dream of our own. We too find ourselves portraits of persons who yearn for righteousness and seek God's response.

The prophet's words speak to us with greater clarity than they did to those first hearing them. We know his words fit perfectly the manger-born bearer of righteousness whose life forever proclaims good news to the oppressed and liberty to the captives. The way forward won't be easy. The way of justice never is, but we know that in Jesus we receive the gift of one who will lead us every step of the way.

Loving One, grant us wisdom and courage to live for the righteousness you bring. Amen.

Today's passage offers a portrait of overflowing joy in our divine adoption. It reminds us that the child in the manger comes to give us a new identity. When Paul writes to the Galatians, Gentiles are flocking to the fellowship. Some insist that new converts conform to Jewish laws, including circumcision. To this, Paul offers a ringing response: God sent the Son so that all might become children of God. Shaped by the Spirit working in their hearts, they are set free from all forms of slavery, including slavery to the law.

As he writes, Paul does more than just stress a key theological point. His words pulse with excitement. In the Greek language in which Paul wrote, his phrases are quick and rhythmic. Bible translators, ever faithful to the ancient manuscripts, rightly hurl in exclamation points. "Abba! Father!" Paul feels profoundly the theology he teaches. He has received a new identity. He is no longer a child of the law nor a child of the society around him with its perpetual conflicts, me-first leaders, and ever-increasing obsession with material rewards that soothe no inner pain and ultimately turn to dust. He is God's child, enfolded in love. Amid his turbulent age, he is free to live the fresh, healing way of love he learns in Christ.

Paul's joy invites our reflection as much as his theology does. What does it mean that we too have a new identity? From what does this set us free in our personal lives and in our own turbulent age? What can we let go of? And what are we now free to embrace? What liberations can we joyfully claim? As God's adopted children, in what fresh, healing ways shall we dare to walk?

Loving One, today may we joyfully claim, and live, the freedom of being your beloved children. Amen.

CHRISTMAS EVE

T hink of what lies behind the gift." My mother smiled as she spoke the words. She always did. I first heard them the day before my fourth Christmas. Presents had appeared in four separate piles under our Christmas tree. Beginning a habit I've never entirely broken, I fiddled with everything in my pile trying to guess the contents. When I finally developed the practice my mother encouraged, I realized she wanted to increase my pleasure. With the gift finally open in front of me I would sense a grandmother's warmth, an aunt's interest in my latest curiosities, a sibling's sly delight at my surprise.

Isaiah offers a sweeping view of the gift we receive at the birth of a son. The prophet carefully develops the scene. To the people of his day, steeped in darkness and sorrow, he announces the coming of light and joy. He points to the birth of a child. With soaring phrases he proclaims this child will embody the life-nurturing names of the Messiah. Then, at the climax of his prophetic portrait, Isaiah focuses on what lies behind it all: "The zeal of the LORD of Hosts will do this." *Zeal* is one of those thickly layered, rich, hard-to-capture biblical words. In Isaiah's prophecy, it conveys single-minded, absolute devotion. What lies behind the gift of this child? What lies behind the gift is God's relentless yearning. Behind is God's stop-at-nothing desire to draw all to the saving ways of righteousness and peace.

As we hover on the edge of Jesus' birth, may we look deeply enough to see the holy steadfastness that brings it to pass. In these next hours, behind any special worship service that moves us, any silence that nourishes us, any gathering that brings us joy, may we see God tirelessly reaching for us all.

God who sends a child, may we know deeply your unstoppable desire for us all. Amen.

CHRISTMAS DAY

I like to imagine the faces of those who first hear the opening verses of John's Gospel. What they hear must astonish them. In the highest philosophical language of their Greco-Roman culture, John declares that the Divine Word, present before the beginning of all else, has become incarnate. And that is not all. To everyone who wishes, the Word made flesh will give us power to become children of God. The listeners stare in rapt attention. Their faces fill with wonder.

Their expressions of wonder reflect precisely what John offers: the portrait of a nearly inexpressible wonder. He does this with captivating images: vast darkness and inextinguishable light; a person rejected, not known by the world yet shining with glory and still bringing that glory into the world. John's words grip those early listeners, hold them still. This has always been so for this passage. It shows no shepherds, no wise men. It offers no angel song. We cannot shape it into an enticing Christmas pageant with costume-clad children and Mary, Joseph, and the baby lying in a manger. John shows none of this, yet his vast panorama pulses with the same world-changing truth as the Christmas narratives of Matthew and Luke. We know what occurs when this passage is read carefully in worship at Christmas. It happens every time. All who are listening fall silent.

That silence points the way to our own appropriate response. In quietness, we can take time to absorb what John shows here. Shall we perhaps read the passage again, very slowly? Perhaps we just sit with the wonder. We need not try to do anything. Let the wonder take hold of us within. Let God, through the wonder, work in us however God wills.

O Loving God, open us to this wonder you have given. Work within us and shape us according to your will. Amen.

Step by careful step, Luke shows us much in this passage. We see the poverty of a couple that offers only pigeons instead of the usual goat. In their determination to do what little they can, we see genuine piety. We see the devotion of an old man who has waited decades for what he finally sees this day. We witness joy as he cradles the child in his arms and his eloquent, aged voice sings praise. For just a moment, Luke points us to the parents. We spot amazement. Then the Gospel writer spreads a complex, climactic image. In a deeply loving act, Simeon offers a blessing, then immediately tells of great pain to come, both for the child and the mother.

As a young artist, Rembrandt painted "Simeon and Anna Recognize the Lord in Jesus." To convey all he found in Luke's account of Jesus' presentation in the temple, Rembrandt focused on a single moment. Simeon has just spoken the harsh words. Mary stares at the child, eyes wide, face frozen. Simeon, crouched on one knee, bends toward her. His right hand reaches out in a gesture of comfort. Rembrandt's painting perfectly portrays the literary scene Luke offers. Both artist and writer present us with a portrait of suffering and love.

This portrait foreshadows the suffering and love that course through all of Luke's Gospel and reach fullest expression on the cross. And it evokes reflection. Where are we, like Simeon, invited to touch with love the suffering of another? Where is the whole family of faith now called to bless with active love others in their need? Where within our most hidden selves do we yearn for the presence of this child who embodies love and will know all our pain?

Loving One, where we suffer, help us to know you are with us. Wherever you beckon through the suffering of others, give us the daring to reach out with love. Amen.

In Rembrandt's *Simeon and Anna Recognize the Lord in Jesus*, Anna is by far the most physically active figure. Positioned behind the holy family and Simeon, she stands straight and thrusts her arms outward, palms open, in a gesture of astonishment and blessing. Her lined face appears to look downward on the small cluster of persons before her and also far beyond them to engage others, including the viewer of the painting. She is a striking presence.

How perfectly Rembrandt interprets Luke's text! After carefully describing Anna's status as a prophet, her great age, and her devotion, Luke makes the key point in a single sentence. The pace of narration quickens, mirroring Anna's energy. Suddenly she's right there, talking about the child "to all who were looking for the redemption of Jerusalem."

If we consider what "the redemption of Jerusalem" means in Anna's world, we see the immensity of her proclamation, for both her age and our own. Cultural, political, and religious divisions fracture Jerusalem. Roman rulers inspire loathing. Corruption allows low-minded persons to take control. The biblical word Luke used for *redemption* also means "freedom." Common folk long for this freeing, life-restoring redemption. Even Anna does not know the fine points of what this newborn will teach. She cannot discern precisely what he will do in the years ahead. In her prayer-tutored heart, however, she recognizes the vast picture. After years of maturing, this little one will free people into a new way of living.

Luke offers a portrait of redemption proclaimed. It brings joy. It also encourages us. Here is Anna. With her voice, her body, every ounce of energy she has, she says it: *Look! This child right here frees us all for a whole new way.* Her very life is proclamation. Unselfconsciously, she beckons.

Lord, by your grace, may our lives and words proclaim the life you free us for in this needy world. Amen.

God's Word Runs Swiftly

DECEMBER 28–31, 2020 • MICHAEL E. WILLIAMS

SCRIPTURE OVERVIEW: The year ends as it began, with celebrations of God's faithfulness. Although Jeremiah lives in a difficult period for the Israelites, God gives him a vision of a time when the Lord will gather together all those who are scattered and restore their fortunes in Zion, the city of God. The psalmist praises God for protecting the Israelites and being faithful to the promises made to their ancestors. In Ephesians, we read of the blessings that God set aside for us even before the world existed, and we are recipients because of the work of Christ. We finish the year by revisiting the opening of John's Gospel. The Word was with God and the Word was God, and in Jesus the Word became flesh and lived among us. Glory to God!

QUESTIONS AND SUGGESTIONS FOR REFLECTION

- Read Jeremiah 31:7-14. When have you failed to comfort or be comforted by someone? How have you recognized who might be able to provide true comfort?
- Read Psalm 147:12-20. How have God's gifts helped you to understand who God is and who you are?
- Read Ephesians 1:3-14. How have you experienced the spirit of adoption into God's family? How has this experience shaped your notions of earthly adoption?
- Read John 1:1-18. When has scripture become intensely personal for you? How might you see the face of Jesus in every child?

Pastor and storyteller; author of *Spoken into Being;* (1948–2018).

The church calendar refers to this day as the Feast Day of Holy Innocents. It commemorates the children who died because of Herod's fear of the birth of another king, a king who would take his throne away. I had known both the story and the name of the feast day for a number of years.

But on December 28, 1989, that date changed for me forever. At 12:35 p.m. on that day, my wife gave birth to our first child, Sarah. When I looked at Sarah, I thought she was the most beautiful baby ever to enter this world. Her mother agreed with me wholeheartedly. Now Margaret and I laugh at ourselves because Sarah's photos from that time picture a red and wrinkled little baby who looks very much like every other newborn. You see, we were looking at her through the eyes of first-time parents, through the lens of a mother's and a father's love.

Since the day of Sarah's birth, the children in the cruel story of Herod's fear have had a face—the face of my daughter. No longer are they faceless, nameless characters. I feel for every parent who has ever lost a child to death, abduction, or poverty. I hear their stories, and the fear wells up inside me. What if one of my children suddenly disappeared?

The holy innocents still die in this country and around the world. God sees each of them with the eye of a mother's and father's love. To God each is the most beautiful precious child that was ever born. Neither the circumstances of their birth, the color of their skin, nor the language and culture they will one day learn matter.

In each child I see the face of my own child. In each child I see the face of the child Jesus who escaped Herod's wrath but could not escape the cruelty of the world entirely.

Gracious God, help me view all your children through the eyes of parental love. May I see Jesus in the face of every child. Amen.

I had gone to visit Hubert at the hospital where he was awaiting the amputation of a second leg. His first amputation had taken place several years earlier. Having been a severe diabetic for some years, he knew that his life might come to this tragic occasion someday. Removing his other leg would extend his life while at the same time transforming it irrevocably.

I was Hubert's pastor and friend, but there seemed to be nothing I could say that would even begin to comfort him. He knew that this surgery was just one more step toward his body's giving out entirely. We talked about his feelings, and he seemed very philosophical about the operation. Yet I still sensed a deep sadness, and as we talked and prayed I wished from the depths of my heart that I could do more. I knew that what I had to offer Hubert was limited.

As I was about to leave, feeling that my visit had brought very little comfort to my friend, there was a knock at his hospital room door. In walked a man on two prostheses, having already lived through two leg amputations. This visitor had a greater authority to speak a word of comfort because of his previous suffering. God had turned his tragedy into a gift, a gift he shared with Hubert.

Generous God, thank you that our tragedies can be turned into blessings for others. Amen.

Several years ago another pastor in my annual conference invited me to baptize her child. This young woman had been a youth in one of the churches I had served years earlier. She had gone on to college and seminary and was now one of my colleagues in ministry. She scheduled the baptism for Sunday evening so both of the small, rural congregations she served, along with her family and many friends, could attend.

She had adopted Daniel from Peru, and the process had been long and difficult. This history of struggle just seemed to make the delight of Daniel's baptism even more joyous. That same day Bishop Peter Storey from South Africa had come into town to teach for a continuing education event I was directing. I invited him to come with me that evening.

I had received directions to the church, but I must have taken a wrong turn somewhere. I drove around on unfamiliar back roads for what seemed to be an eternity. Neither Bishop Storey nor my wife, Margaret, seemed overly concerned. I was getting frantic.

The church was so far out in the country, and I had driven around lost for so long that we arrived just in time for the baptism. As I led the service, looking out on the sea of faces in that little country church, it struck me that this is what the community of faith is all about.

We are all God's children by adoption, as the writer of Ephesians puts it. Our country of origin, our skin color, our native language, and the place on earth we call home make no difference. Baptism makes siblings of us all.

Loving God, I thank you that you have brought me and all your beloved children into your adopted family. Amen.

There was a time in my younger days when I ran ten-kilometer races. Never being a fast runner, I always wound up at the back of the race. In one race, a runner passed me wearing a T-shirt that bore these words: When the going gets rough, sprinters quit.

Psalm 147 affirms that God's Word doesn't quit. God's Word runs swiftly, says the psalm. For the Christian, two questions are basic to our religious quest: "Who is God?" and "Who are we?" To love God and our neighbor we have to be clear about our answers to these questions.

Psalm 147 emphasizes that God's very nature is to give gifts. Finest wheat, snow like wool, frost like ashes, hail like crumbs, the winds that blow, and the waters that flow—all are gifts from God's generous hand.

God's statutes and ordinances represent the most profound of these gifts, though. The commandments God gave to Israel, which Jesus summarizes as love of God and neighbor, are special gifts. They make us partners with God in making the world into the place God wants it to be.

We cannot contain God's Word in any of the boxes we try to put it in. God's Word is a living, breathing reality—not ours to possess but one that runs ahead of us. What an image! We have to run even to try to keep up with God's living Word. This reality makes sense, though, since after two thousand years we've been unable to contain or even keep up with Jesus, God's living Word.

Thank you, God, for your many gifts, especially for your Word that precedes me wherever I go. Amen.

The Revised Common Lectionary* for 2020
Year A—Advent / Christmas Year B
(Disciplines Edition)

January 1–5
Jeremiah 31:7-14
Psalm 147: 12-20
Ephesians 1:3-14
John 1:1-18

> **January 1**
> NEW YEAR'S DAY
> Ecclesiastes 3:1-13
> Psalm 8
> Revelation 21:1-6a
> Matthew 25:31-46

January 6–12
BAPTISM OF THE LORD
Isaiah 42:1-9
Psalm 29
Acts 10:34-43
Matthew 3:13-17

> **January 6**
> EPIPHANY
> Isaiah 60:1-6
> Psalm 72:1-7, 10-14
> Ephesians 3:1-12
> Matthew 2:1-12

January 13–19
Isaiah 49:1-7
Psalm 40:1-11
1 Corinthians 1:1-9
John 1:29-42

January 20–26
Isaiah 9:1-4
Psalm 27:1, 4-9
1 Corinthians 1:10-18
Matthew 4:12-23

January 27—February 2
Micah 6:1-8
Psalm 15
1 Corinthians 1:18-31
Matthew 5:1-12

February 3–9
Isaiah 58:1-12
Psalm 112:1-10
1 Corinthians 2:1-16
Matthew 5:13-20

February 10–16
Deuteronomy 30:15-20
Psalm 119:1-8
1 Corinthians 3:1-9
Matthew 5:21-37

February 17–23
THE TRANSFIGURATION
Exodus 24:12-18
Psalm 99
2 Peter 1:16-21
Matthew 17:1-9

February 24—March 1
FIRST SUNDAY IN LENT
Genesis 2:15-17; 3:1-7
Psalm 32
Romans 5:12-19
Matthew 4:1-11

February 26
ASH WEDNESDAY
Joel 2:1-2, 12-17
Psalm 51:1-17
2 Corinthians 5:20b–6:10
Matthew 6:1-6, 16-21

March 2–8
SECOND SUNDAY IN LENT
Genesis 12:1-4a
Psalm 121
Romans 4:1-5, 13-17
John 3:1-17 or Matthew 17:1-9

March 9–15
THIRD SUNDAY IN LENT
Exodus 17:1-7
Psalm 95
Romans 5:1-11
John 4:5-42

March 16–22
FOURTH SUNDAY IN LENT
1 Samuel 16:1-13
Psalm 23
Ephesians 5:8-14
John 9:1-41

March 23–29
FIFTH SUNDAY IN LENT
Ezekiel 37:1-14
Psalm 130
Romans 8:6-11
John 11:1-45

March 30—April 5
PALM/PASSION SUNDAY

Liturgy of the Palms
Psalm 118:1-2, 19-29
Matthew 21:1-11

Liturgy of the Passion
Isaiah 50:4-9a
Psalm 31:9-16
Philippians 2:5-11
Matthew 26:14–27:66 or
Matthew 27:11-54

April 6–12
HOLY WEEK

Monday
Isaiah 42:1-9
Psalm 36:5-11
Hebrews 9:11-15
John 12:1-11

Tuesday
Isaiah 49:1-7
Psalm 71:1-14
1 Corinthians 1:18-31
John 12:20-36

Wednesday
Isaiah 50:4-9a
Psalm 70
Hebrews 12:1-3
John 13:21-32

Maundy Thursday
Exodus 12:1-14
Psalm 116:1-2, 12-19
1 Corinthians 11:23-26
John 13:1-7, 31b-35

Good Friday
Isaiah 52:13–53:12
Psalm 22
Hebrews 10:16-25 or
Hebrews 4:14-16; 5:7-9
John 18:1–19:42

Holy Saturday
Job 14:1-14 or
Lamentations 3:1-9, 19-24
Psalm 31:1-4, 15-16
1 Peter 4:1-8
Matthew 27:57-66 or John
19:38-42

Easter–April 12
Acts 10:34-43 or Jeremiah
31:1-6
Psalm 118:1-2, 14-24
Colossians 3:1-4 or Acts
10:34-43
John 20:1-18 or Matthew
28:1-10

April 13–19
Acts 2:14a, 22-32
Psalm 16
1 Peter 1:3-9
John 20:19-31

April 20–26
Acts 2:14a, 36-41
Psalm 116:1-4, 12-19
1 Peter 1:17-23
Luke 24:13-35

April 27—May 3
Acts 2:42-47
Psalm 23
1 Peter 2:19-25
John 10:1-10

May 4–10
Acts 7:55-60
Psalm 31:1-5, 15-16
1 Peter 2:2-10
John 14:1-14

May 11–17
Acts 17:22-31
Psalm 66:8-20
1 Peter 3:13-22
John 14:15-21

May 18–24
Acts 1:6-14
Psalm 68:1-10, 32-35
1 Peter 4:12-14; 5:6-11
John 17:1-11

> **May 21**
> **ASCENSION DAY**
> Acts 1:1-11
> Psalm 47 or Psalm 93
> Ephesians 1:15-23
> Luke 24:44-53

May 25–31
PENTECOST
Acts 2:1-21 or Numbers
11:24-30
Psalm 104:24-34, 35b
1 Corinthians 12:3b-13
John 20:19-23 or 7:37-39

June 1–7
TRINITY SUNDAY
Genesis 1:1–2:4a
Psalm 8
2 Corinthians 13:11-13
Matthew 28:16-20

June 8–14
Genesis 18:1-15; 21:1-7
Psalm 100
Romans 5:1-8
Matthew 9:35–10:23

June 15–21
Genesis 21:8-21
Psalm 86:1-10, 16-17
Romans 6:1b-11
Matthew 10:24-39

June 22–28
Genesis 22:1-14
Psalm 13
Romans 6:12-23
Matthew 10:40-42

June 29—July 5
Genesis 24:34-38, 42-49,
  58-67
Psalm 45:10-17 or Song of
  Solomon 2:8-13
Romans 7:15-25a
Matthew 11:16-19, 25-30

July 6–12
Genesis 25:19-34
Psalm 119:105-112 or Isaiah
  55:10-13
Romans 8:1-11
Matthew 13:1-9, 18-23

July 13–19
Genesis 28:10-19a
Psalm 139:1-12, 23-24
Romans 8:12-25
Matthew 13:24-30, 36-43

July 20–26
Genesis 29:15-28
Psalm 105:1-11, 45b
Romans 8:26-39
Matthew 13:31-33, 44-52

July 27—August 2
Genesis 32:22-31
Psalm 17:1-7, 15
Romans 9:1-5
Matthew 14:13-21

August 3–9
Genesis 37:1-4, 12-28
Psalm 105:1-6, 16-22, 45b
Romans 10:5-15
Matthew 14:22-33

August 10–16
Genesis 45:1-15
Psalm 133
Romans 11:1-2a, 29-32
Matthew 15:10-28

August 17–23
Exodus 1:8–2:10
Psalm 124
Romans 12:1-8
Matthew 16:13-20

August 24–30
Exodus 3:1-15
Psalm 105:1-6, 23-26, 45b
Romans 12:9-21
Matthew 16:21-28

August 31—September 6
Exodus 12:1-14
Psalm 149
Romans 13:8-14
Matthew 18:15-20

September 7–13
Exodus 14:19-31
Psalm 114 or Exodus 15:1b-
11, 20-21
Romans 14:1-12
Matthew 18:21-35

September 14–20
Exodus 16:2-15
Psalm 105:1-6, 37-45
Philippians 1:21-30
Matthew 20:1-16

September 21–27
Exodus 17:1-7
Psalm 78:1-4, 12-16
Philippians 2:1-13
Matthew 21:23-32

September 28—October 4
Exodus 20:1-4, 7-9, 12-20
Psalm 19
Philippians 3:4b-14
Matthew 21:33-46

October 5–11
Exodus 32:1-14
Psalm 106:1-6, 19-23
Philippians 4:1-9
Matthew 22:1-14

October 12–18
Exodus 33:12-23
Psalm 99
1 Thessalonians 1:1-10
Matthew 22:15-22

October 12
**THANKSGIVING DAY,
CANADA**
Deuteronomy 8:7-18
Psalm 65
2 Corinthians 9:6-15
Luke 17:11-19

October 19–25
Deuteronomy 34:1-12
Psalm 90:1-6, 13-17
1 Thessalonians 2:1-8
Matthew 22:34-46

October 26—November 1
Joshua 3:7-17
Psalm 107:1-7, 33-37
1 Thessalonians 2:9-13
Matthew 23:1-12

November 1
ALL SAINTS DAY
Revelation 7:9-17
Psalm 34:1-10, 22
1 John 3:1-3
Matthew 5:1-12

November 2–8
Joshua 24:1-3a, 14-25
Psalm 78:1-7
1 Thessalonians 4:13-18
Matthew 25:1-13

November 9–15
Judges 4:1-7
Psalm 123 or Zephaniah 1:7,
12-18
1 Thessalonians 5:1-11
Matthew 25:14-30

November 16–22
THE REIGN OF CHRIST
Ezekiel 34:11-16, 20-24
Psalm 100
Ephesians 1:15-23
Matthew 25:31-46

November 23–29
FIRST SUNDAY OF ADVENT
Isaiah 64:1-9
Psalm 80:1-7, 17-19
1 Corinthians 1:3-9
Mark 13:24-37

November 26
THANKSGIVING DAY, USA
Deuteronomy 8:7-18
Psalm 65
2 Corinthians 9:6-15
Luke 17:11-19

November 30—December 6
SECOND SUNDAY OF ADVENT
Isaiah 40:1-11
Psalm 85:1-2, 8-13
2 Peter 3:8-15a
Mark 1:1-8

December 7–13
THIRD SUNDAY OF ADVENT
Isaiah 61:1-4, 8-11
Psalm 126
1 Thessalonians 5:16-24
John 1:6-8, 19-28

December 14–20
FOURTH SUNDAY OF ADVENT
2 Samuel 7:1-11, 16
Luke 1:47-55
Romans 16:25-27
Luke 1:26-38

December 21–27
Isaiah 61:10–62:3
Psalm 148
Galatians 4:4-7
Luke 2:22-40

December 24
CHRISTMAS EVE
Isaiah 9:2-7
Psalm 96
Titus 2:11-14
Luke 2:1-20

December 25
CHRISTMAS DAY
Isaiah 52:7-10
Psalm 98
Hebrews 1:1-12
John 1:1-14

December 28–31
Jeremiah 31:7–14
Psalm 147:12-20
Ephesians 1:3-14
John 1:1-18

A Guide to Daily Prayer

These prayers imply worship time with a group; feel free to adapt the plural pronouns for personal use.

MORNING PRAYER

In the morning, O LORD, you hear my voice;
    in the morning I lay my requests before you
    and wait in expectation.

—Psalm 5:3

Gathering and Silence

Call to Praise and Prayer
God said: Let there be light; and there was light.
And God saw that the light was good.

Psalm 63:2-6

God, my God, you I crave;
my soul thirsts for you,
my body aches for you
like a dry and weary land.
    Let me gaze on you in your temple:
    a Vision of strength and glory
    Your love is better than life,
    my speech is full of praise.
    I give you a lifetime of worship,
    my hands raised in your name.
    I feast at a rich table
    my lips sing of your glory.

Prayer of Thanksgiving

We praise you with joy, loving God, for your grace is better than life itself. You have sustained us through the darkness: and you bless us with life in this new day. In the shadow of your wings we sing for joy and bless your holy name. Amen.

Scripture Reading

Silence

Prayers of the People

The Lord's Prayer (see Midday Prayer for text)

Blessing

May the light of your mercy shine brightly on all who walk in your presence today, O Lord.

I will extol the LORD at all times;
God's praise will always be on my lips.
—Psalm 34:1

Gathering and Silence

Call to Praise and Prayer

O LORD, my Savior, teach me your ways.
My hope is in you all day long.

Prayer of Thanksgiving

God of mercy, we acknowledge this midday pause
of refreshment as one of your many generous gifts.
Look kindly upon our work this day; may it be made
perfect in your time. May our purpose and prayers
be pleasing to you. This we ask through Christ our
Lord. Amen.

Scripture Reading

Silence

Prayers of the People

The Lord's Prayer (ecumenical text)
Our Father in heaven,
hallowed be your name,
your kingdom come,
your will be done,
on earth as in heaven.

Give us today our daily bread.
Forgive us our sins as we forgive
those who sin against us.
Save us from the time of trial,
and deliver us from evil.
For the kingdom, the power, and the glory
are yours, now and forever. Amen.

Blessing

Strong is the love embracing us, faithful the Lord from morning to night.

My soul finds rest in God alone;
   my salvation comes from God.
             —Psalm 62:1

Gathering and Silence

Call to Praise and Prayer

From the rising of the sun to its setting,
let the name of the LORD be praised.

Psalm 134

Bless the Lord,
   all who serve in God's house,
   who stand watch
   throughout the night.

Lift up your hands
   in the holy place
   and bless the Lord.

And may God,
the maker of earth and sky,
bless you from Zion.

Prayer of Thanksgiving

Sovereign God, you have been our help during the
day and you promise to be with us at night. Receive
this prayer as a sign of our trust in you. Save us
from all evil, keep us from all harm, and guide us in

your way. We belong to you, Lord. Protect us by the power of your name. In Jesus Christ we pray. Amen.

Scripture Reading

Silence

Prayers of the People

The Lord's Prayer (see Midday Prayer for text)

Blessing

May your unfailing love rest upon us, O Lord, even as we hope in you.

This Guide to Daily Prayer was compiled from scripture and other resources by Rueben P. Job and then adapted by the Pathways Center for Spiritual Leadership while under the direction of Marjorie J. Thompson.